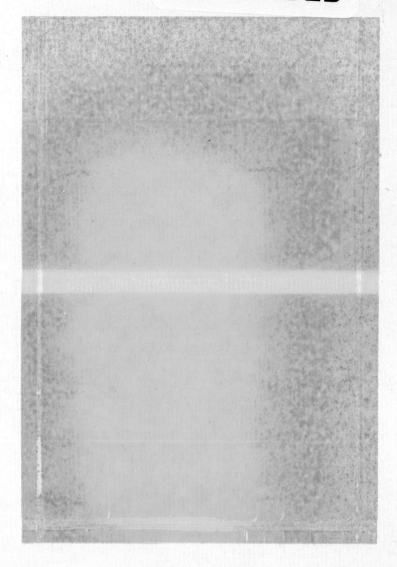

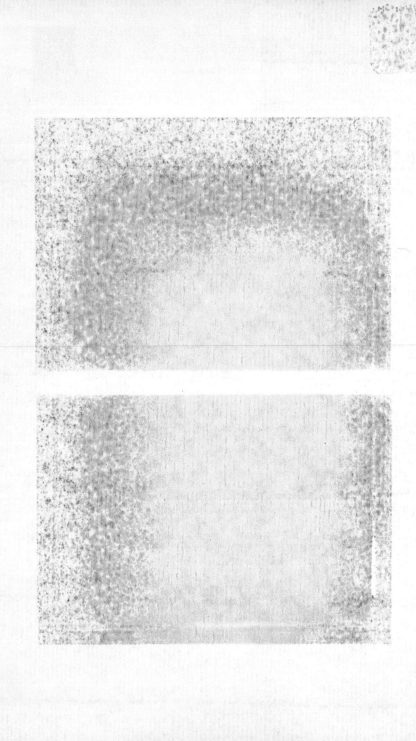

ENGLISH RECUSANT LITERATURE
1558–1640

Selected and Edited by
D. M. ROGERS

Volume 264

ETIENNE PASQUIER
The Iesuites Catechisme
1602

ETIENNE PASQUIER

The Iesuites Catechisme

1602

The Scolar Press

1975

ISBN o 85967 267 o

Published and printed in Great Britain by
The Scolar Press Limited, 59-61 East Parade,
Ilkley, Yorkshire and
39 Great Russell Street,
London WC1

NOTE

Reproduced (original size) from a copy in Cambridge University Library, by permission of the Syndics.

References : Allison and Rogers 596; STC 19449.

THE
Iefuites Catechifme.

OR
EXAMINATION OF
their doctrine.

Publifhed in French this prefent
yeere 1602. and nowe tranflated
into Englifh.
(·.·)

VVith a Table at the end, of all the maine poynts that
are difputed and handled therein.
(*₊*)

Printed Anno Domini.
1602.

TO ALL ENGLISH

Catholicks, that are faithfull subiects to Queene ELIZABETH,
our most dread Soueraigne : The
Secular Priests that are diuersly afflicted,
doe wish all prosperitie, iustice, peace, ioy, and
happines in our Lord Iesus
Christ.

T cannot be vnknowne vnto you all (very reuerend and deere Catholicks) what great and bitter contention (raised vp from hell no doubt through the malignitie of sathan) hath lately fallen out amongst vs, who are your spirituall guides, and ought to haue beene vnto you examples of humilitie, charitie, vnitie, pietie, and a whole schoole of religious vertues. And we are fully perswaded, that the consideration of it, doth very greatlie moue & perplex your catholick harts with manifold griefes: especially, seeing we are on both sides so confident in our owne so contrarie courses.

The Iesuits say vnto vs : *Woe be to that man, by whom the scandale commeth*: We the secular Priests, say vnto them ; *Woe be vnto him by whom the scandale commeth*. Now whether they apply the words of our Sauiour Christ more rightly to vs, or we to them, therein lyeth the doubt, and that is the difficultie : Wee both doe pleade for our selues : and you with the Church, must iudge betwixt vs both as vmpiers of our cause. The woe is of a large extent, & will be too heauie to be vndergone by any. *Expedit ei*, (as the text saith) *it is expedient, or farre better it were* (say some) *for such a man, that a milstone were hanged about his necke, and he drowned in the bottom of the Sea*. In such a contrary application of this so terrible a woe, you (our auncient children and faithfull Catholicks) shall shewe your selues right worthie of these honourable titles, and greatly benefit both vs the Secular priests, and the others the esteemed religious Iesuits, to

the

the preuenting in part of this heauie cenfure; if you continue ſtedfaſt in the doctrine which you haue receiued of vs, conioyned in one a-like vnitie of fayth, hope and charitie; and ſhall take no offence at theſe our quarrells & vnbrotherly garboyles. For as S. *Hierom* ſaith; *Quis ſcandalizatur paruulus eſt*: He that is ſcandalized is but a weakling. *Maiores enim ſcandala non accipiunt* : ſound and reſolute Catholicks doe not take ſcandale at any thing.

There was long ſince an earneſt diſputation amongſt the Apoſtles, *who among them ſhould be greater* : & Chriſt himſelfe was choſen by them as vmpire and Iudge paramount to determine the controuerſie. Who accordingly hearing the matter, propounded vnto him in theſe wordes: *Quis putas maior eſt &c* : *who thinkeſt thou is greater* ? decided their iarre, with ſome ſharpneſſe in this ſort as the text reporteth. *Ieſus calling vnto him a little child, ſet him in the midſt of them and ſaid* : *Amen I ſay vnto you, vnleſſe you be conuerted and become as children*, (that is ſaith *Lyra* in the gloſſe vppon that place) *vnleſſe you be couerted ab elatione ſcil: ſuperbiæ et ambitione maioritatis, from pride and ambitious affectation of greatnes, and become humble and ſimple without malice or gall of ſinne, you ſhall neuer enter into the kingdome of God*. And furthermore, foreſeeing in his diuine preſcience, how ſuch contention for ſuperioritie might proue verie dangerous in the Church, and wound the tender conſciences of manie weake nouices in the catholicke faith : this moſt wiſe Arbitrator (*in whom be all the treaſures of wiſedome and knowledge hid*) doth continue his commination to the better ſuppreſſing of that ſo dangerous an enormitie: ſaying, *Hee that ſhall ſcandalize one of theſe little ones, that beleeue in me, it is expedient for him that a Milſtone be hanged about his necke, and that he be drowned in the depth of the ſea*. Vppon which words the ſaid *Lyra* writeth in this manner; *Et ſi hoc generaliter dicit contra omnes* : *tamen hic ſpecialiter contra Apoſtolos, qui hic de dignitate videtur contendere, et in hoc poterant alios perdere* : Although Chriſt ſpeaketh theſe words generally to all : yet he ſpeaketh them heere ſpecially againſt his Apoſtles, who doe ſeeme to contend here for dignitie : and therein might haue ouerthrowne many a ſoule no doubt, and harmeleſſe hart.

Of theſe things wee haue thought good to put you that be Catholicks in minde ; that thereby you may conſider how the chiefeſt ſeruaunts and children of God haue beene ſubiect to this ambitious humour of affecting ſoueraigntie, and ſeeking for ſuperioritie, dominion, and precedencie. *Iohn* the Patriarch of Conſtantinople, (though otherwiſe a worthie Prelate in the church of God) did cõtende for the ſupremacie with Saint *Gregorie*, that peereleſſe paſtor, prince, prelate, and pope of Rome. And heere at home it is not vnknowne to thoſe that haue read or heard our Engliſh hiſtories, what ſtirre and hart-burning there hath beene in former times, betwixt the

Arch-

Archbishops of Canterburie and Yorke about such matters, being in other respects all of them verie notable men. But neuer was there such an attempt in our opinions for superioritie amongst Catholiques, (for wee will not at this time meddle with any heretiques) since the first preaching of the Gospell of Christ, as now lately is set on foot vnhappily by the Iesuits mischieuous practises. Their order is declared by *Pius Quintus* to be the fifth order, *Mendicantium predicatorum, Of the begging Preachers or Friers.* Ignatius their founder, pretended to haue the called *Fratres minimi, The lowest, least, or meanest sort of Friers :* and termed this company, *Societatem minimam, The meanest or least Societie :* not in regard that they were few in number at the first : but as a great Iesuit saith, *To signifie thereby, that his Societie should yeeld honour to all other sorts of religious persons as to their elder brethrē, ac plane patribus, & as indeed to their Fathers.* But tell vs we pray you; haue these Minimes & begging Friers taken this course ? We wish with all our harts theyhad takē it. ⟨margin: Io. Osorus obitu Ignatij.⟩

That the Apostles before they were fully instructed by the holy Ghost, should haue contended amongst themselues, who should be the greatest, being euerie one of them in so high fauour with their Maister Christ, as they were : it might haue admitted some tollerable excuse, had not our Sauiours *Woe* beene mentioned in the Scriptures, and denounced plainly against them, as a dreadful doome by a sharpe censure of a sorrowfull clause. There wanted not some probable pretences ; why Patriarches and Archbishops might grow into variable oppositions for the prerogatiues of their places, themselues being personages by calling of some equalitie. But that the meanest, least, and lowest order of begging Friers should contend, not among themselues who should be the greatest : but with their elder brethren, auncients and fathers, the most Reuerenced, Respected, and Religious persons of euerie profession : and not that onely, but ouer and besides all this, to striue to bring vnder their girdles the Secular Cleargy, the chiefe state of Priestly preheminency is a wonder as we thinke, the like whereof was neuer heard before amongst Catholiques, Ecclesiasticall, Religious or Temporall, since Christs time till of late daies, that the Iesuits are growne to such a stubborne and vnbridled head, as we feare will breed great mischiefe in the Church of God, before they be well reformed and brought into order againe.

In the other contentions before mentioned, there was no faule as we takeit, eyther in Saint *Peter* for defending his supremacie, or in Saint *Gregorie* the great, for mayntaining the dignitie of the Sea Apostolique : or yet in the Archbishops of Canterburie, for standing vpon their right and interest, granted before vnto them by sundrie of Saint *Peters* successors, for the chiefe primacy in and ouer the Church and ecclesiasticall State in England ; but in those that sought to im-

¶ 3. pugne

pugne them, was all the offence that was committed. And that is
our case iust: who being Secular Priests now in England and
else-where, doe stand at this present in a strong opposition against
the Iesuits. We labour not for any extraordinarie superioritie ouer
them, nor emulate in euill sense any of their vertues or good inde-
uours (if any happily be in them :) nor intrude our selues into their
haruest, nor prie into their actions more then we are compelled, nor
insinuate our selues into their fauours, nor desire to haue any dealing
at all with them. Onely we would be glad to keepe our owne places in the Church of Christ, (which we and all our predecessors Secular Priests haue euer held, since the first propagation of the Gospell
of Christ and Christian Catholique faith and religion, by the holy
Apostles after our Sauiours ascension :) and that now these begging Friers by faction and false pretences might not tyrannise o-
uer vs.

   It is strange to consider how mightily they are possessed, with
pride and ambition, and how farre they haue thereby preuailed. Being men of learning, they scorne to be subiect to the orders of any
Vniuersitie : being preachers, they will be exempted from the controlement of all or any Bishops : being Friers, you kill them, if you
tell them of any cloysters, or wish them to liue retired like right religious men indeed, or to keepe the generall statutes and rules of all
other religious orders. Being naturall borne subiects in many countries where they remayne, no ciuill Magistrate, Prince, or Potentate,
must controll them, nor once seeme to call them to the least account for any of their proceedings. And that which is most, being
men that professe such zeale, charitie, & inward mortification, such
humilitie and godlines : Nay, being men forsooth of perfection (*Est*
*enim hoc institutum virorū plane perfectorum:*this our *institution*,as the
said Iesuit saith : *is of such men as are indeed perfect :*) they refuse notwithstanding to accompanie the rest of the Cleargie both Secular
Regular, and religious, and the whole Church of God in one
of her most soleme and publique seruices done to his diuine Maiestie, which we call our great and solemne processions : because that
by the custome of the Church, they being the youngest and meanest, or minimes of all Mendicants or begging Friers, were to haue
come last behind all the rest in that most honourable seruice.

   But to come to our selues, & to their affectation of superioritie
ouer vs, and that in these dismal daies, & in the middest of our other
domesticall calamities. The Romane Colledge, for the bringing vp
of students to become Priests for England, was no sooner erected,
but by sleights and false calumniations, they got the superioritie and
gouernement of it. Vpon their comming into England, how they
laboured to creepe into mens consciences : to insinuate themselues
into Nobles and great persons estates, and to discredit vs, many Catholiques

Iohn Oso-
rius.

tholiques doe know : Wee our selues from time to time did easily find the smart and inconuenienc of it : and many of vs to our friends haue oft bewayled and complayned with sighs and teares of such their vnchristian dealing with vs . Our brethren then prisoners at Wisbish, who for their vertue, constancie and most Christian Catholique conuersation, & maner of charitable proceeding in all their actions, had worthily merited the name, not onely of the visible, but also of the most afflicted Catholique Church in England : continued in that honour and reputation with all men , euen from the beginning of their duresse vntill some seauen or eight yeeres agon , that Frier *Weston* a Iesuit would needs be their superiour . Frier *Garnet* the prouinciall of the Iesuits in England, was in reasonable tune with some of our brethren (verie auncient, reuerend, and learned Priests) vntill they seemed to dislike this attempt of Frier *Westons:* and then he brake with them in such bitternes as he discouered himselfe verie manifestly : saying, *That he saw no cause why the Secular Priests might not content themselues well ynough to be subiect to the Fathers of the Societie of Iesus,* and added some loose reasons of that his assertion . When both he and his subiect Frier *Weston* perceiued , that their plot was dashed at *Wisbish,* and how odious a thing it grew to be, that men who professe religiō should aspire to such an vnheard of superioritie ; they wrought with their grand Captaine Frier *Parsons,* that what they could not worke one way, they might in effect compasse it by an other . And thence insued the authoritie of our R. Arch-Priest, procured by most indirect, vnlawfull and dishonest meanes . Which authoritie is so limited to the directions of the Iesuits, and as it were confined to their platformes, as whilest he is onely ruled by them, and they by Frier *Parsons:* it had beene peraduenture better for vs in regard of our quietnes & commoditie, that they thēselues had bin appointed our Commaunders, Gouernors & good Maisters : for so hauing attayned directly to that which they aymed at, it is likely they would haue beene content . Whereas now because they want but onely the bare name of our Arch-Prelats ; their minds are so inflamed against vs , as when we tooke exception at the manner of our Arch-Priests aduancement ouer vs, and held that course therein , which hath euer hitherto beene approued in the Church of God : who but the Iesuits that are wholly exmpted from our Arch-Priest authoritie, and ought to haue beene straungers in our affaires (had it not beene vnder-hand , their owne cause) did then, and euer since oppose themselues with might and mayne against vs in that action ?

A principall Iesuit in Spayne telleth vs diuers straunge tales of this his Societie , which to our vnderstanding seeme to smell of worse matter, then we are willing to reueale at this present. Hee saith that : *Ignace their founder, is the Angell of whom Saint* Iohn *spake, when he said :*

John Osorius, in obitu Ignatii.

said: *Quintus Angelus tuba cecinit*, The fift Angell sounded his trumpet. Furthermore, alluding to another Text, he saith : *That Ignatius is
the wearie and weake Aegyptian, whom* Dauid *toke vp to fight the bat-
tels of our Lord* : and addeth, that therefore, *as the souldiers cried* ; Hæc
est præda Dauid : *this is the pray of Dauid* : Ita nunc societas Vniuersa,
quæ a mundi tyrannide liberata est, non præda Ignatij ; sed Dauidis dicitur, non societas Ignatij, sed societas Iesu nuncupatur : *so now the whole
Societie being deliuered from the tyrannie of the world, is not called
the pray of Ignatius but of* Dauid : *not the Societie of* Ignatius, *but of*
Iesus. And the reason followeth : Quia eos in socios Christus admise-
rat, *because* Christ *had admitted them to be his fellowes*. Afterwards
also : Nemo ergo dicat : ego sum Pauli : ego sum Apollo : sed ego
sum Christi : *Let no man say, I hold of* Paule : *I of* Apollo, *but I hold
of* Christ. *And let vs call our selues, the fellowes, not of* Ignatius *but of*
Christ. Also the same great Father affirmeth : that *the Iesuits in Portugall, haue alreadie obtained the name of Apostles, and that this Societie, hath so worthily laboured in* Christ *his vineyard* : Vt Catholici
omnes Iesuitæ dicantur, eo quod Iesuitæ eorum omnium duces ac Magistri sint : *As that in these Northren parts of the world, al Catholiques
are called Iesuits, because the Iesuits are the leaders of them all, and
their Maisters*. In like sort he is of opinion : that the fathers of this
Societie, are the Angels Clouds, and Doues, whereof the Prophet Esay
writeth, saying : Qui sunt isti qui vt nubes volant ; & quasi columbæ
ad fenestras suas? *What Angels, are these that flie like Clouds, and as
Doues to their windowes?* And againe he saith : *They are called Ange-
li, Angels, that is, Messengers*: Eo quod maximarū rerum legatione fun-
gantur : *because they are Ambassadors of the greatest things or affairs
amongst mortall men* : Nubes, Clouds, *for their swift obedience* : *and*
Columbæ, Doues, quia fellis acerbitate caret hæc pacifica societas Iesu,
quo nihil admirabilius: *for that this peaceable Societie of* Iesus, *hath
no gall* : *asmuch to say, as it wanteth all bitternes of gall, splene, ran-
cour, malice and reuenge* : *which is as great a wonder as may be*. But
you will say : quorsum hæc : what of all this : are you sillie men the
persons that eyther wil or dare take vpon you to confute these things
thus published in print by a Spaniard : nay, by so worthie a Iesuit :
and preached for an introduction to make Ignatius a Saint, or at the
least to paint him out for a man fit to be a Saint ? Surely whatsoeuer we can or dare doe (if these follies doe not confute themselues
sufficiently) we will not at this time expresse, as not intending to
deale with many of them. But how true it is, that the name of
Christians is abolished in these Northren Regions, and that we are all
now termed Iesuits : and whether all other orders of Religion that
retaine the names of their founders, are not here verie shrewdly
taxed, and brought to be within the Apostles prohibition : we leaue
it to your further consideration. Onely for the present we say thus
                                                                much :

much : that let the Iesuits be trumpets, *Dauids* pray , Iesus companions, Angels and Clouds, or what elſe this fellow of theirs the Spaniſh Ieſuit would haue them, we much regard not : ſo as againe for
our ſakes he will be pleaſed to ſtrike out the word Doues. For notwithſtanding all the Texts, we doe not find them men of ſuch Doue-
like mindes , and ſpeciall mortification as they doe make ſhew of,
but haue their paſſions and diſtempered humors aſwell as ſome o-
thers haue . Marke we beſeech you , how one of theſe Doues (if
you will needs haue them ſo termed) doth write againſt vs in a little   Ma. Liſter.
treatiſe not paſt two ſheets of paper : becauſe we onely forbore our
obedience to our R. Arch Prieſts verie ſtraunge authoritie (as we
then thought) till we might be further informed of his Holines pleaſure . He calleth vs *Schiſmatikes, and men* (by one of his inferences)
to be caſt into hell : factious perſons , deiected with the griefe of our
owne ruine : and ſaith that we haue loſt our places amongſt Prieſts :
that we are baniſhed from the holy alter and miniſterie of the Sacraments : that our iudgements are to be contemned, and that we are
condemned of the holy Apoſtolique Church He termeth vs triflers,
younglings in Diuinitie , fooles not to be regarded what we ſay :
men that gather not with Chriſt : Newters, that doe belong to the
diuided kingdome, which ſhall be deſtroyed, and rebels againſt the
kingdome of Chriſt. He affirmeth further, that we are become Eth-
nicks and prophane laicall perſons : that we ought to be ſhunned and
auoyded, as the Iewes did ſhunne in times paſt the publicans, notorious & knowne ſinners ; and that we are infamous perſons , nothing
better then ſouthſayers, wiſards, & Idolaters. And whereas amongſt
other things we alleadged, that his Holines , in erecting our Arch-
Preſbiterſhip was miſinformed : *O mendacium: O notable lie* (ſaith this
milde Doue.) and therwithall comes vpon vs againe. *Quid ?* What
(ſaith hee) *Numquid factioſis iſtis licebit in re grauiſsima tam impune,*
tamque impudenter mentiri? Shall it be lawful for theſe factious perſons,
in a matter of moſt importance to lie ſo impudently and go vnpuniſhed ?

There are alſo diuers other Pidgeons of this flight , that out of
queſtion eyther haue galles , or ſome other verie bitter matter in
them, that is equiualent to any gall whatſoeuer : Frier *Holtby* in his
long and tedious letter to a verie vertuous Catholique Ladie written
againſt vs : Frier *Garnet* in ſundrie of his letters both to ſome of vs,
and alſo to others : Alſo Frier *Parſons* in his late Apologie : but eſpecially in his (as we take it) laſt booke intituled : *A manifeſtation*
of the great folly , and bad ſpirit of certaine Secular Prieſts , &c.
Some little taſte we will giue you heere of theſe good Fathers
mortified humour and verie meeke ſpirit, out of the ſaid laſt booke.
You haue heard the title of it : whereunto that the whole diſcourſe
might be ſutable , he inſinuateth directly in this preface, *That we*
are in a ſort poſſeſſed with many wicked ſpirits. And to ſeeme to
haue

haue some authoritie for it: hee applieth thefe words of our Sauiour Chrift vnto vs, where he faith thus. *The vncleane fpirit went
forth, & brought with him feuen other fpirits more wicked then himfelfe, and all entring, dwelt there: and the ending of thofe men was
worfe then the beginning.* Of fixe of thefe diuels the chiefe fubftance
of all his booke doth confift; and therefore he nameth them directly before he commeth to his difcourfe, and fetteth them downe in
expreffe words, for the contents of his treatife. Wherein his whole
drift is, to flaunder more honeft men then himfelfe, and to mif-
leade and feduce you : as though whatfoeuer the Secular Priefts
haue written, in fuch bookes, as they haue beene inforced this
yeere paft to publifh, for their owne iuft defence againft the Iefuits
calumniations, and bad dealings with them, did proceed onely from
their folly : accompanied alwaies with one of thefe fixe lying fpirits. For example, and to vfe his owne words : *From their manifeft
folly & bad fpirit: from their folly & paffionate fpirirt: from their folly
and prefumptuous fpirit: from their folly and vnfhamefaft fpirit:
from their folly and malignant fpirit, and from their folly and deceiued fpirit.* With this folly and thefe fixe wicked fpirits, he raifeth vp
tempefts againft vs by Sea and land, and playeth the Exorcift: in
fuch fort throughout his whole difcourfe: as if hee had beene Frier
Wefton (another Pidgeon of the fame Doue-coate) at Den-
ham, when the time was (whereof wee feare a ftraunge relation) and fo dealeth with our faid brethren, as though eyther hee
himfelfe or they (good men) were diuels indeed. And fhall wee fay
that this man hath no gall in him, but in mildneffe of his fpeech and
fimplicitie of his heart is like a Doue? Hee that fhall with anie
iudgement read his faid treatife, will rather thinke he was brought
vp in a Crowes-neft. Some men are much deceiued, if both he
and many of his crue : might not for their ftinging and poyfoned
writings, be better refembled to Hornets and Dragons, then to fo
milde a fowle as a Doue is reported to be, by all that write of her.

But certaine perfons will fay vnto vs: you fee not that part
of the wallet that hangs at your owne backes. It is true, that
wee are not ignorant how greatly fome of our faid brethren are
blamed, and Maifter *Watfon* chiefely by many of you (how
iuft foeuer their caufe bee) for the bitterneffe of their ftile ; and
we wifh with all our hearts, that they had tempered their pennes
better, not in refpect of the Iefuits, but of your weakenes. God
forgiue vs all our finnes. *In multis enim offendimus omnes : For in
many things wee offend all. Si quis in verbo non offendit hic perfec-
tus eft vir : If any offend not in his fpeeches, he is a perfect man.*
But yet fome further defence may be made of our brethrens faid
bitternes: mens generall imperfections alwaies confidered, wherwith we often ftayne euen our beft actions.

Ia

It muſt bee confeſſed by all men that are of any vnder-ſtanding, that ſharpeneſſe eyther of ſpeech or ſtyle, is not alwaies to bee diſliked. The olde Prophets, Chriſt himſelfe, his Apo-ſtles, many holy Saints and Fathers ; haue vſed this kind of bit-ternes and ſharpe writing when they ſaw cauſe. To which pur-poſe much might be alleadged, as alſo to ſhewe that oftentimes, wounds are better then kiſſes, fretting tents, coraſiues, and in-ciſions, more needfull then gentle, milde, lenitiue, and o-uer haſtie skinning plaiſters. So as hereof there being no queſtion amongſt vs, or any other of diſcretion: the doubt then is, whe-ther the Ieſuits or we, haue the better cauſe : and conſequently, whe-ther of vs may better pretend the teſtimonie of Gods Spirit, a good conſcience, true zeale, perfect charitie, and the practiſe of Chriſt, of his Apoſtles, and of many auncient fathers, for the ſharpenes of our writings.

Maiſter *Parſons* ſpeaketh (in his ſaid manifeſtation) of his owne long and accuſtomed practiſe and experience : where he ſaith : *That an euill argument may ſometimes by cunning and ſmooth handling, or by ſhewing wit & learning, of zeale or modeſty, be made plauſible to the vulgar Reader.* And indeed therein he hath an eſpeciall gift aboue all men that we know. For no mans writings are generally more ſpightfull and galling then his. But it is mixt with ſuch floods of Crocodils teares, when he guirdeth moſt, as that, he then alwaies pretendeth ſuch deuotion and charitie, as though euerie hard word he vſeth, went to his verie heart : and that hee would not deale ſo roughly with any of his brethren for his life, were it not, that (for their good and amendement) hee were driuen thereunto of meere neceſſitie. And with theſe fayre pretences, the ſimpler ſort are greatly blinded. But by his leaue, it is alſo as certain, that if a true cauſe be cleerely and at the full deliuered, although it be done with no ſuch hypocritical skill, but with ſome choller and heat of humour (as zeale ſometime is tearmed :) he is but likewiſe a verie vulgar Rea-der, and of a ſhallow reach, that will therefore be led to diſcredit the truth vpon ſo light a ground. Men of ſound iudgement will alwaies looke to the iſſue of the matter in queſtion, and not to the manner of pleading. More therefore of the cauſe it ſelfe, where-vpon this doubt before mentioned doth ariſe. Wee hope we may truly ſay it, as in the ſight of God, and without all phariſaical oſtenta-tion, that we are not ambitious : that we ſeeke no exemptions from our lawfull ſuperiour : that we honour diſcipline and embrace it : that we craue to haue Biſhops to ouer-ſee, puniſh, & control vs whē we doe amiſſe : and that we labour chiefly in theſe diſaſtrous quar-rels, to withſtand ſo great an innouation & general diſgrace to all the Seculer Cleargie in Chriſtendome, as neuer yet hapned, if we ſhould yeeld to be at the checke and direction either of Frier *Garnet*, Frier

Parſons,

Parsons, or any, or all the Iesuits in the world. And wee are the rather so earnest against both them and their plottings to this purpose: because we likewise know their further practises and most wicked designements, against both our Prince and country , & how they ingaged théselues with the Spaniards, her Maiesties professed enemies. So as might the Iesuits once beare rule ouer al both Priests & people (as let the state look to it in time, for they haue further preuailed here in alreadie then we are glad of:) it would not be long before this kingdom were brought into a general côbustion. Is our cause then so iust, and theirs so impious, and should we be silent? Doe they say vnto vs with *Tobias* the Ammonite: *That do what you can, a Foxe* *shall be able to ouerthrow all your opposition* : The *Infanta* of Spaine shall be your queene, and that sooner then you looke for : and shall we not say as it is there in the Text? *Audi Deus noster quia facti su-* *mus despectui : conuerte opprobrium super caput eorum, & da eos in des-* *pectionem in terra captiuitatis.* Heare vs O our God, heare vs : and *because they doe despise vs and our endeuours, to maintayne both the* *Church and our countrey against their machinations , giue them ouer* *that they may be a despised and contemptible generation throughout all* *the world if in time they repent not.*

Can any true harted English Catholick, seeing how the case nowe standeth betwixt vs and these men , be iustly offended with this our zeale? Hath God made vs annoynted priests here amongst you, *and* *shal we see a sword drawne out against this Land, and not founde out* *our trumpet to summon you to battell?* One telleth you verie plainlie in his Latine Appendix (and we suppose it is our R. Arch-priest him selfe) *that Cardinall Allen and Father Parsons, as Moses and Iosue,* *iam diu proculdubio occupassent promissionis terram : had long since out* *of doubt possessed this Realme of England: nisi quorundam inobedien-* *tia atque ingratissimum obstitisset murmur : had not the disobedience of* *some, and theyr most displeasing murmuring hindred it.* It is the manner of our English Iesuits, and of such as are Iesuited, neuer to mention Frier *Parsons* trecheries, but they ioyne that good Cardinall with him, to mittigate the odiousnes of his proceedings. But howe coulde they haue gotten this land of Promise into their fingers? Meane they by their attempt 1588? or had they before this time layd violent hands vpon her Maiestie? or what had they else doone, if some such impediment as they speake of had not hapned? Blessed was that disobedience, and happy was that murmuring, that deliuered this kingdome from such vncatholick and most trayterous designements. Rather content your selues deere Catholicks to goe & dwell in Babilon : then euer seeke to obtaine the Land of Canaan by such cruell, barbarous, and Turkish stratagems. Are not such Iesuits or persons whatsoeuer Iesuited, worthy to be detested, that dare publish their dislike of such disobedience and murmure, as hath preuented

z. Eldras. 4.

uented such a Chaos of all mischiefes, as the conquering of our little land of promise would haue brought with it? Or if we haue been
too sharpe in our encountering of these Gyants (as they falsly terme
vs) are we not to be excused?

And as wee woulde haue you to iudge of vs and the rest of our
brethren, that whatsoeuer they haue written, it proceeded of theyr
loue and zeale both to our Church and Countrie: so our hartie desire is, that you would thinke and iudge the like of those right zealous Catholicks of other Countries, that haue written against the Iesuits in the like respect, much more sharply then any of our brethren
hetherto haue done. For howe highlie soeuer the Iesuits are yet in
our bookes, because you know them not throughlie: yet are they
alreadie become an odious generation in manie places. In the kingdome of Swecia, their verie names are detested. The Cleargie of
Spayne is in great dislike of them. The religious men generallie in
all countries doe hate them. At this instant, there is a great & most
dangerous contention in particuler, betwixt them and the Dominicans, about a speciall point of grace. At their first attempt to come
into Fraunce, it was fore-seen by the graue Sorbonists of Paris, what
mischiefe they would work if they were admitted there. Afterwards,
they crept into that countrie like Foxes by little and little, and so in
processe of time behaued theselues, as not long since they haue been
banished thence, as men of most pernitious, wicked, and dangerous
conuersation. You haue heard in a word or two, out of *Osorius* the
Spaniard, what the Iesuits thinke of themselues: it woulde make a
large volume to recount the praises which they haue else-where heaped vppon their founder, their societie, & their fellowes; according
as the saying is: Claw me and I will claw thee. You also vnderstand
as well by the premises, as by our bretherens seuerall treatises, what
estimation we haue of them, and some haue beene offended with
them for their plainenes therein. But now wee humbly intreate you
to obserue, howe roundly they haue beene taken vp in Fraunce for
halting, by men of no small credite in that State; for theyr yeres verie auncient, for their experience verie wise, and for their soundnes
in the Catholicke Romane religion, neuer impeached by any but
Iesuits, who condemne all men eyther for Newters or schismaticks,
or hereticks, or at the least for cold and luke-warme Catholicks, that
disclose their impieties.

Maister *Anthony Arnold*, counsellour in parliament, and heeretofore counsellor and Atturney generall to the late deceased Queene
mother, a man throughlie acquainted with the proceedings of the
Iesuits in Fraunce, writeth as followeth, both of them, and somwhat By this the
of their Founder. *Ignatius* (saith he) through the help of the deuill, Iesuits are
hatched this cursed conspiracie of the Iesuits: who haue beene the discouered
causes of such ruine as Fraunce hath receiued. They are a wicked to be no⸗t

onely the fore-runners but also the chiefe captaines of Antechrist; out of whose societie or sect, it is very probable *homo peccati*, that man of sin shall rise, ere all be ended betwixt the secular priests & them the saide sectarie Iesuits, though for the present they remaine catholicke.

race, borne to the ruine & desolation of mankinde. In their fourth vowe to their Generall, they goe thus farre, that in him they must acknowledge Christ present, as it were, If Iesus Christ should commaund to goe and kill, they must doe so. The Generall of the Iesuits is alwayes a Spanyard, and chosen by the King of Spayne. *Loyola* their first Generall was a Spanyard, *Laynes* the second a Spanyard also. The third, *Euerardus*, was a Fleming, a subiect of the King of Spayne. *Borgia*, the fourth, was a Spanyard. *Aquauiua* the fift, now liuing, is a Neopolitane, subiect to the King of Spayne. If their Spanish Generall commaund them to murther, or cause the King of Fraunce to be murthered, they must of necessity do it. They shoote at no other matter, but to establish the tyrannie of Spaine in all places. All the Iesuits in the world, are bound to pray for the King of Spayne, and that once a day, as his affayres doe require. They haue stirring fellowes to be placed in all quarters, to execute whatsoeuer may tend to the good and aduauncement of Spayne. They had no other marke during the warres in Fraunce; but to make the King of Spaine Monarch ouer all Christendome. The common prouerbe of these hypocrits is: one God, one Pope: and one king of Spaine, the great King catholick and vniuersall. All their thoughts, all their purposes, all their Sermons, all their cōfessions, haue no other white they ayme at, but to bring all Europe vnder the subiection of Spanish gouernment. The Ambassadour of Fraunce, when hee was in Spayne and Italie, neuer found matter of weight wherein they had not an oare. There was neuer Letter intercepted during the warres, wherein there was anie pernicious point, but a Iesuits finger was in it. In their confessions and without witnesses, they paint not the faces, but the harts of their schollers, with the tincture of Rebellion against their princes and naturall Soueraignes.

Mathew a Iesuit, was the principal instrument of the League 1585. And from that yeere 1585. they would giue no absolution to the Gentry of Fraunce, vnlesse they would vow & promise to band themselues against their Soueraigne (*Henry* the third) being a most catholick King. *Barnard* and *Commolet*, (the yere before the sayde League) called the King *Holofernes*, *Moab*, and *Nero*: maintaining that the kingdome of Fraunce was electiue, and that it belonged to the people to establish kings: & alledging this text of the old Testament: *Thou shalt chuse thy brother for King.* Thy brother (say they) that is to say, not of the same linage, or of the selfe same Nation, but of the same Religion, as is this great catholick king, this great King of Spaine. The said *Commolet* was so impudent and bold, as to say verie blasphemously, that vnder these words: *Deliuer me O Lord out of the myer, that I may not sticke in it: Dauid* vnderstood prophetically, the rooting out of the house of Burbon. The same Iesuit also, *Commolet*, preaching at the Bastile before the Gentlemen that

were

were then prisoners in the beginning of the yeere 1589, saide vnto
them, after a thousand impudent blasphemies: that he that had been
their King, was not their King, plotting from thence the murther
which they executed afterwards. What voyce is sufficient to expresse
the secrete counsells, the most horrible conspiracies, more dangerous then the conspiracies of *Cateline*, which were holden in the Iesuits Colledge in S. *Iames* streete? Where did the Agents and Embassadours of Spayne, *Mendoza*, *Daguillon*, *Diego*, *Dinarra*, *Taxis*,
Feria, and others, hold their secret meetings and assemblies, but a-
mong the Iesuits? Where did *Lowchard*, *Ameline*, *Cruce*, *Crome*, &
such like notorious manquellers and murtherers, build their conspiracies but amongst the Iesuits? Who made that bloody aunswere
to the catholick Apologie, but the Iesuits? Where did the two Cardinals which termed themselues Legats in Fraunce assemble theyr
counsels but onely amongst the Iesuits? Where was it that *Mendoza* (the Embassadour of Spayne) vpon All-hollow day, in the yeere
1589. (at what time the King entred the Fauxburges) helde his
counsaile, of Sixteene, but in the Colledge of the Iesuits? Who was
President of the counsell (afterwards) of those Sixteene murtherers,
but *Commolet*, *Bernard*, and Father *Ode Pickenar* the vilest Tygar in
all Paris? *Commolet* preaching in S. *Bartholmewes* church after the
murther of the King, exalted and placed among the Angels this Ty-
ger, this deuill incarnate, *Iames Clement*, the murderer. Who imployed all their studies to speake against the person and right of his
Maiestie that now raigneth, as false and slaunderous matters, as possibly their wicked heads could deuise, but the Iesuits? *Commolet* the
Iesuit (when he preached at Saint *Bartholmes*, as is aforesaid) tooke
for his theame the third chapter of the booke of Iudges, where it is
reported, that *Ehud* slew the king of Moab, and escaped away: and
after that he had discoursed at large vpon the death of their late king
(and commended *Iames Clement*) he fell into a great exclamation:
saying, we haue neede of an *Ehud*, we haue neede of an *Ehud*: were
he a Frier, were he a souldier, were he a lackie, were he a shepard, it
made no great matter. Needs wee must haue an *Ehud*: One blowe
would settle vs fully in the state of our affaires, as we most desire.

Alas, their purpose and burning zeale is, to murder the King liuing. Was it not in the Colledge of Iesuits at Lyons, and also in the
Colledge of Iesuits in Paris, that the resolution was last taken to
murder the King in August 1593? Are not the depositions of *Barriere* (executed at Melun) notorious to all the world? Was it not
Varade, Principall of the Iesuits, that exhorted and incouraged this
murtherer; assuring him that he could not do a more merritorious
worke in the worlde, then to murther the King though hee were a
Catholick: and that for this deede he should goe straight to Paradise? And to confirme him the more in this mischieuous resolution,

did

did hee not cause him to be confessed by an other Iesuit? Did not these impious, godlesse, and execrable murderers, giue this *Barriere* the blessed sacrament, imploying the most holy, most precious, and most sacred misterie of our Christian religion, towards the murthering of the chiefest King in Christendome.

As long as the Iesuits remaine in Fraunce, the king of Spaines murtherers, may be exhorted, confessed, housled and incouraged. Their minds are bloodie, & altogether imbrued with the blood of the late murthered king. They filled the pulpits with fire, with blood, with blasphemies: making the people belieue that God was a murtherer of kings, & attributing to heauen, the stroke of a knife forged in hell. The highest poynt of their honour, standeth in executing of murthers, terming them Martyrs which haue spent their liues therein. They are mischieuous counsailors, traytors, wicked inchauntors, firebrands of mischiefe, hypocrits, monsters, watchfull in mischiefe, diligent in wickednes, wretched caytiffes, manquellers, serpents, pernicious, and dangerous vermine, and haue no fellowes in all sorts of wickednes.

And hetherto Maister *Arnold* dispersedly. Vnto whom wee may adde a short, but a notable description of the Iesuits ordinary sermons (as we take it) out of *Petrus Gregorius Tholossanus*, (a great Lawier and a sound Catholick:) which doth so expresly and pithilie set them out vnto vs, nay to all posteritie, and that in so few words, their dispositions, pride and furie, as hee that shall diligently reade them, and throughlie digest them, may euer carrie with him (if his memorie be not verie dull) the right Idea of a perfect Iesuit. But before he cometh to this description, he first setteth downe the iudgments of God against all such kinde of persons, out of king *Salomon* and the prophet *Ezechiell*. *Abominatio est Domini, omnis arrogantia*. *All that are arrogant (without exception) are abhominable vnto our Lord*. *Contritionem præcedit superbia &c*. *Pride goeth before contrition or destruction: and a high minde before vtter ruine*. *Væ pastoribus Israell : woe be to the Sheppards of Israell,&c*. *That which was weake ye haue not strengthened : that which was sicke, ye haue not healed : that which was broken, yee haue not bound vp : & that which was abiected, yee haue not brought againe : and that which was lost ye haue not sought : sed cum austeritate imperabatis eis et cum potentia : but ye did rule ouer them with austeritie and force or potencie*. Secondly, hauing made this way plaine to his purpose, then hee sheweth further what manner of men the Cleargie, by the testimonies of S. *Peter* & S. *Paule* should be : and how farre from such haughtines of minde, such pride and crueltie : and with what diligence, mildnes, & gentlenes, they ought to proceede in the actions and proceedings which doe belong to their calling. *Feede* (saith S. *Peter*) *the flocke of Christ which is amongst you ; ouerseeing them not by constraint, but willingly accor-*

Pet. Greg de Repub. lib. 13. cap. 14.

Prou. 16.

Ezech. 34.

1.Pet.5.

according to God : *neither for filthie lucre sake , but voluntarily.* And S. *Paule : The seruaunt of God must not wrangle, but be mild towards all men, apt to teach, patient, with modestie, admonishing them that resist the truth , least sometimes God giue them repentance to knowe the truth. &c.* Against which Apostolicall rules , hee declareth that the Iesuits (of whom we thinke he speaketh) be great practitioners, rather sorting themselues in the ranke of those that *Salomon* and the prophet *Ezechiel* before spake of, then of the true Pastors of Gods people.

These are his words : *In quo hodie maxime peccant noui quidā Theologastri, et zelo seātraduci mentiuntur : qui in cathedris non verba modestiæ aut verba dei, sed fulgura, tonitrua vomunt : dicteria, scōmata, gladios, ignes, furores, Megæras, cruenta, neces debacchantur : vt potius maledicos, furiosos, dementes coniuratores, seditiosos, inuidos pacis christianæ, milites, prædones, latrones, quam Euangelicæ veritatis predicatores,et enarratores dixeris: similes pastoribus ijs,qui austeritate imperare volunt, qui putant oues potius necandas , quam ad gregem cùm lenitate reuccandas : cum tamen dictum sit de eodem Euangelio , (cuius se enarratores esse mentiuntur eadem superbia) quod ea sit lex gratiæ, et cū misericordia Christique beneficio et bonitate publicata. Sed nihil est impudentius arrogantia rusticorum qui garrulitatem authoritatem putant, et parati ad lites tumidi in subiectos intonant. Hoc habet proprium doctrina arrogantium : vt humiliter nesciant inferre, quod docent : et recta quæ sapiunt, recte ministare non possint &c. Atque statutum, seditionarios nunquam ordinandos clericos, et ordinatos deijciendos.* Wherein (that is to say, both against the prophets and Apostles doctrine) certaine new smatteriug Diuines now adaies, doe verie greatlie offend, who falslie pretend that they are led by zeale, who in their pulpits & Lectures cast out, not words of modestie , or of the word of God, but lightnings and thunderings : who as outragious men in rayling, vtter nothing but taunts, scoffes, swords, fires, rages , furies of hell, matters of blood and murtherings. So as a man may rather terme them cursed speakers, furious persons, mad men, traytors, seditious declamers, enemies of Christian peace, souldiers, robbers , theeues, then preachers and expounders of the Euangelicall truth, being like those pastors that will commaund with seueritie , that rather think it meete to haue their sheepe killed, then to haue them with mildnes recalled to the flocke. VVhereas notwithstanding it is saide of the gospell (whereof lyinglie they call themselues expositors with the same pride) that it is a lawe of grace and published with the mercie, bountie, & goodnes of Christ. But there is nothing more impudent then the arrogancie of base companions, who account their prating a kind of authoritie, and being readie to quarrell , they tyrannise ouer such as are subiect vnto them . The doctrine of arrogant persons hath this property,that they cannot deliuer with humilitie those

A.

things

things which they teach; nor minister rightly their honest conceits. Now there is a statute, that stirrers vp of sedition should not be made Clergie men: and that such as are made alreadie, should be degraded. And thus *Peter Gregorius*. Whereby you may see, that wee are not the onely men that haue whetted their penns against the Iesuits: nor yet that we haue written halfe so bitterlie as others haue against them. It is to be wished, that you woulde take these thinges to hart, & apply them to the Iesuits proceedings vnderhand in England, but more apparantlie in Ireland. There is an old lesson which children learne among their rules in Schoole, and is fit for all persons, times and seasons : *Fœlix quem faciunt aliena pericula cautum* : happie are they whom other mens harmes doe make to beware. Maister *Arnold*, and *Pet: Gregorius*, haue saide sufficient to make all the states in Europe that are not hispanized, to take heede of these fellowes and of their designements. And yet such is their plotting, and Fox-like wilines, as by swearing and forswearing, by fawning and flattering, & by a thousand other sleights, they so inueigle men and women that be of any good or honorable disposition : that an other very singuler wise man of high authoritie, and a sound Catholick, hath thought it very necessarie, to adde much to that which Maister *Arnold*, and *Pet : Greg.* haue written : that thereby all men, especiallie of state and action, may be inexcusable, if either they themselues, or the state wherein they serue, doe euer heereafter take harme by the Iesuits.

The treatise which hee hath written to this purpose, is intituled, THE IESVITS CATECHISME; so termed as wee thinke, to distinguish their newe deuises, instructions, & plottings, from the sinceritie of the auncient and approued forme of Christes Catechisme, which the Church of Rome hetherto hath taught. In this discourse, the Iesuits and their proceedings are more throughlie sifted, and that *ab incunabilis*, from their verie cradle. By reason whereof, all these things falling out at the beginning so badly, and sorting still from worse to worse; the Author of this Treatise is driuen oftentimes in the heate of his zeale, to lay aside his skill in Rhetorick (which is very excellent :) and for the discharge of his conscience to God, and the dutie he oweth to his countrey, as also for a caueat vnto all other countries, to deale very plainly : calling men and matters by their owne names, without any circumlocution or ambiguitie. He that hath eares to heare, let him heare. This gentleman is farre from the said Spanish Iesuits conceit, either of *Ignatius* himselfe, or of his Order.

Fol. 42.

Fol. 39.

As touching *Ignatius*, he saith, *that although for his learning hee was but an Asse : yet otherwise, he was one of the cuningst worldlings that this our latter age hath brought forth: & in deed a very Imposture.* And whereas great account is made of his illuminations, visions,

inspira-

inspirations, extasies, (wherein the bleſſed Virgin and Chriſt himſelfe talked with him,) diuine inſtruċtions,(opening to him the my-
ſteries of the bleſſed Trinitie, and of the holy Scriptures :) all theſe
contēplations(ſaith he)*were meere mummeries or illuſions of the diuell,* Fol.29.
who deſired to preſent vs with ſuch a man,as might by his ignorance trou-
ble the whole ſtate of the Church. The ſaid *Oſorius* the Ieſuit,hauing
in the largeſt ſize commended *Ignatius* his founder : aſcribeth it as a
ſpeciall point of appertayning to his further praiſe , that he left behind him ſchollers of his owne mould, who like waxe, frame themſelues to beare his expreſſe image. To which purpoſe there is a verie fit Text ſought out in theſe words : *Mortuus eſt pater eius,& qua-* Eccleſ.30.
ſi non eſt mortuus,ſimilem enim reliquit ſibi poſt ſe. His father it dead,
and yet he is as if he were not dead , becauſe he hath left behind him
one like to himſelfe . According to which Text, the ſaid Gentleman
in his ſenſe ſheweth very apparantly the great reſemblance betwixt *Ignatius* and his ofspring , and writeth of them, their whole
order , their qualities , and proceedings , as heere in part it in-
ſueth .

They are of the Societie of Ieſus, as *Iudas* was amongſt the A- Fol.23.
poſtles : ſo many Ieſuits, ſo many *Iudaſes,* readie to betray their
Princes or their countries whenſoeuer occaſion ſerues to doe it.
What will you giue vs, will be the burthen of their ſong to thoſe
Princes that haue moſt money, and we will deliuer our Liege-Lord
into your hands, or trouble his State, that it may be yeelded to you?
Ieſuitiſme breeds many complaints among the people: many iarres, Fol.13.
diſſentions, contentions , rebellions , and ſundry ſchiſmes . There Fol.10.
was neuer any ſeċt more dangerous to Chriſtian Religion then this
of the Ieſuits. The diuell vnder the habit of the Ieſuits, doth goe a- Fol.48.
bout to circumuent all the world . The Seċt of the Ieſuits is, a ba- Fol.55.
ſtard religion, and a verie hoch-poch of all religious orders,without
any thing pure in it, or any point of the auncient Church . The di- Fol.13.
uine ſeruice of their Church, is diuided from ours , their priuiledges
make a diuiſion betweene the Biſhops and them ; the Monaſteries
and them : the Vniuerſities and them : the diuines of Paris and them.
Their propoſitions, make a diuiſion betweene the holy Sea and
Princes . Their Colledges are trappes to catch youth : their confeſ- Fol.106.
ſions, ſubornations : their Sermons Mountebanks Markets. Their
whole profeſſion is nothing elſe but a particular coozning of our priuate families , and a generall villany in all the countries where they
inhabit.

To receiue Ieſuits into a kingdome, is to receiue in a vermine : Fol 62.
which at length will gnaw out the heart of the State both ſpirituall
and temporall . They worke vnder-hand the ruines of the countreyes where they dwell, and the murther of whatſoeuer Kings and Fol.59.
Princes it pleaſeth them.The name of the Ieſuits,ought to be odious Fol.20.12.

amongst all Christians : and they blaspheme against the honour of God, when they so intitle themselues . Without wrong to the authoritie of the holy Sea, you may call the Iesuits, Papelards, and their Sect, Pape-lardy : that is, hypocrites, and their order hypocrisie. The Iesuits are Fox-like, & Lion-like. Al their worthy works are but cooznages. In all their negotiations in France, an Asse & a Fox haue been tied together. Iesuits when they lie, doe say, it is to bee borne with: because it is to a good end. All things (saith the Iesuit) are to be taken for good, that are done to a good end. It is a Iesuiticall priuiledge, to vnderset their slanders with the time, by new cogs. In euery matter be it neuer so smal, the Iesuit cannot go by without lying & disguising. The Iesuits neuer lacke new lying inuentions to aduance their owne credit . One *Iustinian* a Iesuit, being found in Rome to be a counterfait, it marred the Iesuits cookery there : for when they did speak of a facer out of matters and an impostor , they were wont to call him, a second *Iustinian* the Iesuit.

Much more might be here added of the particular heresies wherwith he chargeth the Iesuits : also his freenes of speech, *in tearming the first ten Iesuits, Ignatius & his nine felowes, to haue bin in their times verie cheaters:* and likewise how he proueth, *that in the first allowance of their whole order, and the getting since of their priuiledges, they euer vsed cooznage, obreption, and surreption* . But this may suffice to be inserted in a Letter dedicatorie , aswell to giue you a glympse what the demerits, of the Iesuits are in France, & how they are esteemed of amongst the Catholiques there, that draw not with the line of Spaine against their Soueraigne : as also in a sort , to stop their clamorous mouthes and pens that crie out and write so eagerly , against the tartnes of all the bookes which haue beene lately set out by some of our brethren : and especially the *Quodlibets* : as though neuer learned men, being good Catholiques, had vsed the like sharpenes of stile before them : or euer would vse after them . Which immoderate clamors, both of the Iesuits, and of their adherents , together with the confident iustification of all the proceedings which hane beene plotted, and executed against vs and our brethren, by Frier *Parsons* : Frier *Garnet*, our R. Arch-Priest , and other their Iesuited clawbacks, (as though they were indeed Apostolical men sent lately from God that could not erre (in a manner in their course) by reason of a certaine subordination, and sundrie illuminations that are talked of among them :) caused vs when we met with this discourse, and with a translation of it : after that we had perused the translation , and amended it in diuers parts, not onely to put it to the presse, but to commend it also vnto you (that without newfanglenes are truly Catholiques) with this our Preface or Epistle dedicatorie.

The author of this *Iesuiticall Catechisme*, is for his vertue, grauitie, experience, wisedome, Catholique zeale , and great learning, in

these

Fol. 56.

Fol 76.
Fol. 79.
Fol. 17.
Fol. 41.

Fol. 82.
Fol. 19.

Fol. 2 1.

Fol. 39.

Fol. 38.
Fol. 103.

these causes, so imminent, where he is best knowne: and this his discourse is so sutable to such his vertues, so substantiall for the matter, so eloquent for the phrase, so artificially compiled for the method, as neyther of them both haue any need, eyther of ours or any other mens commendation. If the translation doe content you: if the publishing of it may benefit you: if this our Apologeticall preface, or the booke it selfe, or both, may be a sufficient warning, eyther to you, or to the state, or to her Maiesties subiects generally; or to all, or to any good men in particular (that loue their Queene and countrey:) to take heed in time of the Iesuits: to beleeue them by discretion, to trust them no further then they see them: to detest their statizing: to loath their detractions, and to beware of their Forges: (that are euer occupied in hammering out stratageme after stratageme, the second still more pestilent then the first:) it is all wee looke for, besides your Catholique supportation due to the Catholique Priests in times of necessitie, & your daily and Christian prayers: whereunto we commend our selues, and you all, by our daily supplications, to Gods mercifull gouernment for your protecti-on, and to all his heauenly graces for your direction, progression, and happie consummation through our Lord Iesus Christ. Amen.

Your friends alwaies readie
to doe you seruice.

Faults escaped in printing.

Fol.11.b.lin.10.for.*nona*,read *noua*.fo 27.b.lin.2.for perrec dauncer,
read,daunsing dizard. fol.57.b.the last line. for instructed,read, dis-
disproued. fol.117.for,one with another,read,one another. fol.142.
for,cuffe,read ruffe.fol.165.b.lin.17.for, griefe, rage,read,the chiefe
rage.fol.166.a.lin.4.for some were to be. read,some to be. fol.171.
b. lin. 9.for,his poore.read,this poore.fol.174.a.lin.5.for,thich.read,
which.Other small faults haue escaped,which the iudicial readers eye
will easily discouer and amend.

THE FIRST BOOKE
of the Iesuites *Cate-chisme*.

CHAP. 1.

ABout two yeeres agoe departing from Paris, wée met by chaunce vpon the fieldes with fixe in a company that traueld our way : fome of them had been at Rome, fome at Venice. When we had iournied eyght daies together our horfes wearie, one of our conforts told vs, there dwelt a Gentleman not farre off, an olde acquaintance of his, who doubtleffe would efteeme of it as a great honour done vnto him, if (vpon occafion taken to refrefh our felues) we would goe vifite him. How foeuer fome diftafted this aduife at the firft, yet at laft the moft voyces caried it, and all of vs forth-with turned out of our way vnto his houfe, where we found him accompanied with many other Gentlemen. Who efpying, his auncient friend, gaue him many cheerefull embracings, and faid; How commeth it to paffe, that I am fo fortunate, as to behold my fecond felfe this day ? Sir, at a word you are very welcome, and I thinke my felfe deeply indebted to you, for this vnexpected affault, giuen me with fo fayre a troupe.

After we had feuerally thanked him one by one, hee commaunded our horfes to be fet vp, and a cup of wine

B.   10

to be brought vs, and so led vs through the Court into his house : vvhere entertayning one another with enterchangeable greetings, hee gaue order for Supper to be ready in conuenient time, that wee might take our rest : meane-while wee fell into discourse. But as commonly it hapneth, that we lay our hand vpon that part of our body that grieues vs most ; so wee begun principally to complaine of the miseries of Fraunce, brought in amongst vs by diuersitie of Religion, euery man seeking to aduaunce, what himselfe maintaines sutably to his owne priuate passion, which he calls deuotion.

There was a Iesuite in our company disguisd in apparell, a man (without question) very sociable : There was an Aduocate also, whom I well perceiued to be opposite to the Bulles, constitutions, and orders of the Iesuites. The speech when we parleyd, rebounding from mouth to mouth, the Iesuite made demonstration, how much our Church is bounde vnto theyr societie . And belieue me Gentlemen (quoth he) if God had not sent amongst vs our good Father *Ignatius*, and his company, our Catholique religion had been extinguisht : but as it commonly falls out, that in punishing our offences, after GOD hath afflicted a Country with some generall plague, he applies a remedie to it againe, that it may not be vtterly destroied : so hauing suffered *Martin Luther* to infect many Nations with his poyson, it pleased him (for the cause before alleaged) to raise vp another *Daniel* in his Church, to preserue the head thereof, from all the venomous bitings of that Monster. And to speak what I thinke, I am of that mind, that *Ignace Loyhola*, had his name giuen him, not by chaunce, but by miracle, to this end no doubt, that by changing one Letter into another, as *C*. into *R*. calling him *Ignare Loyhola*, for *Ignace Loyhola*, all posteritie might knowe him to be the man, which had made an end of *Luthers* ignorance, and of all his followers, which vppon his grounds should set anie

other.

other herefies abroach heereafter.

At this fpeech of his, euery man began to fmile, for it was deliuered with fo good a grace, as it could not be offenfiue to any, vnlefle the Aduocate, vvho vvith change of countenaunce fayd thus vnto him. Sir, I will not fuffer your fpeech to fall to the ground without taking it vp againe. I would faine knowe what miracles the Iefuits haue wrought; what bounds they haue fet to bridle the courfe of herefie; and what difference there hath beene in the carriage of the one and the other? For if the Hugonotes on the one fide, were the caufe of the troubles in Fraunce, in the yere 1 5 6 1. ftanding as they did vpon their defence; the Iefuite on the other fide affayling vs, in the yeere 1 5 6 5. rayfd vp farre more fierce and great tyrannies than the former. As for your newe Anagram, you abufe your felfe. *Ignace* was in fome good fort a Gentleman of Nauarre, not called *Ignace Loyhola,* but *Ignare de Loyhola,* as much to fay, as *Ignorant of the Law, hold thy peace.* For beeing as ignorant as might be, he thought it better to be filent than to fpeak. VVhich warily acknowledging in himfelfe, hee neuer fhewed his wit in preaching, teaching or writing, except it were at firft within the gates of Rome, where hee taught young children theyr beliefe, as Maifters of pety Schooles are wont to doe.

This fpeech mooued no leffe laughter than the former: then faid the Gentleman our hofte. I fee no great matter of laughter heere; & turning him to the Iefuite, I belieue Sir (quoth hee) that you are of the Societie of I E S V S, the tenour of your fpeech bewraies no leffe. To this the other aunfwered, that it was fo indeed, and theyr order permitted them to be difguifd, the better to found euery man in his humor. I am very glad of thys faid the Gentleman, and I doe belieue, that fome good Angell led you hether into my houfe, the rather for that I haue beene long time defirous of fuch good company, to the end I might know how the case stands with your Order, which I see is balanced betweene two Scales, greatly commended of some, and by the same weights a-gaine much blamed of others. But seeing there is no banquet heere for seruaunts, they shall take away the cloth, and thanks giuen to God for his daily bounty to-wards vs, wee will enlarge our selues with thys poynt a little farther. It was performed as hee had sayd, and all the wayters voyded the place, he desired the Iesuite not to be displeased, if after the manner of a Catechisme, he brought in one like a childe, moouing the question to his Maister, for the better vnderstanding of his first grounds. In this manner dealt the Gentleman with the Iesuite, desirous to be informed of the principall points of his Order, whereunto the Iesuite readily consented. And although in very deed, for any thing I coulde ga-ther by theyr talke, the Gentleman was as skilfull as the Iesuite: yet playing *Socrates* part, he rode after him like a *Platonist*, to draw from him that which hee desired, in such manner as heere ensues.

CHAP. 2.

¶ *What the foundation is of the societie of* Iesus, *which the common-people call* Iesuits.

Gent. Ou say you are a Iesuite, there-fore of a newe Religious Order. *Iesuit.* Nay, rather of a most an-cient, and for this cause haue we taken vpon vs the holy name of the societie of *Iesus*, as imitators beyond others, of our Lorde Iesus Christ and his Apo-stles. *Gent.* You preach & teach freely euery one that will heare you. *Ies.* We doe so. *Gent.* But tell me then, did the Apostles teach little boyes theyr Grammer, or A. B. C.? *Ies.* No. *Gent.* Then haue you great aduan-

tage,

tage of them, and it is not without ſome ground, that
deſpiſing the name of Chriſtians, by which they were
called, you particularly terme your ſelues Ieſuites.

Ieſ. Had they taught as wee doe, their charitie had
beene more compleat, and as for the name of Chriſtians, wee take it to bee too proude a ſtile. *Gent.* Some-
what there is, whereby you paſſe them in charitie and
humilitie. You make three vowes, do you not? of Chaſtitie, Pouertie, and Obedience? *Ieſ.* Neuer doubt of
that. *Gent.* Then are you Monkes. *Ieſ.* By no meanes,
but rather Religious men. *Gent.* Then your houſes be
Monaſteries. *Ieſ.* Nothing leſſe, wee call our habitations Colledges, wherein wee haue our Churches. *Gent.*
What kinde of Cabale is this, that theſe men, who make
ordinary vowes that binde them to their office, as other
Religious perſons doe, yet ſcorne thoſe holy names of
Monkes and Monaſteries, which all venerable antiquitie hath honoured with ſo much deuotion? Peraduenture you ſhould haue cald your Colledges Gods houſes. Yet I thinke you made a conſcience of that, becauſe
we call thoſe Hoſpitalls Gods houſes, where poore beggers are harbourd; and if I be not deceiued, you feare
nothing ſo much as to be poore. VVell, let vs goe on,
you weare a Frock as Monkes doe, you dwell in Cloyſters like other Religious men, doe you not? *Ieſ.* We
know not what Cloyſters meane, we ſhunne them as a
Iakes, which we would be loath to come into; and wee
are apparreld not as Monks, but as Secular Priſtes. It is
true, that by our firſt inſtitution we faſtned a hoode to
our long robes, ſometime with a point, ſomtime vvith a
claſpe, but we quickly left it off againe, after our cauſe
was pleaded, in the yeere 64. againſt the Vniuerſitie of
Paris: For the Heretiques ſaide, our claſpe was a fiſh-
hooke, to catch ſilly peoples goods. And other more
impudent then they, reported we did were a point, like
the women of the Greene Caſtle of Toloſa.

Gent.

Gent. I could wifh, for the honour I beare you, that you had not renewed the remembrance of thofe olde complaints that were made againft you. Let vs leaue thofe bad fpeeches to blacke mouthes, and fuffer vs in good fort to vnderftand what belongs vnto your Order. For I defire nothing more, than to fee you in good conuerfation towards euery man. Although beeing Religious perfons, you refufe the name & habite outwardly appertayning vnto Monkes, yet I doubt not, but for that which is interior, touching Faftes and abftinence from certaine meates, practifd by other Religious men for the taming of the flefh, you obferue thefe very orderly. *Ief.* Quite contrary, for we are exprefly forbidden by our Statutes fo to doe, but it is left free to euerie mans deuotion, wherein is the greater merrit.

Gent. There is fome meaning in this, for hee that fhould leaue the Lent arbitrarie to euery man, might affure himfelfe, it would bring in great diforders: therefore among other Religious perfons, the firft Founders haue beene euer carefull to prouide for this in chiefe, iudging a generall law better than the particuler will of any one or other Religious perfon whofoeuer. But to proceede, what fay you to Proceffions, vvhich the Church hath in all antiquitie much regarded (for as it appeares, they were in vfe in *Tertullians* time) I hope therefore you would not exempt your felues frõ them. *Ief.* We are fo farre from approouing them, that on the contrary our Conftitutions forbid vs to be there, as appeares in the Conftitutions afterward authorized by Pope *Gregory* the thirteenth.

Gent. You are not then as I take it of the body of the Vniuerfitie of Paris? but if you had been matriculated as you defired in the yere 64. would you haue withdrawne your felues from the profeffions of the Rector, where the foure Orders of begging Friers, and other religious men are prefent? *Ief.* We would. *Gent.* Well then,

then, tell mee, If such a sollemne Procession should be made in Paris, as wee see, when they goe to Saint *Geneuiefes* shrine to appease Gods wrath, when all the Parishes, Monasteries, and high Courts also be there, attended on with an infinite number of the Common-people, would ye not goe with thē? *Ies.* No. *Gent.* Make you so small account of the counsell of Trent? *Ies.* Very great, as of that where-vppon stands the confirmation of our whole Order, mauger all our enemies. *Gent.* Know you not what is precisely set downe there, that as well Secular Priests, as Regulers, and all sorts of Monkes cald to publique Processions, are enioyned to goe; they onely excepted, which liue in some straighter inclosure then the rest? Sure, you are not within the compasse of this exception, for in my oppinion, it is made for the Charter-house-Monkes, and Celestines.

Ies. I conceiue it so, but you must likewise vnderstand, that Pope *Gregory* dispensed with vs, in the yeere 1576. to the preiudice of that Counsell, and that not onely by forme of dispensation, but by three expresse prohibitions. *Gent.* And yet, before this dispensation, you neuer kept them company, whereuppon doe you ground your priuiledge?

Ies. Vppon a perswasion that one day wee shall preuaile. *Gent.* Diseasd horses in one stable are put a sunder, are you in that ranke among religious men? I beseech you tell me, euen by way of confession, why were those prohibitions made for you? *Ies.* Because you coniure mee by the holy name of Confession, I will not lie to you. Some one of our Superiors, foisted into Pope *Gregories* Bulls, that it was to this end, to wit, that wee might not be hindered in preaching, reading, & taking confessions: but to speake the truth, seeing the foure Orders of Mendicants did preach, & heare confessions, and reade Lectures in theyr houses as well as wee, and yet forsooke not the said Processions: I take it to bee a

pre-

pretence farre fet, and from the purpofe, and that there was rather fome other caufe of it; namely, that according to the admittance of our Order, our place was to come behind, whereby we fhould haue wronged greatlie the focietie of I E S V S, which wee take to be a fuperlatiue of all others. *Gent.* If it be fo, the fanctitie of your deuotion, is not without fome Feauer of Ambition. Well, yet let vs goe forward. When you fay your canonicall houres in your Churches, do you not fing in two rankes, as wee doe in ours? Haue you not likewife a place appointed for the Priefts office, which wee call the Quier, diftinct and feparate frō the body where the people ftay to fay their prayers? *Ief.* To this I will not anfwer you by roate, but recite the text it felfe of our cōftitutions; *Let not our Company vfe a Quier for theyr canonicall houres, faying of Maffe, or finging of other feruice.* And if you haue well marked the Church in our Colledge at Paris, there was no Quier at all.

Gent. It may be your Law-maker meant by this, that you are fo priuiledged, that when you pray without feeling or deuotion, onely with a kinde of moouing your lyps foftly to your felues, your prayers neuertheleffe are heard of G O D, to ioyne this priuiledge to your other extraordinaries. *Ief.* You are a fcoffer. I will tell you more, that in refpect of Canonicall houres, we haue nothing to binde vs, to doe as other men doe, in finging or faying them out aloude, but we may mutter our prayers as foftly as we pleafe. *Gent.* This prooues our Auncestors to be very blunt, fithence your deuout foules celebrate diuine feruice now, altogether of another fafhion, beyond the practife of antiquitie. But what fay you to your Aniuerfaries? doe you keepe them in fauour of your Benefactors? *Ief.* Wee are very nimble at taking all that is beftowed on vs, yet are we not thereby bound to keepe any yeerely cōmemorations of it. *Gent.* Then are you ftarke fooles. *Ief.* Not fo, but very wife and deuout:

deuoute: for we are not like other men, that ouercharge
themselues with long Mementoes, and are compeld to
passe them all through with one *Fidelium*, as wee say in
the common French prouerbe. To be short, wee make
too great a conscience of deceiuing our Benefactors.

Gent. See heere a new Church, cleane contrarie to the
old. Well, yet let vs goe forward : You tolde mee euen
now, that you make three vowes, of Pouertie, Chastitie,
and Obedience. Nowe amongst the least of many nouelties deuiding you frō vs, you haue 3. vowes in shew
cōmon with other religious persons. *Ies.* Our 3. vowes,
varie much from theirs. *Gent.* Wherein? *Ies.* The first
of our vowes is called Simple, the two other Sollemne.
Gent. I beseech you decyfer your doctrine that I may
vnderstand it, for to say truth, this is high Dutch to me.
Ies. You must know, that in these three vowes, we promise Pouertie, Chastitie, and Obedience, as other Religious Orders doe : but true it is, that in the vowe Simple, there is a peculiar streine, by meanes whereof, for
so much and so long as we are there appointed, we may
be maisters of worldly goods, and take vp successions, as
well in a straight line as collaterall. Moreouer, although
in respect of a religious state, it is not in any of our own
powers to giue ouer our companie, yet after one hath
made aboade with vs, ten twenty, or thirtie yeeres, more
or lesse, our Generall may absolue him, and send him
backe franke and free discharged from his vowe to his
owne house, to marry if he will.

Gent. Good God, what manner of vow is this? *Ies.*
Such as Pope *Gregorie* hath confirmed to vs. It is not
strange to me to finde it so strange to you, for the great
Canonist *Nauarre*, the chiefest of all the Doctors in
matters of the Canon-law, speaking of this simple vow,
giues it the name of Great and Maruailous. *Gent.* He
might rather haue termed it Miraculous, because it lodges ritches and pouertie together in one subiect, a thing

C.   impos-

impoſſible, by common courſe of nature. And that which amazeth me the more, is, that your Generall can releaſe a religious perſon when he thinkes it meet. This in our Chriſtian religion was neuer practiſed. *Ieſ.* None but the Ieſuits may doe it. *Gent.* What is your ſecond vowe which you call Sollemne, and is as I ſuppoſe the firſt of the two ſollemne ones? *Ieſ.* Wee doe nothing in that, that doth ſmell of noueltie, more than in the ſimple: onely from the time a man enters into it, he looſeth all hope of ſucceſſion, or returne to his houſe, and is brought within cōpaſſe of all other religious men profeſſed.

Gent. Before we proceed to that great ſollemne vow, which is your third, I would faine learne of you ſome other particulars of your Order. Seeing you reade Lectures of Humanitie, Phyloſophie, and Diuinitie, not onely to your owne company, but to all ſtrangers that repayre to you. I doubt not, but that ſuch as come in among them, are not all alike appointed to their ſtudies, for charitie begins with it ſelfe: & alſo that to make the Prieſtes (which ſhoulde bee your intention) they muſt heare theyr courſe. *Ieſ.* You deceiue your ſelfe. Wee receiue an infinite company that can neither reade nor write, nor are any way fit for ſtudie afterward, nor yet to be prieſted, whom wee call Lay-brethren, appointed onely to take care of our prouiſion, when wee ſtande in neede. *Gent.* Theſe be voluntaries, like the Oblates, & Mias-Monkes conuerts of other religious orders, which are but halfe Monkes, whom the people call Halfehoods.

Ieſ. Yet you are awry. Our Lay-brethren are preciſely of our Order, like the others as well of the vow Simple, as of the firſt ſollemne Vow. *Gent.* Neuertheleſſe, they profeſſe ignorance, like the Lay-brothers among the Friers of Italie. *Ieſ.* The very ſame. *Gent.* What a mingled religion is this, built with ſuch variety of ſtones?
Bleſſed

Bleſſed God, what would all thoſe good old Doctors ſay, whoſe ſanctimonie hath placed them in heauen, if they ſhould returne into the world againe, and ſee thys Familie rule the roſte, ouer the greateſt part of our Church? Goe to, let vs talke if you pleaſe, of the great ſollemne vowe, which is the laſt. *Ieſ.* That is the perfection of our worke. For in it, beſide the three ſubſtantiall vowes of other religious perſons, wee make a fourth in particuler to our Father the Pope, which wee call the vowe of Miſſion, vvhereby, if it pleaſe his holineſſe to ſend vs to the Turkes, Pagans, Heretiques, or Schiſmatikes to conuert them, or to bring them to the Chriſtian fayth, wee are bound to obey him without reward, taking neyther gold nor ſiluer to defray the charge of our iourney. *Gent.* A very pure and holy deuotion, if it be well imployed. But what true records haue you, that can giue vs ſound teſtimonie of your exployts? *Ieſ.* Let it ſuffice you, that an account thereof is kept in Rome. When the great vowe is made, which is the very cloze of all our vowes, then we begin to be cald Fathers, a dignitie incōmunicable to all the reſt. Yet is there ſo much humilitie among vs, that as ſoone as wee become Fathers, we are wedded to ſo ſtrict a pouertie, that we cannot poſſeſſe any moueables in generall, or particular, but are bonnde to begge our reliefe from doore to doore, not by the miniſterie of brethren conuerts, as the other foure Orders of Mendicants doe, but by men of moſt note among the Fathers.

Gent. Loe here a vowe impoſſible to be imitated. The more you are magnified aboue your fellowes, the more ſubmiſſion and pouerty you take vpon you. When you are qualefied for Ieſuits, as true imitators of the Apoſtles, doe you thinke the Apoſtles by profeſſion went a begging? If you be of that mind, it is an oppinion heretofore condemned by the Church. *Ieſ.* Doe you take it to be euill, that from the abundance of our new zeale,

we

wee should adde some-what to theyr auncient charitie? *Aduoc.* This question is from the purpose (pardon me if I interrupt you) you neuer yet sawe a Iesuite beare a wallet vp and downe the streets. *Ief.* Our state is not worse then the Foules of the ayre, which liue by the grace of God, distributing his Manna to euery man according to his will, as he did in the old time to the chyldren of Israell. *Gent.* You pay vs with very good coyne, I accept of it sithence you are so content. Doe you containe your selues within the bounds of your three vowes of Pouertie, Chastitie, and Obedience. *Ief.* No, for we will not like Atheists, diuorce state affayres and Religion; we thinke all things shall goe well for the glorie of God, & the saluation of our owne soules, when these be ioyned together. *Gent.* What a hotch potch of new doctrine doe you bring vs now? And to say the truth, neuer was any thing better spoken, then that wee learne of *Optatus,* That religion hath beene comprehended in state, not state in religion. Euery one of vs should wish to haue the Gouernours of Common-weales religious, that is, men of fayth & integritie, not playing with theyr consciences to fauour theyr affaires. But for a religious Order, to manage state matters, in the midst of theyr prayers, is great irreligion, or rather heresie. *Ief.* That which you alleage, was *Optatus* his oppinion, not *Ignatius.*

Gent. What say you to Saint Paule, teaching, that *Nemo militans Deo, implicat se negotijs secularibus.* If it be fit so to doe, why did you of late yeres forbid your companie to meddle therein hereafter. *Ief.* That was a statute onely for the time. For perceiuing that in the end of the yeere 93. all Fraunce was enclined to peace beyond our expectation, wee made that constitution to curry fauour with the state. Yet for all this, I would not haue you thinke, that wee haue here stakt our feete into the ground, and goe no farther. For the same constitutions

tions permit vs, to resolue in particuler, as occasion counsels vs. *Gent.* A featefull permission. But what meane you by the worde, State affayres? *Ief.* The day would be too short to vtter it. Let it content you that the greatest and surest counsell we take, is of our owne consciences, which we know to be guided by the line and leading of our Sauiour. By this scrue somtime we remoue Kingdoms, punish Kings and Princes whose manners we mislike, and all for the glory & honour of God, and of his holy Church. *Gent.* All the Christian vvorlde should haue you in wonderfull reuerence for this, and I am sorry you should proue so vnthankfull now, as to abrogate such a holy lawe. *Ief.* It is not so repeald but that it liues in our soules continually. For within these three yeeres, we practisd to kill the Queene of England, and the Countie Maurice of Nassau, and howsoeuer by misfortune we faild of those two strokes, yet we are readie to reach at them againe, there, and elfe where, as wee thinke good, and as opportunitie shall be offered.

Gent. Then you mixe mercenary murders with state matters, call you this ioyning of State & Religion both together? *Ief.* Why doubt you of it? Heresie is a maladie whereto fire and sword should be applyed, as Empiriks deale with desperate diseases. *Gent.* You could not haue pickt out a more fit phrase of speech, than to liken your religion to Empiriks medicines, which the arte of Phisicke condemnes. To vse fire and sworde against an Heretique, is the Magistrates office, into whose hands God hath put the sword, to punish them that are worthy to be punisht, not yours, who as religious men are called to another function. *Ief.* What Magistrate dares proceede against Kings but we, which are inspird with the holy Ghost? *Gent.* Is this a poynt of your first institution? *Ief.* Wee haue put in this our selues, by a rule of Christian-good, to relieue our neighbours. And to shewe you with what pietie wee goe forward, when

wee

wee haue by our holy exhortations gaind any man of worth to execute our diſſignements, before hee depart we confeſſe him, and imploy one part of his penance to confirme him in that holy enterpriſe, wee make him heare Maſſe with deuotion; Wee miniſter the bleſſed Sacrament of the Altar to him; this done, we giue him our bleſſing, for a ſure paſport to goe directly to Para-diſe. VVas there euer a more ſacred and meritorious courſe than this? For to be briefe, it is in defence, and protection, of our Chriſtian Catholike Church. *Gent.* O chriſtian company indeed: I would be glad to learne why our Sauiour Chriſt beeing apprehended, was ſo ſore diſpleaſed with S. Peter when hee had cut off Malchus eare? For at the firſt bluſh it ſeemeth that a man could not haue drawne his ſword in a quarrell of greater merit. *Ieſ.* You ſay well, but you doe not weigh the text. Our Sauiour did not forbid Saint Peter to betake him to his weapon, but after the blow was giuen, he cō-maunded him to put it vp againe. *Gent.* Pardon mee, this aunſwere hath I know not what ſmack of Machia-uell.

Ieſ. Adde this vnto it, that S. Peter prouoked with an vndiſcreet zeale, would haue hindered a miſterie that tended to the redemption of mankind, and wee employ the ſword for the maintenaunce of the Church, with-out which man-kinde would perriſh. *Gent.* O braue and holy expoſition, are you of opinion that this courſe is well pleaſing vnto GOD? *Ieſ.* None but the Here-tiques of our time euer doubted it. *Gent.* I am none of them, neither haue I at any time enclined ſo to be: yet I doubt much of this matter. Is there any thing in your Statutes commaunding you to goe farther? *Ieſ.* There is. *Gent.* What is that? *Ieſ.* We profeſſe to obey the Generall of our Order, blindfolde, (for thoſe be the ex-preſſe words of our Conſtitutions) and wee are bounde to pinne our conſciences to his ſleeue: to ſuffer him to

rule

rule vs like a boate hauing no motion, but that which they giue to it that row it : to leaue off our worke alreadie begun; to obey him, and acknowledge the presence of Iesus Christ in him, as if Christ cōmaunded vs. *Gent.* Pertaines this to your Order ? *Ies.* Yes I assure you. *Gent.* O admirable paradox of obedience, like that of Abraham. *Ies.* So it is. That example was euer in the mouth of *Ignatius*, teaching vs that obedience, is more acceptable to God then sacrifice. *Gent.* O blessed Fathers the Iesuites, nay rather true and onely Patriarckes of our Church. Doubtlesse it is not without reason, that you be called Fathers after the accomplishment of your last vow. Well then, the case so standing, if your Generall should commaund you to procure the death, I will not say of a Prince, (for I doubt not but you would obey him therin) but of our holy Father the Pope, would you doe it ? *Ies.* I would take time to deliberate. *Gent.* If you should do so, this were not to tie your conscience any longer vnto his sleeue. *Ies.* You take me vnprouided, I craue respite to make you an aunswere. *Gent.* Your Order beeing grounded vpon all these godly and holy resolutions, surely our Church is much bounde to you, I meane, not the auncient Doctors of the Church onely, but the Apostles themselues, whom you haue taught their dutie. Nay, what speake I of the Apostles ? you haue taught the great Maister of the Mould, wherein wee ought to fashion all our actions : when contrarie to the expresse cōmaundement giuen S. Peter, you procure the death of Kings and Princes. But what reward haue you got by this ?

Ies. As much as wee can desire or hope for. And amongst others, we are allowed to giue absolution of all sinnes and offences howe foule soeuer they be, except such as are reserued to the holy Sea, wholly extreated & issuing out of Iudgements, Censures, and Ecclesiasticall paines, beside that which is comprised in the Bull vsually
read

read vppon Maundy-Thurfday. And for all that that comes after, to giue fuch order of penance as liketh vs, as in workes of pietie, vowes of Pilgrimage, except in three cafes, of Ierufalem, of Rome, of Saint Iames of Compoftella. Alfo to fing Maffe as well before day, as after twelue a clocke at noone-tyde, when our Superiours fhall thinke it neceffary: To confeffe, and adminifter the Sacrament of the Eucharift: to build Chappels, Oratories, and Churches, in all places where our Generall will: and all this without leaue of Bifhop or Curat: Trauelling thorowe Countries, to haue portable Altars to fay Maffe on in euery houfe, except places interdicted by the holy Sea: That no Bifhop in his owne Dioceffe, may giue prieftly Orders to any of our Company, though he be fit for it, without demiffory Letters from our Generall, who may alfo difpence with forbidden meates without fute to the Bifhops: & in briefe, to abfolue all thofe from cenfures, which are attainted of herefie.

Gent. Heere is a heape of priuiledges giuen you indeed, to the preiudice firft and chiefely of the Bifhops, next of the Curats, and laftly, peraduenture of the holy Sea it felfe. Furthermore, this is a follemne feaft to draw the Common people to you, and pull them from theyr true, naturall, and lawfull Paftors: yea, this is to bring a newe Schifme into the Church of Chrift. *Ief.* Hee that fhall come euery yeere to performe his deuotions one whole day in our houfe, fhall haue plenary indulgence of all his finnes, though hee fay but one *Pater nofter* and an *Aue Marie.* *Gent.* Another bayte to make men feeke after you. *Ief.* We enioy all the priuiledges graunted to all the foure Orders of Mendicants. *Gent.* They may iuftly be difcontented, feeing you gorged with good things vp to the eares, and enioying all their priuiledges. *Ief.* If it be fo, all other religious Orders haue caufe to repine as well as they; for wee enioy all theyr

theyr graunts and fauours. *Gent.* Yet are not you any way tied to theyr vowes and abstinences; this is ill proportiond, for this Aduocate can tell you, the olde Lawyers hold it, *Secundam naturam esse, vt quem sequuntur cōmoda, eundem sequantur incōmoda.* And to say truth, this is another ground of iealousie & grudge between them and you. *Ies.* All that I haue yet deduced, concernes Gods seruice, that which I meane to tell you now, lookes backe towards our Colledges and Lectures. It is lawful for our Generall, or for such as are by him authorized, to build Colledges, to set vp Lectures, euen Lectures of Diuinitie, and other Readers in euery Towne without the Bishops leaue: yea and our company may as well out of the Vniuersities, as in them, take theyr degrees of Bachilars, Licentiates, Masterships, and Doctors, without examination, and be found capable by two or three Commissioners appointed for that purpose by our Superiors, which are not bound to seeke to any Chauncelor, or Rector of other Vniuersities. In stronger termes, we may haue whole Vniuersities of our owne company onely, where the Chauncellor or Rector is a Iesuite, as appeares in the Towne of *Pontumoussen.* We are also allowed to practise Phisique by the authoritie of our Superiors, if they iudge vs to be capable. *Gent.* And craue you no other testimony then theirs that neuer studied Phisick? *Ies.* No.

Gent. I thought your Generall might haue made a Iesuite, but no Phisitian, and I would be loth to put my life into your hands vppon any such warrant. Behold what a fearefull diuision you make betweene the Vniuersities, especially betweene the great, famous, and ancient Vniuersitie of Paris and your selues. *Ies.* What would you more? We may geld, correct, and reforme all manner of bookes, wherein wee finde the least suspition of heresie. *Gent.* What? after the Diuines of Paris haue allowed them? *Ies.* Yea, euen so. *Gent.* I euer

D. tooke

Pius 5. 7. of Iuly. 1571.
Greg. 13.
3, of May,
1575.

Greg. 13.
10. Octob.
1576.
Paul. 3,
1549.
Iulius 3.
22. Octob.
1552.
Pius 4.
19. August,
1561.
Pius 5.
10. May,
1571,
Grego. 13.
1598.
Greg. 13,
11, Feb.
1576.

tooke this to be theyr office, and not to haue appertay-
ned to any other. *Ief.* Doe you thinke that wee care a
poynt for them? Long agoe(except it were in the nonage of our Company) wee had learnd to fet them at
naught. True it is, that in the yeere 1 5 5 4. it fo fell out
that they cenfurd vs, when wee were but beginning to
creepe out of the fhell, yet were wee fpeedilie reuenged
on them, for we made theyr cenfure to be ouer-waighed
by the Spanifh Inquifition. Therefore in Spaine (faith
a braue Hiftoriographer of ours,) *Seeing the Sorbons*

Ribaden. li.
4. c. 11.
*decree was againft the Sea Apoftolique, by which our Re-
ligion is approued and confirmed, the Inquifitors of faith haue
by their decree, forbidden that to be read, as falfe, and offenfiue to religious eares.*

   Gent. You confeffe you fent to the Inquifition to cō-
trole this good and holy facultie of the Diuines of Paris, the auncient pillar, proppe, and fupport, of our Catholique and Apoftolique Romane Church: and you
make a Trophee of it, as of a great victory. *Ief.* Let not
this offend you, for at a pinch wee will grapple with the
Pope, if we take him fwaruing neuer fo little from his
auncient dutie. Wee held oppinion a little before King
Henrie the fourth came to the Crowne, (whom we now
call the man of *Bearne*) that Pope *Sixtus* the fift did erre
a little in fauouring him: and God knowes wee fpared
him not in our Pulpits; fome likewife fought to perfwade the world, that we gaue him a dram to fend him
packing. *Gent.* Regard you not the Pope whofe creatures you are, and haue no authoritie but from him? If
it be fo, I take my leaue of you, and lay my hand vppon
my mouth. Onely I wifh wee had fome *Cneius Flauius*
among vs, to lay open your fecrets vnto Fraunce, or
fome *Tacitus* to fet them downe in writing, with as great
libertie as you put them in execution.

   The Aduocate was fom-what filent vntill vve came
thus farre, but then hee began to breake out. You fhall
hold

hold your peace (quoth hee) as long as you pleafe, fo will not I, I will be that *Cneius Flauius* you defire, for as hee difcouered to the Romanes, the perfumes which their chiefe Prieft folde them at fo high a rate, in acknowledgement whereof hee was created Tribune of the people, that is to fay, A preferuer of the peoples libertie: So will I vncafe by peece-meale, that doctrine which the Iefuites haue fold vs heere-to-fore by golden weight. And I perfwade my felfe that gratefull pofteritie finding it by me recorded, will account mee a Protector of the liberty of the Church of Fraunce. And it may bee it will come to paffe, that as antiquitie made a Prouerbe of *Cneius Flauius*, faying, that he hit the birds eye: fo will fucceeding ages report of mee, that I haue peckt out the eyes of thofe Crowes, that pray vppon the carkaffes and carrion of other beaftes, and of the Iefuits, who now liue not by the bare bones onely, but by the faireft reuenewes of our Families. And that I hold you not long in fufpence, I fay and auerre, there was neuer any Sect more dangerous to our Chriftian Religion then this: and for fuch a one it hath been firft condemned at Rome, afterward at Paris. Neuertheleffe, I will begin with Fraunce, as with her to whom I am moft bound, becaufe fhee brought me forth.

This firft march of the Aduocate made vs ftand vppon our garde: for hetherto fome of the cõpany flept. And for my part, hearing him fo hardie in his promife, I turned towards him, faying; Sir, all this while haue I beene mute, but now I fee you vpon the poynt ready to take Armes, to giue the on-fet vppon thys holy Companie, I recouer my fpeech, as the fonne of *Crafus* dyd when one would haue kild his Father. If you be the Iefuites *Cneius Flauius*, I will be theyr *Tacitus*, to commit thofe things faythfully to writing which I learne of you. I euer tooke this Societie to be one of the ftrongeft Bulwarks of our Catholique Religion, and mee thinkes it

were

were great impietie to flaunder them. *Aduoc.* Call you that a flaunder, when the truth is fpoken? For my part I will fay nothing, which I will not proue by writing, & take my direction from their owne Bulls and Conftitutions, theyr fpeeches and confeffions, drawn out of fuch bookes, as they themfelues haue Printed within thefe 5. or 6. yeeres, allowed by their Generall to come foorth. Whereunto any of the company that ftands in doubt, may haue recourfe if it pleafe him. You promife verie much faid I againe. *Aduoc.* I promife nothing but I will make it good: and there-with he paufd a while, as one that makes femblance to retire, that hee may giue the greater fhocke. On the other fide, I tooke out my tables, to note euery paffage he fhould alleage, which I will fhew to you at large. And fo euery one of vs clayming intereft in the Aduocate to whip him, if we tooke him with a lye: and contrary, if hee fhould fpeake the truth, then all at once to thruft the Iefuites out of France prefently, without refpite. After hee had quieted himfelfe a little, he enterd the Liftes, and made his carrere in this manner.

CHAP. 3.

¶ The cenfure giuen of the Iefuits fect, by the Diuines of Paris, in the yeere, 1 5 5 4.

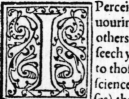Perceiue Fraunce is partiall, fome fauouring the Iefuites aboue meafure, others abhoring them againe. I befeech you my Maifters, (for I fpeake to thofe that of fcrupulofitie of confcience fofter this family in their houfes) that it would pleafe you to giue good eare to mee, and if you finde that to be falfe which I fhall produce, or that I am carried with vnbrideled paffion, you would not fpare me. Likewife, if nothing but

but the truth commaund me, which ought to redownd
to the edification of vs all, doe me the fauour not to credite your first apprehensions, before you giue place vnto the second. You make great account of these men, as
if they were the sole arches that beare vp our Church:
Let me request you to take a viewe of the iudgement of
the Diuines of Paris, in the yeere 1 5 5 4. The Court of
Parliament then troubled with the importunate sutes of
these newe Brethren, bringing the two Bulles of two
Popes, *Paulus* and *Iulius* the third, sent them to this Facultie for their resolution, whether they were to bee receiued into the Realme of Fraunce againe, or not? They
gaue vp their verdict in such forme as followeth.

Anno Domini 1 5 5 4. die verò prima Decembris, Sa-
cratissima Theologiæ facultas Parisiensis, post missam de S.
spiritu, in æde sacra Collegij Sorbonæ, ex more celebratam,
iam quartò in eodem Collegio, per iuramentũ congregata est,
ad determinandum de duobus diplomatibus quæ duo sanctissi-
mi Domini summi Pontifices Paulus tertius, & Iulius Ter-
tius, his qui societatis Iesu nomine insigniri cupiuut, concessis-
se dicuntur. Quæ quidem duo diplomata, senatus seu curia
Parlaamti Parisiensis, dictæ facultati visitanda & examinan-
da, misso ad rem Hostiario, commiserat.

Antequam verò ipsa Theologiæ facultat tanta de re, tan-
tique ponderis tractare incipiat, omnes & singuli Magistri
nostri, palam atq̃, aperto ore professi sunt, nihil se aduersus
summorum Pontificum authoritatem & potestatem, aut de-
cernere, aut moliri, aut etiam cogitare velle. Imò verò om-
nes & singuli, vt obedientiæ filij, ipsum summum Pontificem,
vt summum & vniuersalem Christi Iesu Vicarium, & vni-
uersalem Ecclesiæ Pastorem (cui plenitudo potestatis a Chri-
sto data sit, cui omnes vtriusq̃, Sexus obedire, cuius decreta
venerari, & pro se quisq̃, tueri, & obseruare teneantur) vt
semper agnouerunt & confessi sunt, ita nunc quoq̃, sincere, fi-
deliter, et libenter agnoscunt, & confitentur. Sed quoniã om-
nes, præsertim verò Theologos paratos esse oportet ad satis-

factionem.

*faltionem omni poscenti de his quæ ad sidem, mores, ædificati-
onem Ecclesiæ pertinent, dicta facultas, poscenti, mandanti, &
exigenti curiæ prædictæ satisfaciendum duxit. Itaq́, vtriusq́,
diplomatis omnibus frequenter lectis articulis, repetitis, & in-
tellectis, & pro rei magnitudine, per multos dies, menses, &
horas, pro more prius diligentissimè discussis & examinatis,
tum demum vnanimi consensu, sed summa cum reuerentia &
humilitate, rem integram correctioni sedis Apostolicæ relin-
quens, ita censuit.*

*Hæc nona societas, insolitam nominis Iesu appellationẽ sibi
vendicans, tam licenter & sine delectu quaslibet personas,
quantũlibet facinorosas, illegitimas & infames admittens, nul-
lam à Sacerdotibus secularibus habens differentiam in habitu exteriore, in tonsura, in horis canonicis priuatim dicendis,
aut publicè in templo decantandis, in claustris & silentio, in
delectu ciborum & dierum, in ieiunijs & alijs varijs ceremo-
nijs (quibus status Religionũ distinguntur & conseruantur)
tam multis, tamq́, varijs priuilegijs, indultis, & libertatibus
donata, præsertim in administratione Sacramenti pænitentiæ
& Eucaristiæ, idq́, sine descrimine locorũ, aut personarum,
in officio etiam prædicandi, legendi, & docendi in præiudicium
ordinariorum, & Hierarchici ordinis, in præiudicium quoq́,
aliarum Religionum, imò etiam principium & Dominorum
temporalium, contra priuilegia vniuersitatum, deniq́, in magnum populi grauamen, Religionis Monasticæ honestatem
violare videtur, studiosum, pium, & necessarium, virtutum,
abstinentiarum, ceremoniarum, & austeritatis eneruat exercitium: imo occasionẽ dat liberè Apostatandi ab alijs Reli-
gionibus, debitam ordinarijs obedientiam, & subiectionẽ sub-
trahit. Dominos tam temporales, quã Ecclesiasticos, suis iuribus iniustè priuat, perturbationem in vtraq́, politia, multas
in populo querelas, multas lites, dissidia, contentiones, æmula-
tiones, rebelliones, variaq́, schismata inducit. Itaq́, his omnibus, atq́, alijs diligenter examinatis & perpensis, Hæc societas videtur in negotio fidei periculosa, pacis Ecclesiæ pertur-
batiua, monasticæ Religionis euersiua, & magis ad destruc-
tionem*

tionem quam act ædificationem.

I will not iuggle with you, it may bee fome of thys company vnderftands no Latine, therefore this cenfure beeing the foundation of my difcourfe, I will put it into French apparrell, that euery man may know it.

In the yeere of our Lord 1 5 5 4. the firft of December, the moft facred facultie of the Diuines in Paris, after Maffe of the holy Ghoft was celebrated in the Colledge of *Sorbons* Chappell, according to their cuftome, this fourth time, by oath affembled together, to determine of the two Bulles, which two holy Fathers the Popes, *Paulus* the third, and *Iulius* the third, are fayd to haue graunted to thefe men that defire to be honoured with the focietie of I E S V S. Which two Bulles, the Senate or Court of Parliament of Paris, fent by *Hoftiarius* to the faid Facultie to be perufed and examined.

Before they entreated of fo high and weightie matters, all and finguler our Maifters in pubique with open mouth protefted, that they decreed, deuifd, and intended nothing againft the authoritie and power of the Pope, but all and euery of them, like obedient Chyldren, as they euer acknowledged and confeffed him to be Chriftes chiefe & vniuerfall Vicar, and generall Paftor of the Church, whom all forts of both Sectes are bound to obey, to honour his decrees, and euery one to defend them to his power : So nowe alfo, they doe fincerely, faithfully, and willingly acknowledge & confeffe the fame. But becaufe euery man, efpecially Diuines, ought to be readie to giue an aunfwere to euery one that asketh them of matters appertaining to fayth, manners, and edification of the Church, the faide Facultie hath thought it meete to fatisfie the requeft, commaundement and entreatie of the Court. Therefore all the Articles of both Bulles beeing often read, repeated, and conceiued, & for the greatnes of the matter, many daies, monthes, and houres, according to their cuftome, firft
very

verie diligently difcuſt, and examined, at laſt with one confent, but with great reuerence and humilitie, fubmitting all to the controlement of the Apoſtolike fea, they gaue this doome.

This new Societie chalenging to it felfe the rare title of the name of Iefus, fo licentioufly, and hand ouer-head, admitting all forts of perfons how wicked, illegitimate, or infamous foeuer, diffring nothing from fecular prieſts in outward apparrell, tonfure, canonicall howers, either priuately to be faid, or publikely to be fung in churches, in cloiſtures and filence, in choife of meates and daies, in faſts and other ceremonies (whereby religious orders are diſtinguiſht, and preferued) endowed with fo many and fundrie priuiledges, grants, and liberties, efpecially in adminiſtration of the Sacrament of penance, and of the Euchariſt that without difference of place or perfons, as alfo in the office of preaching, reading, and teaching, to the preiudice of the Ordinaries, of the Hierachicall order, to the preiudice likewife of other religious men, nay euen of Princes & temporall Lords, againſt the priuiledges of the Vniuerfities, and to the great griefe of the people, appeares to defloure monaſticall religion : it cuts the finewes of the painfull, holy, and neceſſarie exercife of vertues, of abſtinence, ceremonies, and auſteritie, it opens a gap to Apoſtacie from other religious orders, it takes away due obedience from the Ordinaries, it vniuſtly depriues the Lords fpirituall & temporall of their right : It breeds a garboile in both gouernments, many complaints among the people, many iarres, difcords, contentions, emulatiõs, rebellions, & fundry fchifmes. Therfore all thefe and other things of like nature thorowly examined and waighed. *This Societie appeares to be in matter of faith daungerous, to the peace of the Church trobleſome, to monaſticall religion ruinous, and more apt to pull downe than to build vp.*

Was there euer a better fentence, mixt with a truer
prophecie

prophecie than this ? And why ? There was no
banding then in the field, euerie man flept fafe in the
finceritie of his confcience towards God, there were no
tumultuary affemblies,but for foure daies togither,& by
them that had determined of it long before. Much leffe
minded they to oppofe themfelues againft the authority
of the holy Sea, as we gather from their humble proteftation. For this caufe,the holy Ghoft after their deuout
inuocation of him by their facrifice, fpake thorough the
organe of this facred facultie. And thus am I perfwaded,
that for thefe thoufand yeers,there was neuer any worke
of the holy Ghoft greater , and more apparant to our
eies than was this cenfure. The Court of Parliament of
Paris fent thofe Buls onely of Pope *Paulus* dated the
yeere 1 5 4 3. And that of *Iulius* the third , dated the
yeere 1 5 5 o. The Iefuites kept all the other clofe, bearing date of the yeeres 43. 45. 46. 49.

Vpon the fight but of thofe two ends of their ware
they iudged wifely what the reft of the whole peece
might be. Without any more a do,remember thofe three
lines. *It breeds many complaints among the people, manie*
iarres , diffentions, contentions , rebellions , and fundrie
fchifmes : and conferre them with your difcouery of their
order,you fhall find the Sorbons fpeech true.The diuine
feruice of their Church is diuided from ours,their priuiledges make a deuifion betweene the Bifhops and them,
the Monafteries and them, the Vniuerfities and them,
the Diuines of Paris and them . Their propofitions alfo, make a diuifion betweene the holy Sea and
Princes. But how be thefe priuiledges maintaind ? By
their Colledges, their confeffions, their preaching.Their
Colledges are traps to catch youth , their confeffions,
fubornations; their Sermons, Mounte-banks Markets.
If you beleeue this Iefuite here, he will fay : we haue no
preachers but them to defend the olde Church. It is not
yet aboue threefcore yeeres fince they were fet a foote.

E.   What

What preachers haue we had of them in Paris? One *Aimond Auger*, and *Iames Commolet*. I remember none but these. On the other side, how many hath the facultie of the Vniuerfitie in Paris bred, of learned and holy men, neuer tainted with innouation? Againe, did euer any man in our time heare a Iesuite handle or expound in Pulpit or open assembly, any one text of Scripture, either to vphold the Apoftolike Sea, or lay herefie in the duft? What is the fumme of their preaching? To bite them that are abfent, not to edifie them that are prefent, except it be to fcandale kings and princes. And that which is moft admirable in this cenfure, is, that our diuines faw the rebellions, these new mafters would raife vp in time to come, againft our king. Therefore while I now embarke my felfe againft them, it is neither giddineffe, malice, nor folly, that caries me with wind and tide. I fet the venerable facultie of the diuines of Paris before mine eies, for my Vice-admirall, to carie the light in my nauigation.

CHAP. 4.

¶ How, at what time, and by what fleights the Iefuites crept into Fraunce.

Hen God is determined to fcourge a whole Realme: he vfeth great and vn-expected means to performe it: it hath fo fallen out with vs. Long before the lamentable death of *Henrie* the fecond, who liued in the yeere 1559. There fprung vp two fectes in Fraunce, the one, in many propofitions as dangerous as the other. That of *Ignatius* which cals it felfe the focietie of *Iefus*: the other of the Caluinifts, who fay they ftand for reformation of religion. Both of them planted in Paris the chiefe citie of the kingdome for a time. It fo fell out that the Iefuites

made

made their assemblies, and the Caluinists had their con-
uenticles. The Iesuites sect is a bastard religion, of our
ancient Catholike & Apostolike Romane religion (for
to say true, it hath a few markes and features of it, though
none such as it ought to haue) this began to be authori-
sed by Ma. *William Prat*, Bishop of Clairmont, legat *du
Prats* bastard, who lodged them in the house of Clairmont at Paris, and at his death, bequeathed them (by
report) threescore thousand crownes. After that they
crouded into more spacious mansions, they bought
the great house of *Langre* in Saint *Iames* street, where
they erected a Colledge and Monasterie both together
vnder diuers roofes, they did read publike lectures without the rector of the Vniuersities allowance, they admi-
nistred the holy Sacraments of penance, and of the altar
to all commers and goers, without leaue of the Odina-
rie. The Caluinists began to preach and teach, if not altogether openly, yet not so couertly as they did before.
Witnesse the great assembly, surprised by the Court of
Parliament before Plessies Colledge, where an infinite
number of men and women were taken, and after that
an Aduocate, a Scholemaister, and a Damsell put to
death. Thus may I say, and say truly, these two sects began to set vp their rests within Paris in S. *Iames* street, re-
ching out to fifteen or twentie houses one after another.
And after this vowed, the one to haue *Iesus* name stampt
vpon their pistolet crownes, the Iesuits to haue it set vpon the gates of their Colledges with a crosse aloft, to
shew that they did lodge at the signe of the crosse. As
the Caluinists cald their religion, the reformed religion,
so the Iesuits gloried, that in some part of Italy, namely
in *Modena*, they were cald the reformed also. And as
the Caluinists whom we terme Hugonots rose vp in
armes in Fraunce, in the yeere, 1561. So the Iesuits tooke example by them, and had recourse vnto
armes about the yeere 1585. to enlarge their bounds.

If

If I be not deceiued in the time, nor miſſe my marke, *Henry* the ſecond died : wherupō the Caluiniſts thought they might make their way faire without noiſe, through the midſt of Fraunce. This good king left behind him foure young princes his children vnder the Queene mothers charge, a ſtranger princeſſe, not allied to the great houſes of France, thereby was ſhe vnfit to ſecond them in gouernment of the ſtate, and education of theſe children. Thus at one inſtant the two ſeĉts began to encreaſe : one by the Kings death, the other by a Biſhops deceaſe. During the minority of our Kings, the Nobility of France couered their ambition with a cloake of religion. New partialities grew among them, ſome taking part with the old religion, others with the new : euerie one of them (by the iudgement of the wiſeſt) ſeeking his owne gaine & aduancement, more then deuotion. In this encounter, the miniſters of whoſe companie ſome were burnt before, put vp a ſupplication to *Charles* the ninth, to giue them audience. This was ſoone granted, & the town of Poiſſy appointed for this purpoſe, where many Cardinals, Archbiſhops, Biſhops, and Doĉtors of Diuinitie were aſſembled on the one ſide : and many Miniſters, of whom *Thodor Beza* was the ring-leader, ſeconded by *Peter Marter, Marlorat, Cimpoll,* and ſome of good place and marke among them, on the other ſide.

Vpon the ſentence of the Sorbons giuen in the yeere 1554. the Ieſuits finding their hope to be forlorne, ſought to Ma. *Noel Brullarte* the Kings Procurator generall, in the court of Parliament of Paris, the ſeuereſt man in his place, that euer was ſeen. Theſe men that ſlip no opportunitie to aduance themſelues, hearing of the great conference at Poiſſy, promiſed to put in their foot among them. At that time one *Ponce Congordan* was their Agent in Paris, of whom *Charles* Cardinall of Loraine was wont to ſay, he was the cunningeſt negotiatior

that

that euer he knew though he had knowne many. He then it was that tooke the matter in hand, presented his request to the Court of Parliament of Paris, not in the name of the Societie of Iesus, but in the name of the Colledge of Clairmount, whereby the Iesuits protested to abiure their vowes, entreating the Court to allow of their Colledge. Which if the Court had done, it had beene a meane to allow their legacie giuen them. The Court according to their prudence and pietie, sent this request to the French Church then assembled at Poissy, to determine of it. Neuer was there a fairer assembly, and neuer did assembly bring forth more mischiefe to the state then that. I feare not to put the Placard into his hands that shall write the Historie of our times, for they authorized both sects without all consideration. And, which I most wonder at, the instruments hereof were two Cardinals, men of great knowledge and zeale, no young prentizes in the misteries of religion, or affaires of state; one of them had been emploied in the greatest matters of this kingdome, in the time of the mightie king *Francis*: the other in the time of *Henry* the second. The two speciall were the Cardinals of Tournon and Lorraine. The first for the grauitie of his yeeres, and consequently for the soundnes of his iudgement, was perswaded that this conference with the ministers was in no case to be admitted, for that the entring into it was a kind of acknowledging them to be a part of our common-weale, whom heretofore we tooke to be rotten members, howsoeuer the nonage of the king might dispence with their opinions vpō this point. The second, in the flower of his yeeres, vpon the confidence he had in his owne wit, seconded by two great diuines *Dispence* & *Salignac*, desired to bring the matter vpon the stage, flattering himselfe, that if they might dispute vpon *Beza*, the matter might easily be drawne to a head.

The

The most voyces went with him. The Cardinall of *Tournon,* spying himselfe supplanted in his oppinion, beganne to drawe vp the Iesuits, a faire and glorious pretence (as seemed) to giue battaile to the newe Religion. Heerein was he followed by a number of other Prelates, not becaufe they did not fore-fee what an infinite number of inconueniences might arife out of it, but becaufe they thought poyfons muft be purged by counterpoyfons. The Scaffolds built, the Cardinall of *Loraine* and *Beza,* played theyr prizes before the young King, in the prefence of many States diuerfly affected. The affembly broken vp, after this wee had three Religions openly in Fraunce. The one, founded nothing but the word of G O D in their preachings : The next, tooke vp the Name of Iefus in their Sinagogues : The third, was our auncient Catholiques, to whom we attribute in our Churches, the honour of our fayth by the onely Gofpell of Iefus Chrift.

CHAP. 5.

¶ *The decree of the French-Church againft the Iefuits, in the affembly had at* Poifsy. 1 5 6 1.

Or all this I would not haue you thinke my Maifters, but that our French church did put many notable ingredients into this Iefuiticall poyfon to qualifie it . For after the recitall all along the Decree, of all the priuiledges and fauours diuerfly giuen them, by *Paule* and *Iulius* the third, and fome Letters-Patents obtayned by them, and reckoning made of theyr requeft prefented to the Court, and put ouer to thefe Prelates, in the end, behold what order they fet downe.

The Affembly, according to the matters put to them by the Court of Parliament of Paris, hath receiued and doth receiue, hath approued and doth approue, the faid

Societie

Societie and Companie, in forme of a Colledge, not of theyr new inftitution of Religion, with expreffe charge, that they take another title then the Name of I E S V S, or of Iefuits, & that the Bifhop of the Dioces, fhal haue all fuperioritie, iurifdiction, and correction ouer this focietie and Colledge, to thruft out and expell from the faide Company, all men of euill life and misbehauiour. Neyther fhall the Brothers of this Company enterprife or performe, any action temporall or fpirituall, to the preiudice of the Bifhops, Chapters, Curats, Parrifhes, Vniuerfities, or other religious, but they fhal be bound to conforme themfelues wholly to the difpofition of the Common-lawe, without hauing any right or iurifdiction, and renouncing all their former priuiledges, expreffly theyr Bulls contrary to the things afore-faid, prouided that if they fayle heerein, or fhall heereafter procure any other; that then this prefent Decree fhall be voyde & of none effect, or exceptions to be taken to the right of the fayd Affembly, & of others in all cafes. Giuen in the Affembly of the French Church, held by the kings commaundement at Poiffy, in the great hall of the venerable religious men of Poiffy, vnder the figne and feale of the moft reuerend Cardinall of *Tournon*, Archbifhop of Lyons, Metropolitane and Primate of Fraunce, Prefident of the faid Affembly, and of the reuerend Father in God, the Lord Bifhop of Paris, the meffenger of this requeft. Giuen vnder the fignes of Maifter *Nicholas Breton* and *William Blanchy*, actuaries and Secretaries of the faid Affembly, vpon Monday the 15. of December, 1 5 6 1.

Pontius *Congordan* theyr Agent, now furnifht with this holy Decree, prefented it to the Court of Parliament of Paris, where it was foorie ratified. Heere I will make a paufe and tell you, that if euer, though not all, yet the leaft part of this decree had beene obeyed, I would here aske them forgiuenes, & affure my felfe that thefe Gentlemen,

tlemen, *Marion, Pasquier, Arnault* & *Dole,*which haue all vowed to make warre vppon them, would doe the like. But if the requeſt they put vp, was but a meere mummery, not onely to mocke the French Church heereafter, but the Court of Parliament, and that they haue made no account of that which was commaunded them, they muſt with one conſent confeſſe,that neither the particular aunſwere made by *Fraunces de Montaignes*, againſt *Arnalts* impleadment,nor the venomous tooth of one *Fon,* (I wot not whō) ſtriken into *Marion* and *Paſquier,* the one, the Kinges Aduocate in Parliament, the other, of the Chamber of accounts in Paris, nor the hipocriticall requeſt made to the King without the Authors Name, ſhall euer be ſufficient to proue thē any naturall or French brood.

The Facultie of the Vniuerſitie of Paris, denounced them at theyr firſt arriuall, to be Schiſmatiques, diſturbers of the peace of the Church, and monaſticall diſcipline. Afterwards, the Church of Fraunce to prouide for their great diſorder, allowed them by way of limitation before rehearſed, notwithſtanding all the ingredients, & coolers, put in to temper this poyſon, the venim ouer-came their vertue. For as ſoone as they had ſeazed vppon this ſentence, they wrote vppon theyr Colledge gate, *The Colledge of the ſocietie of I E S V S.* They followed theyr firſt courſe, which they haue continued & will continue ſo long as they remaine in Fraunce. As it is the nature of the French to be more hardie then men at the beginning,and more cold and feeble then women in continuaunce: So ſuffred wee our ſelues to be led away at laſt, by theſe wit-foundred newe Friers. Euerie man if hee be not hunted hote, abandons the publique affaires, to be wedded to his owne in particular.

CHAP.

CHAP. 6.

¶ *Of the request preferd by the Iesuits to the Parliament,
the yeere 1 5 6 4. to bee incorporated into the Uniuersitie of Paris : and howe many sides
made head against them.*

Ontius Cōgordan for his part, did not lay him down to sleep when he saw vs wearie, but thinking hee had got the day, preferd a petition to the V-niuersitie, in the yeere 1564. the te-nour whereof was this. *The Princi-pall of the Colledge and company of Ie-sus, called the Colledge of Clairmont, beseecheth you to incor-porate thē into the Uniuersitie, that they may enioy the priui-ledges of it.* The Vniuersitie hauing giuen them the re-pulse, they fledde to the Court of Parliament, where *Congordan* chose *Versoris* for theyr Aduocate, the Vni-uersitie entertaind *Pasquier.* The cause pleaded by these two, here was the sport, *Pasquier* at the first push, shewed them, that to read theyr request onely, was enough to o-uerthrow them. For the foundation of theyr cause de-pended vppon the French Churches decree, which for-bad them expresly to take vppon them the name of the societie of Iesus, which title notwithstanding they had inserted into theyr request. This was to strike thē right vpon the visor, by meanes whereof, they were compeld to flie to a deniall, where they tooke sanctuary for the liberty of their actions, as often as they found themselues driuen into any narrowe streight that might preiudice them. *Versoris* denied him that framed the request, that was in plaine termes *Congordan,* who denied himselfe, by the mouth of his owne Aduocate whom hee chose. By this you may see, that in all the negotiations which haue on their part passed between them and vs, to set vp their

F. sect,

sect, An Asse and a Foxe haue beene tyed together.

A meruailous matter, and worthy to be rung into the eares of all succeeding ages. First, they of the newe Religion, troubled vs about the towne of Amboise, against the Lords protectors of the young King, *Fraunces* the second, partly by the conference had at Poissy, and Geneuian preaching insinuated into Fraunce. Lastly, by the surprize of townes, and a bloody battaile fought before Dreux. In briefe, by a ciuill warre of 18. monethes continuaunce, vpon the parcialities of Papists and Protestants, which was afterward luld a sleepe with an Edict of conniuence, our hands beeing yet embrued with the blood of those troubles, and hauing scarce any leysure to take our breath. In this progresse by degrees, the Iesuits request was presented to the Court of Parliament, that had tenne Aduocates, (as *Montaignes* and *Fon* do confesse in their writinges) in respect of 13. aduersaries, which *Fon* reports, were sixe boysterous & mightie limmed bodies, to wit, the Vniuersities, the Sorbons, the Mendicants, the Hospitals, and the Parish priests. With other foure Lordes of great authoritie, namely the Gouernour of Paris, the Cardinall Chastilion, as protector of the Vniuersitie, the Bishop of Paris, and the Abbot of S. Geniueue.

Now, can we be so sencelesse, as to thinke that so many, both of the better and meaner sort, banded against them without cause, in a matter of so great importance? But what were the commons? those which of late memorie plagued the Hugonots, out of all measure, raced the walls of Patriarch and Popincourt, where they had theyr exercise of religion: who by order of Lawe procurd the death of *Gabaston*, the Captaine of their garde, and protector of theyr attempts, together with *Cagres*, both the Father and the sonne. So many Sages of the common people (sworne enemies to heresie) did sette theselues against the Iesuits, lying but yet in the suburbs of

Mont. ca.22
Fon. ca. 4.

of our ciuill warres; againft the Iefuits I fay, who then
vaunted themfelues to be the fcourge of Hereticks. Af-
furedly it cannot be, but that all thofe great perfonages,
who then vndertooke the quarrell againft them, were
perfwaded that this Sect was extreamely to be feared, as
well by the libertie of the French Church and generall
eftate of Fraunce, as of all Chriftendome. Befides thefe
two great parties, there was yet another, more ftrong &
mightie then them both, namely, Mounfieur *Mefnil*
the Kings Aduocate in the Court of parliament, directly oppofite to them.

But for all this great multitude of partakers (fayth
the Iefuite) the matter came not to open triall, but was
put ouer to coufell, as a plaine argument that the good-
neffe of our caufe did craue very much fauour. Poore
foole, and young Scholler, hadft thou been brought vp
in the light of the Royall pallace, or read the courfe of
iuftice of our kings, as thou art nuzled in the duft of the
Colledges, thou fhouldft haue knowne that the high
Courts admit no open triall of great caufes, they haue
no time nor leyfure, duly to informe theyr confciences.
As appeares by a like courfe helde by the fame Court in
the month of Iuly, 94. And for this caufe, Mounfieur
Marion pleading againft the Iefuits of Lyons, in the
yeere 97. faid, that a defectiue and imperfect prudence
of the yeere 64. was in fome fort the occafion that the
affaires of Fraunce degenerated with the time, & waxed
worfe and worfe. As for my felfe, I will fay more boldly with open face, that this matter was in the yeere 64.
put ouer to counfell by the wifedome of men, but thys
counfaile was guided by the hand of God, who to take
vengeance of our finnes, preferued the Iefuits as a deuoted inftrument hung afide in the Temple, fit for the future miferies of Fraunce.

To what purpofe is all this, faue onely this, to fhewe
you that if I deteft & abhorre the Sect of Iefuits, I haue

no small shelters for my oppinion : first the venerable censure of Paris, the yere 1554. wherein were the greatest Diuines that euer were in Fraunce, and by name, *Picard, Maillard, Demochares, Perionius, Ory*, the Inquisiter for matters of faith. The first, an admirable preacher, whose body after his death being layd forth in his house in the Deanry of S. Germins of Lauxerrois, the people of Paris for the sanctimony of his life, did striue to kisse his feete : the foure other his companions, were extreame persecutors of the Heretiks. I haue the great decree of the French church, in the yeere 61. the iudgement that did second it, and finally, many men of marke and communalty, set against them in the yeere 1564. Amongst these, I may speake it for a certainty, which I ought to beleeue because I saw it. There was two honorable resemblances of antiquitie, Solicitors in the cause, *Bennet* the Deane, and *Courselles* the Subdeane of the facultie of the Diuinitie Schooles in Paris ; The one, fourscore yeeres of age, the other, threescore & seauenteene : both ready to depart from hence, to giue vp an account of theyr actions in another world, at which time euery man standes stricte vppon his conscience. With them was *Faber Sindic*, one of the wisest men that euer was among the Sorbons.

In the winding vp of all, I will set downe Ma. *Noell Brullarte*, Procurator generall, the great *Aristides* and *Cato* of his time, which liuing in the yeere 50. withstood the receiuing of the Iesuites. I tell you this, expresly to discouer how like the iugling of the Iesuits of our time, is to the former. For *Fon* is so impudent as to report, that *Ramus* & *Mercerus*, after they became the Kings Professors, reuolted from our auncient Religion, and were solicitors in this cause, and that if they had not encountred them, they had won the field : but to auoid sedition, the Court was forced, warilie to strike saile to the tempest, by putting the matter off to counsell.

Well,

Well, but yet thou lyeſt moſt impudently thou Ieſuit. (Pardon me,for it is very fit I ſhould be in choller.) Neither *Ramus* nor *Mercerus,* for theyr parts euer ſtirred in this, although they tooke part with their brethren, the Kings Profeſſors, becauſe they would not ſeparate thēſelues from the body of the Vniuerſitie.

Moreouer, what likelihood is there, that the mindes generally of the Pariſiens could be ſo ſuddenly changed to take part with the Hugonots. *Mercerus* was ſo farre from faction, that hee had no skill in any thing but Hebrue, wherein he ſpent all his time without intermiſſion: and became ſo great a Superlatiue in that tongue, that by the iudgement of the beſt learned, he was preferd before all the Iewès. In all worldly matters hee ſtoode but for a bare Cypher. But this is a Ieſuiticall priuiledge, to vnderſet theyr ſlaunders with the time by newe cogges. For if this Ieſuit *Fon* durſt, he would ſay that the towne, the Vniuerſitie, and the facultie of Diuinitie in Paris, all the foure orders of Mendicants, & the Pariſh prieſts, were Hugonots, becauſe they hindred the matriculation of this holy Order : what other conſequence can be deduced from his ſpeech ? Oh ſinguler and admirable impudencie, yet to be excuſed, becauſe it proceedeth from a Ieſuit. Neuertheleſſe,to ſhew with what truth & integrity I mean to confound thē in their lying, they cauſed *Verſoris* Plea to be printed in the yere 94. & he to bring the Vniuerſity into hatred,ſaith firſt & formoſt,not that *Mercerus* but *Ramus* & *Gallandius* were made ſolicitors in this cauſe : but this was ſo far frō all likelihood of truth, that euery man tooke it for an hyperbole, by reaſon of the open enmity they caried to all times, which accompanied them vnto their death. This enmity , *Rablays* the *Lucian* of our age, in the preface of his 3. booke, & after him *Ioachim Bellay,* a gallant Poet , in one of his chiefe Poems, ſcoffed at, with expreſſe inuentions, which are the beſt paſſages in all theyr bookes. As for *Gallandius,* he

In the 24. & 32. leafe of Verſoris Plea.

F 3

he was neuer of any other religion, then the Catholique Apoſtolique Romane. I haue quoated out this in particular as I paſſe along, to giue you to vnderſtand,that in euery matter, be it neuer ſo ſmall, the Ieſuite cannot goe by without lying and diſguiſing.

CHAP. 7.

How the Ieſuits were refuſed at Rome, and by what cunning they were afterward receiued.

Euer thinke, that if they were ſo euill intreated in Fraunce, they had any better entertainmēt at Rome. At their firſt comming, *Ignatius* and his new companions arriuing there, plotted(in the yeere 1539) to eſtabliſh a new ſect that ſhould make the three ordinarie vowes of other religious, & a fourth beyond them all,concerning miſſion : and that they ſhould haue a Generall, whom they ſhould be bound abſolutely to obey, without any reaſon yeelded them. I will report it to you word for word, what was the concluſion of their aſſembly, and what *Maffee* the Ieſuite ſaith in the life of *Ignatius*,dedicated by him to *Aquauiua* their Generall, which booke was imprinted by his allowance.

Maffee.lib.2 cap. 9 .de vita Ignacij. *Ergo, without controuerſie, one muſt be choſen to whom all in earth muſt be obedient as if it were to Chriſt, to his word they muſt ſweare, and eſteeme his becke and his will as an Oracle of God.* And after,they concluded that their Generall ſhould continue in this dignitie while he liued. *Moreouer,that whoſoeuer entred this profeſſion, ſhould to the three ſolemne vowes of all other religious houſes, adde a fourth , to go without ſhrinking to whatſoeuer countrey of beleeuers,or infidels,it ſhould pleaſe the Pope to ſend them,and that without fee, or ſo much as petition to defray their charges by the way.* Thus you ſee in the firſt planting of them, another abſolute obedience to their Generall,in all things
different

different from that to the Pope, concerning their miſſion onely. I will leaue the reſt of their rule preſented to *Paul* the third, to the examination it pleaſed his holineſſe to make of it. He committed it to three Cardinals to diſcuſſe, which thought good to refuſe it, ſpecially the Cardinall *Guidicion*. *Ignatius* whom I haue allowed for one of the moſt ſharpe and worldly wiſe men our age afforded, knew he had plaid the Clarke, and in his new ſtatute couched a greater obedience to the Generall, than to the holy Sea. For this cauſe he reformed his rule, and made their obedience to the Pope and their Generall in both alike. Theſe be the words of *Ribadener* a Ieſuit, who hath alſo written the life of *Ignatius*. *The order of* Rib.lib.2. *theſe Clarks muſt be, that by their Inſtitution they be readie to* cap.7. *obey the Pope at a becke, and liue by ſuch a line as he ſhall well conſider and determine of.* Which the Pope, at Tibur, the third of September, in the yeere 1539. was glad to heare. From this paſſage you may gather, that aſſoone as they offered him abſolute obedience in all things, Pope *Paulus* began to lend a fauourable eare vnto them. Neuertheleſſe, he ſtood a while in doubt to open any broad way freely for them to enter, for in the yeere 1540. he alowed them no number aboue threeſcore, afterwards in the yeere 43. he laid the gate wide open vnto them.

CHAP. 8.

Of the inſolent title of the ſocietie of Ieſus vſurped by the Ieſuits, and how many ſundrie faſhions they haue vſed to authorize it.

Vr whole country of Fraunce was very much offended at the proud and partiall name of Ieſuites, which they tooke vpon them. The French Church firſt, next to it the Court of Parliament, expreſly forbad the vſe of it. *Meſſul* the kings great Aduocate pleaded the cause, shewing how odious the name ought to be among Christians: for ripping vp the reasons that moued the Bishop, the facultie of Diuinitie, and the Vniuersitie of Paris to reiect them at their first arriuall; The maine reasons were (quoth he) first the insolent name & title of Iesuits, and verily by how much the more the name may be tollerated among Iewes, Turks, and Pagans, by so much the more it is to be refused among Christians, which do all make profession of the law of Iesus. It is as worthie to be blamed, as if a man should attribute and vsurpe vnto himselfe alone the name of a Christian, among Christians, the name of a French man among the French, or the name of Parisian among the Parisians. Moreouer the name of Iesus is of such dignitie and excellencie, that his Disciples & Followers left it only to their Head, and neuer tooke but the adiectiue of Christian, wherewith they are contented to this day. Vpon the same ground *Pasquier* said as much in a Plea of his. I will begin with their name, and after descend to their propositions. First of all, they call themselues Iesuits in the midst of Christians. Blessed God, is not this an accusation of the Apostles? happie and renowmed were those holy Fathers, seeing our Sauiour Iesus Christ face to face, to heare his exhortations daly, and after his ascension into heauen, to receiue the holy Ghost from him. Neuerthelesse, knowing with what humility they ought to regard and honour that great and holy name of Iesus, they neuer durst call themselues Iesuits, but Christians onely, in the towne of Antioch, where that name was taken vp by them: and as for matters of religion they were afterwards so handled, that as in Rome, the Popes neuer took vpon them the name of S. *Peter*, for the honour & reuerence they bare to their Captain: so in Christendome was there neuer any Christian baptized by the name of Iesus. All the old fathers knew it well, that it had beene

blasphemie

blasphemie to attribute the name due to the onely Creator and Sauiour of mankind, vnto a meere creature. You must acknowledge then (my maisters *Ignatiens*) that you blaspheme against the honour of God, when you intitle your selues Iesuits. It may be you will say we do not take vpon vs the name of Iesus, but of Iesuits, to let the people know that we be Iesus followers. Why ? did the Apostles & other disciples of our Lord, & they that immediatly succeeded him, briefly all the old fathers of the Primitiue Church, trace any lesse after him then you do? so as by some speciall priuiledge you must borrow this title and not they ? Furthermore I would be glad to learne whether we, by withdrawing our selues from the vow of your arrogant superstition, be shut out from the fellowship of our Lord and Maister Iesus Christ ? *Pasquier* said well, that it is to call the Apostles in question. For *Fon* the Iesuit defended afterwards, that the Christians title, was a prouder stile then the Iesuits. *Ignatius* and his companie (as they said) being desirous to draw our Church backe to the steps of the Apostles times, plotted to minister the Sacraments of pennance & of the Altar, and to preach Gods word. And by this deuice they spred farre without the authoritie of the holy Sea, and they likewise desired to be intitled, the company of Iesus. The Apostles ministred these two Sacraments, and caried the Gospell ouer all the world, was it then permitted to these new vndertakers to do the like ? I denie it? For they succeeded not the Apostles, but the Bishops, and vnder them the Curates. The Iesuits deuotion was built vpon ignorance, by reason wherof, they ought not to be called Iesus followers, but his forsakers, as bringers in of a new schisme into the Church. Yet haue they by this erronious proposition, qualified themselues with the title of Iesus company. A stile neuer giuen them by our holy father, but arrogated to themselues, as manifestly appeares in a passage of their request preferd to *Paulus*

G.   the

the third, and interlaced in the Bull in the yeere 1540.
*Whosoeuer in our Society (which we desire to be odorned with
the name of Iesus) is willing to warre vnder the banner of the
crosse.* This clause is repeated word for word, as it lieth
in the Bull of *Iulius* the third in the yeere 1550. which
is the confirmation of their priuiledges. It were absurd to
thinke Pope *Paulus* would honour them with so proud
a title, who refused them at the first, & afterward allotted
them but a certaine number, & that with many scruples
of conscience. Neuerthelesse, as the Iesuits neuer lackt
new lying inuentions to credit them, so they bruted it a-
broad, that they held this title by the faith and homage
of the holy Sea. Indeed the first Chapter of their constitutions begins in this manner. *This little congregation,
which by their first institution was called the Societie of Iesus,
by the Sea Apostolike.* And agreeable vnto this, *Versoris*

In the 30.
leafe of Ver-
soris Plea.

the Aduocate pleading their cause, alleaged this passage,
to shew that the Pope was their God-father, and that
they held their name by humilitie, not by ambition, these
be the words he vsed. I blame not the Aduocate, a man
of account : for he pleaded vpon the aduertisements giuen him, but I excuse not these wise men the Iesuits,
which are made lyers by their owne Buls. There is no
lye so impudent as that, but the authoritie of the holy
Sea was not sufficient to grace them by this forgerie:
they must haue recourse to miracles, that is to say, to their

Maff.lib.2.
ca. 5.
Ribad.lib.1.
ca.12.

iugling casts. Of late yeeres *Maffee* first, and then *Ribadener* found out, that *Ignace* accompanied with *Peter
Faure,* and *Iames Lainez,* going through a Church, not
farre from Rome, being at his praiers, fell into a trance,
wherein God the Father appeared to him, who comme-
ded *Ignace* & his companions to Iesus Christ his Sonne,
then loaded with his crosse, & marked with his wounds,
which promised to take him into his protection, & said
to *Ignace* at that instant, I wil assist thee in Rome. And as
soone as *Ignace* went out of the Church, he discouered

to

to his two companions what vision he had. That this is
but a tale of a tubbe, I haue no doubt at all. *Iames Lainez*
succeeded him in the Generalship, who being priuie to
this miracle, how cōmeth it to passe he neuer signified so
much to *Congordan* his Agent, & *Versoris* his Aduocate,
when the cause was pleaded? Why did he smother this
great miracle when it was requisite to disclose it? For that
which was chiefly obiected against them in the assembly
of Poissie, and afterward in the court of Parliament of
Paris, was the insolencie of this proud title of the Society
of Iesus. Why (I say) did not *Lainez* & his crue, giue vs
notice of this matter, when the French Church and the
court of Parliament forbad them this title. They did not
so much then, because neither the diuell, nor his impostures, built their nests in their pens, as they did at last.
Neuertheles, this lye profited them no more thē another
which we see with our eies. For when *Maffee* had told vs
this tale, marke what he puts to it. *And this was the chiefest
cause, for which after the Society was confirmed, he gaue it e-
specially the name of Iesus.* If that be true which this lyer reports, it followes, that *Ignace* & his companions, tooke
not the title of Iesus Society, but after their order was
cofirmed, yet by their requests put vp to Pope *Paul*, inserted into their first Bull of the yeere 1540. they attributed this name vnto thē. And that which greatly waighes
it, is, that foure or fiue yeeres after, *Montaignes* a Iesuit
roundly confessing that to be false which *Maffee* & *Ri-*
badener haue written, he fathers this inuention vpon the   Cap. 66.
Pope, I answere you (saith he to *Arnault*) *that it is the Pope*   of Truth
which gaue the name to this holy company, & the sacred coū-   defended.
sell that allowed them, which suffices to stop your mouth. The
verie same saith *Fon, The people gaue them the name of Ie-*   Fon. ca. 38.
suits, because the holy Sea called them the company of Ie-
sus. And two leaues after, *The Iesuits tearmed not them-*
selues Iusuits, but the holy Sea termed them the companie of
Iesus. I commend the conscience of these two honest
Iesuists

Iesuits, who speaking nothing of *Ignaces* vision mocke themselues in their soules with these two flatteries. But I cannot chuse but excuse their ignorance, for had they red their first Bull of *Paul* the third, they should haue found that *Ignace* & his companions were intitled the Societie of Iesus when they preferd their petition to the Pope.

The Aduocate standing vpon these contrarieties, one of the company said to him : Me thinks you labour in vaine. They haue this name of Iesuits, neither from God nor from the Pope: but only from the common people, which is a great Philosopher and controuler of our actions. You see *Fon* agrees vnto it: but you must vnderstand at large, how matters passe on this side. Being at the first named the companie or Societie of Iesus, the people marking their behauiour called them *Iesuists*, not Iesuits, pronouncing S. and T. together. For when their cause was pleaded in the yeere 64. The Aduocates cald them nothing else but *Iesuists*. See the counsell Maister *Charles Moulin*, one of the best lawyers in Fraunce gaue vpon the receiuing them. The title was this, *Whether the Iesuits be to be receiued in the Realme of Fraunce, and admitted in the Vniuersitie of Paris*. And all along his discourse speaking of them, he vseth no other terme than *Iesuists*. A matter which you shal find auouched also in *Versoris* Plea, put forth in print by them. *Men qualified their title* (saith he) *and called them the Colledge of Iesuists*. And so it continued a little after. But they could not leaue it, for so much as they ought to haue a common name fitting the whole order and Colledges belonging to them. Which can not bee that of Clairmounte, except peraduenture for the three Colledges sake founded by the Bishop of Clairmounte: It is therefore requisite they should adde the word *Iesuists*. This verie name was afterward in vse in their owne Colledge at Paris, when they were expeld.

Fol. 30.
Versoris
Plea.

It

It is true, that in proceſſe of time the common people for the eaſier pronunciation, diſcarded the S. and called them Ieſuits, in ſteed of *Ieſuiſts*. And when *Paſquier* printed his Epiſtles in the yeere 1 5 8 6. likewiſe when the Plea was printed in the yeere 94. And that of the Aduocate *Meſnil*, they were termed *Ieſuiſts* according to the common cuſtome of time. Neither was this reformed in *Verſoris* Plea. Take it then for certaine, that they were called *Ieſuiſts*, as you may better be informed by ſuch as liued in thoſe daies, & this was done vpon graue conſideration, for no ſparke of true Ieſus being in them, but hypocriſie only apparreld with his name, the people branded them with the name of *Ieſuiſts*. In like manner you know that from the Greeke word *Sophos*, which ſigfies ſage, in old time the word Sophiſter was deriued, to decipher ſuch a one as troubled the waters of Wiſdom. Therfore we do noate by the name of *Ieſuiſts* theſe new diſturbers of Ieſus & his Church. After this manner in our time, from the word *Deus*, ſome haue wreſted a title of men deified, which is a new hereſie. And as God ſhines in his wiſdome, ſo ſhal it not be from the purpoſe to couple a Ieſuiſt & a Sophiſter togither, becauſe a Ieſuiſt is nothing elſe but the Sophiſter of our Catholique religion.

Here ſaid the Aduocate, you haue reaſon, & not only I ſubſcribe to your obſeruatiō, but more, I hold him a heauie beaſt, which ſhal not acknowledge them to be of the Societie of Ieſus. Verely they are, but iuſt as *Iudas* was among the Apoſtles, ſo many Ieſuits ſo many Iudaſes, readie to betray their princes or their countries, whenſoeuer occaſion ſerues to do it. What wil you giue vs (wil be the burdē of their ſong to thoſe princes that haue moſt money) & we will deliuer our Leege Lord into your hands, or troble his ſtate that it may be yeelded to you. Did they not attempt the ſame in Fraunce, and if our famous *Henry* had beleeued them, had they not performed it ?

But

But thanks be vnto God, they met with ſuch a barre
as the neceſſitie of our affaires required.

CHAP. 9.

¶ *That the Ieſuits are called Apoſtles in Portugall, &
in the Indies, and with what deceits they
haue wrought it.*

Veſtionleſſe, he is much deceiued that makes any doubt of
the ſocietie of Ieſus, for there
muſt of force be a Ieſus in theyr
companie, ſithence they haue
had Apoſtles, & ſuch remaine
among them in the Realme of
Portugall to this day : an impietie certainly ſhamefull for our
Catholique Apoſtolique Romane Church, that vnder
cullour of a paynted obedience, they ſay they yeelde to
the holie Sea, vvee haue ſuffered theſe hypocrites to be
called Apoſtles, not in Portugall onely, but in many o-
ther Townes and Citties alſo of the Indies, where they
commaund. Thys hiſtorie, howe diſgracefull ſoeuer it
be to vs, deſerues notwithſtanding, to be vnderſtood &
knowne to all good men, that they may be informed
how the Ieſuits haue not ſpared for any ſleights to rayſe
theyr reputation, by the downfall of the true Church of
GOD.

I muſt tell you then, that *Ignace* beeing at Venice
with his nine companions, *Peter Faure*, which in Latine
is called *Faber*, *Fraunces Xauier*, *Iames Lainez*, *Alphon-
ſus Salmeron*, *Nicholas Bobadille*, *Simon Roderic*, *Paſquier Broet*, *Claudius Iay*, and *Iohn Codury*. One *Hoſius* of
Nauarre, Bachelor of Diuinitie, after many doubts cleered vnto him by *Ignace*, at laſt ioynd hart and companie
with Ignace, and was put into the *Cataloge with the reſt,*

(ſaith

Ribad. lib.
2. cap. 6.

(saith *Ribadener*,) and vppon the poynt of theyr depar- Ribad. lib. 7.
ture from the territorie of Venice, after their first re- cap. 5.
turne from Rome. *Ignatius*, (saith the same Authour) Maff. lib. 2.
Faber and Lainez, went to Viceria, Fraunces Xauier and cap. 4.
Salmeron, to mount Celesius, Iohn Codurus & Hosius (late
said to be put into their nūber) to Tarnisium, Claudius Iay, &
Simon Roderic, to Bassanū, Paschasius & Bobadilla, to Ve-
rona. It pleased God that after *Ignace* was appointed
by his companions to goe to Rome, as hee was saying Maff. lib. 2.
Masse at Mount Cassin, hee saw an Angell carry *Hosius* cap. 4.
soule with ioy to heauen. Thus by his death, their com- Ribad. lib. 2,
panie was reduced to their first Cataloge of tenne, that cap. 12.
number which (I say) preferd their request to Pope
Paule the third, and you shall not finde that they soone
afterwardes gathered any more to make vp eleuen or
twelue, as they did with *Hosius*.

Now, the record tels vs, that as they were at Rome attending the Popes pleasure to giue order for their plot,
Iohn the third of that Name King of Portugall, was
desirous to haue some one of these new Pilgrims to send
him to the Indies, where hee possest a great part of the
Country. The Portugals had by their long and vente-
rous nauigations, opened a way to these newe founde
Lands, (for so our Aunceftors calld them,) and they
made theselues maisters of them, where the most part of
the Commaunders continued in their old idolatry, & o-
thers, although they were baptized, were but rude Christians. By this meanes Ma. *Iames Gouea*, sometime principall of S. *Barbes* Colledge in Paris, aduised the King
to choose some one of these new Pilgrimes at Rome, to
conuert his subiects. *Gouea* by the Kings appointment,
wrote to *Ignace*, who aunswered him againe by Letters,
that he had no authoritie in that case, but that all depended vppon the Popes pleasure. After a little coursing to
and fro, the charge was committed to *Fraunces Xauier* of
Nauarre, and *Simon Roderic* a Portugall.

Thefe

These trauaild to the King, which entertayned them verie gracioufly. Vppon their arriuall, the Pope enlarged this newe companie to the number of threefcore: thefe two men were called Apoftles, a title deriued from them to their Succeffors in that Country. *Horace Turcelin* a Iefuit yeeldes this reafon of it. *Laft of all* (faith he, speaking of *Xauier* and *Rodoric*,) *the excellencie of theyr vertue, and contempt of the worlde, was miraculous in the eyes of the whole Cittie. It was bruted among the common people, that twelue Priefts, (for two were added to the ten) had combined together at Rome. Two of the which company liuing among them, feemed to carrie (I know not what) fhew of an Apostolicall life. This made the people, whether it were for the equalitie of the number, or for the conformitie of life, to begin by too great a title, to call them Apoftles, and continued fo to tearme them though much against theyr wills. For the Portugalls, beeing no leffe conftant in theyr dooings, then religious in determination, they coulde neuer be drawne to recall that name which they had once giuen (as they thought) vnto the truth. Nay the matter proceeded fo farre, that this name grew to be impofd vppon the reft of that focietie, almoft throughout all Portugall.*

Truft me, this paffage is of fuch defert, that I fhould deceiue thefe good men, if I fhould not tranflate it into French, to difcouer with howe great pietie they haue purchaft this title. For *Fraunces Xauier* is honoured for a great Saint among all the Iefuits. Was there euer any impietie or impofture greater then this, that thefe two hypocrits to be counted Apoftles, bruted it abroad, that two new fupplies were added to their Sect, to make vp the number of twelue Apoftles; and that vpon this falfe alarum they were called Apoftles. This was againft theyr will (faith *Turcelline*) belieue the reporter. For *Xauier* tooke fpeciall care not to loofe his tytle when hee came into the Indies. *Therefore, as before in Portugall, fo in India, he began to be commonly calld an Apoftle, and the*

fame

Turcel. lib. 1. ca. 10. of Xauiers life.

Turcel. 2. booke of Xauiers life, cap. 3.

same title afterwards, flowed from Francis as from the Head to the rest of his fellowes. Tell me (I beseech you) whether this be not to renue the heresie of *Manes*, whose followers were cald *Manichees*, he naming himselfe the *Paraclet*, had twelue Disciples whom he cald Apostles, and for such he sent them abroad one by one, to other prouinces, to spread abroad the poyson of his heresie through their preaching. To say the truth, *Ignace* neuer tooke on him the name of *Paraclet*, yet was he willing inough to be accounted for another Iesus by his company: As I wil discourse to you in his proper place, when I come to speak of their blind obedience. He did not only take this authority & power vpon himselfe. But resigned it ouer also to all the Generals of his order that succeeded him, who in like manner haue embraced the title of Apostles, wherewith their inferiours were endowed in Portugall.

This is apparant in Rome, and yet no man seesit, but quite contrarie, this Family is there had in honourable regard, vpon a wrong conceit men haue entertained touching their absolute obedience, whereof these my Maisters make semblance vnto the Pope. And shall we hereafter haue any maruaile to heare a barking at the holy Sea by diuersities of new opinions that fight against it? Pardon me I beseech thee, O holy Sea, for it is the heat of my zeale deuoted to thee, that inforceth me to vtter this speech. Great and vnspeakable are Gods iudgements, to suffer that in the Citie of Rome in your sight and knowledge, there should bee a *Manes*, continued by successions from one to another, which hath not twelue onely, but infinite Apostles dispersed here and there: God will reuenge it early or late, though it be by his enemies.

The Aduocate as a man much wounded in heart, was desirous to prosecute this in a chafe, when the Iesuit interrupting him, said, Verie well sir, you are in daunger to be drawen drie. Marking your difcourfe you put me in mind of thofe young Hiftoriographers which imputed it for folly to *Alexander* the great, that he would haue all men thinke him to be *Iupiters* fonne, they attributed this to his immoderate ouer-weening, neuerthelefle it was an excellent wife drift of his. Can you imagine why ? fo long as the country of king *Darius,* was the marke he fhot at, he was too wife to take that title vpon him, and chofe rather to thruft forward his fortune by ordinaiie meanes of aimes. But as foone as he plotted to paffe into India, a kind of new world deuided from ours, he would haue the people perfwaded by the great Prieft of Ægypt that he was *Iupiters* fonne, and from that time he would be adored as fuch a one, not by the Macedonians his natural fubiects, bred in the liberty of a Greeke fpirit: But by the barbarous people, with fuch refpect and beliefe, that from that time forward they fhould take him not to be a meere Prince, but a great God that came to the conqueft of the Indies: this deuice tooke fo good effect, that he made himfelfe Lord of the country without ftriking ftroke. The Kings, Potentates, and common people, faying, that their countrey was firft vanquifhed by *Bacchus,* then by *Hercules,* both fonnes of *Iupiter*: and that the whole rule and Dominion was referued for the comming of *Alexander,* a third fonne of his. Thinke you our Societie followes not this plot ? you fee we neuer tooke the name of Apoftles any where but in Portugall: but when we were to go to the fame Indies where *Alexander* had beene, we thought as he did, that it was fit we fhould be authorized beyond others, by a more ample, facred, and maiefticall title, which was to be called Apoftles. It had beene ill for vs to challenge it in Portugall, if *Xauier* had not continued it, by an entercourfe of his companie, after his arriuall in the Indies, to the end he might be reputed another Saint *Thomas,* fent thither

after

after the paſſion of our Sauiour Ieſus Chriſt. And it
were impoſſible to recount what conqueſts of ſoules we
made there, vnder this holy perſwaſion. Ha, (quoth the
Aduocate) verily if this be your faſhion, I haue nothing
to do with you: for as when you entred Italy you borrowed I know not what of their Mountebanks, ſo would
you do the like of *Machiauell*, in Portugall and the Indies. Meane while, you my maiſters that haue bragged
much of your knowledge in Diuinitie, haue verie ill
turnd ouer the hiſtory of the kings in the the Bible, from
whence you gather by a continued ranke, that God
tooke away the crownes of all the Kings of Iſrael as oft
as they became Idolaters, eyther while they liued, or in
all time to come neuer ſuffered them to deſcend vnto
their children. How thinke you (I pray ye) that God
hath left the true Kings of Portugall without heires, and
that their Realme came into the hands of the firſt Prince
that caught it? That one *Don Anthonio* a baſtard, one *Ka-*
therine de Medices, Queene-mother of our King, pretended title to it, and laſt of all, that one *Philip* King of
Spaine became maiſter of it without any great reſi-
ſtance. I will not diſcourſe in partriculer of the goodnes
of his title : for mine one part, I thinke that the beſt title
he had, was the iuſtice of God, whō it pleaſed, in reuenge
of the giddie Idolatrie and blaſphemie of the kings and
people, to make this realme, without triall of the cauſe,
paſſe from one family to another, by this holy title of
Apoſtles attributed to theſe hypocrites. And I perſwade my ſelfe, that the King of Spayne now raigning,
will one day fall into the like miſchiefe, if he ſuffer this
impietie.

CHAP.

CHAP. 10.

¶ *The impieties of William Poſtell a Ieſuite.*

Vt why ſhould we thinke this blaphe-mie ſtrange in them, if within few yeeres after they tooke the title of Apoſtles on them, ſome one of them was found ſo abhominable in the ſight of God and man, that he cald the power of our Saui-our Ieſus Chriſt in queſtion, vpon the point of our Re-demption. The man I ſpeake of, is *William Poſtell,* againſt whom *Paſquier* decl aimed in his Plea on this manner.

For ſo much as they buz nothing in the eares of ſimple women but their pietie, which they faſten to their Robes with a claſpe and a poynt, marke whether they they be ſuch indeed as they proteſt in words. We haue the Benedictines, Barnardines, Dominicans, Franciſ-eans, and other like orders. At the beginning of theſe profeſſions, the authors therof were found to be men of ſo holy life, that by common conſent of the Church they were regiſtred in the Kalender of Saints: Where-vpon many drawen by their good life deſired to trace after them. Peraduenture we ſhall likewiſe find, that the firſt of the Ieſuits ſect were men of ſo holy and auſtere life, that we ought to be ſo farre of from any diſlike of them, as on the contrary, we ſhould rather wiſh to be in-corporated into them. About ten or twelue yeeres ago one of your old Factors came to this towne, a man as farre exceeding you in knowledge, as you do the ſimple handy-crafts man. This was Maiſter *William Poſtell:* we heard him preach, read, and write. He had a large Caſ-ſack, reaching down to the middle leg, a long Robe, girt about him, an Epiſcopal bonnet, accompanied with a pale & withered face, which bewraied nothing but great auſteritie: and he ſaid Maſſe with manie nice ceremo-

nies

nies not common in the Church. All this while what
did he bring forth ? One mother *Iane*, an impietie,
an heresie, the moſt deteſtable that euer was heard
of ſince the incarnation of our Lord Ieſus Chriſt.
The Donatiſts, the Arians, the Pelagians, neuer did
ſuch a thing. VVhere preached hee ? Not in moun-
tanie or deſert places, where men are wont to plant
new religions : it was in the fayre hart of Fraunce,
in the Cittie of Paris. Of what Order was hee ? Of thys
venerable Societie of Ieſus. Ha, beleeue mee if your
ſocietie bring ſuch monſters foorth, if you ingender ſo
damnable effects, God graunt wee neuer be of this ſocietie.

The Ieſuits to this day deny it very ſtoutly, that *Poſtell*
was euer of their ſocietie : and not onely deny it, but as
ſoone as *Paſquier* obiected it when he pleaded the cauſe
againſt them, they ſaid it was a new addition put to his
olde Plea when he printed it. *Paſquier* ſhewes himſelfe Chap. 42;
(ſaith the wiſard *Fon*) to haue loſt all the faculties of his
ſoule, his vnderſtanding, his vvill, and his memorie : his
vnderſtanding is full of darkenes, his will full of gale, his
memory fraught with obliuion. For when the cauſe was
pleaded in the yeere 64. *Poſtell* was then aliue, confined
to the Monaſterie of S. *Martine* of the fieldes at Paris,
where hee liued vntill the yeere 1580. Neuertheleſſe,
this good pleader ſpeakes of him as if he had beene dead
long before. And a little after : laſt of all you muſt note,
that *Paſquier* ſpake not this when he pleaded : for he had
beene checkt for ſo impudent a lie, and hiſſed at by the
whole world that ſaw *Poſtell* then preſent; but this was
written one and twentie yeeres after, when he deſierd to
publiſh it. And ſo is he contrary to himſelfe, forgetting
to take that counſell the Prouerb giues, *Oportet menda-*
cem eſſe memorem, to the end he may draw vp the peeces
of falſhood ſo cloſe, that no body might perceiue the
ſeame.

And if you will belieue me, it was not without caufe the Iefuits plaid this Pauin to this Perrie dauncer, for if *Poſtell* were a Iefuite, they are vndone. Therefore I befeech you let vs examine three things: The firſt, whether *Paſquier* made this obiection. The fecond, whether *Poſtell* were of their companie. And thirdly, what vvas that impietie which he fought to bring into our Religion, vnder the name of his mother *Iane*? For as good fellowes vfe to fay, The fport is worthy of a candle. Concerning the firſt, *Paſquier* neuer fpake of *Poſtell* as of a dead man: to prooue it, the beginning of the paſſage is thus. *About tenne or twelue yeeres agoe, one of your companie came to this Towne, a man that paſſeth you, as much as you doe the meane Artificer.* By thefe words you fee, he fpake as of a man then liuing: but hee added afterward, *This was Ma. William Poſtell,* carrying backe all the coherence of this difcourfe, to the time of tenne or twelue yeeres paſt, when *Poſtell* built vp an herefie vppon his Mother *Iane,* as you may gather from the fame paſſage; which fhewes that the Iefuits haue neither vnderſtanding, iudgement, nor memory, ſtumbling in this manner vpon *Paſquier*: and this is it which in the yeere 1 5 9 4. they caufed to be imprinted, in *Verſoris* Plea of the yeere 64. which was an anfwere to *Paſquiers* Plea: if you take vp the booke and reade it, in the 3 6. leafe you fhal finde thefe wordes. *It is obiected againſt vs, that* Poſtell *vvas likewife of our company, & that by thefe bad fruites you may fee what the tree was, I aske them, what were the fruites of* Iudas, *muſt we for them condemne our Lord and his Apoſtles?* And a little after; *Poſtell was neuer profeſſed in our houfe, he was a very Nouice and fent away.*

Would you haue a more euident demonſtration then this, to proue both that *Paſquier* fpake of *Poſtell* liuing, and that he made this obiection. For otherwife, *Verſoris* had fought with his owne fhadow. Let vs nowe confider whether *Poſtell* were of their order. And to make it

good

good that hee was, I apply that which I euen now read
vnto you, *Versoris* & *Pasquier*, were two braue Champions brought to combate in the Lifts before the chiefe
Senate of Fraunce, at the foyles. The blow deliuered a-
gainft *Poftell* offended all the order, in refpect of the
place he helde among them. Had not hee beene one of
them, that great Aduocate *Versoris*, had neuer winded
himfelfe away from this ftroke as he did, but rather had
denied it roundly, as the Iefuits now doe, thinking that
the diftance of time hath raced it out of remembrance,
but knowing that the truth then apparant, would haue
complained of him, hee was not fo hardie. By meanes
whereof, fwimming between two billowes, he acknowledged him to be a Nouice of theyr Companie, but afterward fhut out of doores.

Of this expulfion you fhall not be able to quoate any
time. For after hee printed his booke of Mother *Iane*,
that ftunke in the nofe of all the world, they would neuer haue fuffered him to become a Nouice, as likewife
that is verified, that a little after his booke was condemned, and the Authour confined to the Monafterie of S.
Martins. As before this hee was too great a man in all
kinde of learning, and of the tongues, to fhut him out of
theyr company: fo was he feene publiquely apparrelled
after the Iefuits maner in Paris, in the Colledge of Lombards, with Father *Pasquier Broet*, and the other Iefuits,
in which houfe they had theyr firft aboade. After thys,
when they had a Colledge made ready for them, and
gates open in the houfe of *Langres* in S. *Iames* ftreete,
he did eate and drinke with them daily: before hee was
confined to the Monafterie of S. *Martine*. Heereby
you may fee, that no man then doubted he was a Iefuit.

What was then his impietie grounded vppon his
Mother *Iane*? Beeing nowe to bicker with thefe pretended nauigators of Affrick, euery man muft vnderftand, that they breede as many newe Monfters as men.
When

When *Postell* had beene many yeeres the Kings Profes-
for of the Greeke tongue, in the Vniuerfitie of Paris, he
left his place, defirous to hoift fayle for Palestina, as the
good *Ignace* did: from thence he came back to Venice,
about the time of the good *Ignace*, where hee grew acquainted with a fuperfticious old beldam cald Mother
Iane, whom hee made his Mother. A little while after,
he returned to Paris to the Colledge of Lombards, with
his companions the Iefuits, where hee printed a booke
intituled, *The victory of Women*. In which he maintaind,
that our Sauiour Iefus Chrift redeemed the fuperiour
world onely, that is, Man; and that his Mother *Iane*
was fent from God to faue the inferiour world, that is,
Women, adding *Pythagoras* dreames to his impietie.

Hee fought to perfwade men, that the foule of Saint
Iohn the *Baptift* was transfufed into her. And in another
leafe, that the foule of Saint *Iohn* the *Baptift* was once in
a Gold-fmith. Shee was apparrelled like a Iewe, with a
great Gaberdine of a tawny cullour; fhee went through
the Cittie bare-headed, and bare-footed, wearing a hideous long hayre, crying repentance, for the end of the
world was at hand. This newe S. *Iohn* the *Baptift*, was
afterward burnt aliue by the courfe of iuftice, helde in
the Court of Parliament of Tolofa, which would neuer
take the weakenes of her wit for payment. And in footh,
many men maruailed that *Postell* was not executed in
like manner. For his booke was fold publiquely by Por-
ters, and it cannot any way be excufed; except the Iefuits, (by I know not what externall infatuations, wherwith they doe inchaunt vs,) haue their fafe conduct for
euery thing. I perfwade my felfe, that *Richeome* wil one
day bring in this for a great miracle in his booke of miracles.

Wee haue to this day other remnants of *Postell*, for
the fame *Pafquier* pleading the caufe, faide that *Ignace*
was no leffe factious & troublefome in the Church, then
Martine

Martine Luther, that both the one and the other, were borne in one centenary of yeeres : *Martine* in the yeere, 1 4 8 8. *Ignace* in the yeere 1 4 9 1. Each of them erected his sect, saying, he drew all his principles from the primitiue Church, that thereby they might the more easilie draw the simple people to their line, but that the *Ignacian* sect was more to be feared then the *Lutherans*, running through a ranke of reasons which hee had coucht together. A speciall one was, that euery one of vs would take heede of *Luther*, whom we iudged an Heretique : contrariwise, that in the behalfe of *Ignace*, it was an easie matter for men to be ouer-taken, by I knowe not what kinde of hypocriticall countenaunce vvhich they put on.

This sole conclusion (saith *Fon*) shewes *Pasquier* to be full of ignorance and malice, and if he speak in good earnest, hee is like vnto that Atheist whom I dare not name, that made such a comparison betweene *Moses* and his law, and *Mahomet* and his sect, & called them both deceiuers. How so ? Becaufe he that likens *Ignace* to *Luther*, is as impious as the other, that compared *Moses* and *Mahomet* together. *Moses* was expresly chosen of G O D to deliuer his people out of the captiuitie of Egypt, and the tyrannie of the *Pharaos*. For *Moses* sake, the sea miraculously opened it selfe to make him way. God appeared to *Moses* and talked with him, and by his prayers, all the while he lifted vp his hands to heauen, the same great G O D made the children of Israell victorious. I doe not thinke any man was euer so wicked, that hee durst make comparison betweene *Moses* and *Mahomet* : and if there be any of that stamp, I take our Iesuits to be as bad as he, in comparing *Ignace* with *Moses*. This comparison would be strange to mee, but ouer-looking theyr other Iesuiticall bookes, I found it to be a very familiar matter with them. For Father *Haniball Codret* neuer doubted to write, that his companie

I.   tooke

tooke theyr name from God, who made them the companions of his deere sonne Iesus Christ, which so accepted of them. And in their annuall Letters of the yeere 1589. the Iesuits of the Colledge of our Lady of Loreto writing to theyr Generall, make mention of a little deuill coniurd by one of thē, in the Name of I E S V S, whereat he was some-what angry: but when they pressed him with the name of *Ignace*, then began the deuill to play the deuill indeede, more then he did before, such a feare had he of this holy name. These blasphemies are the least escapes of our Iesuits: this Familie hath good store of others, whereof I trust one day to make you a good and faithfull Inuentorie. But sithence that by leaping from one matter to another, I stept before I was aware vpon the proces and course of times, I will returue to our *Ignace* and his companions, to shewe you vvhat theyr craftie conueiance was to purchase entertainment when they came to Rome.

CHAP. II.
¶ *The Studies of great Ignace.*

THE yeere 1524. *Ignace* began to studie at Barcelona, beeing three & thirty yeeres of age, a course of life which he could not well relish; for hauing (as he bragd) his mind wholy mounted vp to heauen, he could not strike the wing to come downe, so low as the declensions of Nounes, which matter (saith *Maffee*) as it were presaging thinges to come, was furthered by the wicked enemie of mankind, especially at that time offering him many visions, and opening to him the secrete misteries of the holy Scripture. I think that neuer man spake truer then hee, for all these pretended contemplations of *Ignace*, were meer mummeries of the deuill, who desired to present vs with such a man, as

might

Maff. lib. 1.
cap. 17.
Ribad. lib.
1. cap. 13.

might by his ignorance trouble the whole state of the Church. In this conflict hee spent two yeeres at Barcelona, about the expiring whereof, iumping ouer his studies, he remoued to the Vniuersitie of Alcala, where he made a shew of study in Logique, naturall Philosophie, and Diuinitie. *In Logique* (saith Maffe) *he began to turne ouer those whom we call Termini. In naturall Phylosophie, Albert. In Diuinitie, the maister of the Sentences.* I leaue it to your considerations, whether these bookes were fit for him to handle, as a man that had doone all that was for him to doe, who studied his Gramer but two yeeres, when as yet he had employed his fiue sences, without taking his flight to any other dessigne; for the most conuersant in learning, are much cumbred with vnderstanding *Albertus*, much more with the Master of the Sentences, the first foundation of our Schoole Diuinitie. Adde to it, that the two yeres he spent, one while at Alcala, another-while at Salamanca, another Vniuersitie, these were but prisons & extraordinary proceedings for him : that is as much to say, so much interruption of his imaginarie studies hindred in him. I call them imaginarie, because he had no other speculations in his soule, but by faire semblance to fashion a new Sect. All thys vvas partly the cause, that hee perceiuing his drifts to take no place in Spayne, desired to see Fraunce, & came to Paris in Februarie 1 5 2 8. And then (say *Maffe* and *Ribadener*) knowing how little hee had profited in 4. yeeres, as well by reason of the precipitation, as the confusion of his studies, he deliberated to follow the broad way : Let vs take *Maffees* booke into our hands, & marke what he discourseth. *And when by his experience he had found the imbecilitie of mans mind to be such, that he can hardly endure to haue many yrons in the fire at once, condemning his former hast, and forsaking fro thence forth the shortest cut, he entred the Kings high way, and attempted to begin his studies anew. Therefore beeing at mans state, hee disdained not to*

Maff. lib. 1. ca. 18. Rib. lib. 18. cap. 16.

I 2.   *repaire*

repaire euerie day to the *Colledge of Montagu*, and in the company of babling children repeat his *Grammer* rules.

He did also much diminiſh his ſet time of prayer, & taming of his bodie, to recouer the more leaſure and ſtrength : yet ſo, that he principally neuer omitted theſe three things. Firſt, to heare *Maſſe* deuoutly euerie day : Next, to refreſh him with the bread of heauen euery eight day after the Sacrament of pennance : Laſt of all, to call himſelfe twiſe in a day, to a ſtraight account, of all that he had ſpoken, done, or thought : and that comparing the day preſent, with the day paſt, one week with another, & one month with another, he might trie & examin at a hairs bredth how he had gone forward or backward in his ſoule. Let vs follow the traces of the ſame Maſſee.

Lib. I. ca. 19. *Ignace* being come to Paris, fel ſo ſodainly poore, that he was conſtrained to beg his bread euerie day from doore to doore, & to get into S. *Iames* hoſpitall by very humble ſuit, entreating the Preſident of that place, which was indeed a great hinderance to him. Therefore, in *Saint Iames* hoſpitall, which ſtands farre off in the Suburbes, **Ignatius** being driuen to verie great ſtreights, by reaſon of ſo great diſtance of place, he ſtrugled with other incommodities, as well in that the ſchooles began in the *Vniuerſitie* before day, and ended not but within the night, he by the ſtatutes of the hoſpitall, could not get out of the gates eaſily before ſunne riſing, and muſt returne at euening, before the ſunne was ſet : as alſo that by going and comming though he were a painefull and diligent Scholler, yet he loſt much of his Maiſters dictates, and of the exerciſes of the ſchooles. Hauing no other preſent remedy for ſo great detriment, he determined after the manner of poore Schollers, to ſerue ſome of the heads, Doctors of the Vniuerſitie : vpon condition, that ſuch vacant times as he had from his Maiſters buſines, might wholly be ſpent in the ſchooles to get learning. And a little after, ſeeing how *Ignace* went forward with his ſtudies. He tooke a farre better courſe, that when the vacations began, he might runne out into *Belgia*, and ſometime into *England*, or *Britane*, to the Spaniſh factors, by whoſe
bountie

bountie, hauing easily obtained a yeerely summe of money to be paid him by certaine pensions at Paris, all the time of his studies, he might the more commodiously giue himselfe to his booke: *and when he had spent almost eighteene moneths at the Latine tongue in the Colledge of Montagu, he went into a Colledge, cald by the name of Saint* Barbara, *to studie Philosiphie, tarying there three yeeres and a halfe (which is the full time appointed in that Vniuersitie for the course of Philosophy) he profited so well, that by the honourable verdict of his Maister (which was* Iohn Penna *the Philosopher) when he had plaid his ordinarie prizes, he was graced with a lawrell, and other ornaments of learning. After this, he did set vpon the studie of Diuinitie in the schooles of the Domenicans Monasterie, with great trauell. Ribadiner the supply of* Maffees *vntruthes, adds, That hauing gone through his course of Philosophie, he gaue the rest of his time, vntill he was fiue and thirtie yeeres of age, vnto Diuinitie, wherein by Gods goodnes, the haruest was answerable to his seed.* His meaning was to tell you, that he wonne as great honour in Diuinitie, as he did in Philosophie, wherein he said verie true, sithence he got no more commendation in the one profession, then in the other.

I haue here set forth wares which I tooke out of *Maffees* shop, whereby I desire neither to be a gainer nor a looser. It is fit that euerie historie should either containe a truth, or some likelihood of it: this lier hath neither one nor other. For while *Maffee* would here represent the actions of a good and vertuous man, he makes him such a one as knew not well how to speake Latine, or if he did, it was but the verie chattering of a Pye, that spake without vnderstanding. Neuerthelesse, at the end of his studies, he makes him a great Philosopher. It is not inough for a witnesse to depose such a thing was done: he must render a reason of his speech, if he will be beleeued. Let vs go ouer all that I haue here read vnto you. First *Maffee* confesseth, that all *Ignace* his studies for

the

the space of foure yeeres in Spaine were vnprofitable, so that he was constrained to go back to the lowest formes of the colledge of Montaigu with little childrē, to learne the first principles of his Latine Grammer, wherein he spent eighteene moneths onely, before he entred the course of Philosophie. I will shew you that of all this time you shall not find aboue sixe moneths of studie. During these eighteene moneths he neuer lost one Masse, he kept all his Saboths, this could not be done without deuotion, so that he must at the least take vp the Saturday to prepare himselfe : or if he went to lectures that day , it had beene to abuse the Sacrament of the Altar, to present himselfe before it thē day following.

Moreouer, euerie day he fell to examining his conscience, and if you will haue me put him into his circle, a braue studie certainly farre passing all other : but while he gaue himselfe time for it, this was to distract him from his other studie whereof we now speake. His first abode, was at Saint *Iames* of Haultpas, halfe a quarter of a league distant from the Colledge of Montaigu. What a deale of time lost he in going to and fro ? The hospitall gate opened late in the morning, and shut soone in the euening, which made him copie out many lessons euerie day : but that which is much more, when you consider that he was compeld to craue almes at mens houses for his reliefe : his dinner was not readie for him . To quite himselfe of this inconuenience, he was forst to serue a Colledge, a state wherein he might more easily find sustenance for his bodie, but not for his soule : for being come out of a hospital , from a kind of beggerie to seruice, neuer doubt but that he was employed in the most base and vile offices of a Colledge seruant, which are, to make the beds, to sweep the chamber, to brush his Maisters apparrell, and to beate out the dust, to hang the pot ouer the fire, to runne for wine, to

wash

wafh the difhes, and other fmall duties depending vpon this charge. Iudge you what breathing time hee could haue for his booke. In fine, during thefe 18. monthes he made many voiages in the vacations, as well into the Low-Countries, as into England, to recouer exhibition. I would be very glad *Maffee* fhould tell mee what time of vacation was giuen vnto the Schollers, for it is newes to me. Thefe voyages coulde not be made but by long iournies by a foote-man, driuen to begge his liuing, and the very cut ouer the Sea to paffe into England, is fom-what to be confidered.

Put all thefe circumftances together, howe much time had he left him for his Grammer ftudies of the 18. monthes? at the end whereof, they make him leape with a pitch-forke into Phylofophy, which was vnfit for it, and beyond all hope he grew a great Phylofopher, and afterward a profound Diuine. Such Schollers as haue paft the ftreights of Grammer and Rethorique, & haue thereunto ioyned the reading of Oratory, Hiftoriogra-phers, Poets Greeke and Latine, become in fiue or fixe yeeres fpace, hardly able to enter the courfe of Phylofo-phie: and would they haue vs thinke this man, who ne-uer had fixe monthes free leyfure to learne his Gram-mer among chyldren, becam a great Phylofopher? All thefe things giue the lye openly to this hyftorie. For the fame man, during the time of the three yeeres & a halfe of his courfe, was put into the Inquifition, before Fryer *Mathew Ory*, Inquifitour of the fayth; And he was to be whypt in the Hall of the Colledge of S. Barbe, by the hands of Maifter *Iames Gouea*, Principall of the houfe, vpon the complaint of Ma. *Iohn Penna* his Tutor, be-caufe he put his fellowes out of theyr ordinarie courfe of ftudies. *And I know not with what emptie fhewe of holines, he peruerted the excellent ftate and difcipline of that Schoole,* faith *Ribadener.* Furthermore, in the three yeeres of his courfe, he intangled in his net one *Faure, Xauier, Lainez, Salme-*

Maff. lib. 1.
cap. 20.
Rib. lib. 1.
cap. 3.

Ribad. lib.
2. cap. 3.

Salmeron, *Bobadilla*, *Roderic* his first companions, or rather to say truth, his first Disciples, with whom he afterward made the first stampe of his Societie at Montmarter.

I learne all this, specially of *Maffee*, yet is this braue calculator, so vnaduised to tell vs, that to make himselfe capable of Philosophie, hee forgot all the old illusions of the diuell, to giue himselfe the better leasure to studie, without consideration calling that the diuels illusion, which *Ignace* auouched to be deuotion. Lay aside his Philosophie, and call to mind his studie in Diuinity. He proceeded Master of Arts in March 1532. then he fell into a long and tedious sicknes, & by the Phisitions counsell he changed ayre, and went into Spayne in the moneth of Nouember 1535. Can you make him a great Diuine in three yeers, which neuer laid any foundation in Grammer or Philosophie? And to shew you that he was a great Asse, I meane in respect of all kind of learning, and not concerning the wisedome of the world, wherein no bodie came neere him, this is couertly acknowledged by the Iesuits themselues, who feed you with no fables. When Painters draw the picture of S. *Hierom*, they lay a booke open in his hands, to shew he was a man reputed the most learned of all our Church Doctors. And when the Iesuits represent the figure of their *Ignace*, they giue him a paire of beads in his hand, in token of his ignorance, for vpon these, silie wome say their praiers, which can neither read nor write. So shall you find him portraied by a sweet Ingrauer, before a Crucifix, in the forehead of *Ribadiners* booke, printed at Lions by *Iames Roussin* in the yeere 1595. *Rene de la Fon*, with a kind of synceritie of conscience, a matter very familiar with him, frankly acknowledges the like, when he saith, That neuer any disgraced Saint *Anthonie*, nor Saint *Frances*, nor the Apostles (a speech surely worthie of so deuout a Iesuit, to set the Apostles behind

Fon lib.1.
cap.38.

hind Saint *Anthony* and S. *Frances*.) Were the Apostles
studied, saith he? they drew their Diuine knowledge
from the holy Ghoft: also *Ignace* set his from the same
holy Ghoft, & though it were leffe in quantitie, yet was
it deriued from the same fountain. And truft me, I know
in good earneft, that *Fon* is a confcionable man, to a-
uouch his *Ignace* to be learned like Saint *Anthonie*, who
gloried that he knew nothing. It is not fo with *Ignace* of
whom I take hold for his ignorance, but with thefe two
ignorant Iefuits, *Maffee* & *Ribadiner* which would make
vs beleeue he was a great Philofopher and Diuine, not
confidering that by publifhing this in groffe, they belye
him by retayle, in reckoning vp the parcels of his ftudies. Neuerthelefle, I would euerie man fhould vnderftand after what fafhion the holy Ghoft was lodged
in *Ignace* and his companions, when they put vp a
fupplication to Pope *Paul* the third, for the approbation
of their order.

CHAP. 12.

℣ *That when* Ignace *and his companions came before Pope*
Paul the third, they were plain Mounte-banks, and that
the titles they gaue thēfelues were falfe.

Hich way foeuer I turne me, I find nothing but trecherie in this Iefuiticall Family, euen from the beginning of their
order, when *Ignace* & his fellowes preferd their requefts to Pope *Paul* the
third, for the authorizing their holy
company to take the name of Iefus: the promife they
made to him, was to bring the heretikes backe againe into the bofome of the Church, and to conuert the Turks,
and other mifcreants vnto our faith. A worke that not
onely required they fhould bring a willing mind with
them, but fufficiencie and capacitie to performe it. For
this caufe they were euer carefull not to be counted
K.   fimple

simple schollers, for then men would haue mockt them
and neuer haue called them Diuines. They were too
weak to grace themselues so far, hauing no ground, therfore after a smoother manner, they tearmed themselues
Maisters of Arts, not of Spaine or Italy, but of the great
& famous Vninersity of Paris. And in the neck of it, they
added, that they had studied Diuinity many yeeres. The
Pope, to be resolued what fruite this newe order might
bring forth, committed the matter to three Cardinals. Of
these three, one was of Luca, *Barthelmy Guidicion*, a very
learned & holy man (by the Iesuits own testimony) who
a little before this, had made a booke against new orders
of religion. This man standing as it were vpon his own
ground, became a puissant aduersary of theirs, & drew
the two others to his opinion. But in fine, *Ignace* won the
al, as wel by long importuning them, as also by a million
of *Masses* which he made his fellows say. These Cardinals
did but dispute the question in general, touching noueltie of orders, without sounding the bottom in particular,
to know whether these great votaries issued out of *Horace* mountaine, that was brought a bed of a Mouse. Let
vs now supply their want. *Montaignes* speaking of their
comming, saith thus : *First I answere, that this company of*
Mont. ca. 30 *Iesus began in Paris, and that it tooke the first roote there in
ten Maisters of Arts of the said Vniuersity, of which Maisters
one was a Biscaian ,* Ignace de Loiola, *one a Nauarean,*
Frances Xauier, *two were French men,* Pasquier Broet, &
Iohn Codury *: Three were Spaniards,* Iames Lainez, Alphonse Salmero, & Nicholas *Bobadilla: two were Sauoians,*
Peter Faber, & Claudius Iaius *: & one a Portugall,* Simon
Roderic. *It pleased them all to go forth Maisters of Arts in
the Vniuersitie of Paris. And that you may learne, by reading
the first Buls of Pope* Paul *the third, the tenor of which was
this. For we haue beene of late informed that our beloued
sonnes,* Ignatius de Loyola, *and* Peter Faber, *and* Iames
Lainez, *also* Claudius Iaius, Paschasius Broet, *and* Frances

ces Xauier, *with* Alphonsus Salmeron, *and* Simon Roderic, *&* Iohn Codury, *&* Nicholas *Bobadilla, Priests of the
Cities, & Dioceses of Pampilon, Gebennen, Seguntin, Toledo,
Visen, Ebredune, and Palestine, respectiuely maisters of Arts
graduated in the Vniuersitie of Paris, & many yeers exercised
in the studie of Diuinitie, long since departing out of diuers regions of the world, by the inspiration of the holy Ghost agreed
in one.* I leaue that that remaines, containing the admirable vow of these wandering Knights, and that which
they obtained of the Pope. All these were also inspired
touching the life & comming of Pope *Iulius* the third to
the Supream sea, of whom they obtained their confima-
tion in the yeere 1550. By the same quality also you shal
find in *Ribadiner* his 3. booke & 12. chapter, where the
Bull is all at large inserted, all of them say, they proceeded
Maisters of Arts in the Vniuersitie of Paris, all studied
Diuinity many yeers, and all were inspired by the holy
Ghost. I neuer vnderstood that the holy Ghost taught
vs to be liers, but by these vndertakers. To proue them to
you to be such, I will haue no recourse but to their two
great historigraphers. For if you beleeue *Maffee*, neither
Lainez, nor *Salmerō*, nor *Bobadilla* went forth maisters of
Arts in Paris, but in a Vniuersity bordering vpon Spain,
which they call *Complutensem Academiā*, in the Spanish
tongue, Alcala. Let vs heare what *Ribadiner* saith. Iames Rib.lib.2. cap.4.
Lainez *a yong man, hauing gone through his course of Philosophie, came to Paris from the Vniuersity of Alcala, with* Alphonsus Salmeron *also a verie stripling, that came both to
study & to seeke out &see Ignace.* In this passage, I cannot
perceiue that *Iames Lainez* was made Ma. of Arts at Alcala, & as for *Salmerō*, he was a yong boy that cam to Paris, as wel to studie as to see *Ignace*, yet *Maffee* more aduē-
terous in this point thē his cōpanion, hath declared thē to
haue taken their Maistershipss of Arts in Spain. *Iames La-
inez*, who next after *Ignace* gouerned our Society, & *Al-* Maff. lib.1. cap.4.
phonsus Salmeron of Toledo, very expert in the Greek &

K 2.   Latine

Latine tongues, each of thē hauing ended his courſe of Phyloſophie at Alcala, trauaild to Paris, partly to ſtudie Diuinitie, partly to ſee *Ignace.* Make theſe two paſſages agree. *Ribadiner* makes *Salmeron* a young lad, not promoted to any degrees; at the leaſt, hee makes no ſuch mention of him as he did of *Iames Lainez*: and *Maffee* publiſht him to be accōpliſht in al knowledge of Greek and Latine, and to haue receiued his degree of Maiſterſhip in Spayne. Let vs dwell vppon this opinion, for I take no pleaſure to make them lyers, but vpon good gages.

The ſame *Maffe,* puts after theſe two heere, *Nicholas Bobadilla,* and *Simon Roderic,* ſaying; Vnto theſe, came *Nicholas Bobadilla* a Paleſtine, a learned young man, that had publiquely profeſſed Philoſophie in Pintia, a towne in Spayne, and alſo *Simon Roderic* a Portugall, a man of excellent wit. I will therefore place *Bobadilla* among the Spaniſh Maiſters of Artes, becauſe hee read a Phyloſophie Lecture before he came into Fraunce, but not *Roderic,* whom he makes to be a young man of great hope, and no more in theſe wordes *Præſtanti indole.* I know it well, that *Ribadiner* ſpeaking of theſe 7. all at a lumpe, ſaith; that after they were Maiſters of Artes, they made theyr firſt vowe at Montmartire, in the yeere 1 5 3 4. vppon the Aſſumption of our Ladie : but he ſaith not, that they were all made Maiſters of Arts at Paris. The truth is then, if you belieue them, that foure of theſe ſeauen, proceeded Maiſters of Art at Paris, *Loyola, Faure, Xauier, Roderic,* and the three others in Spayne, *Lainez, Salmeron,* and *Bobadilla.* And a yeere after, *Claudius Iay, Iohn Codury,* & *Paſquier Broet,* ioynd themſelues to their ſoeietie. You ſhall not finde eyther in *Maffee* or *Ribadiner,* that any of theſe tooke any degree of Schoole.

Thus if you giue any credit to them, of theſe tenne companions, 4. were Graduats in Paris, three in Spaine, and the three other without degree of Maiſterſhip. And

Eod. cap. 4.

I

I will shew you as I passe along, that *Pasquier Broet* was a great Asse for all his porredge. I speake of him, because I once turnd & wound him, and put him out of breath, when he, in the house of Clairmont in Harpe-streete at Paris, was President of the Iesuits. This fellowe was a great Idole, of whom a man may say, as in old time *Ausonius* said of *Ruffus* the Rethoritian.

Hæc Ruffi *tabula est ? nil verius : ipse vbi* Ruffus *?*
In cathedra : quid agit ? hoc quod et in tabula.

Is *Ruffus* picture heere ? most true : where's he ?
He's in his chayre : what doth he ? that you see.

And for all this I deceiue my selfe, for he neuer durst come into a pulpit to preache or read a Lecture, knowing his own insufficiencie. Behold now what time these ten Champions spent in the study of Diuinitie : for they tolde Pope *Paule* that they had studied it many yeeres. Maffee testifies vnto vs, that when they made theyr first vowe at Montmartir, the greatest part of them had now gone through theyr course of Diuinitie, and the others had begunne it with a good minde to finish it, that they might march forward together, to the conquest of Turkish soules in Palestine, by our holy Father the Popes leaue. The passage deserues to be viewed here at length. *Ignatius* hauing by the goodnes of God gotten these companions, (speaking of the sixe first companions) determined to put that in practise with al speed, which he had long hamered & cast in his mind, that by the Popes permission he might goe to Ierusalem, & either call the bordering Nations, which in time past sincerely profest Christianitie, & after were deceiued by Mahomets wicked superstition, frō their miserable error to the truth of the Gospel : or take that which followed, shed his blood, and loose his life in so holy and glorious a cause. Neither

K 3   was

was it hard for him to bring the reft to the bent of his bow, which came forward already of their own accord, and were inflamed with the loue of God. And becaufe moft of them had not yet finifht their ftudies in Diuinitie, that the zeale now begun in them might not coole againe, and alfo that their obedience might be fo much the more acceptable to the maieftie of G O D, by how much the greater neceffitie of feruitude & religion they impofed vpon themfelues, calling vpon the bleffed Virgine for her protection, & vpon S. *Denife* the Areopagite, the Parifians Patron, in a Church in the fuburbs, called Montmarter, by the mifteries of confeffion & of the Eucharift, euery one bound himfelfe, that at the end of his diuinity courfe, when he fhould goe forth Doctor of Diuinitie, prefently he fhould forfake the world, and feek the faluation of foules, in perpetuall pouertie; & by an appointed time faile to Ierufalem, with an intent to imploy all theyr endeuours to conuert the Infidels, and with care and ftudie purchafe a crowne of martirdome.

If this refolution fhould any way be hindered, they fhould goe to Rome at the yeeres end, & offer their trauaile to the chiefe Bifhop, Chriftes Vicar, for the fpirituall good of their neighbors, without any contract for reward, or exceptions of times or places. This vow they made in that Church, with great confent & alacritie, in the yeere after Chriftes natiuitie 1 5 3 4. 18. Kalends of September, vpon which day, the anniuerfary gratulation of the virgin Maries affumption is celebrated. And they celebrated the fame vow in the fame place, the fame day together, the next and the third yeere after.

Tis fit this fhould be tranflated into French, for it is neceffary for my difcourfe that euery man fhoulde vnderftand it. I haue tranflated thefe words, *Emefo Theologiæ curfu*, at the end of their courfe, when they had proceeded Doctors of diuinity. For I fee Maffee in like maner, defirous to fhew that *Lainez* & *Salmeron* proceeded

maifters

maſters of Arts in Spaine, vſeth the ſame form of ſpeech, *vterᵹ, cõfeƈto Philoſophiæ curriculo.* And *Ribadiner* repor-ting *Ignace* and his companions, to haue taken the like degree in the yeere 1 5 3 4. *Confeƈto* (ſaith he) *philoſophiæ curſu.* From this paſſage you may gather, that in the yere 1534. the moſt part of theſe 7. companions, were now Doctors in Diuinitie, and that the others had a purpoſe to finiſh their courſe. That any one of thẽ was a Doctor at this time, is too loude a lie, for if it had been ſo indeed, this title had neuer beene ſmothered, when they put vp their ſupplication to Pope *Paulus*, in reſpect of thoſe which had already taken this degree, & they would haue taken good heede to challenge no other ſtile then Mai-ſters of Arts. I wil goe farther with you, for I wil make it appeare, that none of theſe 7. or of the other 3. that after came to them, had euer ſtudied diuinitie. For if they had euer begun the courſe, as Maffee auoucheth, & ſtudied it many yeeres, this word *many* imports not two or three yeeres onely, but foure or fiue at leaſt ; we neuer ſay, that a man is in companie of many perſons, which is accom-panied but with 2. or three. The manner of the Diuines of Paris, is, when a man hath begun his courſe, at the 2. yeeres end, hee muſt defend publiquely in the diuinitie Schooles appointed for this purpoſe, where he anſwers vnder a Doctor, his moderator, to helpe him when he is hard driuen by the Opponent. Hauing plaid his ſchol-lers prizes, which is called his probation, he is made Ba-cheler, and from that day allowed to were a hood vpon his ſhoulders when he goes into the towne; and a redde habite of Bachelers in Schooles. When our ten Ieſuits came to Pope *Paule* the third, they neuer told him they were Bachelers in diuinity, they had not thẽ begun their courſe, nor ſtudied diuinitie ſo much as 2. yeeres : where ſhall we now finde theſe many yeeres they ſpeake of?

There can be no anſwer to this obiection but one, that is, to cõfeſſe freely, that Maffee lies, when he ſaith ſom of
them.

them were Doctors of diuinity,& some had begun their course. It may be some will say, that without matriculation in their Diuinitie course in the Colledge of Sorbons, euerie one of them particularly had studied it some more, some lesse, after they were Maisters of Arts. For my part,I striue not for the victory,but for the truth, and I doubt not, but that *Maffee* & *Ribadiner* also haue made no bones to lye in this point. Let vs then examine what time *Ignace* and his companie could spend in Diuinitie,without entering into this course. *Maffee* and *Ribadiner* talke of this matter, as blind men speake of colours. I will deliuer you the true historie. I haue searched the old Registers of Paris,for those that proceeded Maisters of Art,in and after the yeere 1 5 2 0. vntill the yeere 1 5 5 6. when *Ignace* his companions, went out of Fraunce to meet him at Venice. I searched the records of *du Vale*, the Vniuersities Register, and *Violet* the beadle of Fraunce, for they two keepe the bookes. This did I in the presence of other men of account : And marke what I found according to the order of the Alphabet which they obserue.

Peter Faure and *Frances Xauier* went forth Maisters of Arts in the yeere 1 5 2 9. so saith the Register booke. *Petrus Faber Geben : Franciscus Xauier Pampil : Ignace* in the yeere 1532. *Ignatius Loyola Pampil : Claudius Iaye* and *Simon Roderic*, in the yeere 1 5 3 4. *Claudius Iayus Gebon : Simon Rodericus Visensis : Alphonse Salmeron, Iohn Codure* in the yeere 1 5 3 5. by these words *Alphonsus Salmeron Tolet : Iohannes Codure Ebrun.* I haue faithfully drawn all this out of the Register of the French Nation,where,in the matter of Licentiats, are comprehended Spaine, Sauoy, Prouence and Italy. As for *Maffees* and *Rabadiners* speech, auouching *Pasquier Broet* to be of the Dioces of Amiens, were that true , they would haue remembred it in their supplication to Pope *Paul,* where no mention is made of this Dioces. The truth
then

then is, that among three of them, two, without doubt, neuer tooke degree in Fraunce, but in Spayne; *Lainez* and *Bobadilla* : and *Pasquier Broet* which is the third, proceeded in neither of both. For that, that remaines touching the studie of Diuinitie, what is become of those many yeeres of *Iay* and *Roderic*, who proceeded but Maisters in March, 1 5 3 4. and of *Salmeron* and *Codury*, which came after them in the same degree in the yeere 1 5 3 5? for both our Historiographers agree, that in the moneth of Nouember 1 5 3 6. they forsooke Paris, to tender themselues in Italy to their Maister *Ignace*. As for *Ignace* himselfe, you cannot tell how to giue him aboue three yeers time of studie in Diuinity at the most, and much of that lost by a lingring sicknes, for which the Phisitians councelled him to chaunge the ayre, whereupon he returned in o Spayne, in Nouember, 1 5 3 5. yet did these great Clarkes promise by their learning, to conuert heretiques and infidels to our religion. Thinke you that if the three Cardinals put in commission by the Pope to examine them, had sounded the bottome of them, they should not haue descried, that vpon their comming into Italy, they had euen with the ayre, drunke downe I know not what manners and dispositions of the Mounte-banks, who vtter their Triacle in euerie towne, & take vp their standing in the market place, with a long Oration promising to heale al manner of griefes and diseases, with their oyntments, pouders, oyles, and waters : faire shewes, that commonly come to nothing.

L.   CHAP.

CHAP. 13.

❡ That we haue great likelihood to proue, that the approba-
tion of the Iesuits sect made by Paule *the third,*
is nothing worth.

He aduocate hauing ended his discourse,
the Iesuit replied and said: Why haue you
held vs so long with this friuolus matter ?
I see our first Fathers the founders of our
order, were not all Maisters of Arts in Pa-
ris : I see some of them were no Graduates : I see neuer a
one of the was Bacheler, much lesse Doctor of Diuinitie:
I see none of them studied it : Briefly, if it may pleasure
you, I grant all you would haue me. What of all this I
pray you, sith Pope *Paule* the third authorized them, &
ten yeeres after, *Iulius* his successor confirmed our new
profession ? Popes that deserue to be beleeued, aboue all
the rules of Lawe, by reason of their absolute power
and dignitie . Let me tell you freely, that though
our good Fathers were but simple Schollers, men
should hardly finde you match them, sith you inde-
uour by your curious speech, to call their state in question after it was allowed. You must vnderstand, that
the Pope supplies, by the scroule of his thoughts,
whatsoeuer wants, either in law or action.

This had beene well spoken (quoth the Aduocate)
if the Clarks of the Court of Rome coppying out the
Bull, had by some expresse declaration, put in a clause
derogatorie to the truth of the matter. Yet is not this
proposition altogether approued; as for my selfe, I will
take good heed that I neuer doubt of the authoritie of
the holy Sea, confirmed by infinite places as well of holy Scripture, as of the works of the auncient Doctors of
the Church. Yet the case standing as it doth in that
which followes, we haue great reason to be perswaded
that

that the approbation *Paule* the third made of their Sect,
is of no force, not for lacke of authoritie in him, but by
reason of a plaine surreption vsuall among you. Marke
I beseech you what I shall say vnto you, assoone as euer
Ignace forsook the warres, to betake him to another kind
of life : he had a purpose to become a Captaine of our
Church militant. The first shew he made of it, was a-
bout the yeere 1 5 3 6. in the Vniuersitie of Alcala,
where he drew three Spanish Schollers to him, *Artiague,*
Calliste, Cazere: and from that time had he a motion of Maff.lib.1.
Iesuitisme in his head. He had heard, that Saint *Iohn* the cap.17.
Baptist pointing to our Sauiour Iesus Christ, in the sight cap.14.
of the Iewes, cald him the Lambe of God that came
downe from heauen, to take away our sins : Hereupon
this wise man, taking the barke from the sappe, thought
he could not immitate our Sauiour Christ more truly,
then by wearing a wollen garment that was neuer died,
but of the same colour it hath when it is taken from the
sheeps back, thus were his three companions, and hee
sutably clad in Say, *Quos propterea* (saith Ribadiner) *à*
panni similitudine, Ensaialados vulgò Hispanico vocabulo ap- Cap.14.
pellabant: that is, Men in Say. And before him, *Maffee*
reported, that *Natiui coloris lanea veste cuncti vtebantur.*
Marchants ordinarily call it cloath, serge, or wooll, bearing the colour of the beast. These foure were all of one
companie, and among other things, they made a shew of
studying Diuinitie. Imagine you what a pretie maske
it was to see these foure great Clarkes in the Diuinitie
Schooles without gowne or cloake, onely suted in Say
of one colour. One *Francis* ioynd himselfe to these, who
had no leasure to apparrel himselfe like the rest . This Maff.lib.1.
new kind of habit, cast them into the Inquisition, from cap.17.
whence they were brought before Master *Iohn Figuero*
Viçar generall to the Archbishop of Toledo, who charged them to change their habit, commaunding *Ignace*
and *Artiagu* to go in blacke, *Callist* and *Cazere* in tawny,

Rib.lib.1.
cap.14.

as for *Francis*,he altered not his at all. A few moneths after, perceiuing *Ignace* to be vnlearned, he forbad him
to catechize the people for the space of foure whole
yeeres, in which time he might grow capable of that office. His Disciples being vnwilling to come within the
compasse of law any more,forsooke him vtterly, and he
spying his affaires go backward, after the same manner
that a little before certain hipocrits,called the *Illuminates*
were suppressed in Spaine, he determined to come
into France, hoping to haue better successe here; and
that he must be singular in some point whatsoeuer it
were, if he would preuaile. I haue told you what his cariage was in Paris. At the last, he, *Faure, Xauier, Laniez,
Salmerō,Bobadilla,*& *Roderic*,made a vow in the Church
of Montmarter, in the yeere 1534. vpon the day of the
Assumptiō, that as soon as they had proceeded Doctors
in Diuinitie, they should go to Palestine at the Popes
pleasure, to conuert the Infidels, as I told you of late:
and if any thing fell out crosse to hinder this enteprize,
they should put the matter into the Popes hands,to giue
such order for it, as he thought meet. There must be
much time to furnish them for the accomplishment of
this vow; For by the order of the facultie of Diuinitie in
Paris,after the degree of Maistership,there was a surcease
of fiue yeeres,which was afterward reduced to foure, before a man might begin his Diuinity course.Of the seuen
first,& three last companiōs,there were but two,that according to this graue order,were fit to begin this course:
that was,*Peter Faure*,and *Francis Xauier*,Maisters of the
yeere 1529. and so were not to be admitted before the
yeere 1535. As for all the rest, not one of them had
made his fiue yeeres preparation after his Maistership:
and one of them, *Pasquier Broet*,was no Maister at all,
and two others, *Lainez* and *Bobadilla*, hauing gone forth
Maisters in Spaine,were not adopted in the Vniuersitie
of Paris,& so consequently were incapable of admission.
Notwith-

Notwithstanding the tenor of their vow, they neuerthelesse to the preiudice therof, left France in the yere 1536.
and in 37. they were at Venice, where when they had
rested a fewe months, at mid-lent they went to Rome,
as well to get leaue of the Pope to take holy Orders of Maff. lib.
priest-hoode, as also to goe to Ierusalem to preach the 2. cap. 3.
Gospell, faining themselues, not onely to be Maisters of
Arts, of the chiefe Vniuersitie of Europe, but to haue
studied diuinitie there for many yeeres. The Pope en- Ribad. lib.
tertaind their request without any great sifting the cause, 2. ca. 7.
forasmuch as they confined themselues to Palestine, &
that without charge to his holinesse coffers, many of the
Spaniards themselues contributing to this matter, in fauour of them.

Thus these newe Pilgrims receiued 210. Ducats, by
bills of exchange at Venice, to set their new pilgrimage
afoote. I haue portraied out *Ignace* to you, for one of the
cunningest worldlings in our age. Finding his cause
drawne vp to such a head, he beganne to forget his first
vowe, and to feede many townes in the state of Venice
with new assemblies. There it was cōcluded among thē,
to diuert their voiage backe againe to Rome, to shewe
Pope *Paule*, that newes was come of warre between the
Venetians and the Turke, vvhich vvas a great barre
to their pretended pilgrimage. In the Cittie of Rome,
they erected a new frame of their societie, much different from the former, and they followed it two whole
yeeres; in which space, Pope *Paule* coulde not by anie
meanes finde in his hart to graunt them theyr peticions,
although he were vrged and importuned by many, and
by Cardinall *Contaren* himselfe: for neuer was yet noueltie destitute of a Patron.

Now let me tell you an expresse miracle of God, that
happened about the same time, to discouer these tenne
newe enterprizers to be very cheaters. They reported
that the Seas were stopt, by reason of the warres against

the

the Turke, & that by this meanes they could not effect theyr first designe. Behold here a new way, beyond all expectation opened to them, for the conuersion of Infidels to our religion, without any danger. All that I haue spoken of in this place, concernes their two Euangelifts, and doubtlesse this historie deserues to be sent by sound of Trumpet through all the world.

I remembred vnto you before, that *Iohn* the third of that name King of Portugall, possest a great part of the East Indies, ill peopled, which he desired to haue conuerted to the truth. The fame of the deuotion of this newe companie, that said they had vowed these conuersions, was spred ouer many Nations : the King summoned them by Letters to come to him, that vnder his protection they might be difpatcht into the Indies. But *Ignace* beeing subtile & wilie, turnd the deafe eare to this motion, remembring no more his first vowe made at Montmarter, nor his second vowe renued at Rome, by which hee got a good sum of money, and sent forth *Xauier* and *Roderic* onely, keeping the other seauen about him. Doe not you see by this, that *Ignace* was a states man, no religious man, who dalied with his vowe made at Montmarter ?

By the matters heere discourfed, you haue heard what was their vow at Montmarter, to goe for the conquest of soules after their doctorfhip in Diuinitie. That some of them said they were Maifters of Arts in Paris; that they had bestowed many yeeres in the studie of Diuinitie; meere fables. The paufe *Iulius* the third made in their allowance, euen when hee tooke them at theyr word, to be such men as they reported themfelues to be, and that he was verie much pressed by Cardinall *Contaren*, their Solicitor and Protector, what would hee haue done then think you, if his holines had receiued any true intelligence of their history ? Me thinks that with admirable maieftie, of those venerable yeeres hee carried, I

see

see him speake to them in this manner.

All new orders of Religion are to be suspected, and for this cause were they forbidden by two generall counsels, the one held at Rome, the other at Lyons; you present vs a new religious Order, vnder the name of the societie of Iesus, as true followers of him and his Apostles. Your intention is derogatorie to your profession, or to speake more properly, your profession is contrarie to your petition, and implies a contradiction. For if you be the Apostles Schollers, one of the first lessons they taught vs was, that looke what hath beene ordred in a generall Counsell by the heads of the Church, ought to be kept inuiolable, vntill it be repeald by another Counsell vppon iust occasion. As if all did shoote out of one stocke of the holie Ghost, *Placuit spiritui sancto et nobis,* they spake in such cases, as men that diuorced not the holy Ghosts cause frō the Churches, nor the Churches cause from the holy Ghosts. If you trace after the Apostles so precisely as you protest, how comes it to passe that by a new found order, you goe about to breake the auncient canonicall cōstitutions of the Church? I know it well, that beeing Christes Vicar, I may dispence with you, and I much commend your obedience to the holy Sea. But setting aside that which hath beene decreed in generall, & looking in particular toward you, all things degenerate from that you now intend: I perceiue that your beginning had some taste of God, your proceeding sauours much of man, and your end smacks three or foure times more of the deuill.

Betaking your selues to a deuotion full of perrill, you made choice of the Martirs Church neer Paris, to shew you would all be ready to shed your blood for the truths sake, as oft as occasion serued. A braue and holy resolution, which cannot be praised enough. Vpon this point you went to confession, all of you heard Masse deuoutlie, after that you receiued the Sacrament, vpon the day

of

of the Assumption of our Lady, the most solemne feast of hers: desirous that the blessed virgine should bee a witnesse to your vow, you continued it two yeeres after, the selfe same day and place. Heere be holy circumstances enow to tie you to the vow you made then: Let vs consider nowe what this vowe was. You promised to God, that when euery one of you had ended his diuinitie course, you would renounce the world, and goe to Palestine to conuert the enemies of our fayth, and that if you should within one yeere after your Doctorships, be any way hindered of your voyage, you should seeke vnto me to receiue my direction. For the first execution of so faire a plot, you made choice of the Citty of Venice, for the generall *Rende-vous* of these Pilgrims that were to goe to Ierusalem.

Maff. lib. 2. capit. 2.

Before you proceeded any further, thou *Ignace*, (for to thee I speake in particular, as to the ring-leader of them all) didst wisely take thy iourney into Spayne, to take order for your affaires and fellowes. And after that, with great zeale you tooke shippe at Valentia to goe for Venice, without any feare of *Barberosse* the Turks scouring of the Seas, all of you met at Venice; you came after that to me to receiue my blessing, and passe for your trauell and inhabiting Palestine. You obtained at my hands all that you craued, you receiued much gold and siluer, giuen you by diuers men for your first earnest of the voyage, vpon this blessing you returned back to Venice, with a purpose to performe your promise. I would faine know who diuerted you? You say the warre suddenly made betweene the Venetians and the Turke. What Gallies mand, what ships rigged, what preparation sawe you for this exployt? The Turke and wee are continuall enemies, yet doth hee not refuse to giue pasport and safe conduct to poore Pilgrims, paying him his auncient trybute: did this warre driue away the religious persons that dwell neere the holy Sepulcher?

Further-

Furthermore, who compeld you to alter your vow, for that which is prolonged from one yeere to another, is not quite broken off. Likewise, the Venetian and the Turk are now vpon entreatie of peace, & the matter either already concluded, or at a point so to be. Besides, if the passages be stopt that way, they lie open for you to the Indies, there is no feare in that passage, the King him selfe leades you by the hand, why doe you draw back? You that so late made shewe to goe to Palestine, a voyage subiect to a thousand dangers of your liues, go now in Gods name to this new world, and come not heere to plant a new world in our old Church.

Paul. Ioui. lib. 32. hist.

It is not the warre betweene the Venetian and the Turke that driues you frō your first vow, it is your selues that vow what you lust. This sauors of man more then I would it did. At your first comming frō Venice to my Court, you little knowe what cheere was made you by me and mine: and whether good or bad, which of the two, I haue no leasure to tell you; you founde more fauour then you looked for; good countenaunce, kinde entertainement, gold & siluer to spend by the way. For this cause you returned to Venice, you tooke your shortest cut to recoyle back againe to Rome, with more promises of submission to the holy Sea, forgetting your originall vowe. But let vs yeelde a little to you as you are men, & let vs take your new excuse for payment. How can I winke at the lies you flap me in the mouth withall, to circumuent mee and betray mee. You say you are all Maisters of Arts, of the great & famous Vniuersitie of Paris, I find three of you neuer tooke degree. You say you haue studied diuinitie many yeeres: where shall I finde these manie? in two of the companie, that vvere but Maisters in the yeere 1534. & two others in the yere 1535. and these came to Venice in the yeere 1536. Where shal I find then (I say) these many? in *Ignace*, that forsooke Paris three yeeres before he was Maister, or in

M.   that

that other, that neuer tooke degree ? To be short , I see
but two of your companie, *Faure* and *Xauier* that euer
could haue any leysure to follow this studie. I knowe it
well, that if you make any lie on your part , you will say
it is to be borne withall, because it is done to a good end.
A ghostly deceit, and I tell you at a word , that Chistia-
nitie brookes no fraudulent pietie.Set these two particulers apart, let vs come to the naked truth. Howe can I
dissemble the breach of your vow, wherein it cannot be
but the deuill had a finger ? You promised and swore to
God, that you woulde goe no further with your enter-
prizes , before you had ended your Diuinitie course :
where is the end,nay where is the beginning of it ? Prick
mee out the time , when euery one of you seuerally began it.If you began it,who hindered your finishing of it?
for there was nothing in Paris to feare you. The vvarre
betweene the Emperour and the French King, God be
thanked, is ceased : Nothing constrained you to make
such a hote vow at Montmarter,it proceeded from your
zeale,which tied you to nothing at the first,but now the
vow is made, you are bound to keepe it.

Before it was made,was not this worke necessarie for
the winning of soules, which you promise to performe ?
You like auriculer confession in our Ministerie , a most
holie thing : the transubstantiation of the bodie of our
Sauiour Christ in the Sacrament, a most holy thing : If
the word (most) import no more. These be meanes to
keepe the Catholiques to theyr old religion, yet are they
not sufficient, to conuert men of a long time nousled vp
in Idolatry and Mahometisme. Euery one of them hath
in his impious superstition, certaine Maximes contrarie
to the Christian fayth. Besides this, doe not you know,
that the deuill *Martine Luther*, (so I meane to call him,
as an impe of the deuil of S. *Martins*) is in complet Ar-
mour against the two Sacraments, by an infinite sort of
Sophistications , ill deduced from the holie Scripture,

if

if you learne of him to dosse out your hornes, as you haue promised, this is no young Schollers worke, nor for a simple Maister of Arte, but for one of the wisest and best learned Diuines to take in hand. For otherwise, while you thinke to defend our cause, you will betray it. What weapons must you haue to foyle these miscreants? The foure Euangelists, with the Commentaries of the good Doctors of the Church, S. *Hierom*, S. *Ambrose*, S. *Augustine*, S. *Gregory Nazianzen*, *Gregory* the great, the first Pope of that name, S. *Iohn Chrisostome*, S. *Bernard*, and many others, whom the Church hath enroled in the Kalender of Saints.

All these hold a course of morrall Theologie, a verie trenchant sworde to destroy the euill life of Christians: but that blade which I meane to speake of now, is fittest to bring you to close fight, with poynt to poynt; One *Peter Lombard*, maister of the Sentences, and S. *Thomas* of *Aquine*, men worthy to be followed in Schoole learning. These be two Champions, by whose help we may be sufficiently armed to buckle with our enemies, & this is no studie of two or three yeeres, ancient discipline requires at the least sixe yeres trauell in them for publique exercise, besides all the rest of our life in particular.

Sith you haue vowed to G O D to distill your wits through this Limbec, why would you haue me dispence with you? You that haue dedicated your selues, as wel to conuert Infidels as Hereticks, why haue you not doone it? It became you to doe it, except you meant to present vs with *Phaetons* fable of newe Coach men, who vndertaking to driue the horses of the Sunne, cast the whole earth into a combustion. Had you any sparke of religion in you, you haue no power at all to reuoke your vow made alreadie vnto God; the place, the day, the misteries, the Church, (twise or thrise frequented) the things you bring with you, bind you, without hope of dispensation. As for me, I neither wil nor can dispence with you,

the

the law of God, and the Gospell, our canonicall constitutions, my fayth, my religion, & the vniuersall Church
whereof I am the head, forbids mee.

Howe thinke you, would not Pope *Paule* haue flatly
reiected them, if hee had beene aduertisd of theyr false
degrees, and their fained studies of diuinitie, and of their
vowe made at Montmarter, seeing there belongs much
labour to gaine it before it be consented to. Heereupon
I doubt not, but that their order beeing receiued and allowed by a manifest surprize and obreption, theyr au-
thorising is voide. Consequently, that all that is built vppon thys foundation, is of no effect or validitie. That
the Iesuits, let them fortifie themselues as much as they
will, by the Bull obtaind of him successiuely after the
first, of the yeere 1540. seeing the roote it selfe it rotten, the tree can beare no fruite at all.

Hetherto I haue shewed you what an **Asse** *Ignace*
was, and what notable lyers hee had to his companions,
men altogether ignorant in diuinitie. I will nowe make
plaine to you, that theyr sect, which they call the societie
of I E S V S, stands vppon ignorance of the antiquitie
of our Church.

CHAP.

CHAP. 14.

That the Oeconomie of our Church consistes, first, in suc-
cession of Bishops: secondly, in the ancient orders of religion:
thirdly, in the Uniuersities: and that the Ie-
suits Sect is built vpon the igno-
rance of all these.

Ot only the religious orders allowed by
our Church, but true Christians, by what
name or title soeuer they be called, are
not of the Iesuits Sect, (Christian humilitie forbids vs to speake so proudly) but
follow our Sauiour and Redeemer Iesus Christ, after
whose example and his Apostles, we ought to frame our
life as neere as we can : that of his great & infinite mercie, he may take pleasure in vs. *Ignace* a very nouice, and
young apprentise in the holy Scriptures, made choise of
nine companions, as raw in these matters as himselfe.
They bringing in their Sect, imagined themselues euerie
way to be cõformable to the first grounds of the Primitiue Church, & for this cause, cald themselues the Societie of Iesus. Let vs then examine what were the first, second, & third sort of plants by which our Church grew
and what the Iesuits institutions be: that by matching &
confronting the one with the other, we may iudge of
ther title, they attribute to themselues this partiall and arrogant name of the Societie of Iesus, aboue all other
Christians . When our Sauiour was to ascend vp into
heauen, he commaunded all his Apostles to haue a care
of his flocke. This charge was three times giuen in particuler to Saint *Peter*, as to the rocke vpon which
he had before promised to build his Church. After that,
hauing cast the fiery flames of his holy spirit vpon them,
their whole intent and purpose was, to sow the seeds of
his gospell ouer all the world. Their ordinarie seat was

M 3. at

at Ierufalem, from whence they fent foorth at the beginning, heere one, and there another of their company, into diuers parts of the Eaft, which after their trauell, came backe againe to giue vp an account of their labours, in a courfe held by them. And although Saint Iames were by common fuffrages chofen (faith *Iuftus*) particularly to be gouernour of the Church of Ierufalem : yet had Saint *Peter* fuperintendance and generall primacie among the Apoftles, which was not taken from him. And in the whole hiftorie of their acts written by Saint *Luke*, the principall miracles were done by him, and the generall rule of this holy company was put into his hands.

Among them, were many perfons deuoted to religion : fome cald Bifhops, fome Priefts, of the Greeke word that fignifies Elders. This we learne of Saint *Luke* chap. 15. & 16. of the Acts, and in the 20. following, Saint *Paule*, who taking his leaue of the Ephefians in the end of the Oration made to them, cals them Bifhops whom he named Priefts in the beginning. Tis true that this gouernment continued not long among them, in fo much, that as well for the good of the Paftors of the Church, as for the flockes, the feuerall charges of feuerall prouinces, were giuen to fuch men as were moft fit, they were called Bifhops, and to men of meaner gifts were committed Townes, Villages, & Parifhes. Thefe the Church cald Priefts, who exercifed their minifterie by the Bifhops authority, & they were in time cald Curates, you may fee a verie faire picture of all this antiquitie drawen by venerable *Beda*. *Sicut duodecem Apoftolos,*

Bede in. 10. & Luc. *formam Epifcoporū præmonftrare nemo eft qui dubitet, fic & hos feptuaginta Difcipulos figuram presbyterorum, id eft, fecundi ordinis facerdotes geffiffe fciendum eft. Tametfi primis Ecclefiæ tēporibus, vt Apoftolica fcriptura teftis eft, vtriq̓ Presbyteri, vtriq̓ vocabantur Epifcopi. Quorum vnum fapientiæ maturitatem, alterum induftriam curæ paftoralis fignificat.* As

no

no man doubts but that the twelue Apostles represented the state of Bishops, so must you vnderstand that the 70.Disciples were a figure of the Elders,that is of Priests in the second place, although as the holy Scripture testifies,both sorts of Priests, the first & second were in the Churches infancie cald Bishops : yet the one of them signifies soundnes of iudgement, the other pastorall trauell in his Cure.I haue quoted the words expresly,to bewray the ignorance of a new Iesuit, which affirmes,that Bishops and Priests were at the first both equall; herein renuing the heresy of *Ærius*.Our Church general,rested fifteene or sixteene yeeres in Hierusalem, which was the common resort of all their missions. And after, the Apostles chose diuers prouinces to themselues, and bestowed the others vpon Bishops ; among others, the prouince of Ægypt was allotted to Saint *Marke*, Saint *Peters* scholler ; his Sea was establisht in Alexandria, the eight and fortith yeere after the natiuity of our Sauiour : that is, about fourteene yeers after his ascention.Lo here the first plant of our Church, wherein you may gather agreeably to the course of times, the primacie and authoritie of the holy Sea of Rome : the Patriarches of Constantinople, Alexandria, Antioch,and Hierusalem, the Archbishopricks,& Bishopricks, the particular Rectories,and Curates,of Townes, Burroughs,& Villages.

The Church continued long in this state, but afterward, the extraordinarie persecutions of some Emperours,draue them to flye into the Deserts,to saue themselues from those cruelties,where beyond all expectation of the common people,they deuoted themselues by vow to a solitarie life. Their Patrons were two great Prophets, *Elias* in the old Testament, & *S. Iohn* the Baptist in the beginning of the new : but this latter was speedily put to death by *Herods* commandement, & with his life, as much as lay in him,caried away with him from hence this great deuotion. *Philo* the Iew, seemes to attribute a
renouation

Fon.ca.27.

Euseb lib.3. Eccle.Hist. ca.1. & 4.

renouation to the Sea of Saint *Marke* in Ægypt, when he saith, that some one or other of his nation, forsooke their goods, and vowed a societie recluse, in the exercise of prayers and Orisons: which was a kind of shadow, but no liuely picture of the Monasteries that afterwards grew vp in the Church. They that *Philo* speakes of, were Iewes, which being Christians, seated themselues about the lake *Marie* in Ægypt, where, not being throughly instructed in our religion, they iumbled Christianitie and Iudaisme togither: so *Sozomen* and *Nicephorus* teach vs, and *Eusebius* himselfe swarues not farre from this matter.

Soz.lib.2. ca.16. Niceph.li8. ca.39. Euseb.lib.2. ca.16.

    The first of our side, which vpon deuotion entertaind a solitarie life, hetherto not put in practise, was *Paule* the aged: so saith Saint *Ierom*, that he learned it of *Macaire* and *Aneathas*, Saint *Anthonies* schollers, who farre exceeded him in holines of life & deuotion: *Huius vitæ* (saith the same S. *Hierom*) *autor Paulus, illustrator Antonius, & vt ad superiora veniam, princeps Iohannes Baptista.*

Saint Hier. in vita S. Anthonij. Saint Hier. epist ad Eusto.begin. audi. filia.

This course of life, tooke beginning (saith he) of aged *Paule*, Saint *Anthonie* promoted it, and if you will go higher, S. *Iohn* the Baptist was standard-bearer to them all. A matter worth the nothing, that as God establisht in his Church two great and holy companies, one of Bishops and Priests, the other of Abbots, Monks, and religious persons: so it pleased him to make Saint *Paule* a chosen vessell of his in the first ranke; and to lay the first planchers, & open the first doore, to our Monasteries, by the other Saint *Paule*, in the second ranke. Saint *Anthonie* (as I tolde you) succeeded him, from whom, as from one great fountaine, there issued many riuers, *Macharius*, *Aniathas*, *Iulian*, *Paule* the younger, and others, in whom, God made himselfe knowen by many miracles. This extraordinarie solitude, could not easily be embraced by all deuout men, but by such as were (if I may so terme them) Paradoxes.

    Thus

Thus some vowed a solitarie life, but after the manner of Monkes. For although they withdrew themselues from the common people, yet liued they in a Societie shut vp within themselues, sequestred from the rest of the people, which course being more easie to be borne withall, was more frequented then the first. Saint *Hierom* writing to *Rusticus*, a man desirous to betake himselfe to a solitaie life. *Primum tractandum est, vtrum solus, an cum alijs in Monasterio viuere debeas. Mihi quidem placet, vt habeas sanctorum contubernium, nec ipse te doceas.* You must first be aduised (saith he) whether you will liue alone, or in the company of others in a Monasterie. For my part, I thinke it best you should haue companie, and not be your owne Maister. When Sant *Anthonie*, liued in Ægypt, Saint *Hillarion* led the same life in Syria and Palestine that he did: and prouoked by the great fame that was spred of him ouer all Christendome, he went to see him, and returned verie well instructed from him: Neuerthelesse, by a new deuotion, he began to make himselfe more sociable after, then he was before: On this manner many Monasteries, neuer knowen before, were by his example erected in Palestine, which he visited at certaine times, as the Generals of religious orders doe, accompanied with many Monkes. Saint *Hierom* discourseth this at large, in his life: and this brings me halfe into a beliefe, that the Monasteries tooke their first beginning from him, and grew to be such as we see at this day. I may well say, that at one and the selfe same time, there were Anacorits in Ægypt vnder Saint *Anthonie*, and Monkes in Palestine vnder Saint *Hilarion*, of whom I will speake anone. *Ante Hilarionem nulla Monasteria erant in Palestina, nec quisquam Monacum ante sanctum Hilarionem nouerat in Syria: ille fundator huius conuersationis & studij, in hac prouincia fuit. Habebat Dominus Iesus in Aegypto senem Antonium, habebat in Palestina* *Saint Hier.* *iu vita Hilarionis.*

N

Iestina Hilarionem iuniorem. Before *Hilarion* came, there
were no Monasteries in Palestine, nor Monks in Syria:
he was the first founder of this Societie and studie
in this Prouince; our Sauiour Iesus Christ had aged
Anthonie in Ægypt, and *Hilarion*, younger then he,
in Palestine. Saint *Anthonie* was foure-score and
tenne yeeres when hee died, and Saint *Hilarion* foure-
score.

Now had all these men (I meane such as dwelt
alone in the Desartes, and such as liued in Couents)
apparrell distinct and different from the Common
people. This made *Cyprian* say (speaking of badde
Monks) that neither the solitarie life, nor the frocke
in steed of other rayment, nor the fastes, defended
Monks : but vnder this habite, many times a verie
worldly minde is couered. And Saint *Hierome* in
the life of *Hilarion*. *Igitur Hilarion* 80. *ætatis suæ
anno, cum absens esset Hesechius, quasi testamenti vice,
breuem manu sua scripsit Epistolam, omnes diuitias suas
ei derelinquens, Euangelium scilicet & tunicam sacceam,
cucullum & Palliolum*. Therefore *Hilarion* at foure-score
yeeres of age (*Hesechius* being absent) wrote a short
Epistle to him, in steede of his last will, bequea-
thing him all his riches, to wit, the Gospell, his garment of sack, his hoode, and his cloake : This kind
of habite hath beene continued to this day in the Monasteries, their exercises consisted in Fastings, Prayers, and Orisons, not so much to get their liuing by
it, as to shunne the snares and temptations of the Diuell : Hereupon none might be admitted into their
companie in Ægypt, that was not skilfull in some
manuarie trade. Thus likewise, the least part of their
care, was to become learned; this lesson they learned
of their great Patron Saint *Anthonie*, who professed that hee knew nothing, beeing of opinion, that
the studie of learning, would hinder spirituall meditation

Sanct. Cyp.
serm. de
dupl. martir.
Ep.104.

gations, and being such kinde of men, they tooke no orders of Priesthood.

This made Saint *Iohn Chrysostome*, (comparing a Priest and a true Monke together) say, that a Priest in respect of a Monke, is like a King sorted with a simple man that liues a priuate life : therefore the Monks office was, neither to preach, nor to teach the common people. Saint *Hierome* writing to *Paulinus* a Monke, saith, If you will take the charge of a Priest vpon you, if you desire to be called to the high degree of a Bishoppe, dwell in townes and Castles, that by winning other mens soules, you may saue your owne: But if you will be a Monke, that is to say, solitarie, what make you in townes, which are no habitations for sole men, but for troupes and multitudes?

The Bishops and Priestes, haue a looking glasse of the Apostles, they then succeeding in their charge, make themselues successors of their merits. And as for vs, let vs set before our eies Saint *Paule*, *Anthonie*, *Iulian*, *Hilarion*, *Macharius*, Captaines of our profession ; and not to forget what the holy scripture tels vs, an *Elias* and an *Eliseus*. Our Table is the ground, our diet is hearbes, and sometime a fewe small fishes, which wee account for great banquets. The same Saint *Hierom*, beeing intreated by a good sonne, to preach to his Mother, thereby to reconcile her to a daughter of hers ; you take me for a man (saith hee) that may croud into a Bishops chaire, you vnderstand not that I am shut vp in a Cell, sequestred from companie, by vow deuoted onely to lament my sinnes past, or shunne the sinnes present.

Sanct. Hier. tract. de vitand. susp. cont.

Time (as I haue told you) culd out two sorts of these men, the one dwelt solitarily in the desartes, cald Ancors, the others, in Couents, which the Greeks cald *Cœnobites*,

N 2   whose

whofe order and difcipline Saint *Hierome* defcribes in that notable Epiftle, that begins (*Audi filia.*) And although the Monkes were neither Priefts nor Clarks, yet by courfe and compaffe of time, their fuperiours were permitted to be Priefted, that they might admini-fter the Sacraments to them.

Thus became Saint *Hierom* an Abbot and Prieft togither : Likewife *Iohn*, Bifhop of Conftantino-ple , reproouing *Epiphanius* Bifhop of Cypres his in-feriour , for Priefting fome Monkes in Saint *Hie-romes* Monafterie, hee made his excufe by the mul-titude of Monkes, which then wanted Priefts to mi-nifter vnto them. And Saint *Ambrofe* in a funerall Oration he made for *Eufebius* Bifhop of Vercellis, a-mong other particularities for which he commended him, this was one, that he had Priefted all the Monkes of his Dioces. In proceffe of time, Religious per-fons, ioyning holy orders to deuotion, became great nurferies of our Church : In that fome of them were made Archbifhops, fome Bifhops, who by their holy liues, and deepe learning, promoted Chriftian Religion greatly. Such were *Gregorie Nazianzen*, and *Bafill*, both Monkes, and both Bifhops , which feuerally erected an infinite number of Monafteries, and re-ligious orders, the one, in the Realme of Pontus the other, in Cappadocia : and in them begunne the dif-cipline of Religions, which is in part tranfmitted ouer euen vnto vs. I omit heere of purpofe to touch the nouelties brought in by time, contenting my felfe with fhewing you the firft roote of all.

It remaines, that I fpeake a word or two to you of our Vniuerfities, erected as well for diuinitie Lectures as o-ther humaine Sciences. Neither in the Apoftles times, nor long after, was our Church particulerly charged with Lectures. The Apoftles office, & fucceffiuely the

Saint Amb.
ferm.69.

Bishops, consisted in preaching the Gospell and adminiftring the holy Sacraments. VVee are debters to the Church of Alexandria for this firft inftitution: where, in the dayes of *Commodus* the Emperour, *Panthen*, a man of great learning, firft opened a Diuinitie schoole, by the authoritie of *Iulian* the Bifhop. And frō that time, (faith *Eufebius*) the cuftome begun in the Church of Alexandria, was continued vnto vs : namely, to haue men that excelled in all knowledge and learning, to be Doctors, & Diuinitie Readers.

Eufeb. lib. 5, hift. ecclefi. ca. 9. 10.

Clemens Alexandrinus fucceeded *Panthen*, a man verie famous for his learning among the beft learned in his time. After him came *Origen*, who tooke to him *Heraclas* the beft of all his Schollers, thefe two parted the publique Lectures between them. *Origen* read Diuinitie, Aftronimie, Geometrie, and Arithmatique, leauing the meaner Lectures of the Church of Alexandria to *Heraclas*. The other Bifhops borrowed this commendable cuftome of trayning vp of youth : this cuftome fpred fo farre in this manner, that the Vniuerfities beginning to fet learning abroach, the Bifhops became the firft and laft Iudges of theyr endeuours : and for this purpofe haue they a Chauncelour ouer them, with whom the examination of this courfe, and thefe matters dooth refide. As for Monkes, and religious perfons, they haue no authoritie to read Lectures but to their own companies.

I haue heeretofore related, what was the firft and originall Oeconomie of our Church, in Bifhops, Abbots, and Vniuerfities, vpon which three great Pillers our religion ftands. Now let vs bring the Iefuits to the touch, that we may know what they are. They be men apparrelled like our Priefts, bearing no outward marke of Monks, yet do they make the three fubftantiall vowes of Chaftitie, Pouerty, and Obedience, common with other religious perfons, and they ioyne pouertie with it, as well

N 3   in

in generall as particuler, by them of the last vow, which are called Fathers, men aboue others deuoted to preach, to administer the holy sacraments of Pennance, and of the Altar, to reade publique Lectures in all Sciences to all sorts of schollers, without any subiection to the auncient statutes of the Vniuersities: yea and without acknowledgement of superioritie of the Bishops ouer thē, hauing their prerogatiue apart. But in conclusion, for the accomplishment of their deuotion, they offer to goe into all quarters of the world, where it shall please the Pope to commaund them, to conuert Infidels and vngodly men, thereby to renewe in some sort, the ancient practise of the Apostles. Therefore let vs now consider, whether this innouation of theyrs, may by the auncient order of the Church, deserue any place among vs, and whether they may be calld the companie of Iesus; if not by priuation, at the least by preuention of al other Christians.

CHAP. 15.

¶ That no man can tell, where to place the Iesuits among all the three auncient orders of our Church: and that this is the true cause, for which they neuer yet durst set in theyr foote into Processions.

En say, that dreames for the most part arise out of a long meditation imprinted in our heads the day before, by a reflection vppon some subiect, which hath presented it selfe againe in the night vnto our fantasies: Thus hath it happened vnto mee of late, for as one of the principall things I bent my mind vnto, was the Iesuits proceedings, so it fortuned, that one night among the rest, I dreamed this which I will rehearse vnto you. And I beseech you my Maisters, not to thinke

I

I tell it you, to make you merry, but in the soberest manner that I can; the matter is of such moment, that if I should doe otherwise, I should deserue to be punisht. If you will not accept it for a dreame, take it at the least for a heauenly vision, such a one as *Ignace* had, when God the Father appeard to him, recommending him to his sonne Iesus Christ: or els, when hee shewed him all the tooles with which hee made this great frame of the world: or when *Durus, Xauiers* first disciple, sawe in a desolate Chappell, our blessed sauiour Iesus Christ in the shape of a childe, come to reconcile himselfe to the virgine his Mother that was angry with him.

As I was asleepe, me thought I saw G O D take a generall surueigh of his Church, from the passion of our sauiour & Redeemer Iesus Christ, vnto this day: where (as it were) in a great procession, the Apostles went formost, followed by Popes, Patriarches, Archbishops, and Bishops, Curates, priestes, and all those Ecclesiasticall persons which are calld Seculars, because they bee no Monks. In the second ranke, marched those good olde Fathers, the Hermits, vvho were the first founders of Monasteries. After them, traced many great Abbots & religious Orders of *S. Augustine* and *S. Benet*, from whom as from two great conduits, flowed all other religious Orders, called Regulars.

In the reareward, came the Vniuersities, led by their Rectors, and the foure faculties, of Diuinitie, Law, Phisick, and Arts, with all their Officers, & a huge companie of schollers great and small. *S. Peter* carried the streamer before the first, Saint *Anthonie* before the second, and because some haue thought good so to place him, *Peter Lombard*, Bishop of Paris, and Maister of the Sententences, before the third; a man framed for this purpose at this time, without looking backe towards Maister *Iohn Gerson*, Doctor of Diuinitie, and in his time Chancelor of the Vniuersitie of Paris.

Last

Laſt of all came the good *Ignace*, with his equipage of *Faure, Xauier, Salmeron, Bobadilla, Roderic, Broet, Iay,* and *Codury,* his firſt companions. And after them, *Iames Lainez, Fraunces Borgia, Euerard Marcurian, Claudius Aquauiua,* all of them ſucceſſiuely, Generalls of their order. Behind theſe, were the Prouincialls, Rectors, Fathers, Principalls, Regents, Preſidents, ſpirituall & temporall coadiutors, and ſchollers admitted. All which, marching after theyr Captaine *Ignace*, deſired to bee marſhald vnder the banner of S. *Peter* firſt, next vnder S. *Anthonies*; laſtly, vnder the Vniuerſities.

At the firſt, *Ignace* neuer doubted to be receiued of the Apoſtles, becauſe their preaching, adminiſtration of the ſacraments of Pennace & of the Altar, and the great vowe of Miſſion made by the Fathers to the holie Sea, ſeemed to paue the way thether very faire for them; this made him ſteppe boldly to S. *Peter.* You ſhal be partakers of the whole diſcourſe that paſſed between them. I beſeech you let it not diſpleaſe you to ſee my Dreame enioy the priuiledge of dreames, which make what perſonages they luſt, play theyr parts with thoſe that come into our fantaſies, without reſpect of any rule or interpoſition of time, which commonly we obſerue in other matters.

S. Peter. Good Fathers, you are very welcome; for the maine ſcope of our calling, hath beene to winne as many ſoules to God as poſſibly wee could. *Ign.* This is the marke we aime at, by the particular vow of Miſſion which wee make to your ſucceſſors in Rome. *S. Peter.* This is well done, howe are you called? *Ign.* As our vocation craues, to wit, *The ſocietie of Ieſus.* In reſpect whereof, the common people, by inſpiration of the holie Ghoſt, haue called vs Ieſuits: a name which at thys day, appeares to be miraculouſly ſpredde oner all the world, it hath pleaſed God it ſhould be ſo. *S. Pet.* Nay rather the deuill; which hath vnder your habite, gone

about

about to circumuent all the world, this is not the firſt taſte we haue taken of his trecheries, neither will it be laſt: he watches euerie day to ſurprize the Church of God. How cōmeth it to paſſe? We which were foſtred euerie day in the companie of Ieſus, to whom he imparted all his ſecrets, all the while he was debaſed here in the fleſh, and after he aſcended vp to heauen, made vs pertakers of his companie by his holy ſpirit, we (I ſay) neuer durſt take this name vnto vs, but the name of Chriſtians; firſt in the Church of Antioch, where our holy brethren *Paule* and *Barnabas* did gouerne: A title approoued by the Church from our time to this day: and do you that deſire to be among vs, by a new and arrogant title call your ſelues Ieſuits? *Ign.* I beſeech you hold vs excuſed, it is not pride but humilitie that prouokes vs to it: our Sauiour had two names, one proper, which is that of Ieſus, this at that time was a common name to many Iewes, though men of baſe and vile condition: the other is that of Chriſt, much more noble and honourable: for it appertaind to none but Kings, Prieſts, and Prophets, men cald Gods annointed: for which cauſe you haue choſen this name, and we contrarywiſe, the other of Ieſus, for the ſmall account the Iewes made of it, as meaner and lower then the other. Thus if there be any greater pride in the choice of the one, then of the other, it may eaſily be iudged from whence it comes. Moreouer, we doe not thinke, that the name of Chriſtian was impoſed vpon you by the Church of Antioch, but accidentally by the voice of the common people without iudgement, it was receiued to be by a ſecret inſpiratiation of God.

Fon.ca.38.

At this ſpeech a great many ſaints and deuout men ſtanding in the firſt ranke, began to murmour ſoftly one to another, and ſome mutined out aloud: ſaying, that without giuing any further hearing vnto *Ignace*, he and all his followers were to be baniſhed our Church.

And

The first Booke of

And that by this propofition, (the foundation of their order) there is much Iudaifme, in Iefuitifme: for iuft as the olde Iewes arraigned our Sauiour Iefus Chrift: fo deale thefe new Iewes at this day with the Apoftles. The Primitiue Church vfurped not the Name of Iefus, although it feemed to them to be common among the Iewes, but becaufe the Apoftles, and other true and faithfull Difciples of Chrift Iefus, knew the force, energie, and exceeding greatnes of this holy name. Then Saint *Mathew* and Saint *Luke*, ftepping forth, defended, that God the Father himfelfe gaue this name by the mouth of the holy Ghoft his Embaffadour, expreffly fent by him, when he told the Virgin *Marie*, that he that fhould be borne of her pure wombe, fhould be called Iefus, (a name that fignifies a Sauiour,) becaufe he fhould be the Sauiour of the world. Hereupon, *Eufebius* Bifhop of Cefarea, made a faire commentarie vpon the difference of the two words. And Saint *Auguftine* that famous Bifhop of Hippon, fhewes, that if God the Father gaue this name of Iefus, it was done by a fecret myfterie prophecied by his great Prophet *Mofes*, whom GOD told, hee had chofen him to lead his children of Ifrael to the land of promife: and for this caufe, did he take another to fucceed him in his place before he died. *Mofes* made choice of *Aufes*, but in the choice, chaunged the name of *Aufes* into that of Iefus, that in time to come (faith this notable Affricanian, Bifhop) men might know, that not by *Mofes*, but by Iefus, that is to fay, not by the law, but by grace, Gods people fhould enter the land of promife. And as the firft Iefus, was not the true Iefus, but onely a figure of him: fo the land of promife, was not the euerlafting land of promife, but a figure of it.

There was no Bifhop of note, nor any of the auncient Doctors of the Church, in all the firft fquadron,

which

Math.ca.1
Luc.ca.1.

Eufeb.lib.1.
ca. & lib.2.
ca.6.

Aug.tom.
1 c.hom.27

which was not of this opinion, or brought not out some matter of attainder against *Ignatius*. Then Saint *Peter*, by his authority and primacy ouer all the Church, spake to them with an admirable Maiestie on this manner. It is neither for you, nor for vs, to yeeld a reason of that which was done at Antioch, when the Church of God gaue the name of Christians: this was a worke of the holy Ghost. And as it is not the seruants duty, to aske any reasons of his Maister, why he commaunds him this or that, but he ought only to obey him: so God hauing charged vs by his holy Spirit, to call our selues Christians, it is not fit for any man whatsoeuer, to enquire the cause of it. There is no speedier way to make men heretiques, then to become curious questionists in such matters. Therefore neuer thinke, that this name was imposed vpon vs by the Suffrages of simple people.

As the name of Iesus came from God the Father, so I may speake it for a certaine truth, that by the faith and homage I yeelded to our Sauiour at the first, vpon this word Christ, he built his Church vpon me, and gaue me the Keyes thereof, among the rest. For hauing asked the question of vs all, what men reported of him, some of the Disciples aunswered, that some tooke him to be Saint *Iohn* the Baptist; others said, hee was *Elias*: others one of the olde Prophets. But whom doe you (quoth hee, to vs his Apostles) iudge me to bee? I, taking the tale out of the mouth of all the rest of my fellowes, by the greatnes of zeale wherewith I was transported, aunswered him, Thou art the Christ, the Sone of the liuing God: and presently he replied, that I speake not this of my selfe, but by Reuelation from God his father. And after this he declared me to be *Peter*, and that vpon this Rocke, he would build his Church, and whatsoeuer I bound on earth, should be bound in heauen. Sith that vpon this confession of Christ, he

Math.16. Luc.8.

built

built his Church vpon me, this was a silent leſſon he taught vs of his will and pleaſure, that after his aſcention into heauen, he would haue his Church to bee called Chriſtian; and vpon this proiect, all our brethren doubted not to take vp that name at Antioch. I my ſelfe afterward, making *Euodus* Biſhop of that Sea, confirmed that name of Chriſtian in the Church. I maruell ſaid Saint *Peter*, (turning himſelfe to *Ignace*) that you honouring, as you ſay ye doe, the Sea of Rome, where my ſucceſſours ſway the gouernment, and yet at the firſt daſh, you haue deſpiſed my decrees: were there nothing elſe but this to be weighed in you, you may not ſo be admittted into this ranke. *Ign.* Will you not receiue vs vpon the three vowes we haue with great holineſſe made, of Chaſtitie, Obedience, & Pouertie, and that which is more, of generall and particular pouertie, when we became fathers of our order ? S. *Peter* This is another barre that ſhuts you out, for although Chaſtitie, Obedience, and Contempt of the world, were familiar matters with vs, yet did we not this by vow; that was brought into the Church after our time, by thoſe whom you ſee ſtand in the ſecond ranke, and to ſay the troth, wee neuer tyed our deuotion to pouertie.

Suidas in verb. Chriſtianus.

Ign. Wee miniſter the Sacraments of pennance, and the communion as you did, and we are readie to go foorth for the aduauncement of Chriſtianitie, whither ſoeuer it ſhall pleaſe your Succeſſours to ſend vs. S. *Peter* Theſe two Sacraments are likewiſe miniſtred by the Mendicants, of which order there be many now in the Indies, in Paleſtine, and at Pera, neere vnto Conſtantinople, to conuert the Infidels, yet are they not ranged in our Squadron; you muſt go to them, and let them know, there is too great oddes betweene vs and you, to yeelde you anie place heere.

Ignace

Ignace, finding himselfe excluded from the firſt ſtati-
on in this proceſſion, he was ſome-what amazed, neuertheleſſe, he thought to ſpeed better with the ſecond, becauſe he ſhould there haue to doe with *S. Anthonie,* the
honour of all the firſt Hermits. For I know (quoth he)
that in the heate of his holy meditations, hee gloried in
ignorance: & I am ſure, that if he doe but trie me therein, he ſhall find me nothing inferior vnto himſelfe. Thus
deuiſing with himſelfe, what might beſt bee doone to
creepe into his fauour, he ſhewed him, that he had paſſed his time in heauenly contemplations, and not in learning, as hee had done before. Yet true it was, that hys
ignorance had made many learned men, which were all
prieſted. miniſtring the holy Sacraments, ſome of them
were Preachers, and ſome Regents.

The holy and venerable yeeres of this good Hermite,
gaue *Ignace* this aunſwere: Brethren, I commend your
intention, but it is nothing like vnto ours. Our deuotion, and the deuotion of all the good Fathers, firſt founders of the religious orders, was a ſolitarie life, without
ſchollerſhip or prieſthood: our wiſedome conſiſts in
continuall lifting vp the minde toward God, taking all
humaine learning to be meere vanitie. And as for Eccleſiaſticall functions, we take no charge of them, they depend vpon the Biſhops, that feede vs by theyr inferiors
in the Church. Your Rulers are not like ours.

In Gods name my good brethren, goe your way in
peace, leauing vs to our ſweet life, in quietnes of conſcience, within our Cells. Neuertheleſſe, it may be you ſhall
find behinde vs, ſome ſhreds and remnants of ours, in
in whom you may take ſome roote, namely, thoſe which
by permiſſion of the holy Sea, are called to the orders of
prieſthood, and may both preach, and miniſter the holy Sacraments of Penance and the Alter, as you doe.

Ignace paſſing from them to the other, Saint *Benet*
perceiuing him comming by his gate, tooke the ſpeech

to himſelfe, and ſaid ; If you be of our companie , you muſt either be Ancors and Hermits, or Monks & Conuentualls. Your profeſſion, denies you to be Ancors, & we may be eaſily entreated to excuſe you of it , becauſe that life is too painfull. But if you be Monks and Conuentualls, as we are, where is your frock , your hood, & your cloake ? For *Elias*, the firſt image of our Order, and after him *S. Iohn* the Baptiſt, both differd from the cōmon people in apparrell. VVhere is the great ſhauen crowne vpon your heads, by which *S. Hierom* ſaid, that in pouertie we are like to Kings and Monarches ? where be the extraordinarie faſts your ſocietie keepes, not onlie beyond the cōmon people, but beyond the Biſhops and Curats ? Where be the Cloyſters within your Monaſteries ? Heereto *Ignace* and his companions briefely and roundly anſwered him, that they were no Monkes, but religious perſons onely.

Is it euen ſo, (ſaide *S. Benet*) then are you a kinde of quinteſſence of Monks. And as the facultie of Phiſicke admits none of theſe Paracelſian abſtractors of quinteſſences into their ſchooles : ſo may not we receiue the Ieſuits. To reiect a Paracelſite and a Ieſuite, both rime and reaſon will beare vs out . Therefore get you ſome whether els : for as you diſdaine the holy name of Monks, ſo are you diſdained by Monkes. You proceeded Maiſters of Art in the Vniuerſitie of Paris , at the leaſt, you preſented your ſelues for ſuch men to Pope *Paule* the third, I counſell you to returne as Maiſters of Art to the Vniuerſitie, you ſhall finde ſome of your acquaintance there, it cannot be, but that ſome one or other of them wil entertaine you.

Ignace perceiuing his caſe grow worſe and worſe, miſtruſted ſome misfortune in his attempts, whereuppon, turning himſelfe to his companions, he ſaid : Nowe wé are in queſtion to goe toward the Vniuerſitie, I knowe what my behauiour muſt be ; and although it will bee

eaſie

easie for them to goe beforme me,if I come to the great
Doctors,yet sith at the first I tooke no course, but to
teach pettie schooles for children,and you after me,haue
read Lectures to all sorts of schollers against our first institution, I pray you (quoth he to Father *Claudius Aquauina,*) seeing that now all my superioritie ouer our companie rests in you, that as Generall of thē all, you would
take the charge to sway Maister *Iohn Gerson,* it may bee
you shall find more fauour at his hands then all the rest.
Aquauina, not onely gaue him no deniall, but thought
his commaundement very fit to be obeyed.

Then began hee and his to bragge, that they taught
freely,wherein he thought his companie had very much
aduantage of the other Regents, but his feete were in-
tangled:for he was more roughly handled by them then
by the former,and when they came to pell mell, because
both sides had beene nousled in Schoole *Ergoes,* there
was the best sport of all. Nowe let vs see them beginne
theyr disputations. *Aquauina* hauing framed his proposition, and propounded his question, *Gerson,* one of the
chiefest Doctors of Diuinitie that euer were in Fraunce,
spake thus to *Aquiuaua.* *Ger.* You would faine be of
our companie, will you then acknowledge our Bishop,
for your superiour and ours, especially in matters concerning the instruction of youth: for hee is our chiefe
Iudge in this cause. And now as his substitute in the office of a Chauncellour, and Chanon of the Church of
Paris, I cary the flagge of the Vniuersitie of Paris,which
is the chiefe of all others. *Aqua.* I doe not vnderstand
your speech, we haue a greater Maister our holy Father
the Pope, which hath dispenced with vs in this point, a-
gainst the Bishops authoritie. *Gers.* You faile in the
first marke, this one poynt must send you backe againe
to Rome, to learne your lessons, and banish you out of
all the Vniuersities in Fraunce. But let vs proceed: our
Vniuersities are compounded of two sorts of men, the
one

one are Seculars, the other Regulars, in either of these, the rule and gouernment differs. The Seculars may be Maisters of Art, Doctors of diuinitie, Law, or Phisicke, and read Lectures after they haue theyr degrees, to all commers, as well within as without the Colledges; the Regulars are permitted but to goe forth Doctors of di-uinitie, and to reade to the nouices of their orders onely. Which of these two sorts are you ? Aunswere mee not I beseech you, as in the yeere 1 5 6 4. you aunswered the Rectors, and officers of our Vniuersitie of Paris: they moouing the like question to you, you replied twise or thrise, that you were, *Tales quales vos curia declarauerat.* For the Aduocate that pleaded against you, standing vpon this poynt, argued that you were such as were vn-worthy to be enrolled in the Vniuersities register.

Aqua. I maruell not at that, we were at that time like vnto the Beare, whose whelps seeme at the first to be but a rude lumpe of flesh, but by the Dams continuall lick-ing of them, in time they recouer the shape of a Beare : so was it once with vs; for (to tell you truth) *Ignace* and his companions, neuer prickt it out perfectly what wee were; but after we had many wayes exercised our wits, vppon an obscure platforme of theirs, we were not cal-led Monks, but regular Clarkes: for so hath our great *Ribadinere* entiteled vs; and before him, if I be not de-ceiued, the Counsell of Trent gaue vs the same stile, which was publisht a fewe months after our cause was pleaded, to haue recourse to the first day of May follow-ing.

Rib. lib. 2. capit. 17.

Gers. This is not to aunswere my question, you must aunswere categorically, to bring you into one of these two predicaments, of Seculars, or Regulars. *Aqua.* Did I not aunswere you at large, when I tolde you wee are Regular Clarks ? For beeing such, we are not bound to stand to the old statutes of your Vniuersities, beeing neither pure Seculars, nor pure Regulars. And we may
with

with all our vowes, be graduated throughout all your faculties, and read publique lectures to youth in all sciences, without seeking to, or acknowledgement of, the authoritie of your Bishops. *Gers.* Then are you a kind of Hermophroditicall order, such as *Pasquier* hath publisht you to be in his researches of Fraunce, for being Seculars and Regulars both together, you are neither of both. And sith you are not bound to obey our statutes, we likewise are not bound to immatriculate you in our Vniuersities. *Aqua.* Why do you refuse vs, that teach freely? *Gers.* Because you be verie coniecatchers. The first that euer came to teach in Paris, were *Alcuin*, *Raban, Ian*, and *Claudius*, venerable *Bedaes* schollers, they made proclamation, that they had learning to sell: you quite contrary, bestow it gratis. Yet is it true, that in three score yeeres space, you haue got more treasure twice or thrice told, then all the Vniuersities in France euer had, since the first stone of their foundation was laid. Moreouer, were you not censured by the Vniuersitie of Paris? in the yere 1554? *Aqua.* You may say what you wil, but of later memorie, the same facultie of Diuinitie, allowed vs against the old censure; for some particular persons, hauing abused the name of the Vniuersity of Paris in the yeere 1594. in the Court of Parliament; the Sorbons made a Decree in fauour of vs, by which the pursuit of our aduersaries was disalowed.

At this speech all the Sorbons shouted, you be lying Sophisters, and verie bad Grammarians. We know it well that the Aduocate that first pleaded for you, would faine haue beene your buckler, and after him, *Montaignes* of your companie, then *Fon:* But this is to enioy your ordinarie priuiledge, you know whereof. Let the Beadle bring out our Decree and read it, for this is too much impudencie to be laid vpon Christian people. *Die nona Iulij, Anno Domini,* 1 5 9 4. *viso & audito a facultate Theologiæ Parisiensi legitimè congregata, in maiore aula Sorbonæ,*

P.   *libello*

libello supplici, à venerabilibus patribus sociotatis Iesu, ipsi facultati proposito, quo quidem exposuerunt superioribus mensibus, D. Rectorem, tam suo, quam omnium facultatum nomine, libellum supplicem supremæ Parlamenti Curiæ obtu-lisse, quo petierit vt ipsi, corumáz societas vniuersa, ex toto Galliæ regno pelleretur, ac credibile non esse sacratissimam facul-tatem, huic petitioni consensum prebuisse. Ac propterea sup-plicarunt quatenus placeret dictæ facultati, declaratione tes-tificari, huius petitionis & litis intentæ, nullo modo participes esse. Ipsa facultas, matura deliberatione super hoc habita, in hunc modum censuit. Se quidē censere prædictos patres redi-gendos et recensendos esse in ordinem & disciplinam vniuersi-tatis, regno autem Gallico esse nullo modo expellendos.

Signed, *Panet dictæ facultatis Bidellus*.

This Decree was inserted at large in your Plea of the yeere 1 5 9 4. and in the 4 4. Chapter of *Fons* Booke: it is fit that euerie man should vnderstand it.

The ninth of Iuly, in the yeere of grace 1 5 9 4. a view being taken by the faculty of Diuines in Paris, then law-fully assembled in the Sorbons great Hal, of a bil of sup-plication, put vp to the facultie, by the venerable fathers of the society, wherein they declared, that a few moneths since, the Rector of the Vniuersitie, as well in his owne name, as in the name of all the faculties, preferd a sup-plication to the high Court of Parliament, wherein he required, that they, and all their societie, might be thrust out of Fraunce, and because it was not credible that the most sacred facultie had consented to it, therfore they desired the said facultie, to testifie by some speciall decla-ration, that they had no hand in this matter. The facul-tie vpon good consideration had, certified in this man-ner, that for their parts they iudged it fit, that the said fa-thers should be brought into the order and discipline of the Vniuersitie, but not by any meanes to be cast out of Fraunce.

The word *redigere* is more significant, then to bring.

or reduce, which I haue vsed for lacke of other : for the Calepins of the Latine tongue teach vs, that, *Redigere, est vi quadam vel industria ducere ad aliquid vel aliquo.* Cal you this an approbation of your companie, when by strong hand we would haue you brought in subiection to the Vniuersitie, and that in this case you are not to be hunted out of the Realme? Away with the whole cluster of new vowes, draw your selues into the Vniuersities orders, acknowledge the Bishop your superiour, as we do, take degrees in Diuinitie onely, and read to none but to your owne Societie, as other religious do, euery one in their place : we shall then agree with you, and take your parts stoutly in the highest Courts in Fraunce, that you ought then to liue among vs . Meane while, by your writings , you doe impudently and falsely , make a Trophee of this Decree, as if wee had laid the bridle in your necks; but the verie sight and reading of this, foyles you. Therefore get you packing , your Rules and Maxims impeach ours, which we of a long time haue kept in all holy and venerable antiquitie.

When *Gerson* had pronounced this sentence, *Ignace* and all his first companions vanisht out of sight , and presently after that, *Aquauiua* spying himselfe and those that were with him, left in the lurch, he cried. Sith you afford vs no place in earth, maugre all the rout of you, we will haue place in heauen with *Ignace* and *Xauier* : or it shall cost vs all the treasure we haue here and there in banke, but they shall be canonized. Then began all the little frie to hisse, & the greater sort of schollers whoopt; A Foxe, A Foxe, will they giue money to make *Ignace* a Saint ? *Aquauiua* somewhat dismaid, thought they had cried, *Osanna, Osanna,* and to requite them, set him down in a chaire, offering his hand vnto them to kisse, as he did to all those that came to his chamber, the same day he was made Generall : but sodainly he saw that he was

decei-

deceiued: For this company of wilde youths baited him worse then they did before. *Gerson* to pacifie them, said, My sonnes, neuer thinke that in Rome they will haue so little wit as to make these two men Saints. The Iesuits haue desired it a long time, and to compasse it, they haue imployed not their coyne (for I thinke there is no such trafick in Rome about sanctifying of soules)but all manner of lies, cogs, & hypocrisies, to surprize the holy Sea. For how comes it to passe thinke you, that within these few yeeres, the pens of *Maffee, Ribadiner* and *Turcelline,* haue hatched so many fabulous visions, & miraculous tales of *Xauier,* but to make their false testimonies seruiceable for this canonization? But the best sport I see, that as plaiers, to grace their Enterluds, bring them vpon the stage by day, with the windowes shut, and candles lighted; So the Iesuits spare for no burning Tapers in Rome, about *Iguace* Tombe, to make some better shew

Turcel.lib.1 of the sanctimonie of the place. And the same *Tur-*
ca.16. *lelline* saith, that when *Xauiers* bodie was carried into the Towne of *Gouea,* where it now lieth, there was a great waxe Candle onely of a Cubite length, lighted and set in the place, which burned continually two and twentie dayes, and as manie nights without wasting.

Yet haue not all these Torches, to this day beene able, to lighten the hearts of the Consistory of Rome, to make these two new Saintes, neyther will they euer doe it, as I am perswaded. Neuer thinke so Sir, said a little wagge in the companie, for lyes, and importunate suits, (matters proper to the Iesuits) will worke it out at last. Haue you forgot in *Boccace,* how *Chappellet de Prat,* a notable knaue, was canonized for a Saint, by some silly soules in the Cordeliers Monasterie at Dijon? And why may it not so fall out with *Ignace Loyola,* founder of the Iesuits order, seeing *William du Prat,* Bishop of Clairmont was their first benefactor here in Fraunce?

Presently

Presently vppon this speech they made such a noyse, that if it had thundred, you would scarce haue heard it. Continuing this hurly burly, some of the best Schollers began to clap their hands, as they doe in the Schooles, when the one side and the other haue argued long, and disputation ceaseth.

With this I waked, very much astonied at this dreame, wherein I find that verified, which one *William* of *Lorrey* spake, in the beginning of his *Romant* of the *Rose*, saying, that euery dreame is not false. My dreame doth make it good: I know what account the Iesuits doe, and ought to make of the counsell of Trent, as that where-vpon the approbation of theyr societie is partly groun-ded. Although they haue expresly commaunded all Clergie men, as well Seculars as Regulars, to goe the processions, except the close Monks, Carthusians, and Celestines. Neuerthelesse, the Iesuits neuer came there, eyther before that Counsell was held, or after. It is verie true that they coggd a Die, when they got a Bull from Gregorie the 13. to forbid them this matter: But thys was before their constitutions bare anie prohibition.

I come nowe to another matter, which is, that *Elizabeth Rossell*, one of *Ignace* fauourers, seeking to erect a Iesuiticall order of women in Rome, *Ignace* would ne-uer agree to it; hee knewe it well, that this would haue ministred matter of laughter to all the world: for what kinde of habite or place should these women haue had in their Monasteries? The religious men of Saint *Benets* order, *S. Barnards, S. Dominicks,* and *S. Fraunces,* do all weare the habite appertaining to their orders. The Ie-suits are apparrelled as priests, if women should haue ta-ken that attire to, you must haue called them vvomen priests.

Let vs returne to our processions, which all good and free Catholiques religiously embrace, *Ignace* bragged euery where he was a Catholique, why then did he for-

Rib. lib. 3.
cap. 14.
Maff. lib. 2.
cap. 17.

P 3   bid

bid his focietie the proceffions? Becaufe hee knew, that
if they came among other Ecclefiafticall orders, they
were vncertaine what place they fhould take, theyr fect
being a newe baftard religion, a very hotch potch of all
our orders, without any thing pure in it, or any poynt of
our auncient Church. Therefore, to call them the focietie of Iefus, is to goe out of the way, but I wil now giue
them a name more agreeable vnto them. I remember I
haue read in the *Romante* of the *Rofe*, late alledged by
me, that when Saint *Lewes* brought the Carmelites into
Fraunce, from Mount Carmell, they vvere called the
Pied-coats, becaufe their cloakes were ftriped & welted
with black & white. Sith then we fee the Iefuits to be a
partie-colourd religion, of diuers peeces of our ancient
Church, ill futed & fowed together, you may call them
and theyr religion, the new Motley.

Heere the Aduocate held his peace, which miniftred
matter of talke vnto the Gentleman, who faid to him, I
know not how true it is, that you had fuch a dreame as
you haue told me, yet I may well fay, there is much truth
in it. And more then that, you cannot paynt out thefe
matters more liuely, then by the picture of a dreame.
But feeing you make reckoning of the *Romant* of the
Rofe, me thinks by the modell of it, wee may more fitlie
call the Iefuits, Papelards, and theyr companie, Papelardie. Heere-vnto faide the Aduocate, I befeech you
let vs not ingage the authoritie of the holie Sea, by the
quarrell of thefe hypocrits. I will not, faide the Gentleman, fith you haue bound mee to harken till you haue
made an end.

CHAP.

CHAP. 16.

❡ That without wrong to the authoritie of the holy Sea, you may call the Iesuits Papelardes*, and theyr sect,* Papelardie*, that is, hypocrits, and theyr order hypocrisie.*

Ee haue euer yet in Fraunce embraced Poperie, with all honour, respect, and deuotion, and euer yet in Fraunce, hath this holy name, by many men, been by false shewes abused. VVhen you see a soaking Vsurer, & adulterer, or a thiefe, mumble manie *Pater nosters* daily at the Masse, without amendement of his euill life; or a Monk within his cloister, vnder his habite, his sad looke and thin visage, nourish rancor, auarice, enuie, and brocage in his hart, wee call both the one and the other Papelards, and their actions, Papelardie, what say you then to Poperie? It is the cleere spring and fountaine, from whence we ought to draw the vnitie of our Christian fayth. What is this papelardie? A maske of poperie in them, which outwardly would be esteemed to be better men then others, and inwardly are worst of all.

This one lesson haue I learned in that *Romant* of the *Rose*, where *William Lorrey* represents vs an Orchard, enuirond with high walls, painted with the portraitures of Hate, Enuie, Robberie, Auarice, Sorrow, & Pouertie; among which, was the picture of Hypocrisie, drawn in this manner: I will set you downe the old language, with the newe of *Marot*, the first for his authoritie, the second for his grace.

> Here was an Image in my sight,
> *That well became an hypocrite,*
> Papelardie *it was nam'd:*
> *Because in secret it is fram'd,*

To

To feare no mischiefe to atchiue,
If none spie what it dooth contriue.
The lookes were like a penitent,
And it appeared to lament :
A creature sweete it seemd to be,
Yet vnder heauen no villanie
Is found, but that it dares performe :
And it resembles much the forme
That hath beene made to this semblance,
Set out with sober countenaunce.
In apparrell it was clothed
Like vnto a woman yealded :
In the hand it held a Psalter,
The hart did groane, the eyes did water,
With prayers to God that fained be,
And to the Saints both he and shee.
It was not merry, it was silent,
As if the thoughts were euer bent
To shewe deuotion euery where,
Inuested in a shirt of haire.
Fat fed she was not you must know,
Fasting had brought her very low :
She grew so pale and wan of late,
That vnto her and hers the gate,
Of Paradise denied them passe.
For many people haue a glasse
Of flesh abated, saith Gods booke,
That many others they may hooke :
And for a little glory vaine,
Gods kingdome they shall neuer gaine.

VVhen this *Romante* was compilde, *Wickliffe*, *Iohn Hus*, *Ierom* of Prage, *Martin Luther*, and *Iohn Caluine*, were not yet borne, to make warre vppon the holy Sea; for *William* of *Lorrey*, liued in the time of S. *Lewes*, yet was the word (Papelardie) then in vse, marke whether

all

all these particularities set downe by him, doe not encounter our Iesuits? I confesse, that none of them lye in hayre, and likewise, that they take no knowledge of the extraordinarie fasts which other religious persons keep. They are wisely dispenst withall, by their statuts, but to passe ouer all other poynts, they repose theselues whollie vpon the authority of the holy Sea, as if they were the first-borne children of the Popedome. And at other times, when you see them vpon theyr knees, saying ouer their Beades one by one, before a Crucifix, or an image of our Ladie, and after, marke theyr confessions & communions before the people, with I knowe not what leaden lookes, fraught with hipocrisie, and notwithstanding, they worke vnder-hand the ruine of the Countries where they dwell, and the murder of whatsoeuer Kings and Princes it pleases them: and that theyr Masses, confessions, and comunions, are the directorie starres of their Machiauelian tricks, what better name can we giue them then Papelards? As for the name of the societie of Iesus, it is so proude a title, as no good men can make agree with them, except it be to grace their hipocrisie the more. Their sect (as they say) was first cosorted in Paris, and sworne at Montmarter in the hart of Fraunce. The words of Papelard and Papelardie, are French words, I thinke we shall find very many that will resigne them ouer vnto them, as words euery way fitting theyr profession. Neither is it any disparagemet to the merit of Christes crosse, that these men haue abused the name of Iesus, nor by their counterfet mortification (that I may speake as *William* of *Lorrey* doth) vnder the false shew of poperie, is the authority of the holy Sea encreased or diminished: it is strong enough to beare vp it selfe, without any helpe of this new seruice, or rather of this new deuice of the deuill, to surprize vs by the name of Iesus, & so ruinate & turne topsie turuie, all religious orders, and the holy Sea it selfe.

Q.   You

You ſhall neuer be inhibited by me, (ſaide the Aduocate) nor by any in this company, for ought I know : for
if, to folow your propoſition, a Papelard be ſuch a one, as
makes a faire ſhew outwardly, vpon his ſtall , but hath a
falſe ſhop behind, within his ſoule, where all is contrarie,
you haue proceeded maſter of the Art of hipocriſy, making vs vnderſtand that of Ieſuitiſme, which wee neuer
knew, and you are able to read a lecture of it. And ſith I
ſee you forward enough to ſecond me, let mee end that
which I haue begun, and when I haue ſpoken of the Ieſuits ſect in generall, let mee like an Aduocate ſpeake a
word or two of good Father *Ignace*, who is the marke I
ſhoote at.

CHAP. 17.

¶ *Of the fabulous viſions of* Ignace, *and the miraculous*
fables of Xauier.

N O body durſt write the life of *Ignace* after
his death, which hapned in the yere 1556.
it was too great a taske . The firſt that e-
uer attempted it, was *Iohn Peter Maffee,*
a prieſt of that ſocietie , that dedicated 3.
bookes of this argument, to *Claudius Aquauiua* theyr
Generall. This fleſht *Peter Ribadiner* , another prieſt of
the ſame ſocietie, to make a reflection vppon his fellow,
with fiue other bookes, ten yeeres after ; wherein, at the
firſt ſetting out, hee endeuours to make his hiſtorie appeare to be without check, becauſe that before the eſta-
bliſhing of their company, he, beeing not yet 14. yeeres
of age, followed *Ignace* at Rome , ſo throughly deuoted
to him, that he brags he could ſpeake of many things he
ſawe himſelfe , and faithfully reckon vp others, vvhich
Lewes Gonſalua, a man to whom *Ignace* diſcourſed them
at large a yeere before, had reported to him. Both the
one & the other, were diuerſly inſtructed in the Latine
tongue,

tongue, the first, by *Christopher Seuere*, the other, by *Christian Simon Liton*, both men of an other religion, whom I may not belieue more then the Iesuits, which be naturally lyers, in whatsoeuer they thinke wil serue to aduance their sect; perswading themselues, that it is no fraude offerd vnto God, when they beguile the world with a lie for aduantage.

I will rip vp heere, the most famous visions, which they say theyr great Sophy had. *Ignace*, by theyr computation, descended of the noble house of *Loyhola*, was in his tender yeeres, sent by his Father & Mother to the Court of King *Fardinand*, surnamed the Catholique, & in the yeere 1522. put in trust to keepe the towne of Pampelune, then besieged by the French, where one of his legs was shiuerd with a shot, and the other verie sore hurt: the towne deliuered, and hee taken prisoner, our Nation sent him away with much kindnesse to his owne house. And beeing so sicke, that the Phisitions and Surgions almost dispaired of his recouerie, in the night of his great crisis, Saint *Peter* (in whom hee did euer put his trust) appeared to him, promising to cure him, as he did indeede: for from that time, his sicknes beganne miraculously to decline, and hee grewe better and better. And when hee was recouered, spending his time in reading amorous discourses, because he could get no other bookes, one gaue him the life of our sauior Iesus Christ, and the Legend of the Saints, which he read; and from that time grew admirable deuout, desirous to change his old life, into a more austere & religious course: wherevpon, the virgine *Mary* appeared to him night by night, with a smiling countenaunce, holding her little babe in her armes: vpon this vision, hee forsooke the world for euer after. But *Ribadinere* goes farther, and hee reports, that *Ignace* being at his prayers and Orisons vppon his knees, before the Image of our Ladie, there happened a great earthquake in the house where he prayed.

Maff. lib. 1. capit. 2.

Q 2.   Now

Now while he was drownd in his deuotion, the deuill appeared to him, sometime faire and beautifull to looke vpon, sometime gastly & hideous, seeking to diuert him from his purpose, now by faire promises, anon by feare and terror, presented to his eyes. Entring the Dominicans Church, he was so rauisht, that rapt into heauen, he saw the holie Trinitie in three persons and one essence, a matter that ministred argnment vnto him to write a booke of the Trinitie, *Quoquo modo potuit stilo* : & here was not the end of his miraculous visions, (saith *Maffee*) for G O D shewed him the patterne he laid before him when he made the world. Moreouer, hearing Masse in the Dominicans Church, as the Priest lifted vp the host, *Ignace* saw Iesus Christ in it, in body and flesh, iust as he was when he liued vpon the earth.

Maffee sets it downe better in Latine, *Dum à sacerdote de more salutaris hostia attollitur , vidit* Ignatius *illa specie* Christum, Deum eundem , et hominem verissime continere. *Ribadiner* saith, that *Ignace* being very attentiue to a sermon he heard in Barcellona, *Isabel Rousset*, a Lady of honor, saw his head crowned with glistering beames, like vnto the sunne. And in another place, that he continued 7. daies together and would eate nothing, and hee spent seuen houres euery day in continuall prayers, and in the meane while , whipt himselfe thrice euerie day . Hee would haue held on this course, with the expence of his life, if his Confessor the Sonday following, had not commaunded him to take sustenaunce, or els he would giue him no absolution, as a murtherer of himselfe: This he did broad waking, but harken to another history more admirable then this.

Vpon a Saturday at euen-song, hee fell into such an extasie , for the space of seauen vvhole houres, without moouing hand or foote , that euery man iudged him to bee dead; at the last , some one or other, perceiuing his heart to beate a little , they resolued to waken him: And

Side notes (left margin):

Maff. lib. 1. capit. 6.
Ribad. lib. 1. capit. 6.

Maff. lib. 1. capit. 7.
Rib. lib. 1. capit. 7.

Maff. lib. 1. capit. 8.

Ribad. lib. 10. ca. 10.

Rib. lib. 1. capit. 6.

Rib. lib. 1. capit. 7.

And the next Saturday, about the same time of Vespers, as if he had beene rouzed out of a dead sleepe, he began to open his eyes, calling vpon the holy name of God. Both the one and the other Historiographer, speakes of the apparitiō of God the Father, & Iesus Christ his Son beaten and wounded, bearing his crosse, and that God the Father, recommended him to his sonne, entreating him to take the Iesuits cause in Rome, into his protectiō; which accordingly he promised to doe. And that *Ignace* being retired into the Monasterie of Mount Cassin, to spend forty daies togither in deuotion, as soone as he had said Masse, *Ozius*, one of his companions that died at Padua, appeared vnto him, mounting vp to heauen with some other cōpanie, *Splendidiore quam reliqui, habitu, gloriaᶢ, multò illustriore. Ignace* hearing that *Simon Roderic*, one of his crue was sick, going to visit him, he was certified from heauen, that he should recouer, wherin he was not deceiued. He assured *Peter Faur* of this matter, one that gaue much credit to him. See here in effect, the visions and miracles of *Ignace*, nothing inferiour to those that are spoken of in the Gospels, and in the Acts of the Apostles, nay rather in some points, far exceeding them.

Margin notes: Maff.lib.b. ca. 5. Ribad.lib.b. ca. 11.

Maff.lib. 2. cap. 6. Rib.lib. 2. ca. 12.

Rib.lib. 2. ca. 9.

To make vs way to Paradice, we passe through the Sacrament of Baptisme, & when our Sauiour was baptized by Saint *Iohn* the Baptist, at his comming out of the water, he saw the heauens open, and the holy Ghost descending in the shape of a Doue, and resting vpon his head, and therewithall, a voice was heard, Thou art my deere sonne in whō I am well pleased. When *Ignace* deuised to open a way to his company, he saw God the Father & Iesus Christ his son, who said to him, Go in peace, for I wil take thy part in the citie of Rome. Whē the holy Ghost was represented by the shape of a bird, it was inough: but me thinks it is more, that *Ignace* saw God the Father, and God the Son also, in his proper body. Iesus Christ was tempted but once, one maner of way by

Q 3. the

the diuel: *Ignace* twice tempted diuersly, & by very perswasiue speech. Iesus Chrift fasted fortie daies in the wil-
dernes without meat or drink : *Ignace* fasted only seuen
daies, & to counterpoize the rest of Chrifts fasting, he
disciplind himself thrice a day, & spent seuen houres of
the day vpon his knees in praier. The man whom our
Sauiour singled out for a chosen vessel to himselfe, was
S. *Paule* : when he wrought his conuersion, he appeared
not to him, but assaulted him only with sharpe speeches,
Saul, Saul, why dost thou persecute me? and he was three
daies blind, & did neither eate nor drink. This miracle is
nothing in comparison of *Ignace,* whose soule was caried
into heauen, where he saw the Trinitie in three persons,
and one essence : and after that, was in a traunce seuen
whole daies together, without sight, meat, or drinke.
Beside all this, he had one thing in particular shewed to
him (beyond all that is spoken of in the olde Testament)
he saw the tooles God himselfe occupied when he fashioned & fitted this great frame of the world : A blessing
neuer bestowed vpon any man, but *Ignace.* All we confesse the tranfubstantiation of the body and bloud of
Chrift in the Sacramēt of the Alter : a matter we cannot
see with bodily eies, but by the eies of faith. *Ignace* herein
passed vs all, when at the eleuation of the host, he saw Iefus Chrift there, God & man. I leaue the shaking of the
house where he was, by an earthquake, like vnto that of
Paule and *Silas.* I omit many other visions, specified by
me heretofore; and credit me, when I had read ouer *Ribadiner,* I found nothing in his sir-name and his booke,
but baldarie. And as for *Maffee,* I thinke he is transformed into *Morpheus,* which presents sundry shadowes
to men asleepe.

I doubt not, but that God was able to worke all these
miracles by *Ignace,* and much greater to, if it had so plea-
see him : he is the same God now that he was in the A-
postles daies : God without beginning, and without
end :

end : but that he hath done any such thing, I vtterly denie, and auouch these to be blasphemous impostures,
dropt by the Diuell himselfe out of the pennes of two
Iesuits, to snare simple people with their cursed superstition. I will make this matter cleare and euident. The
most pregnant proofes of all, are those, which we call
presumptions of law and of fact, which arise out of manie particularities, when they meet together, and when
they do not agree with them, this is to deceiue, against
the common sence and vnderstanding of the people.
The greatest iudgement that euer was giuen, was that
of *Salomon*, betweene the true and the supposed
mother, for which hee was called *Salomon* the wise,
yet was this grounded vpon presumption. For my part,
I thinke I haue greater presumptious than that *Salomon* had, to proue, that the pretended visions, wherewith these two hypocrites bleare your eyes, are mists and
illusions.

I will make this matter manifest, and omit the scruple
tucht by me before, that the writers hereof be Iesuits:
no, this is not the point whereupon I meane to rest. I
could be content to tell you, that I make no reckoning
of *Maffee*. He hath written so, therefore it is true, I
denie it ; & desire to be enformed who told it him : and
I will shew you my reason hereafter. The reason is, because in the historie, I build more vpon *Ribadiner*, who
saith he was in his young yeeres in *Ignace* company at
Rome, and that whatsoeuer he reports : he heard it of
Lewes Gonsalua, to whom *Ignace* imparted it a yeere before he died.

Therefore this honest man the Iesuit, might well
speake of all those things which *Ignace* did at Rome, after he was chosen Generall of their order, and of that
which fell out before. I should be a scrupulous gaine-
sayer, if I should say, that you may not beleeue *Ribadiner*,
when he tels you, *Gonsalua* spak it : neither is *Gonsalua*, if
he

he were aliue, any Saint, but such as for whom we keepe no holy-day, although he auouch he heard all these tales of *Loyola*. I will tread all these matters vnder foot, I do beleeue that *Ribadiner* heard it of *Gonsalua*, and *Gonsalua*, receiued the newes of all these miracles from *Ignace*. Let vs now giue credit to *Ignace* in his own cause, for none but he can say, that Saint *Peter* appeard to him first, and then the Virgin *Marie*; that he was two seuerall times visibly tempted of the diuell : that he saw the Trinitie in heauen, Christ Iesus in flesh and bodie in the host, the soule of *Hozius* his companion caried to heauen, that God shewed him how he made the world, that Christ promised him to assist him in Rome : all this rests vpon *Ignace* onely, none but he can giue vs testimony of it, and this makes me say, that if we should beleeue it, we were verie heauie headed.

If I were to rest vpon this point, I should haue inough to prooue you ought neither to receiue nor reiect all these miracles, but I will proceed. When *Pasquier* pleaded the cause, one of the fairest parts of it was that, with which he stoutly chalenged the Iesuits, to choake him with any one miracle that euer *Ignace* wrought : he said, that all the holy Fathers, Saint *Benet* , Saint *Dominic*, Saint *Frances*, and others , confirmed their new orders by many miracles done by them, as we read in their Legends : but not any one could be found done by *Ignace*. I haue deliuerd you that passage, word for word, wherin he spake of *Posties* impiety . *Ignace* was dead eight yeeres before this was pleaded. After his death, all hatred towards him ceased, when men talked of his miracles ; for we cannot speake so freely of the liuing. This cause was prolonged seuen moneths and more, both in the Vniuersity of Paris, and in the Court of Parliament, when they stood vpon the maine making or marring of their order. *Iames Laniez*, companion & successor of *Ignace* in his generalship, either knew these things, or ought to know them, and leasure and time inough had he to certifie. Neuerthelesse, in all *Versoris* Plea, there is not one word spoken of visions or miracles. A signe, that these lies, were new coyned by these Papelards after the cause was pleaded. Put this to it, that all the visions *Maffee* and *Ribadiner* reckon vp, hapned in Spaine, before *Ignace* either had the Popes blessing, or his order was allowed. And that after hee was chosen Generall, you shall not find in these two Iesuiticall Priests, any vision shewed him from heauen, nor any miracle done while he liued, nor after his death : yet if any miracle came from him, of force it must be either then when the holy Sea confirmed him, or after. In Rome, you see *Ignace* his forecast was good, to bring a new tyrannie into our old religion, but no marke of miracles at all. And why thinke you? because all his visions hapned to him in Spaine, two of them onely excepted, which he had in Italie, in corners : but neither durst he, nor his ministers, broach so grosse matters in Rome. I speake expresly of Rome, where, *Iuuenesq́, senesq́,*

Et pueri nasum Rinocerotis habent.

Turf.lib.5. ca.16.

Will you haue me lay this imposture open to your eies, by some other issuing from the same root? Among the companions or disciples of *Ignace*, there was one *Frances Xauier*, appointed by him to go to the Indies at the request of King *Iohn* of Portugall. *Ribadiner* wrote his historie, onely vpon report of the countrie, as the farther a Iesuit goes, the louder he lies : so *Horace Tursellin*, comming after the rest, reflects vpon his companion, with great increase and interest. For neuer did our Sauiour Christ while he was vpon the earth, nor after his ascension, nor Saint *Peter*, not Saint *Paule*, worke so great miracles as *Xauier* did in the Indies. He was a Prophet that foretold the things to com, he did read means thoughts, he made the crooked to go vpright, the dumb to speake, the deafe to heare, he cured the leapers, he rid the sicke

Turf.lib.6. ca.1. Turf. lib.2. cap.18.

R.   of

of their difeafes when the Phifitians had giuen them o-
uer: faying but a Creed, or a Gofpel ouer men, he had a
facultie to raife the dead. For in the feuenth Chapter of
his fecond booke, he finds, that he had raifed fix : another time, vpon his returne from Iappon, fpying one of
his companions laid out vpon the Bere, and ready to be
put into the ground, he reftored him to life againe, as he

Turf. lib. 4. cap. 3.

had done a Pagans daughter. But the grace of the tale
is, that fhe returning on foot, knew *Xauier*, and told her
father, this was the man, that had puld her foule
backe againe out of hell. And that which was neuer

Turf. lib. 4. cap. 7. & lib. 5. cap. 7.

heard of before in our religiõ, he cõuerted many people
by Mediators and Interpretors. Likewife, he wrought
many miracles by the minifterie of others, namely, by

Turf. lib. 2. ca. 7.

fuch as fcarce had any knowledge of our Church. For
after he had Baptized and Catechized little infants,
he gaue them his beads, wherewith the ficke being touched, they recouered health. Being at Meliopora, there

Turf. lib. 1. ca. 7.

was a rich Citizen poffeffed with many diuels, *Xauier*
was intreated to go to him, but hauing other bufines, he
fent a little child to him with a croffe, which being laid
vpon the poffeffed, and a Gofpel faid ouer him, in fuch
manner as *Xauier* had commaunded, prefently all the diuels were caft out, very much angred, that they were eicc-
ted by fuch a one as was yet but a nouice in Chriftianity.

Lib. 2. ca. 7.

Hoc magis indignantes (faith the author) *quod per puerum*
pellebantur, & eum Neophylum. Another time it fell out
fo, that being requefted to helpe one that was poffeffed, becaufe he could not goe himfelfe in perfon, he put
fome little children in commiffion, teaching them their
leffon what they fhould do, and putting a croffe in their
hands. Thefe came to the poffeffed, whom they made
to kiffe the Croffe, according to their direction, faying
certaine prayers ouer him, which they had learned by
heart, and prefently, as well by the faith of thefe little
brats, as by *Xauiers*, the diuell went out of the man, but

he

he was reuenged on him at the laſt : For when *Xauier* was vpon his knees before the Virgin *Marie*, the diuell ſo ſcracht him by the backe,& belly,that the poore man had none to flie vnto but the Virgin , crying vnto her : *Domina opitulare* , *Domina non opitulaberis ?* And after this, was conſtraind to keepe his bedde vntil his skinne was healed.

I omit a great many particulars, that I may come to other of *Xauiers* miracles , as well in his life as in his death : for departing this life at *Siues,* his bodie was rold vp in quicke lime , that beeing ſpeedily conſumed, it might not putrifie : neuerthelesſe, being ſixe moneths after caried to the Towne of Goa , where he lieth , hee was found to looke as freſh and ſound,as when he liued. **Lib.5.ca.12.** After he was brought to this Towne, there was a waxe Candle of a cubit long, placed at the foote of his Tombe, which burnt two and twentie daies, and as many nights, and was not waſted. A man that neuer ſaw further then the length of his owne noſe , hauing got ſo much fauour of the Prieſts, as to open him *Xa-niers* Tombe, tooke the dead mans hand and rubbed **Lib.5.ca.4.** his eies with it, and preſently recouered his ſight. Many other miracles were done by his dead corps : But I find none ſo famous as theſe two : for one of his Diſciples, hauing ſtollen away the whip wherewith he beat him-ſelfe, and a woman called *Marie Sarra* did cut of a peece of his girdle, which ſhe wrought into ſiluer, and wore it about her necke, theſe two deuout perſons, cu-red an infinite number of all ſorts of diſeaſes, by the bare touch of theſe two reliques.

All theſe miracles were done in the Indies, and ma-ny other moe if you beleeue *Turſellin.* After the appro-bation of their order , *Xauier* was not to be compared in ſanctitie with *Ignace*, his Superiour and firſt foun-der of that ſocietie, being inſpired with the holy Ghoſt, although not in ſo great meaſure as the Apoſtles were,

R 2   (ſaith

(saith the wisedome of *Fon.*) And all visions ceased in him, that day that his order was allowed, and he seated in Rome ; but contrariwise, they budded a fresh in *Xauier*: what causeth this difference ? I will tell you : If *Ignace* had set downe his staffe in the Indies, and *Xauier* abode in Rome, *Ignace* had wrought many miracles, and *Xauier* none, for in these cases, it is a great deale better cheape to beleeue them, then to trauell from place to place, to enquire whether they be true or no.

All these stories, are in verie deed such, as by common prouerbe we call old wiues fables, that is to say, fit to be told to simple women, when they sit spinning by the fire side. One *Iustinian*, a Iesuit in Rome, called Father *Iustinian*, counterfeited himselfe to be leaprous, to make his cure miraculous : Againe, he would haue made men beleeue, that being shot with a Pistoll through his garment, the bullet rebounded backe againe from his body, without hurt, and so by the wonderful grace of God, he was not wounded. These matters were beleeued by the simple people at the first, but after they were found to be false, this marred the whole roast of the Iesuits cookerie in Rome, for when they did speake of a facer out of matters, and an Imposter, they were woont to call him, a second *Iustinian* the Iesuit.

It may be you will iudge it straunge I tell you, we need not looke into Spaine, nor the Indies for their forgeries, sith of late yeeres they bruted it abroad in Fraunce, that *Theodore Beza* was dead, and that at his death, he was conuerted to our Catholique Apostolique Romane Religion, by one of their companie : by whose example, many Citizens of Geneua had done the like, through the trauels of the Iesuits. We tooke it to be true a while, but after that *Beza* was knowen to be risen againe, hee wrote certaine French and Latine Letters, by which he conuinced their impudencie. Wha a

mint

mint of fables will they haue in strange countries, which euen in the midst of vs, feare not to feede vs with such bables?

Last of all. to make the matter plaine, what notable lyers *Maffee* and *Ribadiner* are, (for as I begunne with them, so will I end,) *Ribadiner* shewes vs one *Ignace* in Spaine, who all vppon the suddaine hauing abandoned the world, *cæsariem elegantem habebat, solutam et impexā reliquit, vngues et barbam excrescere siuit.* He had a fayre head of haire, which he layd out loose & vnkempt, flaring in the wind; he neither cut his beard, nor pared his nayles. Looke vpon his picture in the beginning of *Ribadiners* booke, there is nothing so slick as hee, neyther his locks, nor his beard, nor his nailes growne. You may imagin by this, what is in the rest of al theyr bookes. And to say the truth, when I see *Maffee, Ribadiner,* and *Turcelline,* bestow so good Latine vpon such lying matter, it makes me remember our old *Romants,* of *Piers Forrest, Lancelot Dulac, Tristram* of *Lyons,* and other aduenturous Knights of the Round-table, which had all strooke hands in amitie, and sworne reciprocally on to another: in honour of whom, many gallant pennes haue been set a work to make idle tales, in as good French as that time afforded. In like manner haue these three Iesuits written, not a historie, but a *Romant* full of fables, touching the life of *Ignace* & his fellowes, all wandering Knights of the trauailing Robe, linked together in a band of indissoluble societie; it is fit that euery thing should haue his turne.

Rib. lib. 1. capit. 5.

R 3   CHAP.

CHAP. 18.

¶ *Of* Ignace *his Machiauelismes, vsed to set*
his Sect a floate.

Hen the Aduocate had ended his difcourfe, the Gentleman faid to him. You
may iudge what you will of thofe two
that haue written the life of *Ignace,* if you
can perfwade me, that our age neuer afforded a brauer man, nor more fit to
make a new fect then he, I will take no exceptions to *If-*
maell the Perfian Sophie. When I fpeake of a fect, I befeech you my Maifters be not you offended : for I take
the word in his natiue fignification, for fuch a forme of
life and difcipline, as in old time was attributed to the
Philofophers. I fee three men combined by the myfterie of our time, *Martin Luther,* a Germane, *Iohn Caluin,*
a French man, and *Ignace de Loyola,* a Spaniard, all three
great men, I will not fpeake of the doctrine of the two
former, which I condemne ; yet neither was *Luther* nor
Caluin, fo great as *Loyola.*

The firft, made an vproare in all Germanie : the fecond, fo troubled Fraunce, that there was no fafety for
him but in Geneua : & the laft, hath made a pudder, not
onely in Spaine, and the prouinces depending vpon that
Kingdome, but in many other Nations alfo. And that
which is more admirable, the two former, got their credit with their pen, and the laft, by writing nothing. For
as you your felfe haue truly difcourfed, *Ignace* was aboue
thirty yeeres of age before hee learned his Accedence.
Long before this time, he compiled three books in Spanifh, one of them was intituled, *Spirituall exercifes :* another, was of the Trinitie, and the third, was of the life of
Iefus Chrift, the virgin *Marie,* and fome of the Saints :
neuerthelefle, hee did wifely to ftop the breath of thofe
bookes

bookes againe betimes, hee knewe well the weakenes of the stile, and with what broken timber they were built. *Luther* and *Caluin* were brought vp, the one in a Monasterie, the other in Colledges, where they began to push at the chiefe Gouernours of the Church of Rome, and scholler-like spent their time, in contentious wits and writers. *Loyola*, borne of a noble familie, in his youth trained vp in a great Kings court, drew his busines to a head very Gentleman-like. For beeing desirous to continue the newe tyrannie which he had plotted, in sted of writing, which happily might be confuted, he drew all out of heauen, that no body might speake against it.

Doe not you remember, that *Minos* King of Creete, going about to make new lawes to his subiects, perswaded them that he had conferd with *Iupiter*: *Lycurgus* in Sparta, with *Apollo*: *Numa Pompilius* in Rome, with the Nymph *Ægeria*: and *Sertorius*, to purchase the more authoritie with his souldiours, said he was familiar with a Doe, as if one of theyr imaginarie Gods had beene transformed into her. These are the Machiauellismes of which the old world was deliuered before *Machiauell* was borne. And there be a great many *Machiauells* among vs at this day, who neuer read his bookes; I think the same deuises glided through the soule of this great *Ignace*, & I assure my selfe, that hee reckned vp to *Lewes Gonsalua* before he died, (for so *Ribadiner* tell vs) all his visions of God, of the virgine *Marie*, of S. *Peter*, and of our sauiour Iesus Christ, promising him all the helpe he could to further him at Rome; whereby hee grew in hope that in time to come, all the Generals his successors, should become the highest Commaunders.

And that which makes mee wonder more, is a matter I will now acquaint you with. We read, that when *Augustus* had lockt himselfe fast into the saddle of the Romane Empire, yet tenne yeeres after, to auoyd all enuie, he counterfeited before the Senate, that he would giue

vp

vp his gouernment, betake himselfe to a priuate life, and
lay aside all that imperiall maiestie which he had gotten:
hee was much hindred herein, by the humble sute of all
the Senators his slaues; and thus by the consent of all the
chiefe Rulers of the Cittie, he held without feare or ielo-
sie, the extraordinary power hee had got into his hands
ouer that state.

Ignace had the like conceit of his Generalship: for
when he had gouernd tenne yeeres, or there about, with
absolute authoritie, hee called together the greatest part
of the Fathers the Iesuits at Rome, and before the whole
assembly, desired them to dispence with him in the gouernment heereafter, because the charge was too heauie for his shoulders: But they with all meekenesse,
commending his modestie, denied him his request, as a
matter very preiudiciall to theyr Order. And contrariwise, they entreated him to take care of theyr constitutions, to augment, or diminish, or qualifie them as hee
thought good. From that day, he tooke the reines into
his hand, to commaund them in such maner as you see:
but hee would not haue his statuts publisht, before they
were confirmed by a generall meeting. Meane while, he
left a writing in a little coffer, in manner of a Iournall,
how things passed betweene the holy Ghost and him,
and the visions set downe, where-with hee was inspired
when he made his constitutions.

These remembrances were found after his death, and
with great wonderment presented to the generall congregation held at Rome, in the yeere 1 5 5 8. where all
that he had ordred was considered of, and from thence passed through the hands of theyr Printers and Stationers.
You blame Ignace in your discourse, for all his appariti-
ons, & you say they were impostures contriued by him,
vpon which ground his societie hath coyned manie fables. Pardon mee, I pray you, for you iudge of these
matters like a Punie, not like a Statesman. I tell you a-
gaine,

Rib.lib. 4.
capit. 2.

againe, I doubt not but that *Ignace* hath told you all his visions, whereof he himselfe alone was witnesse. But when? Not in the flower of his age, when he was in action; but when sicknes and age had broken him, and he saw himselfe at the graues brinke; perswading himselfe, there could be no better meane to establish his order after his death, and confirme his statutes, then to feede them, not with these holy, but rather fained illuminations, which he opposed without printing of Bookes, against all *Martin Luthers* & *Iohn Caluins* vaine disputes and *Ergoes*. Was there euer playd a brauer, a wiser, and a bolder pranke then this?

CHAP. 19.

¶ The conclusion of the first booke.

He Gentleman had scarce ended his discourse, but the Aduocate answered. You and I will enter the List together to fight it out. For all that *Maffee* and *Ribadiner* haue written of *Ignace*, is false, & all that you haue said is true. That which I haue spokē hetherto, is by way of an introduction to the sport, I am determined to shew you now what theyr vowes be, which I will proue to be stuffed with erronious and hereticall doctrine, and an infinite mingle mangle of Machiauellismes and Anabaptistries, vvhich time hath measht together.

The Aduocate prepared himselfe to goe forward, not remembring that it was high mid-night, then said the Gentleman: If you haue any such purpose, it is best to deferre it vntill to morrow morning, the night is farre spent, and you my Maisters (my new guests) are wearied with your iourney, & you in particular my good friend, (quoth he to the Aduocate) are tired with talking, and we with hearing. I arest you all, you are nowe my prisoners,

S.

prisoners, and thinke not that I will let you go to morrow: let vs take a little truce with our eyes, our tongues, our eares, and our thoughts, me thinks this difcourfe deferues to be profecuted with a fafting wit : it were fit, it fhould not be taken vpon a fudden, but that you fhould paufe vpon this which is already fpoken, if fleep will fuffer you. Neuer yet was good Aduocate, how well foeuer he were prouided for a great caufe, agreeued to haue put it off to another day, that he might be better furnifht : and I think you neuer fpake to a matter of more importance then this.

The Gentlemans aduice was taken, and euerie man retyred him into his chamber, vntill feuen of the clocke in the morning, then euerie one hauing been at Church to render vnto God, not what euerie man is bound, but what euerie man was able to performe: the whole companie met in the Hal. The Gentleman gaue his feruants ftraight commaundement, that none of them fhould be fo hardie as to interrupt them, whatfoeuer bufines fell out . Now let vs go on with our tale (quoth he) for we cannot doe a better deed then this : but vpon this condition, that in our fpeech, we raile vpon no bodie . We may not eafily be drawen to perfecute fo harmeleffe a companie, as many men take the Iefuits to be.

The Aduocate promifed to deale honeftly herein, protefting againe that he would not fpeake for any particular grudge he bare them, but for the common good of all men. And to make it fo appeare to you (quoth he) I leaue all affectation, and flowers of Rhetorique, wherewith men of my profeffion vfe to grace their fpeech. I will read thofe paffages plainely to you, vpon which, all that I intend to doe, is grounded ; and if anie man will put any better ftuffe to it when I haue done, I giue him leaue . For the beft Art I obferue, is to fhew no Art at all. But fith the Iefuits do now fue for a re-eftablifhment of them in

Fraunce, I will begin with that, that toucheth vs neerest. The Aduocate hauing in one of his Portmantewes all the Buls, and constitutions, that concerne the Iesuits, and many other bookes of like argument, as well with them, as against them, he laid them forth vpon a greene Carpet, thus as he had done the night before, so proceeded he now to verifie his speech. Let vs see him play his part vpon the stage.

The end of the first Booke.

S 2.   THE

The second Booke of the Iesuits Catechisme.

CHAP. 1.

❡ That our Church of Fraunce, and the Sect of the Iusuits, cannot stand together.

(∵)

Et vs tread all choller vnder foote, (saith the Aduocate) not as if it were not verie fit to be angry with heresie, yea and to sleep vpon that anger, but becaufe choller fometimes befots vs, & makes vs faile in the duties of our vnderftanding. The Iefuits defire to be fetled againe in Paris, where-into they entred at the firft like Foxes, and afterward, fild themfelues like rauening beafts with the blood of the French : and yet, if their order haue any poffibilitie of agreement vvith our Church of Fraunce, let vs forget all the miferies and calamities, that haue been brought vpon vs by their means in our laft troubles ; and let vs not enuie thē their aboade in the principall Cittie of Fraunce. It is no fmall aduantage for them, that would plant and fpread a new religion, to be placed in the chiefe Cittie of a kingdome, by the authority of the foueraigne Magiftrate.

They caft in our way two great words, to ftoppe our mouth altogether ; the name of Iefus, to which euerie knee muft bow, and the name of the Pope, which wee muft receiue with all fubmiffion and honour. But to whom doe they fell theyr trafh ? Are wee any other but followers of Iefus ? Are we any other then the children of the holy Sea ?

1. All of vs acknowledge, by a common and generall faith, that we are a part & portion of the church of Iesus, by the merit of his passion, euer since that we haue been regenerat by the holy sacrament of Baptisme.

Conference at Poissy, 1561. Act of parliamēt in the same yeere. They, by an arrogant name applyed, entitle themselues and their sect, the societie of Iesus : a title forbidden them, both by our Church of Fraunce, and by the Court of Parliament at Paris, in the yeere 1561.

2. Wee in this country of Fraunce, auow with all humilitie and readines, our holy Father the Pope, as Primate, but not as prince of all Churches. In this fayth we liue and die vnder him, renewing the oath of allegiance, from the day of our baptisme, to the day of our death.

Part 7. of their const. c. 1. arti. 2. The Iesuit, as a vassaile peculiar aboue others, acknowledges him for his prince, to whom hee specially renewes the oath of his allegeance, at the change of euerie Pope.

3. Our church of Fraunce holds, that our holy father the Pope, is vnder a generall & oeconomicall counsell : so we haue learned of our great diuine *Gerson* : so of the councell of Constance : and so, when in former times any decree came out from his holines, to the preiudice of our Kings, or their realme, our aunceftors appeald from it, to a generall Councell to be held afterward.

Cap. Noui de iudic. ext. cap. ad Apostolicæ de re iudic. capit. vnam sanctam de maior. et obed. The Iesuit maintaines a cleane contrarie opinion, & that in the same sort as the courtiers of Rome doe.

4 With what dissimulation soeuer the Iesuit cloakes his writings now a dayes, hee acknowledgeth the Pope prince of all kingdoms, as well in matters temporall as spirituall, becaufe the Popes haue acknowledgd themselues for such, in their decretall sentences, and namely, of late, in their Bull of the great Iubile, publisht for the yeere 1600. S. *Peter* and S. *Paule*, whose successors they are called, princes of the earth : if the Iesuite doubt of this article, he is an hereticke in his sect.

Our church of Fraunce, neuer belieued that the Pope had

had any power, ouer the temporal estate of our Kings.

5 The Iesuit obayes the Pope, by an obedience which he calls blindfold : a proposition of a hard consequence for the King, and all his subiects. Looke the chap. of this book, where wee entreat of blindfold obedience.

A proposition also which we obserue not, but stoutly improue in our Church of Fraunce.

6 By an auncient tradition, which wee hold as it were frō hand to hand frō the Apostles, euery Dioces hath his Bishop, ouer whō it is not lawful to vsurp any authority.

The whole sect of the Iesuits, is nothing els but a generall infringing of the authoritie of Archb. and Bish : yea they hold, that the Bishop hath no other iurisdiction or power, then that which he holds of the Pope. Bellam. lib. 1. de indulg, cap. 11.

7 The administring of the word of God, and of the Sacra. appertaines principally to the Archb. & Bishop : after, to the Curats within their parishes, & to none other, except a man haue permission of some of them within their charges.

The Iesuit giues to himselfe, full power to preach the word of God, and to administer the holy sacrament of Pennance and the Eucharist, wheresoeuer it please him, to the preiudice of the Ordinaries. By the Buls of 1540. & 1550.

8 Only the B. in his dioces, can dispence with the vse of meats forbidden, according as necessitie requires.

The Iesuit acknowledges herein, none but the Superiors of his order. The Buls of Iulius the 3. 1552.

9 We admit not to the order of priest-hood, any that are borne in adultery or incest.

The Iesuit admits them without difference. The Buls of Paule the 3. 1546.

10 By our ancient canonicall constitutions, Churchmen may not say Masse but before noone.

The Iesuit may sing Masse after none. if it please him. The Buls of Paule the 3. 1545.

11 Our priests are forbidden to say Masse any where but in our Churches, except for the succouring of them that are sick, and that by the permission of the Curat.

The Iesuit may make a particular oratory within his
house,

houfe, and in all places where foeuer he comes : & there fay Maffe, and haue an Altar to carry about with him.

Tert. lib. 2. ad vxorem. Sid. Apul. lib. 5. epift.

12 One of the auncienteft parts of deuotion, that we haue in our Church, are the Proceffions, for euen *Tertullian* makes mention of them : and we find, that *Mamercus* Bifhop of Vienna , brought in the Rogation, which wee obferue euery yeere, in the weeke of the Afcention of our Lord Iefus Chrift.

The Buls of Greg. 13. 1576.

The Iefuit, doth not onely difalow of them, but maintaines that they are forbidden him.

13 We celebrate Anniuerfaries in our Church, in the remembrance of them, that lately beftowed any goods on vs by way of almes,

Part 6. of their conft. ca. 3. art. 6.

The Iefuit receiues a pace what foeuer almes are giuen him to this end ; but yet he admits not of the Anniuerfaries, nor the Obits.

14 We haue in our Church , a certaine place neer the Altar, which we call the Quire, where our priefts fay diuine feruice, apart from the common people.

Part 6. côft. ca. 3. art. 4. Rib. lib. 3. cap. 22. The bull of Gre. the 13 30. of Octo. 1576.

The Iefuit hath no fuch place.

15 We fay our canonicall houres aloude in our churches, of ordinary, that euery man may pertake thereof.

The Iefuit is not bound, but that he may fay them in a low voyce.

16 As our country of Fraunce hath alwaies abounded in deuotion aboue all other Nations ; fo it hath had fpeciall priuiledge of God, that all the heads of religious orders, that haue been graffed vpõ the ancient orders of S. *Auftin* & S. *Benet*, haue vowed theyr perpetuall houfes amongft vs French men : as the orders of Clugnie, the Ciftercians, the Premonftratenfes, and Gramont.

The Plea of the Kings Aduocate of Mefnil.

There is neuer an order but that of the Charter-houfe Monks, whofe General hath not taken his habit in Dauphine. And if there be any that make not their abode there, at the leaft they come often times to vifit their fheep in this our countrey of Fraunce. Befides that, the

Generals

Generals of the Iesuits haue vowed their abode within Rome, neuer any of them is seene to come into Fraunce to visit theirs : so little of any French nature haue they in them.

1 7 We receiue no Prouincials in France, of what religious order soeuer they be, vnlesse they be Frenchmen.

The Generall of the Iesuits sends vs such, as it pleases him : A Marchandize that cost vs deere in our last troubles.

1 8 We in our Church of Fraunce, allow of no religious persons, which vow themselues to the saying of Diuine seruice in the Church, but such as weare their habits and other monasticall weeds, assigned to them by reuerend antiquitie.

There is no difference betwixt the habit of a Secular Priest, and a Priest Iesuit.

1 9 We haue alwaies confin'd our religious men within the cloisters; as well, that there they might lead a solitary life, as also, that they might serue them for walkes, and refreshings, after their studies.

The Iesuit should haue wrongd his greatnes, if he had conform'd himselfe to the fashions of other orders.

2 0 After that our religious men haue made the three ordinarie and substantiall vowes, of Pouertie, Chastitie, and Obedience, they may not returne to the world, to follow againe their former course of life, no not with the consent of their Abbots.

The Iesuits, hauing added to the simple vow of Ie-　Greg. 13. suitisme, after the two yeeres of their Nouiceship, the Bull. 1584, three vowes common to all religious orders; may notwithstanding, be turnd ouer to the world againe by their Generall, whensoeuer it pleaseth him.

2 1 Our religious persons, after they haue made those three vowes, are vncapable of all kinds of succession.

Greg. 13.

The Iesuit as long he continues in his simple vow,　Bull. 1584.

T.　may

may enioy any of them, as if he had not at all giuen ouer the world.

22 No man enters into other orders of religion, but with an intent to studie, that he may in time be preferred to the order of Priesthood.

The Iesuit receiueth men into his order, vnder the name of temporal coadiutors, which make profession of ignorance, and are neuer admitted into holy orders.

23 All other religous persons, haue certain daies, wherin they keep extraordinary fasts, & abstaine from meat, which daies are not cōmon for fasting to the rest of the people. The Iesuits, though from their verie entrance they take the name of religious persons, yet at no hand obserue any such day.

Rib. lib. 3. ca. 22.

24 The auncient ordinances of our Kings, *Charles*, 5. 6. 7. admit no principals of Colledges that are straungers, and borne without the Realme, vnlesse at the least they be made denezens.

The General of the Iesuits establisheth in the Colledges of his order such Rectors and Principals, as pleaseth him, without respect whether they be French, or no.

25 In our religious orders, the religious are not suffered to read Lectures of humane learning, to any but those of their owne order.

The Iesuit reads to all goers and commers.

The Bull of Pius 4. 1561

26 The degree of Maisters of Arts, is not giuen with vs to any religious person, but onely the Doctership of diuinitie, if they be fit for it.

The Iesuit takes the degree of Maisters of Arts, as well as of Doctor of Diuinitie.

Bull of Pius 2. 1552. and Pius 4. 1571. Pius 4. Bull 1556. Greg. 13. Bull in May. 1578.

27 The order, that we obserue in our Vniuersities, is, that the Bishop is the chiefe Iudge: and for this cause, in euerie Cathedrall Church, where there is an Vniuersity, there is also a Chauncellor of the Vniuersitie, to whom there is a Prebend annexed, which giues the degrees of Bachilers, Licentiats, Maisters, and Doctors, after

the

the disputations and publike trials made, in the places of old hereuuto appointed.

The Iesuit is ignorant of this forme: he must haue a stable by himselfe. At the first, the Generall made Maisters and Doctors of his absolute power: afterward, these degrees were take by the authority of the Prouincial, vpō examination by 2. or 3. deputed by him to that purpose.

28 Yea more then that, in this our country of France, no man may receiue the degree of Maister or Doctor, but in famous Vniuersities. The Iesuit, turning topsie turuy all our ancient discipline, may make Ma. of Arts, and Doctors of Diuinity, wheresoeuer they haue Colledges, though they be not in any Vniuersitie. Pius 4. 1561.

29 In al alienations of the Church goods, which depēd vpon Bishopricks or Abbies, the communalty must assemble theselues togither with the cōsent of their heads, to contract, & afterward, the authority of the superiour must concurre; who must depute a Promoter as he that is proctor for the good of the Church: al which is done, to discusse & examine, whether it be fit that such alienation be made. To the alienation of the goods of the Iesuits, there is nothing required, but the will and absolute power of the Generall, without any other ceremonie. Pius 5. 1568 Cōst.par.9. cap.3.art.5.

30 Our kings receiue a subsidie of beneuolence, from the churches of their Realme, which we cal Tenths.

If you will giue credit to the Iesuits priuiledges, they are exempted from it. In their first confer. Generall.1558. Greg.13.18. Decemb.

31 Our kings may not be excommunicated by the Popes, as we will proue in his place.

This rule is charged to be vntrue by the Iesuits. 1 5 7 6. Pius 4.1561. 19.Art.

32 It is not in the Popes power to translate our Realm to whom it pleases him, for default of obedience to him, as I hope also I shall proue. The Iesuit maintains formally, that the Pope according to the occasiōs of matters, may transfer, not onely kingdomes, but the Empire also. And to the end I may file on a row other propositions, Monta. in his booke of the truth defended. cap.15. Bellar.de transl.imp. Montaign. Chap.15.

wherein

wherein they contradict vs.

Bellar.de
exem. Cler.
cap.1.
Propo.3.
Propo.4.
Propo.5.

33 Cleargie men may not be iudged by a Secular Iudge, although they kept not ciuill lawes.

34 A Cleargie mans goods, both ecclesiasticall, and temporall, are free from tributs to secular Princes.

35 The exemption of Cleargie men in matters politicke, as well for their persons, as their goods, was brought in both by humane and diuine law.

That which I will certifie to you in my speech following, is, the doctrine of *Emanuel*, a Doctor of Diuiniy, a Iesuit of Antwerp, in his Aphorismes of confession; wherein, as he declares in his Epistle by way of preface, he laboured 40. whole yeeres : and sets downe his vndoubted propositions of confession, by order of Alphabet.

36 A Cleargie mans family, is of the same Court with himselfe.

37 A Cleargie mans goods, may be confiscated by an ecclesiasticall Iudge, in such cases as a Lay-man may be so punisht by the law.

38 A Cleargie man may not be punisht by a Secular Iudge, for a false testimonie giuen before him.

39 A Clergie man being smitten by on of the Laitie, may sue him before an ecclesiasticall Iudge.

40 A Cleargie man may vse the custome and statute of Lay-men for his owne profit. His meaning is, that the custome binds him not, vnlesse it please himselfe.

41 A Bishop may constraine men vpon paine of excommunication, to bring in the Testaments of the dead, and see they be executed.

42 A Bishop may charge a benefice, which hee bestowes, with a yeerely pension for the maintaining of a poore scholler, or Clarke.

43. A woman is not vsually to haue succession in Fee.

44. A Cleargie man dying intestate, and hauing no
kinred,

kinred, the Church which he serued, must be his heire : but now perhaps, the chamber of the Apostolique Sea inherits.

45. A prisoner going to execution, is not bound to confesse that, which before he vntruly denied, vnlesse otherwise some great harme may ensue.

46. A prisoner is not to be compelled by his confessor to confesse his fault.

All which Propositions, directly derogate from those, which we obserue by the common law of Fraunce. And yet, that which is more mischieuous & intolerable, is that which he hath in two other Articles written in this sort.

47 The rebellion of a Cleargy man against his Prince, is not high treason, because he is not subiect to the Prince.

48 If a Priest in confession, haue intelligence of some great daunger intended to the state, it is sufficient to giue a generall warning to take heed. He also against whom euill is intended, may be warned to take heed to himselfe, at such a place and time, so that the penitent be not in daunger to be discouered thereby.

Good God : Can we abide this order in our countrey of Fraunce ? I know, that although (God be thanked) our kings were neuer tyrants, yet the Iesuits propound two Maximes, which if they should take place, euerie soueraigne Prince, must stand to the mercie of his people.

49 A King may by deposed by the State for tyranny, and if he do not his dutie, when there is iust cause, an other may be chosen by the greater part of hepeople. Yet some thinke, that tyrannie onely is the cause for which he may be deposed.

50 He that gouerns tyranously, may be deposd by the peoples sentence, yea though they haue sworne perpetuall obedience to him, if being warned, he will not amend.

If

If thefe two Articles take place,there is no Prince,be
he what he will, that can be affured in his eftate. And I
pray you fuppofe,that this confeffionary was printed
in the yeere 1589. that is to fay, to confirme & authorize,that which was purpofed againft the King deceafed,in the beginning of the yeere, when certaine ill
difpofed perfons would haue declared him to be a tyrant.

51. We haue in this countrey of Fraunce, an appeale,
as it were a writ of Errour,of the thundring of the Apoftolike Buls; when they are found to enterprize anie
thing,eyther againft the maieftie of our Kings,or againft
the auncient Councels, receiued and approued in our
Church of Fraunce,or againft the liberties thereof,or a-
gainft the authoritie Royall, or Acts of the high Courts.
This appeale as from the abufe, I tell you,is one of the
principall finewes of the maintenance of our eftate.

The Iefuit will not acknowledge it, for many caufes,
which touch him neere, which I will not here difcouer.

52 The Iefuits acknowledge none for their Iudge,
but the Pope,or their General,defiring by this means,to
fend vs backe againe to that old labyrinth of Rome,
wherof our good Saint *Bernard*, complaind to Pope
Eugenius in his bookes of confolation. And thereof we
faw a notable example in Burdeaux, when *Lager*, Rector of the Colledge of the Iefuits,declared that he would
not obey the Maire and Iurats, who had fent for him
for the preuenting of a certaine fedition : faying,that he
acknowledged them for ciuil Magiftrates ouer the Bur-
geffes of the Citie, but that neither they, nor any other
Iudges, of what nation,qualitie, dignitie, and authority
foeuer, had any power ouer their focietie,but onely our
holy Father the Pope, or the Generall of their order.
And fhall we then fuffer this family to liue in the midft
of vs ? That were indeed to receiue in a vermine,which

at

at length will gnaw out the heart of our estate, both spirituall and temporall.

Then said the Iesuit to the Aduocate, I will not be long in aunswering your curious collections. For against all that you haue said, I oppose in one word, the generall counsell of Trent, by which we are approued and authorized.

Sess.25.ca. 16.de regular.

5 3 Whereto the Aduocate aunswered, I grant that you haue thirtie on your part, but we haue 4 5. aboue you. This Councell concerning the doctrine, is an abridgement of all the other auncient Councels, therfore it is in that regard, to be embrast by all deuout soules: but wholy to be reiected concerning discipline, as well Secular as Ecclesiasticall; as that Councell, by which our whole Realme of Fraunce would be set on fire, if it should be receiued. And they that can sent well, smell that all which was then decreed, came from the Iesuitish foules: I meane, as concerning matter of gouernment. If there were no other respect but this, ye were to be banisht out of Fraunce: because we cannot allow of you, without allowing of this Councell: and the approuing of it, were to make a great breach, both into the Maiestie of our Kings, and into the liberties of our Church of Fraunce.

CHAP. 2.

That the Popes authorizing the Iesuit, at his first comming, neuer had any perswasion, that eyther he could, or ought to inhabit in Fraunce.

Hen the Aduocate had made an end of this discourse, the Iesuit, thinking he had some great aduantage against him, began to speak thus to him. Let vs lay aside the counsell of Trent, though it be a strong fort for the confirming of our order. At

the

the leaſt, you cannot deny, that we are aſſiſted with an infinite number of the Buls of diuers Popes, *Paulus* and
Iulius the third, *Pius* the fourth and fifth, and *Gregorie*
the thriteenth : by all which, they do not onely approue
vs, but gratifie vs with many great priuiledges, ſuch as
neuer were granted to any other order of religion, as you
might vnderſtand by me yeſterday. Whereupon it followes, that you and all other, that ſet themſelues to fight
againſt vs, ought to be held for heretiques.

   Aduoc. A great obiection forſooth : for you could
not poſſibly fight againſt me with any better weapons :
& I am right glad, that my whole diſcourſe, begins, continues, & ends, according to the authority of the holy ſea.
    Abs Ioue principium, Iouis omnia plena.

The holy Sea hath approued of you, (ſay you) I grant
it, only to pleaſure you. Therefore they that allow not
of your ſocietie, are heretiques : I denie that. The Colledge of Diuines, and the Vniuerſitie of Paris, our whole
Church of Fraunce, ſo many ſocieties, ſo many of worth
and honour, made themſelues parties againſt you, in the
yeere 6 4. and diſalowed of you : yet for all that, ye neuer
heard, that they were declard at Rome to be heretiques.
Inſomuch, that the Popes which authoriſed you, neuer
thought that you were to inhabit in France. They knew
that their dignitie, is the mother of vnitie in the Vniuerſall Church. They were not ignorant of the liberties of our Church of Fraunce, wholy contrarie to the
profeſſion of the Ieſuits : and that to ſettle them in
Fraunce, had beene to plant a huge ſort of ſchiſmes and
diuiſions. Whereby you may perceiue the reaſon, why
they repeald not the iudgements that had paſt againſt
theſe goodly Maiſters, as well in the conuocation of our
whole Cleargie at Poiſie, as in the Parliament at Paris.
Following herein, by a good inſpiration of God and his
holy Spirit, the ſteps of *Paulus* the third, to whom
when the Ieſuits preſented themſelues at the firſt, fai-
                       ning

ning that they would goe into Palestine, and there settle theyr aboade for the couerting of the Turkes, they were not onely fauourably entertaind by him, but, which is more, he caused money to be deliuerd to them for the defraying of the charge of theyr voyage. But when they returnd the second time, to haue a confirmation of their new determination, Pope *Paule* was two whole yeeres before hee could yeelde to it. And why so? Because in theyr first proiect, there was no danger to Christendome, but onely to themselues, that were the vndertakers of this matter. In the second, there was assurance for their persons, but great hazard & danger to all Christendome. And after many denialls & refusals, although he suffered himselfe to be carried away by Cardinall Cōtarens importunitie, yet he was of opinion, that not onely they were not to take vp theyr dwelling in Fraunce, but not to continue in any other part of Christendome, but verie sparingly.

Howe then? Shall wee thinke that this great Pope, would leaue desolate this new Order approued by him? No truly. And if you will examine this storie aright, you will rest satisfied. If in the yeere 1 5 3 9. the Iesuits had made promise of no more, but the 3. substantiall vowes of other religious orders, he would neuer haue admitted them in such a fashion as they presented themselues: Munks, who by a title appropriated to themselues, were termed of the societie of Iesus, wearing no religious habite at all. Munks, that would not tie themselues to their Cloysters, there to leade a solitarie life, nor reduce themselues to the extraordinarie abstinence from meates, and to the fasts of other religious orders. Munks, that would preach and administer the holy Sacraments, without the permission of the Bishop. For all these circumstances layd together, promise (I cannot tell what) great dissolution, rather then edification.

What then prouokt him to receiue them? First, their

V.   vow

Maff. lib.2. capit.3. Ribad. lib.2. capit.7.

vow of abſolute obedience to the holy Sea : afterward, that of their Miſſion : by which *Ignace* and his compa-nions promiſed, that when ſoeuer they ſhould be com-maunded by the Popes, they would goe into all heathen Countries, to diſpeople them (as it were) of Idolatry, & to plant Chriſtianitie in them. They were a company of Argonautes, which promiſed to embarque themſelues, not to goe conquer the golden Fleece, like *Iaſon*, but to tranſport abroade, the fleece of the Paſchall Lambe, vn-der the enſigne of Ieſus.

A goodly profeſſion doubtleſſe, in fauour whereof, Pope *Paulus* ſuffred theſe newe pilgrims, which tooke the croſſe for the glorifying of the Name of Ieſus, to terme themſelues the ſocietie of Ieſus, to weare the ha-bits of Prieſts, not of Munks, not to ſhut themſelues vp in Cloyſters, to miniſter the word of God, and the holy ſacramẽts, one with another : for as much as they vowed themſelues to the conqueſt of thoſe Countries, wherein there were no Biſhops nor Curats : a conqueſt to be made, not with materiall armes, but only with ſpirituall. Send them to the new found Lands, according as they promiſd to goe, neuer was there order in greater requeſt then this, prouided, that they acquit themſelues of their promiſe, not by word, but effect. Tranſplant them into the midſt of the Chriſtian Churches, & eſpecially of this our Church of Fraunce, in ſted of order, you ſhall make diſorder, of as dangerous a conſequence, as the ſect of the Lutherans.

And that no man may thinke I make fantaſticall and idle diſcourſes, in the Bull of the yere 1540, repeated all at large in that of 1550, they promiſe to goe, without ſhifting or delay, whether ſoeuer the Pope will ſend thẽ, for the ſauing of ſoules, and aduauncing our fayth, whe-ther to the Turks, or to other miſcreants, euen to thoſe parts, which they call the Indies; or to any heretikes or ſchiſmatiks, or to any belieuers.

If

If the meaning were, to make new feminaries of them through all Chriftendome, it were a ridiculous thing, to fet the coûtries of belieuing Chriftians, in the laft place : befides, it feemes, that thefe words [or to any beleeuers] are added but by the way, and as it were for a fafhion. But thefe great promifers and trauailers, forgetting what theyr firft inftitution was, haue fet vp onely fome doo-zen Colledges, fuch as they be, in Countries vnknowne to vs, (at the leaft if we muft belieue them) & haue erec-ted an infinite fort in the midft of vs, to plant thereby a newe Popedome, and to trample vnder foote the old, vnder which, the Church militant hath triumphed.

Wee are not out of the Church of S. *Peter*, becaufe we condemne thefe new Friers in Fraunce, but we con-forme our felues without Sophiftrie, to the originall and primitiue wills of the Popes, *Paulus* and *Iulius* the third; and though their wills had been otherwife, yet our Ch. of Fraunce, hath time out of minde, beene accuftomed, moft humbly to make the cafe knowne to the Popes, when they were to be carried away by the vniuft impor-tunitie of particuler men, to the preiudice of the church. So did S. *Martine*, Bifhop of Tours, an Apoftle gar-dian of our Country of Fraunce : fo did our good Saint *Lewes* : and yet they were iudgd to be hereticks there-fore, no more then Saint *Paule*, when hee withftood S. *Peter*, who in that cafe yeelded vnto him.

V 2.   CHAP.

CHAP. 3.

❡ That it is against the first institution of the Iesuits, for them to teach all sorts of Schollers, humaine learning, Philosophy, and Diuinitie : and by what proceedings & deuises they haue seazed vppon this new tyrannie, to the preiudice of the auncient discipline of the Vniuersities.

E may not thinke Gentlemen, that *Ignace* and his companions, when they presented themselues to Pope *Paulus*, made offer to teach the youth, in such sort, as the Iesuits since that time haue done. I haue shewed you what his suf-ficiencie was in all parts of good learning. It was he that set the first plant of theyr societie, and knowing his own small forces, hee promist onely to teach little children theyr Creede, as our Curats doe, or their Vicars in pettie Schooles : which I wil proue to be true by the course of this storie.

When they came first to Rome, to receiue the Popes blessing against their pretended voyage into the holie Land, *Maffee* saith, that during their aboade, according to the auncient custome of the Church, they endeuourd to catechize the common people and the children from streete to streete. And afterward, when they were assembled to draw theyr articles for their future societie : *Ac simul concepta verborum formula sese obstringerent, puerili ætati per Catachesim instituendæ.* The same thing is repeated by *Ribadiner*, who saith, that this article was then agreed on by them, *Pueros rudimenta fidei doceant.*

Let vs come nowe to theyr Bulls, and first to that of 1540. by which, the wise *Paulus* 3. fearing all the affaires of these new Associats, after much importunitie, signed their Bill, but with this charge, that they should

Maff. lib. 2. capit. 9.

Ribad. lib. 2. cap. 13.

not

not be aboue three-score. See what the beginning and promise of this supplication was, *Quicunque in societate, quam Iesu nomine insigniri cupimus, vult sub crucis vexillo, deo militare, et soli Domino, ac Ecclesiæ ipsius sponsæ, sub Ro. Pontifice, Christi in terris vicario, seruire, post solemne castitatis, paupertatis, et obedientiæ votum, proponat sibi in animo, se partem esse societatis, ad hoc potissimum institutæ, vt ad fidei defensionem, & propagationem, et profectum animarum in vita & doctrina Christiana, per publicas prædicaciones, & verbi dei ministerium, spiritualia exercitia, & cantus opera, & nominatim per pueroru, & rudiu in Christianismo institutione.* And because this latter clause might receiue some doubtfull construction, it is in a fewe wordes expounded, a little after in the same Bull. *Et nominatim commendatam habeant institutionem puerorum et rudium in doctrina Christiana, decem præceptorum, et aliorum similiter rudementorum.* Thys is cleere, & yet they might haue Colledges, not euery where, but in approoued Vniuersities; and not to receiue for schollers, all commers and goers, but onely them that are of their Seminarie.

Possint (saith the same Bull) *in Vniuersitatibus habere Collegium, seu Collegia habentia reditus, censús, seu possessiones, vsibus & necessitatibus studentium applicandas, retenta penes Præponu & societatem omnimoda gubernacione, seu superintendentia super dicta collegia.* Sith the goods of the Colledges, were appointed for them that should be students therein, it cannot be vnderstood of strangers, but onely of them, that vow to be of their order: whom since, they haue called schollers approoued. As for others, they were onely to teach little children their creed, as we see the Maisters of our Presbyteries doe. That appeares by this word (*Puer*) which signifies an age, somwhat, but not much, exceeding the whom the Romans calld Infants. And indeed, whe we would noate an old man, who by the feeblenes of his yeeres becomes a child againe, we say that he doth *Repuerascere.* An infant is he

that

that can neither goe nor speake. *Puer*, is an infant that begins to goe and speake, and so is he exprest by *Horace*, in his booke of the Art of Poetry.

> *Reddere qui voces iam scit puer, & pede certo*
> *signat humum.*

In the yeere 1543. it was permitted the Iesuits to receiue, without any limitation of number, all them that would be of theyr order. And as Pope *Paulus* opened the doore to them on this side, so did hee shut it on another. For in the Bull of 43. there is rehearsal made, word by word, of the priuiledges that were graunted them by the first, of 1540. but cōcerning the instructing of children in their Creed, there is no mention at all, which I beseech you to consider. In the yeeres 45. and 46. theyr priuiledges were greatly encreast, and singulerly in the yeere 49, yet there is no speech in any of them, of teaching children, although in these latter, there is expresse mention made againe, of Colledges ordayned for them of theyr Order.

If you desire to know the reason, and whence this diuersitie proceedes, I will tell you. When by theyr first creation, there might be but three-score of theyr society, Pope *Paulus* made no great dainties to open the pettie Schooles for them, to teach little children theyr Creed: but whē he set open a wide gate for all men that would, to be of their societie, then his meaning was, they should be framed after the fashion of other religious orders and Monasteries, which may teach no other youth, but such as are of their seuerall Orders.

In this estate they liued till the yeere 49. in which Pope *Paulus* died, whom *Iulius* the third succeeded. They had to do in the beginning with a Pope, who, albeit being ouercom by the importunities of a great many, he yeelded in the end, yet still kept them vnder. But vpon the suddaine, after his dicease, they learned *Lisander* the Lacedemonians lesson, who saide, that a good

Cap-

Captaine muſt be clad in the skinne of a Foxe and of a Lion : a leſſon afterward recommended by *Machiauell* in his inſtitution of a Prince. Looke not in the courſe of this ſtorie following, for any thing in your Ieſuits, but Foxe-like, and Lyon-like : and ſo doing you ſhall finde that they haue proued braue ſchollers of *Machiauell.* *Ignace* a verie wiſe worldling, vnderſtanding that there were many nouelties brought into the ſocietie, which he had deuiſed, contrary to the auncient order and diſcipline of our Church : ſo that a man could verie hardly like of them, conceiued that it was needfull for him to haue a new confirmation by *Iulius* ; marry he would get ſome new priuiledge by the bargain. I told you, that by the firſt Bul of *Paulus*, the Ieſuits were permitted to teach little children the firſt enterance into their Creed, to preach and to haue Colledges founded to bring vp, and inſtruct their youth, the nurſerie of their Societie, and none other, & that afterward, in al the other Buls following, although all their priuiledges were confirmed, yet there was no mention of this ordinaunce for inſtruction.

They preſented their ſupplication to *Iulius*, declaring at large their former, of the yeere 1 5 4 0. and with a tricke of foxerie foiſted in this word *Lectiones*, which was not mentioned in the former Bull, and then they ſet downe all that, which had paſt in the other Buls : and for their Colledges, they bring in a new paſſe-right. But it is beſt to read the places themſelues. *Iguace* by this new ſupplication, takes vp againe his *Quicunque in ſocietate noſtra &c. Proponat ſibi in animo ſe partem eſſe ſocietatis ad hoc potiſſimum inſtitutæ, vt ad fidei defenſionē & profectum animarū, in vita & doctrina, Chriſtiana per publicas prædictiones Lectiones, & aliud Dei quodcunq́; miniſteriū ac ſpiritualia exercitia Puerorū, ac rudiū in Chriſtianiſmo inſtitutionē.* Behold the firſt ſurpriſe, which lies in two points, the one in this word *Lectiones,* newly put in, after the word, *Prædicationes* ;

Prædicationes; the other, in the Catechizing of young children, which hath beene taken from them euer since the yeere 1543. And yet, all this is not inough for the establishing of their Colledges, & their ordinary teaching of the youth, in such sort, as they afterward encrocht vpon these things. By these Buls, they were permitted to read now and then publikely in Diuinitie, as we see their fellow *Maldonatus* did, twise vpon festinall daies : first in expounding the Canon of the Masse, afterward, vpon the Psalme, *Dixit Dominus Domino meo.* Otherwise, that last restaint to the teaching of little children, had beene in vaine, if the word *Lectiones*, might reach to the publike exercise of all sorts of learning, such as is in other Colledges.

And in these publike Lectures of Diuinitie, that were to be read, as Sermons and Instructions for the adunacing of our faith, there was no innouation at all against our auncient discipline. For although religious persons might not teach any, but them of their owne order, humane learning and Philosophie, yet they were not forbidden to read publiquely in Diuinitie : and so our Fathers, saw one *Cenomani* a Iacobin, and one *De Cornibus* a Franciscan, and we of late yeres, *Panigarole*, read publique Lectures of Diuinitie in Paris.

All the alteration that I gather, out of this Bull 1550, is, that whereas by that of 1540. they were forbidden to haue Colledges any where, but in approued Vniuersities, in this of *Iulius* the third, they are permitted to haue them in all other places. Let vs read the text of the Bull, *Quia tamen domus, quas Dominus dederit ad operandum in vinea ipsius, & non ad scholastica studia, destinandæ erunt, cùm valdè opportunum fore alioqui videatur vt ex iuuenibus ad pietatem propensis, & ad litterarum studia tractanda, idoneis, operarij eidem vineæ Domini parentur, qui Societatis nostræ, etiam professæ, velut quoddam Seminarium existant, possit professa Societas, ad studiorum ccmmoditatem, Scholarium*

larium habere Collegia, vbicumque ad ea construenda & do-
tanda, aliqui ex deuotione mouebuntur. Quæ simulac con-
structa & dotata fuerint (non tamen ex bonis quorum colla-
tio ad sedem Apostolicã pertinet) ex nunc authoritate Apo-
stolica erigi supplicamus, ac pro erectis haberi. Quæ Collegia
habere possint reditus, census, seu possessiones, vsibus & necessi-
tatibus studentiũ applicandas, retenta penes Præpositũ, vel So-
cietatem omnimoda gubernatione, seu superintendentia super
dicta Collegia, & prædictos studentes, quoad Rectorũ seu Gu-
bernatorũ ac studentium electionem, et eorundem admissionẽ,
emissionem, receptionem, exclusionem, statutorum ordinatio-
nem, & circa studentiũ instructionem, eruditionem, ædificati-
onem, ac correctionẽ victus, vestitusq̃, & aliarum rerum ne-
cessariarũ eis ministrandarum modum, atque aliam omnimo-
do gubernationem, regimen ac curam, vt neq̃ studentes dictis
bonis abuti, neque societas professa in proprios vsus cõuertere
possit, sed studentium necessitati subuenire.

This was the supplication which they presented, and
Iulius signed, wherein you may find some obscuritie in
these words [Societie profest] and in other, which I will
cypher vnto you when opportunitie shall serue. Let it
suffise, that in this passage, there is no other noueltie, but
that wheras by their first Bull, they might haue no Colledges, but in approoued Vniuersities, by this, they are
permitted to haue them in all places, wheresoeuer anie
man will found any Churches of theyr Societie, which
they in their language, call Houses. These words, Churches and Monasteries, offended their daintie eares. And
moreouer you see, that the Colledges which are spoken
of, annexed to their Houses, are not ordaind but for the
schollers of their Order. And in this new alteration, yet
this was not to alter any thing in the auncient gouernment of the Vniuersities. For all other orders of religion
in theyr Monasteries, scattered heere and there in theyr
Prouinces, teach their Nouices, & afterward send them
to the Vniuersities, there to perfect their studies, and to

X. take

take degrees in Diuinitie, if they be found fit for it. And thence it comes, that there is not a Monasterie of anie noate, that hath not a house in that great and famous Vniuersitie of Paris, to lodge the religious of their Order, which are to proceed in Diuinitie.

See heere the beginning of the ruine and generall change of the auncient estate of our Vniuersities. Wee knew not what it meant, to make religious persons Maisters of Arts, and much lesse, to make them take theyr degrees in Diuinitie, other where then in Vniuersities, whether all sorts of publique trialls for learning are brought. *Iulius* the third ouerthrew this wise custome, in fauour of the Iesuits. For hee ordaind that a Iesuit, wheresoeuer hee haue beene student, in Vniuersitie, or otherwise, should take gratis all degrees, of Bachiler, maister, Licentiat, Practitioner, and Doctor, in any facultie whatsoeuer; and that if any man would exact of him, that which by an honest & laudable custome hath been receiued of antiquitie, notwithstanding, hee should goe out Maister or Doctor, vpon the onely credit & authoritie of his Generall, and should enioy from thence forward, all the priuiledges, freedoms, and liberties that others doe.

This Pope was of a very fantasticall iudgement. You know the storie of his great Ape, that would not be ruld by any body, but a little begger boy, of which hee, beeing then Cardinall *de Monte*, tooke such a liking, that afterward beeing made Pope, hee gaue ouer to him all his Benefices, and made him a new Cardinall: whereupon, the vertuous & honourable personages of Italie, called him Cardinall Ape. I doe not thinke it strange then, that this Pope, pricked forward by such an other fancy, would needs aduaunce to extraordinary degrees, and neuer before seene in the Vniuersities, these Apes of our Catholique religiō. And that you may not think, that I will encroch vpon the Iesuits priuiledges, & feede

you

you, as they vse to doe with an impudent lye, let vs read
the text of the Bull, *Nec non scholaribus* (speaking of the
schollers approoued of their Colledges) *Collegiorum So-*
cietatis huiusmodi, in Vniuersitatibus alicuius studij genera-
lis existentium, quod ipsi (si præuio rigoroso & publico exa-
mine eisdem Vniuersitatibus idonei reperti fuerint, Rectores
Vniuersitatum huiusmodi, & eos gratis & amore Dei, absq;
aliqua pecuniarũ solutione promouere recusauerint) in Col-
legiis prædictis à Præposito Generali pro tempore, existente,
vel de eius licentia à quouis ex inferioribus Præpositis, vel
Rectoribus huiusmodi Collegiorum, cum duobus etiam, vel
tribus Doctoribus, vel Magistris, per eosdem eligendis :
scholaribus verò Collegiorum eorundem, extra Vniuersitatis
existentium, studiorum suorũ cursu absoluto, ac rigoroso ex-
amine præcedente, à dicto Præposito Generali, vel de eius li-
centia à quouis ex Præpositis, vel Rectoribus huiusmodi Col-
legiorum cum duobus etiam vel tribus Doctoribus, vel Ma-
gistris, per eosdem eligendis, quoscunque Baccalaureatus, &
Magisterij, Licentiaturæ, ac Doctoratus gradus accipere,
Præpositis, vel Rectoribus, cũ Doctoribus huiusmodi, vt eos-
dem Scholares ad gradus ipsos promouere, eisdemq; schola-
ribus, vt postquam promoti fuerint, in eis legere, disputare,
ac quoscunque alios actus ad hæc necessarios, facere, exequi,
omnibus & singulis priuilegijs prærogatiuis, immunitatibus,
exemptionibus, libertatibus, antelationibus, fauoribus, gratijs,
indultis, ac omnibus & singulis alijs, quibus alij in quibusuis
Vniuersitatibus studiorum huiusmodi, rigoroso examine præ-
uio, ac alias iuxta inibi obseruari solitos & requisitos vsus,
ordinationes, ritus ac mores, pro tempore promoti, de iure
vel consuetudine, aut alias quomodolibet vtuntur, potiuntur,
& gaudent, ac vti, potiri & gaudere poterunt, quomodolibet
in futurum, non solùm ad ipsorum instar, sed pariformiter, &
æquè principaliter absq; vlla penitus differentia, vti potiri,
gaudere in omnibus & per omnia, perinde ac si gradus huius-
modi in eisdem Vniuersitatibus, & non eorum Collegijs acce-
pissent.

They

They that haue been brought vp in the Latine tongue, shall finde, that *Iulius* speakes onely of Iesuits schollers. It is a clause that hath relation to all other the former Bulls, wherin there hath been speech of their Colledges, and in this particularly it is ordaind, that, although the schollers of this Order haue been students in Vniuersities, or out of them, if after they haue been well and duly examind, they be found fit, they should be freely admitted to the degrees of Practitioners and Doctors, (a word which cannot reach to strangers) and that, if any man would make them pay duties, it should be in the power of their Generall, to creat them, or to cause them to be created: and after they haue taken their degrees, they may read, dispute, and keepe all other acts heerunto requisit; in short, that they may receiue the same prerogatiues that others doe.

What? will you stretch this worde (read) to all goers and commers, as in other Colledges of Maisters that are Secular? No truly. For what power soeuer is here granted them, it was graunted as to persons that were Regular, (for so they haue termed themselues) and therefore, it was to giue these new Maisters and Doctors, leaue to read to theyr schollers allowed, as if theyr degrees had beene giuen them by the Vniuersities. Let the Iesuit, according to his good custome, bring all the shifts of Sophistrie hee can, this passage, (if a man read it from the beginning to the end) can not be otherwise vnderstood. If *Iulius* had meant that the Iesuit graduated, might read to all goers & commers, as the Seculars doe, assure your selfe, hee would not haue forgotten to make expresse mention of it.

But you see (will some man say to mee) howe manie termes he hath giuen to the Iesuits Lectures to authorize them. Doe you thinke that strange? how could he doe lesse? sith that by a new deuise, neuer seene before, hee ordained, that vpon the simple credit of the Generall of

this

this Order, the Iesuits might read Lectures to them of their order. This pollicie, that so weakens all the auncient sinewes of the Vniuersities, could not be sufficiently exprest for the authorizing of it.

I haue hitherto declared vnto you, what, as then, was the estate of their Buls, concerning their Colledges, you shall now vnderstand their historie to this purpose. Although neither by the auncient custome of the Vnuersities, nor by the new grant of their Buls, they were permitted to set open their schooles to all sorts of schollers, nor to haue in their Colledges any other but of their seminarie : yet finding themselues to be supported by Maister *William du Prat*, Bishop of Clairmont, they setled themselues in one of the Townes of his bishoprick, called Billon, where they opened their Colledge not only to them of their order, but also to all other the students. O singular obedience of French-men to the Church of Rome ? They bragge that they haue Buls from *Iulius* the third, permitting them so to doe. At this word we thought, that the onely alledging of the title, ought to be held for a good and sufficient title : And yet they had no title but of their owne Villaine, quoth I to a Gentleman of Gascoigne : who aunswered me very readily, that he be beleeued it, because they had chosen for their chiefe, Colledge in Fraunce, the Town of Villon. They vsed this word for Billon, as the Gascoigns are wont to pronounce *U*. for *B*: and *B*. for *U*. To which I replyed, that we need not to make any change of the letter ; because by our lawes, we were commaunded to bring into Bullion, all false and counterfait moneyes, and that the Colledges of the Iesuits, were of that stampe.

In the Towne of Billon this villanie tooke beginning, which afterward they spread abroad : first to Tolosa, thē to Paris, by meanes of the great legacies, that *du Prat* had giuen them. Neither durst any of vs make head a-

gainst

gainſt any of their vnlawful enterpriſes, ſo much did our coũtry of France honor the Sea Apoſtolik, vnder which they ſhielded themſelues, though falſely. We are indeed reuerently to yeeld obedience to that Sea, but cooſeners are not to be ſuffered to abuſe it for their aduantage, and there is none, whom it more concernes to looke to this, then our holy Father the Pope, if he meane to preſerue his authoritie ouer all, and againſt all. Good God, where are our eies ? Let vs runne ouer all their Buls of 1 5 4 o. 4 3. 4 5. 4 6. 4 9. if you find, that they are permitted to hold and open their Colledges, in ſuch ſort as others of the Vniuerſities, I will yeeld my ſelfe to any ſentence, that ſhall be giuen againſt me. All their worthie actions are but cooſinages, and if you ſpeake of them in ſecret to them, they will tell you, that they are the miracles which God hath wrought by their Saint *Ignace*. When they firſt preſented themſelues to *Paul* the third to be admitted, they termed themſelues Maiſters of Arts, proceeded in the Vniuerſitie of Paris, and at this day, *Maffee* flouting the whole conſiſtorie of Rome, is of opinion, that three of them had proceeded Maiſters in Spaine, and that himſelfe and *Ribadinere*, would not giue any place of maiſterſhip to *Broet*, *Iaye* and *Codury*. And ſetting open their Colledges in Fraunce, they did but ſhroud themſelues vnder the authoritie of the Sea Apoſtolike ; an authoritie falſely ſuppoſd by them. Whence came theſe illuſions ? From the miracles forſooth of great *Ignace*, who blinded all mens eies.

I will now returne againe to the courſe of their Buls, that you may vnderſtand, when this power to read Lectures to all ſchollers, was graunted them. After this, enſued the troubles in Fraunce, 1 5 6 1, about diuerſitie of Religion : in the beginning whereof, the Ieſuits finding this a fit time for their aduantage, not by reaſon of any fauour to theyr ſect, but becauſe of diſpleaſure againſt that ciuill warre, obtayned by a manifeſt forgerie, newe

Bulls

Bulls of Pope *Pius* the fourth, the tenure whereof is this.

Insuper tibi moderno, & pro tempore existenti Præposito,
Generali dictæ Societatis, vt per te, vel illum, vel aliquen ex
Præpositis, vel Rectoribus Collegiorum vestrorum, tam in
Vniuersitatibus studiorum generalium, quam extra illas v-
bilibet consistentium, in quibus ordinariæ studiorum, artium
liberalium, & Theologiæ lectiones habentur, cursusq̃ ordina-
rij peragentur, vt dictæ Societatis Scholares & pauperes ex-
ternos, qui dictas lectiones frequentauerint, & etiam diuites
(si officiales Vniuersitàtum eos promouere recusauerint) cùm
per examinatores vestræ Societatis idonei inuenti sint (solu-
tis tamen per diuites, suis iuribus, Vniuersitatibus) in vestris
Collegijs Vniuersitatum quarumcumque, & alijs extra Vni-
uersitates, consistentibus Collegijs vestris, alios quoslibet Scho-
lares, qui inibi sub eorũ obedientia, directione, vel disciplina
studuerint, ad quoscunq̃ Baccalauriatus, Licentiariæ, Magi-
sterij, doctoratus, gradus, IVXTA IVLII PRAE-
DECESSORIS NOSRI TENOREM,
promouere, ipsiq̃, sic promoti, priuilegijs, alijsq̃, IN EIS-
DEM LITERIS contentis plenariè vti, potiri, gau-
dere liberè ac licitè valiant, authoritate præfata cõcedimus, &
ampliamus: nec non præsentes literas, & in eis contenta, de
subreptionis vel obreptionis, aut nullitatis vitio, seu intentionis
defectu, puonis prætextu quæsitoue colore, nullo vnquam tem-
pore notari, vel impugnari possint.

This decretall, was the first opener of their Colledges
to all manner of schollers: but whereupon was it grounded? Vpon the Bull of *Iulius* the third, as it is twice repeated. Was there euery any greater forgery, or more
craftie conueiance then this? For Pope *Iulius* neuer had
any such thought; and that is the reason why these Sophisters, haue caused to be added in the end of *Pius* the
fourths Bull, that no man may accuse them of obreption, or surreption, or of any wilfull fault; being desirous
that euery one of vs should shut his eyes, and blindfolde
his vnderstanding, that wee might not take any knowledge

ledge of that apparant shame, which is brought in a new, against the auncient honour of the Vniuersities, by which our Church hath alwayes beene kept in strength. But the Pope hath added this word (*Ampliamus*) will some Iesuite of the lowest forme say to me. Was there euer any poynt either of state or Religion, more important, or of greater consequence then this? I let passe that these newe Maisters were permitted to be Graduats in all faculties, as it was graunted by *Iulius* his Bull.

I graunt, that by this last Bull of *Pius*, there Colledges were opened to all commers and goers: both the one & the other notwithstanding, being new schismes in our Vniuersities. But who can abide this, that theyr schollers must be admitted to practise, whether they be Iesuits or strangers, vpon the testimonie of two or three of their order, so they pay their duties to the Chauncellours, Rectors, Presidents, & vnder-Gouernours of the Vniuersities? Is not this to make the Superiors of Vniuersities, no better then Registers to the Iesuits & theyr schollers? Is not this to disgrace the Gouernours of the Vniuersities without desert?

Is not this, by submitting them to the conscience of their Generall, and two or 3. of his, to bring in a Chaos, hotch-potch, and confusion of all thinges in our Vniuersities? And to say the truth, there is no better meanes then that, by making a Seminary of Iesuits, to make altogether a nurserie of Hereticks, by committing the Doctorships & Maisterships of schollers, to the iudgement of these new Templars. Sith this depends vppon this one word (*Ampliamus*,) which was craftilie foysted in, by these maister workmen in such tricks of legerdemaine, we shall admit this new disorder: thereupon the Pope shall stop his owne eares, and our mouthes, that the shifts, obreptions and surreptions of these reuerend Fathers in God, may not be discried, & all because this last clause was added, by a Clark of the Court of Rome,

that

that copied out the graunt. Read all the 7. former Buls,
ye shall find no such clause in any of them. Why did
they cause it to be added in this? Because they knew in
their conscience, that this last Bull was obtained by
obreption, contrarie to all reason. If I should appeale
to their consciences, they would make a mocke at me.
For the same yeere, that they got this Bull at Rome,
(which was 1 5 6 1.) they promist in a full assembly
of the Church of Fraunce, that they would renounce
all the extraordinarie priuiledges, that had beene graunted them at Rome. This abiuration they confirmed by
publique oath in a full Court of Parliament, but they
neuer performed it. And that which is especially to bee
considered, they lookt to themselues verie carefully, for
presenting the Popes priuie Buls, either to our Cleargy,
or to our Parliament. For if they had shewed them, they
had beene not only derided, but also abandoned, as men
that had no wit. Hitherto you haue descried in them,
good store of the Foxes craft, now you shall see how
they haue playd in Lions. For, the yeere 1 5 7 1. they
got other Buls of Pope *Pius* the fift, of this forme and
substance.

Decernimus & declaramus quod præceptores huiusmodi
Societatis, tam literarum humanarum, quàm liberalium ar-
tium, Philosophiæ, Theologiæ, vel cuiusuis earum facultatũ,
in suis Collegijs, etiam in locis vbi Vniuersitates extiterint, su-
as lectiones, etiam publicas legere (dummodo per duas horas
de mane, & per vnam de sero, cum lectoribus Vniuersitatum
non concurrant) liberè & licitè possint : quodã, quibuscumq̃,
scholasticis liceat in huiusmodi Collegijs, lectiones, & alias
scholasticas exercitationes frequentare, ac quicumque in eis,
Philosophiæ vel Theologiæ fuerint auditores, in quauis V-
niuersitate, ad gradus admitti possint, & cursuum quos in eis
Collegijs fecerint, ratio habeatur. Ita vt si ipsi in examine suf-
ficientes inuenti fuerint, non minus, sed pariformiter, & absq̃,
vlla penitus differentia, quam si in Vniuersitatibus præfatis

Y. *studuissent*

studuissent, ad gradus quoscumque, tam Baccalaureatus,
quàm Licentiariæ & Doctoratus, admitti possint & debeant,
eisq́, super præmissis licentiam & facultatem concedimus.
Districtius inhibentes, Vniuersitatum quarumcumque Rec-
toribus & alijs quibuscumq́, sub excommunicationis maio-
ris, alijsq́, arbitrio nostro, moderandis, infligendis, & impo-
nendis pœnis, ne Collegiorum huiusmodi Rectores & Scho-
lares in præmissis, quouis quæsito colore, molestare audeant,
vel præsumant. Decernentes quoque præsentes litteras, vllo
vnquam tempore, de subreptionis, vel obreptionis vitio, aut
intentionis nostræ, vel alio quopiam defectu notari, vel impug-
nari nullatenus posse, minusq́, sub quibusuis similium, vel dissi-
milium gratiarum renocationibus, limitationibus, & alijs
contrarijs dispositionibus comprehendi posse.

O admirable, not Philosophers, nor Diuines, but pe-
tifoggers in the Court of the Church. He that shal haue
need of a forme of petifoging, were best haue recourse
to these Buls, wherein notwithstanding with an infinite
hardines, they haue coucht the furie of the Lion. To the
other they added, I know not by what sophistrie, the
word *Ampliamus*; but in these last, there is nothing
but thunder from heauen, and Superlatiue excommunications against any man, that shall but dare to looke
vp in opposition against their tyranny. True it is indeed,
that least I should fall foule on thē by mistaking, I could
wish, that some *Oedipus* among the Iesuits, would disci-
pher and expound to me, that last clause : which they
should not haue added, if they thought that this Bull
was such an one, as that men could not be discontent
with it. In this Bull *Pius* the fift, had made exception
of two houres in the morning, & one in the afternoone.
Gregerie the thirteenth by another of 1 5 7 8. in steed of
the two houres in the morning giues but one. There
hath alwaies beene in our Iesuits, enteprise vpon enterprise, to the preiudice of antiquitie. You see in effect
the whole historie of the pretended instruction of the
youth,

youth, by the Iesuits, and how by little and little they
haue got ground, againſt the auncient orders of the V-
niuerſities. Hauing employed all ſorts of vnlawfull deuiſes and ſhifts,which are familiar, not to learned men,
but to the baſeſt of the people; who abuſing the abſolute power of the holy Sea, bring, if I may dare to
ſay ſo, the Popedome and the reſt of the people to liue
vpon almes. By theſe clauſes of the Chancery of Rome,
they thinke to fight with vs, with edge tooles. And a
Procter generall,might rebate them brauely by an appeale, as by abuſe, becauſe theſe Buls were not onely
wrung out by deuiſes,but doe alſo,directly vſurpe vpon
the liberties of our Church of Fraunce, the ordinarie
rights and priuiledges of our Vniuerſities. For why
ſhould not this appeale be receiued,ſith that the Signo-
rie of Venice, according to their wiſe carriage in all
their actions, knowing the diſorder, that theſe newe
people bring with them, haue expreſly forbidden them
by an act made the 23. of December, 1591. to reade
publique or priuate Lectures to anie, but thoſe that
are of their Societie? Which act, a man cannot ſufficiently commend,and which proues,that we are verie dul-
lards if we doe not follow their example. It is a light
which ought to ſerue all nations as a Lanterne to bring
them into a ſafe Hauen.

CHAP. 4.

⁋ That the foundation of the deceits of the Ieſuits, proceeds
from the inſtruction of the youth: and why our aun-
ceſters would not that the young folke ſhould
be taught in houſes of Religion.

ALL things (ſaith the Ieſuit) are to be taken for
good,that are done to a good end. What skils it
that there haue beene deuiſes and ſhifts in our
Buls, ſo long as the Pope diſpenceth with vs for
them?

them: and that our intent was not grounded but vppon a Chriſtian charitie, ſuch as the inſtruction of youth is, the very plant of our Order, wherein we deſire to be alwaies the principall labourers.

It is well ſaid, (quoth the Aduocate,) and for my part, I thinke that all the charitie that you haue brought with you to this worke, is a very cooſinage. Let a man take your charitie away, and by the ſame meanes he ſhal take away your cooſinage. Pardon mee, I pray you, if this word haue eſcapt mee, it ſhall heereafter be familiar to me. For, by ill hap, thinking that all your profeſſion is nothing but cooſinage, and hauing no dexteritie in varietie of my ſpeech, as many of you haue, I am one of thoſe, who call that bread and wine, which is bread and wine, and ſo cooſinage, that which is cooſinage; vnleſſe you like better, that I ſhould rather call it ſometimes villanie: and becauſe this poynt lies heauie vpon my ſtomack, I will to the depth of it out of hand. If the diſcipline that is tollerated in your Order be good, why is it not generall in all other, who eſteeme as much of charitie as you doe? Why are they not ſuffered to receiue all ſorts of ſchollers, though ſtrangers, as well as you? Can it be, that our good old Fathers, faild in iudgement, and that wee are now conſtrained to haue recourſe to theſe new Fathers. There neuer was wiſer diſcipline then that of theirs. For they thought, that alwaies the firſt obiects ſeeme faireſt to children, & that their wits, like wax, receiue very eaſily all ſorts of impreſſions.

They thought, that they ought not to ſuffer them to be ſeduced, but to let them enter into religious Orders, with an honeſt libertie of their conſciences, whereas by going ordinarilie to the Munks lectures, they might be conuerted in haſt to that, whereof they would repent themſelues afterward at leyſure, when there was no time for it. And by this deuiſe, the Ieſuits verie eaſily ſurpriſe many children of good houſes, there being no ſnare ſo
easie

eafie to entrap them as this. If they perceiue any of their
fchollers begin to affect them, them they drawe to their
net, and as foone as they haue taken them, they make
them vanifh out of their Parents fight, to the end they
may not be recouerd. It is a good coofinage, you will
fay, that frees a child frõ the vaine feruice of the world.
Nay rather, it is a coofinage woorthy to be punifht for
example fake, as you wil confeffe when you vnderftand
the proceedings. The Rectors informe themfelues by
the Regents, of the capacitie of thofe in their formes, of
their wits, and of their behauiours. Hereof they make a
Catalogue, the figure wherof I will fhew you, for I haue
one here readie printed, as followeth.

Wit.	Iudge-ment.	Pru-dence.	Expe-rience.	Profit in lear-ning.	Natuall compex-ion.	What talents he hath, wherof vfe may be made in any feruice of the Societie.

And vnderneath the titles, they fette in euerie Cell, the name of fome childe, his forme, and his age, acccording to the qualitie which they fuppofe to bee in him. Now fo it is, that euery yeere, they fend from euery Colledge Letters to their Generall, which they call, yeerelie Letters, by which they aduertife him how great a number of foules they haue gained, & how much their confeffions haue auailed them in this regard; and their Letters they accompanie with this Catalogue, which being aduifedly confidered by their Generall, he commaunds the Prouincialls or Rectors, to beware that they fuffer not this bird to efcape out of theyr cage. After this warning, they all employ themfelues in diuers maner in this goodly and fruitfull labour, one, by auricular confeffions, another, by allurements, a third, by priuate exhortations in his chamber, and it is meruailous hard for a poore youth to rid himfelfe out of their nets, efpeciallie beeing fo watcht.

Yet I will tell you a ftorie of a young man of great hope, in the furprifall of whom, they faild of their purpofe. They perceiued, that hee had many good parts, & yet had his mind greatly inclind to deuotion: they imagind thereupon, that hee would be a very fit pray for them. This youth, being pencioner in their Colledge at Paris, one of their Fathers began to fet his fowling Nets for him, and among other talke, askt him, if it fo fel out that it fhould pleafe God to call him out of the world, what would moft difquiet him at the houre of his death. The feare of the other world, (quoth the youth) becaufe of the finnes I haue committed. What would you fay then, (replies the Iefuit) to him that fhould free you of this feare? I would think my felfe greatly bound to him, faid the youth. You may affure your felfe of deliuerance from this feare, (concludes the Iefuit) if you will wholie become one of ours. For our focietie of Iefus, is an acquittall from all finnes. This young boy beeing thus
managed,

managed, gaue full credit to his speech, and had quickly
truſt vp his pack to be gone, according to the inſtructions hee had receiued, which were, that without taking
leaue of Father or mother, he ſhould firſt goe to one of
their houſes which they would name to him, and there
he ſhould receiue certaine money to ſerue his turne, till
he came to another; & ſo hauing in euery of theſe houſes mony to defray the charges of his voyage, he ſhould
come at the laſt to Rome, there to receiue ſuch inſtructions as theyr General would giue him.

When hee was vpon the very poynt of his departure,
by good hap his Father came to ſee him, and found him
quite changed: hereupon, he was deſirous to know the
cauſe of his change: the boy refuſd to tell him, but the
Father preſt him hard, and coniurd him with a fatherly
ſeueritie, not to hide the matter from him. At the laſt, he
vnderſtood all that had paſt, whereupon hee preſently
tooke him away from that houſe, and after that all theſe
fumes were vapourd out of his braine, ſent him to another Colledge, where hee profited ſo well, that I aſſure
my ſelfe, he will proue very rare in the vocation which
now he followes, and will prayſe & thank God as long
as he liueth, that it pleaſed him of his gracious mercy, to
deliuer him from ſo dangerous a ſhipwrack.

CHAP. 5.

❡ *With what cunning the Iesuits enrich themſelues with
the ſpoyle of theyr Nouices.*

He Ieſuits winning in this ſort the youth
of their Colledges, as well pencioners as
ſtrangers, would thinke this a ſmall matter, if they did not alſo enrich themſelues
with their ſpoiles. It is a generall rule, verie well vnderſtood by them, That he that conſiſcates
the body, conſiſcats the goods.

I

I will not here make an Inuentarie of the great wealth they haue gotten, as hauing not been in theyr purses to fee it, but this I will tell you, that this practife hauing been often obiected to them, hee that made *The humble fupplication to the King*, affirmed, that of three or foure hundred that haue vowed themfelues to their Societie, there are not aboue three or foure that haue prefented it with their goods: and *Frances Montagnes*, that made the booke *De la veritè defendue*, faith, that of two thoufand, there were but two hundred. The art of wife lyers is, not to difagree in their tales, & yet both thefe reports are faultie: They fhould fay, that of three or foure hundred there were not foure, & that of two thoufand there were not 2. hundred that had not beftowed their goods on them. And indeede it were vnpoffible for the Nouice to keepe his goods from theyr fingering. For they haue a meruailous art, and that infallible for this effect. They haue two bookes of Statuts, the title of the former is, *Couſtitutio Societatis Iefu*, which is deuided into two parts : the fecond is entituled, *Conſtitutiones & Declarationes examinis generalis*. Thefe Bookes I haue in my poffeffion, as alfo that, in which all their Bulls are regiftred. In their Examination, you fhall find in the fourth chapter, and in the firft, fecond, and third Article, that which followes for the diftributing of their goods that enter into their focietie.

1. *Quicunque Societatem ingredi volunt, antequam in domo aliqua vel Collegio eius viuere fub obedientia incipiant, debent omnia bona fua temporalia quæ habuerint diſtribuere & renuntiare, ac diſponere de his, quæ ipfis obuenire poffent : eaﳳ diſtributio primùm in res debitas & obligatoria, ſi quæ fuerint, & tunc quàm cirtiffimè fieri potuerit, prouidere oportebit. Si verò tales nullæ fuerint, in pia & ſanɛ̌a opera fiet, iuxta illud : Diſperſit, dedit pauperibus : & illud Chriſti ; Si vis perfeɛtus eſſe, vade & vende omnia quæ habes, & da pauperibus, & ſequere me. Diſpenſando tamen hæc bona*

*bona iuxta propriam deuotionem, & à se omnem fiduciam
submouendo, eadem vllo tempore recuperandi.*

2. *Quod si statim propter aliquas honestas caussas non re-
linquet, promittat se promptè relicturum omnia post vnum
ab ingressu; absolutum annum, quandocumque per Superio-
rem ei iniunctum fuerit, in reliquo tempore probationis, quo
completo, post professionem professi, & ante tria vota publica, Coadiutores re ipsa relinquere debent, ac pauperibus, vt
dictum est, dispensare, vt consilium Euangelicum, quod non
dicit, dà Consanguineis, sed pauperibus, perfectiùs sequantur;
& vt melius exemplum omnibus exhibeant, inordinatum erga parentes affectum exuendi & incommoda inordinata di-
stributionis, quæ à dicto amore procedit declinandi, atque vt
ad parentes & consanguineos recurrendi, & ad inutilem ipsorum memoriam, additu præcluso, firmius & stabilius in sua
vocatione perseuerent.*

O holy and Christian lesson of the Iesuits, who would
haue a young man, that vowes himselfe to their society,
to dispose, before he enter thereinto, not only of all such
goods, as are fallen to him, but also of all such, as may fall
to him: and it is yet more holy & meruailous, when they
teach him to forget all that affection, which God commaunds the child to beare to his father and mother; and
after them, to his neerest kinred, and that they call this
affection disordered. And that further they otdaine
that within the two yeerers of his probation, he giue all
his goods in almes to the poore, & that he doe not leaue
them to those, who being next of kinne, should he his
heires. And all this is, because he might neuer after vpon any loathing of their new rebellion, returne home to
his fathers house. But I beseech our Iesuits to remēber
this holy lesson: for I hope to put them in minde of it
hereafter, to better purpose in his proper place. In the
meane while, let vs marke what the Catastrophe of this
deuout Comedie will be.

3. *Si tamen dubitaretur num maioris foret perfectionis,*

Z. *dare*

dare vel renuntiare conſanguineis, huiuſmodi bona, quàm à-
lijs propter pacem, vel maiorem ipſorum penuriam, & iuſtas
alias ob cauſas, nihilo minus ad declinandum errandi in hu-
iuſmodi iudicio periculum, quod ab effectu ſanguinis ſolet pro-
ficiſci, contenti eſſe debebunt hoc, arbitrio vnius, duorum aut
trium, qui vita & doctrina commendantur (quos vnuſquiſ-
que cum Superioris authoritate elegerit) relinquere, & in
eo conquieſcere, quod illi perfectius, & ad maiorem Chriſti
Domini noſtri gloriam eſſe cenſebunt.

This is that I lookt for of them: after that they haue
made their approach ſtep by ſtep, they are at laſt come
to the wall, and there lacks nothing but to ſcale it, or to
enter the breach, for the winning of the Towne. What
may we looke for of this award vpon arbitrement, but
that we read of *Q. Fabius Labeo*, who being choſen
Arbitrator by the Senate of Rome, to decide the controuerſie betwixt the Nolans and Neopolitans, concerning their bounds, after he had ſurueyed the place, talking with each of them apart, he councelled thē not to
be wedded to their own wils, but rather to chooſe peace
then purſue their quarrell. To which when both parts
had condeſcended, for reſpect they had to him, after he
had ſet each of them their bounds as pleaſed him, he adiudged to the people of Rome, all the ground which
remained betwixt them, and for which they had beene
in ſtrife. Wherein they could not complaine (ſaith
Valerius) becauſe they had put the matter to his honeſty,
and ſo (ſaith this author) by a diſhoneſt ſhift, the Citie
got a new tribute. I know well, the iudgement I giue
of them, will be ſubiect to cauelling, and that ſome will
ſay, that the Gloſſe goes beyond the text, for ſome particular grudge I beare them. But I call God to witnes,
that I wiſh not their hinderance in any thing, but as I
conceiue it makes for the common good. I enuie not
other Monaſteries, for that they which enter into
them, preſent them with their goods, becauſe I do not

ſee

see that they enter thereinto by craftie enticements, but vpon deuotion guided by the holy Ghost: but as for the Iesuits, they take quite another course. There is nothing but the hand of man that cunningly workes the matter by a long traine. First of all, in teaching the yong boyes, whether Pencioners or others, they cast their eyes vpon them that are for their purpose, and make a Catalogue of their sufficiency and capacities, which they send (as I told you) to their Generall, winning them afterward with sweet allurements. When they are once won, they steale them away from those, to whom they appertaine, and send them into other countries, to make them forget their friends. After, when they are fast in their nets, and are now readie to giue their farewell to the world, they are perswaded by force, to leaue nothing to their father, mother, or kinred, but to giue all to the poore. But to what poore? That is not exprest. And surely, he were of a verie dull capacitie that would not iudge, that vnder this generalitie, they meane to speake for themselues in particular; and that in this choise, the young man wil ayme chiefely at their society, vnto which he is about to vow himselfe, and which he thinks to be the vpholding of the Catholique Church. To conclude, if his timorous conscience, haue any scruple by reason of the pouertie of his parents, yet is he not suffered to extend his liberalitie to them, but this doubt or perplexitie is committed to the iudgement of two or three of their Iesuits. What is all this, but to tyrannize ouer this poore man, by a long trayne of words and cariage of matters, and to constraine him, when all comes to all, to bestow his goods on this poore Societie, vpon which so much wealth is heapt? But if hee would contest to the contrarie, they will make him at his first enterance beleeue, that hee will prooue a disobedient childe, and one that neuer will haue anie deuotion to their order.

Z 2   But

But (as thought is free) let vs suppose that these two or three pretended wise men hauing giuen sentence in fauour of their societie, what appeale shall this new Iesuit goe seeke to plead against them? He (I say) who for his first lesson, receiues commaundement, to forget that holy trust committed to him by God, I meane, the loue of his father and mother, to obey his superiours, will he think you, dare once lift vp his eye lid to make head against them? And yet notwithstanding, why should we blame them for this sentence? For they may say without going so about the bush, that they are the Apostles of our time, as they haue caused themselues to be called in Portugall, and that as in the primitiue Church at Ierusalem, they that would be Christians, were bound to bring all their goods and reuenewes to the Apostles feet; so these holy and deuout soules, will haue all bound, who will enter inter into their societie, to make them partakers of all their goods. And for all this doe you say that I am not their most humble and most affectionnate seruant? To concolde, in all *Riba-ner*, I find nothing so fine, as when he tels vs, that *Igna-tius*, and his fellowes, hauing for a time setled their a bode with the Venitian, went twice a day through the Citie to begge almes: and that one of them, ordinarily stayed in their house, to prouide for them of that little, which was giuen them vpon almes : And that it was *Ignace* that gaue this charge, who declared thereby, that what deuotion soeuer he made shew of, he had a moneth mind to the kitchin too. This lesson his suc-cessors haue learned verie perfectly.

Rib.lib.2. cap.2.

CHAP.

CHAP. 6.

¶ That the craftie liberalitie of the Iesuit, in teaching the
youth, hath brought the Vniuersitie of
Paris to ruine.

 Will be more charitable to them then
they are to vs. Let vs not enuie them
the good that they get by theyr newe
guests, if by theyr Lectures they haue
furnisht vs with many braue men for
the gouernment of our Realme. I pray
you tell me Gentlemen, whether your children, vvhich
you haue committed to their teaching, haue gone before their companions, in matter of learning or publique
charge, or no? Shall you finde in the high Courts, anie
Presidents or Counsailers of the Iesuits bringing vp,
that excell others? I do not only see none such, but quite
contrarie, eyther we haue none such at all, or very few;
in whom likewise, you shall finde no other disposition
but sad and heauie, no way sociable with pubilque persons.

They that are brought vp in other Colledges, not
with fantastique assemblies, but with courage, in our ancient religion, are preferd to all places of charge, as well
temporall, as Ecclesiasticall. The Iesuits shoote at no o-
ther marke, but the growth and greatnes of theyr owne
Cōmon-weale, because (that I may not lie to you) theyr
Schoole brings forth some men of marke, pickt & chosen among their schollers. These are such, as in theyr
youth suborned by the auncients, haue beene taken by
craft, in whom age cannot quench the naturall fire that
was in them. Afterward vnprofitable for the Common-
weale.

And verily, it was fit that God should muffle our eies,
when we first suffered the Iesuits, not onely to read, but

to read gratis : that we might not perceiue, that the offer they made to the Vniuerſitie of Paris, was like the artificiall horſe the Greeks ſaid they had made to offer to *Palladiũ*, the Image of the goddeſſe *Pallas*, which was in Troy. A horſe, which notwithſtanding, caried in it ſelfe the ruine and deſtruction of the Citie. In this manner are we beguiled by the Ieſuits, who counterfeating to preſent a *Pallas* to Fraunce, in Paris, to wit, their Colledge, they haue laid our famous Vniuerſitie in the duſt.

A generation of Vipers, no ſooner brought forth, but they killed their mother. For *Ignace* and his nine companions, when they preſented themſelues to Pope *Paule*, were no further qualified then Maiſters of Arts in Paris, as I told you of late. But with what eies ſhal we ſee, that they who by their vowes promiſed pouerty, as well in generall, as particular, either would or could, ſhew liberalitie worthie of a Monarch, that is, to teach and take nothing? Before they came here, the Vniuerſitie flouriſht, it was a common Port, where the greateſt part of all the Nations of Europe did ride at ancor. Which you may perceiue, as well by the foure ancient and great ſchooles ſtanding in Straw ſtreet, as by the Proctors of the Nations, next the Rector : For there is one ſchoole and one procter for for the Germane Nation, vnder which is comprehended, the Engliſh, Scotiſh, and others. If any ſpeake of this Vniuerſitie, they ſaid, learning was come to found Athens in Rome, and Rome in Paris. The ofspring of the good houſes of Fraunce, eyther when they were firſt ſent out to learne, or if they had begunne their ſtudies in other Townes, yet at laſt, their generall *Rende-Vous*, was in Paris, to attaine to the accompliſhment of learning there.

The Principalls, lodgd in their Colledges the ſchollers, whom they call Pentioners, with moderate pentions ;

ōns; and of ſtrangers, they tooke for theyr admiſſion,
one ſhilling, or two at the moſt. The Regents had certaine beneuolences of their Auditors, which they called
Fayrings, of one more, of another leſſe, as it pleaſed their
Parents to beſtow : for no man was bound, but onely by
a certaine ſhame, which hee conceiued by the honeſt liberalitie of his fellowes . The Regent had no action at
all againſt them for the recouering of one penny , and
yet the matter was carried with ſuch modeſtie , that the
Regents hauing ſwet and trauaild about the inſtruction
of their youth, they were bound to feaſt them one day
in a Garden, where they brought into practiſe that auncient libertie, which the Maiſters of Rome were wont to
giue to their ſchollers in their Saturnalia.

No man can ſay, that there was one iot of couetouſ-
nes in all theſe proceedings , neither did you euer ſee a-
ny Principalls or Regents growe to great wealth: and
yet euerie one ſtudied to his vttermoſt endeuour , with
no other intent, but to enrich himſelfe with a good report, by beeing compaſt about in his Lectures with a
great multitude of Schollers : as indeed there is no ſhar-
per ſpurre to well dooing then honor. The Principalls
ſtroue by a certaine enuie one with another, who ſhould
haue the beſt Regents to winne commendation, and by
this means, the fame of the Vniuerſity of Paris was ſpred
euery where.

But vpon a ſuddaine, when it was not permitted, but
tolleraʇed in the Ieſuits , that they ſhould open theyr
ſhops, all this honorable ambition, vaniſht into ſmoake.
They calld themſelues Protectors of the Catholique religion : by meanes vvhereof, the Fathers of Children,
that could ſee no farther before them then the length of
their noſes, ſent theyr ſonnes thether, to abide and be inſtructed by them.

The ſchollers being not well confirmd , were verie
glad to ſaue their Gate-mony, their Fayrings, and their
candles:

candles : and so their Colledges being stuft full, these li-
berall Iesuits, beganne to take twice or thrice so much of
their schollers for pention, as they tooke in other Colledges; which the foolish fathers besotted, neuer denied
them. Hereupon, by little and little, the Readers & Regents of the Vniuersitie, waxt cold in that desire which
before they had to make themselues famous. This was,
as it is with the Spleene in our bodies, which cannot
grow, without the decay of other parts. In like sort, the
growing of the Iesuit by this vnlawful cunning, was the
ruine of the Vniuersitie of Paris, which God be thanked, now riseth againe, euer since the Act of the Court
of Parliament, in the yeere 1594.

But what is become of all this? The Principalls and
Regents, in the midst of their famous couetousnes, remaine poore, and the Iesuits, in the midst of their craftie
liberalitie, are become exceeding rich. And this is that,
which Monsiure *Du Mesnill*, the Kings Atturney generall, very wisely said to *Versoris* and *Pasquier*, when as
they reasond of the case of the Iesuits, and the Vniuersitie at the Kings-bench barre; *Timeo Danaos & dona fe-*
rentes. I know that the meeke Iesuit, in his supplication
presented to the King, affirmes, that our holy Father the
pope, hath in Rome cõmitted to them, the instruction of
the young Romane Nobilitie, amounting to the nũber
of 2000. schollers, and of fiue Seminaries of young men,
Romans, Greeks, English, Dutch, Scottish. Wee enuie
not either Rome or Italie this great happines, much lesse
the Iesuits, who finde themselues there to be very well
and warme. They are permitted to become wholly Ita-
lionate, so they get them out of Fraunce, and let vs liue
in quiet : and to that end, I giue them these two verses
following, to serue them for Letters demissories.

Vos qui cuncta datis (rapitis tamen) ITE ALIO, ite :
Cœlestes immò procul abs IESV ITE scelesti.

Or

Or rather, by way of amplification, let them take this heere.

> YOu that doe brag you freely *learne & teach,*
> *Houses & hiues for drones you freely reach.*
> *The course of iustice freely you corrupt,*
> *And Kings Edicts you freely interrupt.*
> *Mens wills and farmes, by you are freely caught,*
> *By you the people freely are made naught .*
> *And when your noses greater gaine doe wind,*
> *You sing your selues, others to mourne you bind,*
> *Whom you haue coosend of their ancient seates,*
> *Your craft, the Father of his child defeates.*
> *Most willingly (loe heere) I honour you,*
> *O, of our Sauiour* IES VS *holy crue :*
> *New Idols, of a new and foolish age,*
> *Freely depart, with all your equipage.*

Nay more, to passe the time as they trauaile ouer the Alpes, I will giue them with all my hart a Latine Poëm, that *Adrian Turnebus* made in fauour of them, a fewe months after their cause was pleaded, translated since that time verse for verse, by *Stephen Pasquier.*

¶ *A Poëm of* Adrian Turnebus, *vpon the liberalitie of the Iesuits.*

AMong the most principall and woorthy personages of our age, as well for good life, behauiour, & Catholique Religion, as for all sorts of good learning, we had in the Vniuersitie of Paris, that great Clarke, *Adrian Turnebus,* the Kings Professor : a man prayfed and honourd by the pennes of as manie, as since his death euer writ of him, and among other religious men, *Genebrard,* Archbish. of Aix, in his Chronographie . *Adrianus Turnebus* my Maister (saith hee) in the Greeke tongue, and the Kings Professor, at 53. yeeres of age, dyed in Paris, the 12. of Iune 1565. a Catholick, though the hereticks gaue out the cōtrarie of him. This learned religious perſon, makes it his glorie, that he had *Turnebus* for his Maiſter, and beares witneſſe of his Catholique fayth, whoſe witnes alone is woorth a hundred others. I truſt the Ieſuits will not be grieued, to take this honorable commendation that he gaue of them in Latine verſe, a little before his deceaſe, tranſlated then into French, verſe for verſe, and printed at Paris.

¶ *Against* Sotericus, *that will needs read without ſtipend.*

THou *Soteric*, who freely vaunts to read,
Perſwade thy Lawyer for no fee to pleade,
Which ſells his ſpeech by weight of golden hire,
And make thy Proctor no reward require,
But let him cap and curtſie for nothing :
Try if thou canſt the ſacred Senate bring
To aske the King no ſtipend for theyr paine,
Nor benefit : If Proctors talke for gaine,
And euery Lawyer by his breath doe thriue,
And Senators vpon allowance liue,
Let each good Order then be kept with them,
The Courts thy Stoick paradox condemne.
None thee beleeue that profit dooſt deſpiſe.
The ſeates of iuſtice heere before thine eyes
Proſper by gaine, and grow maieſticall,
Take away this, the Courts will haue a fall.
Men will iudge thee a fained hypocrite,
Not well contented with a little mite,
But ſay you gape for dead mens wills and treaſure,
And lie in wait to hunt it out of meaſure ;
Thus from the poore their almes is ſwept away,
Small things you ſcorne, to get ſome greater pray.
I wiſh at meaner gifts you would not grutch,
Nor heape and hale from Clairemont halfe ſo much.

What

VVhat you by wicked shifts doe scrape and racke,
Belongs vnto the poore, not to your backe.
Your pietie and bountie doth appeare,
You craue great gifts, shun small ; Deuotion deere.
The loue of this, hath set your hart on fire,
None willingly becomes a thiefe for hire,
But soares aloft, in hope to part the spoyle
He makes faire shewes, and with a goodly foile
Drawes them along, whom in his nets he shuts,
And then himselfe with blood and murder gluts.
Thus while you carelesse seeme to teach for price,
Whom you may rifle of their goods, you tice.
Kindreds disherited, their wealth you share,
Whereof the lawes and iustice should take care.
Come now to sale, make market of your skills,
Take treble wages, giue vp dead mens wills,
Abstaine from theft, let their bequests goe free,
No scratching Harpie heereto will agree.
Then let your labours be no longer vaunted,
By your Societie our lands are haunted.
Though foure or fiue doe teach, yet in your Cells
A thousand heauie-headed Drones there dwells,
Not apt to teach others, nor themselues to learne,
When ours, no maintnaunce haue, but what they earne.
Not one with vs that idle is, can liue,
Why doe you then the name of Maisters giue
Vnto your selues, in such a Towne where more
Maisters haue been then schollers heretofore ?
Mention of this their monthly records make,
Not a Denier of Schollers will you take.
And shall such Locusts with so easie sute
Lodge in our bosome to deuour our fruit ?
He that no recompence will haue, there-while
Watcheth the Realme and people to beguile.
Who will no burden be, yet hath no stay
Of liuing : this of him will wise men say,

He is a shifter, and his gaine is cheated,
Whats due to him he takes not, though entreated,
What is not due, he doth exact. See now
What tricks your rifled Schollers learne of you.
Their Legacies haue made you fortunate,
They be the props and pillars of your state.
Of Lands and Lordships you desire good store,
With power of life and death ouer the poore
And blockish vulgar sort : Then if you please,
Epicures Gardens you may haue for ease.
Grammarians, Maisters, Doctors, and the Schooles,
Schollers & Chayres must weepe, you make all fooles.

CHAP. 7.

⁊ That the sect of the Iesuits , agrees in many things
with the heresie of Peter Abelard.

Fter that *Pasquier* had by his Plea layde
open, the impieties and blasphemies of
the Iesuite *Postell,* he set himselfe to buckle with their Metaphysicall *Maldonat,*
who some sixe weekes , or two months
before, in a great auditorie of young
boyes, playing with his wit to the dishonour of G O D,
had read contrarie Lectures. In the first , he labourd to
proue by naturall reasons, that there is a God. In the second, that there is none. The Iesuits maintaine at this
day, by the pen of *Rene de la Fon,* that the God-head
must be prooued by naturall reasons, & that a man may
dispute both pro & contra, and that hee which thinkes
otherwise , and relyes onely vppon fayth, is impious.
Thys proposition, together with theyr practise, which I
haue obserued since their comming to abide in Paris,
makes me remember *Peter Abelard,* who was so toucht
to the quick by S. *Bernard :* and I thinke I shall not at all
wander

wander from my purpose, if I recount you the storie, the better to make comparison betwixt him and the Iesuits; especially, because *Ignace* had for his first Regent in Barcelonne, one called *Ardebal*, in whose name you shall find *Abelard*, without difference of any one letter.

Peter Abelard, comming of a verie auncient and noble house of Britaine, being the eldest of fiue brothers (which is no small priuiledge in that countrey) gaue ouer all and euerie whit of his goods, that he might dedicate himselfe to learning: wherein he was verie forward, before he went out of the countrey. But to the end he might be better furnisht, he came to Paris, which then began to be the fountaine of all good litterature. There he found two Maisters, *William Campellensis* in Philosophy, and *Anselm* in Diuinitie, who read diuers lectures in the Bishops Pallace, where the Vniuersitie then was. *Abelard* had not studied Philosophie, but that, as he was of a great, but a running wit, so he farre out-stript his companions, and became equall euen to *Campellensis* his Regent. And as one that was so, without taking any degree of licence, of his owne priuate authoritie, he tooke the Doctors Chare: which being forbidden him, he went and read at *Corbueil*, afterward, at *Melun*; from thence he came backe to Paris, where he read in the Suburbs. A certaine space after, he studied Diuinity vnder *Anselm*, wherin he profited exceedingly, and vpon like extraordinarie confidence in himselfe as before, he vndertooke to teach, without the approbation of the Vniuersitie, to the great mislike of all the auncients, yet not of the younger sort, who commonly take pleasure in such nouelties. As he grew wonderfully in all things, so there befell him a verie great mishap. For he got a maide of good sort with child, called *Heloise*, whom he was constrained to marry priuily, to satisfie her vncle, being a Canon of the Church of Paris.

Maff.li.br. cap.16.

Afterward

Afterward, being defirous to conceale the marriage, and hauing put his wife into a cloyſter of Nuns at Argētueil, her vncle taking offence thereat, cauſed him a little while after to be taken at vnawares, and thoſe parts to be cut off, by which he had offended. In the end, ouercome with ſhame, his wound being perfectly whole, he became a Monke in the Abby of Saint *Denis* in Fraunce, and *Heloiſe*, a vailed Nunne in the Nunnery of Argentueil: yet could not this working ſpirit be reſtrained by the auncient diſcipline of our Church. For he began to ſet open a ſchoole, as well of Philoſophy, as of Diuinitie, within his Monaſterie, drawing to him an infinite ſort of ſchollers. This thing made the Vniuerſitie of Paris to ſtirre againſt him by complaint to the Prelates, Which himſelfe alſo conceales not, in a long Epiſtle being the generall ſtorie of his life, out of the which I haue copied this paſſage.

Cum autem in diuina Scriptura non minorem gratiam, quam in ſeculari, mihi Dominus contuliſſe videretur, cœperunt admodum ex vtraque lectione ſcholæ noſtræ multiplicari, & cætera vehementer omnes attenuari. Vnde maximè Magiſtrorum inuidiam atque odium aduerſum me concitaui. Qui in omnibus que poterant, mihi derogantes, duo præcipuè abſenti ſemper obijciebant: quod ſcilicet propoſito Monachi valdè ſit contrarium, ſecularium librorum ſtudio detineri, & quod ſine Magiſtro ad Magiſterium diuinæ lectionis accedere præſumpſiſſem, vt ſic inde omne mihi doctrinæ ſcholaris exercitium interdiceretur. Ad quod inceſſantur, Epiſcopos, Archiepiſcopos, Abbates, & quaſcumque poterant Religioſi nominis perſonas incitabant. This paſſage I eſpecially note vnto you, as ſeruing meruailous fit, to be employed in this my diſcourſe. As he made his fame to grow by reading, ſo did he alſo by writing; for hee wrote a booke, *De Vnitate, & Trinitate diuina,* in fauour of his ſchollers, as he ſaith. *Qui humanas & Philoſphicas rationes requirebant, & plus quàm intelligi, quàm*

quæ

quæ dici poſſint, efflagitabant . Dicentes quidam verborum
ſuperfluam eſſe prolationem, quam intelligentia non ſequere-
tur : nec credi poſſe aliquid niſi prius intellectum, & ridiculo-
ſum eſſe aliquem alijs prædicare, quod nec ipſe , nec illi quos
doceret , intellectu capere poſſent : Domino ipſo arguente,
quod cæci eſſent ductores cæcorum.

This booke offended all the Cleargy of France. Wher-
vpon, there was a Councell aſſembled in the Towne of
Soiſſons, where *Conan*, Biſhop of Preuoſte, and Legate
in Fraunce for the Sea Apoſtolique, was Preſident. *A-*
belard being heard ſpeake for himſelfe , and his booke
being read; that was condemned as heriticall, and appointed to be burnt in open market, and he the author
of it, was confined for euer into the Monaſtery of S. *Me-*
dard, and expreſſe charge giuen him not once to come
abroad. He had many ſchollers, whereof ſome were
become Cardinals, and were neere about Pope *Innocent*
the ſecond. Inſomuch, that by their intreatie, he found
means to be receiued again into the Monaſtery of Saint
Dennis; where again he plaid the foole, though he ſcapt
puniſhment for it . Thus he continued, till at laſt , hee
had leaue of the king to withdraw himſelfe into Cham-
paigne, and there he built an Oratory, which he dedicated to the trinitie, rather for reuenge, then deuotion,
that he might ſet himſelfe againſt them that had condemned his booke . But percerceiuing that it diſpleaſed the Prelates, and that he brought himſelfe into
danger to be cenſured againe, he changed his name into *Paraclet* (which ſignifies Comforter) a name particularly conſecrated to the holy Ghoſt : meaning, that
this place had beene the Hauen of his comfort, after he
had paſt many tempeſts and ſtormes. Which againe
offended our Church; as he himſelfe confeſſeth. For although all Churches, (as I gather out of of him) had
beene conſecrated in the name of the Father, of the Son,
and of the holy Ghoſt : yet there neuer was any conſecrated

crated to God the father, to God the Sonne, or to the
blessed Spirit. To this obiection, he being a great Sophister, aunswered, that if Saint *Paule* to the Corinths,
commaunded that euery man should build in himselfe
a spirituall Temple to the holy Ghost, no man should
thinke ill of it, that he had made a materiall temple. In
this place, as he that sought for nothing but nouelties,
he opened publique schooles of Philosophie and Diuinitie. Whereof many schollers, that were curious, being aduertised, they left the Townes to come to
him, and to stay with him, building themselues little
Lodges and Cels, where they lay vpon the straw : *et pro
delicatis cibis* (saith he) *herbis agrestibus, & pane pro cibario
vtebatur.* This indeed was, for him to set vp a new Sect,
who had beene condemned by the Church and Vniuersitie. The preachers declaimed against him, as a principall heretique, that displeased by his meanes, the
Lords Temporall and Spirituall : but aboue all other,
Saint *Bernard* tooke this quarrell in hand, as we see in
his Epistles. For perceiuing, that notwithstanding the
sentence of condemnation giuen by the Councell,
Abelard continued opinionatiue in the teaching of his
error, vnder the shadow of supports, and fauours he had
in the Court of Rome, writing to Cardinall *Yues. Dam-*
*natus est Suessione, cum opere suo, coram Legato Romanæ
ecclesiæ, sed quasi non sufficeret illi, illa condemnatio iterum
facit, vnde iterum damnetur, & iam nouissimus error pe-
ior est priore. Sequutus est tamen, quoniam Cardinales
& Clericos Curiæ se discipulos habuisse gloriatur, & eos in
defensione præteriti & præsentis erroris adsumit, à quibus iudicari timere debuit, & damnari.* And further :
*Magister Petrus Abelardus, sine regula Monachus, sine
solicitudine Prælatus, nec ordinem tenet, nec ab ordine tene-*
*tur. Homo sui dissimilis est, intus Herodes, foris Ioannes,
totus ambiguus, nihil habens de Monacho, præter nomen
& habitum.* And writing to Pope *Innocent* the second.
Habemus

Bern. Epist.
193.

Habemus in Francia nouum, de vtere Magistro, Theolo-
gum, qui ab ineunte ætate sua, in arte Dialectica lusit, &
nunc in scripturis sanctis insanit. Olim damnata & sopita
dogmata, tam sua videlicet, quàm aliena suscitare conatur,
insuper & noua addit. Qui dum omnium quæ sunt in cœlo
sursum, & quæ sunt in terra deorsum, nihil præter nescio quid
nescire dignatur, ponit in cœlo os suum, & scrutatur alta Dei,
rediensq; ad nos refert verba ineffabilia, quæ non licet homini
loqui. ET DVM PARATVS EST DE OM-
NIBVS REDDERE RATIONEM, &
contra rationem præsumit & contra fidem. Quid enim magis
contra rationem, quam rationē transcendere? Et quid magis
contra fidē, quam credere nolle quicquid non possis ratione at-
tingere? Deniq; exponere volens illud Sapientis: Qui credit
citò leuis est corde. Citò credere (inquit) est adhibere fidē ante
rationem. Cùm hoc Salomon non de fide in Deum, sed de
mutua inter nos dixerit credulitate. Nam illam quæ in Deu-
um est fidem, B. Papa Gregorius plane negat habere meri-
tum, si ei humana ratio præbeat experimentum. Laudat au-
tem Apostolos quod ad vnius iussionis vocem, sequuti sint Re-
demptorem. Scit nimirum pro laude dictum: in auditu au-
ris obediunt mihi: Increpatos è regione discipulos quod tardi-
us credidissent. Denique laudatur Maria quod rationem
fide præuenit: & punitur Zacharias, quod fidem ratione
tentauit. Et rursum commendatur Abraham qui contra se
in spem credidit. At contra Theologus noster: Quid (inquit)
ad doctrinam loqui proficit, si quod docere voluimus & ex-
poni, exponi non potest vt intelligatur.

Doth not Saint *Bernard* heare bring proces for our
new Iesuits, when by their naturall reasons they prooue
and disproue, *pro & conta* concerning the Dietie? Saint
Bernard (I say) whom in this the Archbishop of Reims
followed, and the Bishops of Soissons, Challons, and
Arras, who in the end of their letters, write thus to the
Pope: *Qui ergo homo ille multitudinem trahit post se, &*
populum qui sibi credat, habet, necesse est vt huic contagio,

B b. *celeri*

celeri remedio occurratis. In the end, Pope *Innocent* in-
terposed his decretall sentence in these words : *Commu-*
nicato fratrum nostrorum Episcoporum & Cardinalium
consilio, destinata nobis à vestra discretione, capitula, & vni-
uersa ipsius Petri dogmata, sanctorum Canonum authoritate,
cum suo authore damnauimus, eiq̃ tanquam hæretico perpe-
tuum silentium imposuimus. Vniuersos autem erroris sui
sectatores & defensores, à fidelium consortio sequestrandos,
excommunicationisque vinculo innodandos esse censemus.

Fon. ca. 36.

The Iesuits say, that *Pasquier* impiously accuseth
Maldonat the Iesuit, of impietie, (these are the words
they vse) because in one of his Lectures, he had proued
to his schollers by naturall reasons, that there is a God,
in another, that there is none. And they themselues
are wholly heretiques, by the proposition they maintaine, when as thinking by the wings of their wits, to
lift themselues vp aboue Heauen, they fall downe
into the bottomlesse pit of Hell; or else Pope *Innocent*
the second, Saint *Bernard*, and our whole Church of
Fraunce, are deceiued. But because this is not the marke
I ayme at, my intent being onely to examine, the like-
nes and vnlikenes, that was betwixt *Ignace* and his fellowes vpon the one part, and *Abelard* that great heretique and disturber of our Vniuersitie of Paris, on the
other: I will put you in mind, that both the one and o-
ther, came of great and noble houses. The difference be
tween them was, that *Abelard* was the eldest of his brethren, *Ignace* the yongest : he learned, & of a great spirit,
Ignace vtterly ignorant of all good learning. Thence it
came, that the one would violently set vp his Sect like
a Lion ; and thereby sunke vnder the waight of his
hope : the other like a Foxe, who by that meanes,
enlarged his.

But if you take away these differences, they were very
like in many other things. *Abelard* writ a booke of the
Trinitie, which was condemned by the Church, *Ignace*
made

made another of the same matter, which he himselfe condemned; shewing himselfe therein more wise and aduised then the other; *Abelard* without any degree of licence, would needs at the first marry himselfe to the Chair, to read in the Vniuersity of Paris. The very same thing did, not *Ignace*, who was a meere ignorant fellow, but his followers, the Iesuits. So that you shal neuer find, any one of their first Regents which read in the Vniuersity of Paris, to be a Graduate. *Abelard*, being a religious person of the Abbey of S. *Dennis*, taught both Philosophie and Diuinitie: the verie same that our religious Iesuits do. The Vniuersitie at that time tooke it ill, that Philosophie was read by a Munke, to forraine schollers and strangers: and it is also one of the principal articles of controuersy with the Iesuits. *Abelard* read Diuinitie without any degree of licence, whereof the Vniuersitie complaind to the Prelats of Fraunce, yet did he nothing which the Iesuits did not afterward, and do euen to this day: and it is one of the principall complaints of the Vniuersity against them. *Abelard*, was condemned by our Church of France: *Ignace* & his fellowes, first by the facultie of Diuinitie in Paris, afterward, by our Church assembled at Poissy. *Abelard*, brought in the heresie, to proue that by natural reasons, which depends vpon our Christian faith: the Iesuits, not only follow this damnable opinion, but maintaine that he is an Athiest, & impious, who beleeues in God with all humility, & likes not that a man should by naturall reasons, proue to boyes, that there is a God, & that there is none. *Abelard*, was greatly supported in the Court of Rome by Cardinals; and that is it, which spoiles vs at this day. For the Iesuits finding all fauour there, abuse it, and call all the heretiques that rely not vpon their heresies. *Abelard*, was a religious, not religious, hauing indeed, nothing of a religious but the habit: Which gaue Saint *Bernard* occasion to say, that hee was, *Sine ratione Monachus, qui nec ordinem*

tenebat,

tenebat, nec tenebatur ab ordine. I pray you tell me what order the Iesuits keepe, and by what order they are held. True it is, that *Abelard* was in his habit religious, and these men know not what it meanes. Saint *Bernard* said, that *Abelard* represented *Iohn Baptist* outwardly, and inwardly *Herode*. As for our Iesuits, I neuer could acknowledge any thing of Saint *Iohn* Baptist in their sermons, but much of *Herode* in their cruelties, to make Princes be murthered, and to driue them out of their Realmes and Dominions. Yet there is one difference, for these fellowes liue fat and faire, and are not bound by their constitutions to keepe extraordinarie fasts, as other orders doe: contrariwise, *Abelards* schollers and followers, lay vpon the straw in little cabins, and for their dyet, contented themselues with bread and hearbs.

To conclude, *Abelard* tooke to himselfe apart, the great and holy name of *Paraclet*, for which he was condemned by our Diuines: and with a like zeale, the Iesuits haue taken the name of Iesus, which was forbidden the. The conclusion was alike, for notwithstanding the mislike of our Prelats, the name *Paraclet* remaines yet to *Abelards* Oratory, which at this day by a corrupt name we call *Paraclt*; and it is a house of Nuns, whereof *Heloise*, *Abelards* wife, was the first Abbesse: in like sort the name Iesus continueth with the Iesuits, that they may in all points enioy *Abelards* priuiledges. And in my opiniõ, there is not any one of them, that hath hit righter vpon their agreement with *Abelard*, then he that in the yeere 1594. defended the Colledge of Clairmont. Who, when *Arnault*, had freshly obiected against them in a full Court of Parliament, the name & quality of a Iesuit, answered in scorne, that, that obiection, had beene made against them before, by Master *Stephen Pasquier*, and that it was out of date. One thing onely is wanting in this generall corespondence of *Abelard* with our
Iesuits;

Iesuits; namely, such a worthy personage as S. *Bernard,* to be a meanes to the holie Sea, against these new trou-blers of our Church, and our Vniuersities. For when I speake of him, I dare be bold to say, that God did spread in his hart, the beames and rayes of his holy Spirit, as much & more then in any man that liued since his time.

CHAP. 8.

¶ That the Iesuit giues himselfe licence to bring into his
Colledge children, out of the bosoms of their
Fathers and Mothers, without
theyr leaue.

S the Iesuits put euery peece of holie scripture in practise, not for maintenance of our Church, but onely of their sect, so doe they maintaine, that they may drawe all children to them, whether theyr Fa-thers & Mothers wil or no, (their consent being a thing not necessarie) for the loue and honour of God. Thys rule they put in practise very religiously vppon all chyl-dren of good Houses, or at least, vpon as many as by a-ny means they may lay hold on. Among whō, hauing conuayed away out of sight a youth, of 15. yeeres old, the eldest sonne of *Airault,* Lieuetenant criminel in the siege Presidiall of Angers, a man of especiall reckning. He put vp a supplication to the Court of Parliament of Paris, that his sonne might be restored to him.

The parties being heard at large, the Court tooke or-der by an act of the 20. of May, 1586. that a commission should be graunted him, to informe himselfe of the in-ticements vsed by the Iesuits to his son : & in the meane while, inhibitions & restraints were sent, to the Prouin-ciall, Rector, and Principall of the Colledges of Clair-mont, forbidding them to attempt any thing to the pre-iudice of the supplication presented by *Airault,* or to re-

Bb 3   ceiue

ceiue his sonne into theyr Societie, vppon paine of a-
mends : and it was farder enioyned them, to giue knowledge of this act, to the other Colledges of their Societie.

This notwithstanding, these holy Fathers would not
deliuer the youth againe, so that the poore Father vvas
faine to comfort himselfe, first with his teares, and then
with his penne, by writing and printing a booke of the
power of a Father, wherein hee shewed, that it was impudently to abuse the holy Scripture, to take them raw-
lie, according to the Letter onely, as the Iesuits did, to
the disaduantage of Fathers. He spake like an honest &
worthy man, as hee that felt no small griefe, for the stealing away of his sonne. I will speake without passion, &
say, that it is a hard thing, that the child should enter into orders of religion, against the will of his Father and
Mother, of whō himselfe is a good part. And yet I think
it not onely excusable, but commendable, when beeing
of a competent age, a man betakes himselfe to a Monasterie, though his Father and mother consent not to it :
but when these things are carried by the crafty conuey-
ance of Munks, the matter deserues extraordinarie punishment.

A fewe yeeres since, there was great blame lay'd vpon the Charter-house Munks of Paris, for hauing without the Fathers knowledge, receiued a young man into
their Order, The Prior being sent for about the matter,
by the Court of Parliament, maintaind with a wonderfull resolution, that hee was not bound to turne him a-
way. We goe not to seeke them (quoth he) we liue a solitarie life, seuerd from the Towne, within the Towne :
we allure them not to vs by Lectures or by conferences.
Yea, contrariwise, wee make expresse profession of silence, and they of our order, speake to no man without
leaue of their Superiour. If any man of ripe age, moued
by the grace of the holy Ghost, be desirous to become

one

one of our Order, why should wee goe to procure any others good will, whom wee know from his infancie by the instinct of nature, not to be disposed to such deuotion. This were to enuie God a goodly sacrifice, readie to be offered to him, and wee should be coutned traytors to the generall good of the Church, if wee should deale otherwise.

The Court hauing heard his defence, dismist him, without pressing him any further, which they did not on the behalfe of the Iesuits, in *Airaults* case. You shall vnderstand hereafter the reasons of this diuersitie. Surelie, if wishing might preuaile in such matters, I could desire, that all children, before they make theselues Munks, would followe the example of *Elizeus*, who would not become seruaunt to *Elias*, till hee had taken his leaue of his Father. Which if perhaps they doe not, beeing not won to that course but by themselues, through the inspiration of God, I doe not thinke (I will say it yet once againe,) that a man can blame them, or the Monasterie that receiues them. But for the Iesuit, the matter stands quite otherwise; and I remember, that I was one day with a poore Father enraged, who, hauing his sonne stolne & caried away, letting loose the reines to his choller, with a troubled minde, spake on this manner to the Rector of the Iesuits in Paris. I did not commit my son to thee to make a Iesuit of him, but to instruct him in humane learning, that hee might not stray from our Catholique religion, with intent to make him heyre of my will, of my goods, and of my estate, supposing that thou hadst some religion in thee. But where hast thou found (thou lewd fellowe) that it is permitted thee, by auricular confession, by a counterfeit deuotion, by hypocriticall speeches, to seduce my poore child, to steale him frō himselfe, to steale him from his Father, to steale him from GOD? For why should I not call it, stealing from God, when as for the first worke of his deuotion,

thou

thou teacheſt him, to ſteale himſelfe from his Father? An innocent I may call him, to whom by reaſon of the weakenes of his age, and vnderſtanding, thou haſt giuen no leyſure to bethinke himſelfe in conuenient time, of that which he hath promiſt to God, by making a vowe to liue a Munks life. Thou Iugler in matters of Chriſtian religion, which playeſt tricks of paſſe and repaſſe, to make a child paſſe, by inuiſibilities, (it is, it is not,) to the end thou maiſt withdraw him, both frō his Fathers preſence, and alſo frō the Magiſtrats. And when thou haſt thus done, thou haſt vp thy generall prouerbe, Theſe be the works of thy holy ſpirit; whom thou haſt alwaies in thy mouth, as harlots are alwaies prating of their chaſtitie.

Dooſt thou thinke (thou wretch) though my firſt proiect was to bring him vp in mine owne calling, yet if after he was come out of thy houſe, and come to yeeres of diſcretion, he would haue forſaken the world, that I would haue enuied him that felicitie? Not to make him a Gypſie, to rogue about as thou dooſt all ouer the world, feyning that hee can tell euery man his fortune, whē he cannot tell his own: but to frame him after the mould of our auncient orders of religion, and at once to ſhut him vp in a Cloyſter, there to leade a ſolitarie lyfe, to giue himſelfe to faſting and prayer, to weare hayrecloth, & ſo to behaue himſelfe, that his Cloyſter ſhould be a Pallace to him, fiſh as Manna from heauen, and hayre-cloth, more ſoft then the fineſt Holland ſhirt of Linnen.

And, that after hee had employed his ſolitarineſſe in long watchings, and deuotions, hee might come out of his Cloyſter, as a worthy and valiant warriour, not to murder Kings, not to conquer Realmes, and to ſel them to him that would offer moſt, but to kill ſinne, to ſubdue diſordered ſoules, by preaching in the midſt of the churches, that which appertaines to euerlaſting bleſſedneſſe.

nesse. I call not to the Iudges of this world, for reuenge of this wrong, thou detestable coosner, the great Iudge of Iudges shall be my auenger, euen then, when after he hath chastizd the Magistrate, either for his feare, or for his long winking at thy lewdnes, he shall cast thee into the fire, as the Father doth the rod, when he hath beaten his childe there-with.

I saw a poore Father, in the Iesuits Colledge in Paris, play hys part in this sort : and to say the truth, I coulde haue wished, that the good olde man, had some-what brideled his choller, which me thought past the bounds of modestie : but what modestie can a man looke for in a Father, that hath his sonne stolne from him ? There is no remedie, but he must needes be out of patience. In a worde, consider I pray you the first griefe of a poore desolate Father, who complaines not that his sonne is become a religious person, but that it is wrought by the Iesuits seducing, alluring, and coosning.

Did you neuer heare it sayde, that it is a great burden to our conscience, when wee marry our Chyldren vnder age, because it is to teach them to hate theyr vviues, before they can vnderstand what it is to loue them ? So stands the case with these young youths, enticed to this spirituall marriage. For howe soeuer at theyr first entraunce, euery thing laughs vppon them, by reason of the charmes and sweet entertainment of theyr ghostlie Fathers, yet afterward, there settles an imperfection in theyr mindes, of a long repentance for their hastinesse : and they fall to curse the yere, the month, the weeke, the day, the houre, and the moment, in which they were so deceiued. And if there be any that scape this repentance, alas they are very few.

To conclude, as long as wee mingle the bringing vp of our youth with this pretended Munkerie, wee shall neuer be able to saue our selues from this vnhappy confusion, wherof the Cittie of Paris, (thankes be to God)

Cc. is

is at this day difcharged. But I fpeake to them, who being coozned, protect, as yet, this new monfter with their authoritie.

CHAP. 9.

¶ Of the vow of the Iefuits, which they call the simple vow.

Ntending to entreate now from henceforward, of the Iefuits fimple vowe, I heere vow, not to deale with them, but at their owne weapons. They haue bin alwaies hetherto fo cunning that fewe men haue had any knowledge of theyr dealings. Their Bulls and their ftatuts are, to this day, printed within their Colledges, fo that no man knowes the Printers name, neither can they eafily com into any ftrangers hands: which hath beene the caufe, that no man heeretofore, durft fpeake fo boldly of them. But as the force of truth is fuch, that in time it wil be difcouerd, fo the Caball of thefe Rabbines, could not be kept fo fecret, but that in tract of time, their bookes haue gotten out of their Colledges, vpon which I haue framed thys prefent difcourfe. I will begin with their fimple vowe, a vow, which I may fay is new, and monftrous, and which cannot be tollerated in our Church, without the ouerthrowing thereof, at the leaft in regard of religious Orders and Monafteries.

By the Lecture which the Iefuit read vs yefterday, you vnderftand, that the firft vow of their Order, is that which they call the fimple vow, by which, hee that will vow himfelfe to their Societie, makes at the firft the 3. ordinarie vowes of all other religious Orders, namelie, of Chaftitie, Pouertie, and Obedience. And although, in refpect of himfelfe, hee may not after this vow, giue ouer his profefsion, yet is it in the power of the General,

when

when he will to difmiffe him, though hee haue beene a
Iefuit 25. yeeres : and, which is more, as long as he goes
no farder then this fimple vow, he is capable of all inheritances direct and collaterall , notwithstanding the
vowe of pouertie hee hath made. Let vs not detract any
thing from the honour due to the one and to the other,
but let vs fee what difcourfe *Montaignes* hath made of
thefe matters.

By this difcourfe (faith he, fpeaking to *Arnault*) two
lyes that you haue made fhal be refuted; The one is, that
no man euer makes this vow of pouertie, but that thereby all hope of fucceffion is loft. For it is made in the end
of the Nouicefhip, as hath been faid. Now, if notvvith-
ftanding this vow of Pouertie , they retaine fometimes
for many yeeres the proprietie of their goods , by theyr
Superiors leaue, and are capable of inheritances, be not
offended thereat, neither call the Iefuits couetous therefore. For this retayning , is not for them who haue renounced this right, as I faid before, but for the benefite
and commoditie of thofe, that are vnder theyr gouernment. For if it fhould chaunce, that vpon iuft caufe they
were to be difmift out of the Societie, according to the
priuiledges thereof, they fhoulde thereby receiue no
wrong, but bee able to liue of themfelues : whereas o-
therwife, beeing depriued thereof, they fhould be driuen eyther to begge, or to continue in the Societie, not
onely to the hurt and preiudice thereof, but alfo to the
endangering of their owne bodies, yea and theyr foules
to.

It is a nevve Lavve (you will fay,) true. It is new and
vvonderfull, fayth the great Canonift *Nauarre*. It is a
new Lawe, as alfo the fimple vow of Chaftitie is, which
this Societie makes, vvhich hinders marriage to be contracted, and difanuls it after it is contracted. But it ceafeth not to be right, by beeing newe, as long as it is ratified by the Prince and head of the Church, who made

Montag. ca. 50. de la verite defendue.

C c 2.   the

the Lawes of other religious Orders, and the reſt of the Canon Law.

The newnes of a thing, hinders not the nature of it. The newe Raiſins are Raiſins, as wēll as thoſe of the Vine that *Noe* planted. All right was nevve in the beginning, and yet ceaſt not thereby to be right. Sixteene hundred yeeres hence, this will bee more auncient then the Canons of the Apoſtles are at this day, which were as young fifteene hundred yeeres a goe, as this is now. The other lye, which is alſo refuted by this diſcourſe, is, that the Ieſuits caſt men off, when they are ſpent with trauaile. For as they are not retayned for hope of theyr goods, ſo are they not caſt off by reaſon of theyr pouertie, but for ſome other iuſt cauſe. Otherwiſe, at the laſt, they muſt needes diſmiſſe all that make profeſsion, becauſe they are depriued of all their goods; and they ſhould receiue none that is not rich, neither of which they doe.

If there be any of ſo obſtinate a nature, that he wil not be amended, after that he hath beene lookt to, and medicind a long time, it is reaſon that hee ſhould beare the puniſhment of his ſtubbornneſſe, and that the ſocietie ſhould vſe their right. VVhich notwithſtanding is not done but very ſildome, and that by the authoriue of the Generall onelie, and almoſt alwaies with the liking of them that are diſmiſt : whom we haue not ſo much emploied, as endured, and waited for their amendment, 10. and ſometimes 20. yeeres. With ſuch griefe of hart doe they vſe this remedie; and ſo deerely loue they the ſaluation of thoſe that are damageable to thē. And ſo it is plaine, that you are in all things altogether vniuſt to the Ieſuits, in ſlaũdering thē, that they ſeduce men, by receiuing thē into their ſociety, & diſmiſsing them out again.

Some man more ſcrupulous, & of better vnderſtanding then you, will demaund, vvith what conſcience they can be diſmiſt and abſolued, that haue once made

VOW

vow of religion, since the vow is a bond to God, which he onely can release, as a right belonging properly to him. To that I aunswere, that a vow binds, according to his intent that makes it. If any make a vow to fast after the order of the Chartehouse Munks, he binds himselfe to fast, as the Charterhouse Munks do, not as one of another order, who obserueth no such fast. They that make vowes in this Societie, make them according to the intent and fashion thereof; the intent is, that they should be in such sort bound to ahide in it, as that, when there shall be any iust occasion, they may be dismist, and acquited of their bond. Wherefore, hee that is bound, hath no wrong done him, if he be constrained to keepe his promise, or if hee be dismist, because he cannot, or will not doe his endeauour, to amend himselfe and accomplish it. For he hath made his vowe with such a condition, *& volenti non fit iniuria :* and he that forsakes the Societie without leaue, is an Apostata, and beares reproach, and the marke of his sinne. But he that departs, by the aduise, or good pleasure of his Generall, who thinks it meete, vpon some necessitie of minde or bodie, or of his parents, or for the publique good, or for some other iust cause, that hee should be licenced to giue ouer, is thereby absolued from his vowes.

CHAP. 10.

That it cannot be excused, but that there is heresie and Macchiauelisme in the Iesuits simple vow.

Hus much the Iesuit *Montaignes.* Now I instantly beseech our holy Father the Pope, and adiure all Kings, Princes, Potentates, and Lords, which fight vnder his banner in our militant Church, that they

they would open their eies, and euerie one particularly examine his conscience, for the good of our Christian world. With whom haue I here to do? with the Iesuits; who making aunswer to *Arnaults* Plea, would haue thought they had wrongd their holinesses, if according to the ordinary simplicity of others, they had intitled their discourse thus, *A defence against* Arnaults *Plea*; but with a proud title, they haue set on the front of their booke. *The truth defended for the Catholik religiõ, in the Iesuits cause, against the Plea of* Anthony Arnault. I take them at their word, & wil labour for the Catholike religion with them: there is nothing more commaunded vs by God & his Church, then the performance of our vowes. I should abuse both the time & my pen, if I would proue this by texts out of the old and new Testament, and by the authorities of the auncient Doctors of the Church, sith deuotion first brought into our Church, the orders of Religious Monasteries, by which wee enter the three substantiall vowes of Pouertie, Chastitie, and Obedience. This rule hath beene so strictly obserued, that the Pope himselfe, though hee haue fulnesse of power ouer our consciences, yet neuer gaue liberty to himselfe, to dispense wholly with a religious person; vnlesse it be in fauour of some soueraigne Prince, for the succouring of some verie vrgent necessitie in his estate. And our Lord being desirous to shew, that such dispensations please him not, sometimes interposes the rigour of iustice verie manifestly. That was seene long since in the Realme of Naples, where, when all the royall line was ended in *Constance*, who had beene a long time a professed Nun, the publique necessity seemed to claime, that she should be disuayld, that the blood royall might be renewed by her. She was absolued from her vow by the holy Sea, and presently married to the Emperour *Fredericke* the second, of which marriage, *Manfrey* was borne, and of

<u>him</u>

him *Conradin.* But neuer marriage brought greater ruine to Italy then this : becaufe the Pope and the Emperour were thereby in continuall diuifions vnder the
names of the Guelfes and Gibbilins, which lafted an infinite while. And as for the children that came thereof,
Manfrey was flaine in a pitcht field, & afterward, *Conradin* his fonne taken by *Charles* of Aniow, king of Naples, who caufd him to be beheaded vpon a fcaffold. I
haue purpofely toucht this example, to fhew how little
God likes thefe vnmunkings, what authoritie foeuer he
haue giuen to our holy father the Pope : who alfo hath
beene drawne thereto with an infinite number of re-
fpects, before he yeeld. But aboue all, it is a generall rule
in Rome, that in all other families not foueraigne, the
Pope neuer makes a religious man lay, but only chan-
ges the rigour of the firft vow, into an other more eafie
to beare; as we faw of late in this our country of France.
When as the Lord of Bouchage, comming of a verie
noble houfe, had made himfelfe a Capuchin, and that
after the death of all his bretheren, the neceffitie of the
time feemnig to call him again to worldly affairs, all that
his friends could obtaine at Rome, was, the chaunging
of his vow into that of Saint *Iohn* of Ierufalem. It was
neuer permitted, a religious man in our Church, that
had made the vowe of pouertie, to fucceed his parents : much leffe to be releaft out of his Monafterie
to enter againe into a fecular life. The Pope giues not
himfelfe this libertie.

And fhall wee fuffer in our Church, a religious Iefuit to fucceed, and his Generall to giue him leaue to
doo fo, when it pleafeth him ? *Dij talem terris auertite
poftem.* This is no priuiledge, this is a new monfter, Montaig.
which is brought into our Chriftian profeffion. For ca.50. & 51.
all this, the Iefuit thinkes to bee acquitted by God,
of this herefie; when hee faith, that there is no more
in anie vowe, then a man puts into it : hee fhould
say

say there is no more in the play. For by rendering this reason of simple vow, hee playes with God ; and is one of those scorners, of whom *Dauid* speaketh in in the first Psalme. In summe, the Iesuits would say, that there simple vow is a vow, of a pettie dissimulation, and that they thinke to deceiue God by the same Sophistrie, which the old Pagan vsed, when he said, *Iuraui lingua, mentem iniuratam habeo* : Which protestation, was condemned by them of the time, though they were not Christians. So saith that Iesuit, I vowed pouerty with my tongue, but in my mind I had a bird that sung an other song.

And thinking by this shift to make vs like of their new doctrine, hee playes three parts at once, the Iesuit, the Heretique, & the Macchiauelist. And whereas they say, that the great Canonist *Nauarre* calleth their simple vow, *Nouum & mirabile*. Saint *Bernard* reprouing *Abelards* heresie, said no lesse, that, *Ambulabat in magnis et in mirabilibus.*

CHAP. 11.

Of the Iesuits engaging the authoritie of the holy Sea, to excuse the heresie of their simple vow.

Vt these two priuiledges (saith *Montagnes*) are granted vs by the Head & Prince of the Church. See how these honest men wrong the authority of the holy Sea; and into what disorder they bring it , by making it a defence of their heresie. I will neuer abide, that this come to the ears of the enemies of our Church, but that withal, they shal vnderstand how al things haue past. The truth is, that before *Gregorie* 13. neuer any Pope was of aduise to grant them these priuiledges, and yet euer since the comming of *Ignace*, they haue practised

fed this simple vow, as we may see by the same *Gregories* Bull, 1 5 8 4. Whereupon euerie good Catholique will maintaine, that it was a new heresie brought in by them, against the holy and auncient decrees. Tell me honest men, what is become of the soules of your Saints *Ignatius Loiola, Iames Lainez, Frances Borgia,* & *Euerard Merouie*, the foure first Generals of your Sect? Where is *Frances Xauier*, that was canonized a Saint amongst the barbarous? Where is *Peter Faure, Nicholas Bobadilla* and *Pasquier Broet*? In briefe, where be the soules of all them of your Sect, that liued from the yeere 1540. vntill the yere 1584. and died in this heresie? In which yeere, you obtaind permission for the time, to come, not absolutiō for that which was past: so that it came too late, for thē that died before. In the meane while, we haue these for Maisters, & Lecturers of our youth in their Colledges, for holy fathers, & Diuines in our Church, to preach to vs. And yet, as profest heretiques, in steed of establishing againe our afflicted religion, by establishing their owne greatnes, they haue wholy ouerthrowne ours altogither: and haue had no other foundation of their heresie, but their owne detestable couetousnes.

This indeed might haue beene obiected against vs heretofore (will the Iesuit say) but not now, by reason of this new Bull. This answere at the first sight may seeme verie sufficient to stop our mouthes: but when you shall vnderstand how, at what time, and by what cunning it was gotten, you shall find nothing in it, but sauours of a Iesuit. They haue diuers vowes, but I find none so solemne, as that which I will presently declare to you; which is, to put in execution their deuises, be they good or euill, of their own priuate authoritie, without any respect had of the holy Sea: and when they haue a long time vsed this verie ill, they spy out occasions of troubles for the authorizing of that their practise, as men most necessarie for the maintenaunce of our religion.

Dd. gion.

gion. By doing wherof, they giue law to him, of whom
they make shew to receiue law. The fisherman fishes in
a troubled water, and the Iesuit in our troubles. In this
sort began their Societie, and after many refusals, was
confirmed by Pope *Paule* the third in the yeeres 1540.
and 43. in consideration of the troubles that were at
that time in Germanie, betwixt the Catholiques and
the Lutherans. In this sort they obtained of Pope *Pius*
the fourth, their great priuiledge, to disturbe the ancient
discipline of all Vniuersities, in the yeere 1561. That
is to say, when the troubles began to rise in Fraunce, betwixt the Catholique and Hugonot. The same was
practised by them in 84. when father *Claudius Ma-*
thew, their Prouinciall of France, stirred the humours of
Rome, not only against the Hugonots, but also against
the most Catholik King deceased, as if he had fauoured
them. And feeding Pope *Gregorie* with an infinite sort
of vaine hopes, they thought they might without daunger, pull of their maske, and get that approued by him,
which they neuer durst discouer to any Pope before,
namely, the dishonestie of their simple vow. In such sort,
that in Iune 1584. they obtaynd the confirmation of
this vow, and fiue moneths after, the deceased King
Henrie the third, who wanted not his spies, made a
Commission to be publisht in open Parliament, against
them that practised any league in straunge countries. If
there were nothing but the opposition of this time, it
were sufficient to deface the memorie of that Bull of
Pope *Gregorie*, and also many decretals of *Boniface* the
eight, which was a profest enemie to Fraunce.

But I haue yet stroger reasons on my side, for I see not
that any man thinks, that Pope *Gregorie* euer gaue any
sufficient consent thereto. And that it is so, after he hath
briefly discourst of the Nouiceship, he saith, that the religious making their first simple vow: *In Societatē cooptan-*
tur acquantū est ex parte ipsorū perpetuò, ex parte verò So-
cietatis

cietatis IVXTA APOSTOLICA INDVL-
TA, ET CONSTITVTIONES PRÆ-
DICTAS, tamdiu obligati sunt, quandiu Præpositus Ge-
neralis eos retinendos censuerit. Quod ad Societatis conser-
uationē maxime est necessariū, IDQVE AB ILLI-
VS EXORDIO PROVSVIM, & post, experi-
mento cōprobatum est. Idq̃; initio ingressus, illis explicitè mani-
festatur, atque ipsi conditionē hanc amplectuntur: quæ eis si
quos dimittere oporteat, multò est commodior, vt liberi potius,
quàm votis obligati dimittantur, aliisq̃; iustis & rationalibus
de causis. That is to say, that after the time of their Nouiceship, and when by vow they haue sworne Pouertie,
Chastitie, and Obedience, they are incorporated into
our Society, for as much as to theselues belongs, for the
whole terme of their life: but forasmuch as appertaines
to the Societie, according to the Apostolicall indults
and constitutions spoken of before, they are bound to
abide with vs so long, as it pleaseth the Generall to
retaine them. A matter verie necessarie for the preser-
uation of the Societie, and prouided for in the first beginning of this order, afterward, found to be very profitable by experience. And this is at euery mans first enterance, expresly made known to him, and he accepts the
condition; which is the more commodious for such as are
to be admitted, that whē theyshal be sent away, they may
depart acquitted & discharged of their vow, vpon some
iust and reasonable considerations. By this Article, you
learn not, that a religious person hauing made his simple
vow, may inherit: but that is supplied by an other that
followeth in these words: *Et licet qui ad gradus professorū*
& Coadiutorū formatorum nondū peruenerunt, bonorū suo-
rum iis atq̃; dominium, tum alias ab iustas causas, tum etiam
vt maiorē habeat Societas libertatē, illos si opus fuerit remit-
tēdi, & cum minori offensione dimittēdi. And although (saith
the Latine) that they which are not yet come to the degree of those that are professed, and of formed coadiu-

tors, may poſſeſſe their goods & demaines, for many
waighty reaſons, eſpecially, that the Societie may haue liberty, to turne them out again, if it ſhal be needful, & diſmiſſe thē with the leſſe ſcruple, or doubt of conſcience.
Out of theſe two Articles you may gather; Firſt, that it
is permitted to the General to abſolue his religious from
their ſimple vow, whenſoeuer it pleaſe him, and to ſend
him backe to his owne houſe, freed and acquitted from
his vow. Secondly, that this religious man, may poſſeſſe
tēporall goods, which clauſe they haue ſtretched to ſuc-
ceſſions, as you ſee in *Montaignes*. Thirdly, that ſince the
beginning of their order, they haue vſed to do ſo. And
laſtly, that *Gregory* hath cōſirmd theſe two priuiledges to
thē, according to the grants that before were made thē,
& their conſtitutions. I wil make this controuerſie very
plaine. Let vs run ouer the Buls, that they had obtained
before, there is not any one wherein you ſhall finde, that
their Generall was permitted, to diſmiſſe them, when he
would, or they to inherit during their ſimple vow. There
are 23. of thē, thoſe of Pope *Paul* the 3.1540.43.45.46.
49. Thoſe of *Iulius* his ſucceſſor, 50. & 52. of *Pius* 4.61.
of *Pius* 5. 65. 68.71. in March & Iuly, of *Gregory* 13.72.
73.75. in Ianuary & May 76. in February, Iuly, October
December 78. in Ianuary & May. There is no mention
in any of theſe, either for diſtinguiſhing, or for inheriting
or poſſeſſing of goods. All theſe Buls haue beene printed
by them, in one volume, that of 84. is inſerted at large
in the ſummary of Buls, gathered by *Mathew Toſcan*
and in *Ribadiner*, in the third booke of *Ignace* life, Chap.
23. If they pretend that they haue any other, let them
ſhew them, becauſe, where none are ſhewen, it is preſumed there are none. If I haue proued as I haue, that in
all the former Buls, there is neuer a word ſpoken of theſe
two priuiledges, the truth is, that by theſe laſt Buls, they
haue circumuented the religious care of the holy Sea: as
they did before, in the yeere, 1 5 6 1. when to diſturbe all
the

the auncient customes of the Vniuersities, they gaue
Pope *Pius* to vnderstand, that, that which hee granted
them, was but a confirmation of a grant made to them
by *Iulius* the 3. This then was a cooznage, obreption,
and surreption, and consequently, there is no reckning
to be made of this Bull of 84. I am of opinion with thē,
(GOD forbid that I should steale away any part of the
truth frō them in this matter, or in any other) that in their
constitutions, there is speech that the Generall may dismisse when he wil. But Pope *Gregory* put in his permission, not onely in consideration of these constitutions,
but of the former Apostolique graunts, which notwithstanding cannot be found. For a simple constitution of
their Order, would neuer haue beene sufficient to make
Pope *Gre.*cōsent to the infringing of all the ancient constitutions of the Church, in fauour of these new people.

*Part. 2. de
const. ca. 4.
art. 3. &
form exam.
ca.6.art. 8.
& c. 7. art.1.*

I acknowledge also, that, as for this poynt, the Nouices, when they entred into the course of Iesuitisme,
were not ignorant of it : For 4. or 5. dayes after that the
Nouice entreth into the house of Nouiceship, there to
accomplish his two yeeres of probation, the Exami-
ners are charged to deliuer to him all their letters Apostolick, theyr Statuts, and Constitutions ; yea, the generall examination that is to be made of him : to the end,
that hee may informe him-selfe of the weight of the
burden hee must beare ; vvhen hee shall bee admitted
into this Order, and that hee may not haue any ground
to repent himselfe afterward. Now sith it may be found
by their constitutions, that theyr Generall is permitted
to absolue the religious from theyr simple vow, whensoeuer he will, and sith these constitutions are imparted
to them, it cannot be sayd, that they are ignorant of this
priuiledge of their General ; and a man may say of them
in this regard, as the Iesuit *Montaignes* doth, *volenti non
fit iniuria* : if so be that this permission be lawfull to be
admitted into our Christian Church, and that *Gregorie*

*Const. part.
3. c. 4. art. 5.*

D d 3.   was

was not coozned in grauting it to the Iesuitish Church.

But for the second priuiledge, whereby the religious is permitted, during the simple vow, to inherit and posfesse temporall goods, not onely there is nothing for it in theyr auncient Bulls, but also, not in any of theyr conftitutions : Yea, all things fight against this intention. At the entrance into this Order, they are bound to make a vow, both particularly and generally, of Pouertie, say the Bulls of *Paule* the third, 1 5 4 0. and those of *Iulius*, 1 5 5 0. And because that perhaps may require a more precife explication, they expreffe it at large in the 4. c. of their generall Examination, where they enioyne them, as I said ere-while, to difpose, not onely of the goods that they haue in poffeffion, but also of thofe, which they haue no otherwife but in hope. *Debent omnia bona fua temporalia quæ habuerint diftribuere & renunciare, ac difponere de his quæ ipfis obuenire poffent.* They muft (fayth the Latine) renounce all the temporall goods they haue, & diftribute them; and likewife difpofe of all that hereafter may fall to them.

You fhall note by the way, thys wife refolution of the Iefuit, who appoynts, that he, which will enter into this order, fhall difpofe of goods which hee hath not. They are commaunded to giue their goods for almes to the poore, and not to leaue them to their kindred, to renounce all loue they beare them, euen that which is due to their Fathers and Mothers, and all this is, to the end they may take from them, all mind of returning to their Fathers houfes. *Vt ad parentes & confanguineos recurrendi, & ad inutilem ipforum memoriam, firmius & ftabilius in fua vocatione perfeuerēt.* That the way to returne to their kindred, and the needleffe remembrance of them, may be ftopt, and they may perfeuer the more firme & ftable in theyr calling.

In the conclufion of all this, they haue no sooner abandoned all their goods, during the firft yeere of theyr

Cap. 4. de Examin. art. 42.

Nouice-

Nouiceſhip, but that they are permitted, after their vow
of pouertie, to be heyres vnto them whom they were cōmaunded to forget, yea the loue and memory of them.
Therefore I conclude, that this priuiledge, for him to in-
herite that hath made the vow of Pouertie, is firſt againſt
the holy decrees of God, and of his Church. Secondly,
againſt common ſence. Thirdly, grounded vppon two
inexcuſable and very manifeſt lyes, The one , when it is
ſuppoſed by the Bull , that their Conſtitutions permit
them to inherit, during theyr Simple vow , The other,
when according thereto, they giue their Nouices to vnderſtand, that they may inherit after they haue made the
ſimple vow. For contrariwiſe, all theyr Conſtitutions
gaine-ſay it in very plaine termes. Turne therefore and
wind this Bul of *Gregory* which way you wil, there is nothing in it, that engages the holy Sea in fauour of them.

I confeſſe freely, that when the Ieſuit *Montaignes* alleaged, that the Prince & head of the Church, had permitted them this vnhappy vowe, I beganne to tremble,
weighing with my ſelfe, of what conſequence this permiſſion was to all Chriſtendome : but when I had ſatis-
fied my ſelfe by reading the Bull, ô impudent coozners,
(quoth I then) who draw in the holy Sea for warrant of
your impietie. Did euer any man ſet the popedom for
a fairer mark then this, againſt our aduerſaries ? I would
not wiſh any other thing in their hands then this, to try-
umph ouer vs , if it were true. This is the charitie that
you honeſt men , which preach nothing but charitie,
ſhew, to the deſolation of the holy Sea , of which you
make ſhew to be the only Protectors. And yet, if Pope
Gregorie had otherwiſe made this grant, then to gratifie
you at that time, when you promiſt nothing leſſe, then
to giue Lawes to all ſoueraigne Princes, and to the
Pope himſelfe, I would not ſeeke to preuaile againſt
his Bull, eyther by the auncient liberties of our famous
Church of Fraunce, which cannot beare in Fraunce
ſuch

such extraordinary permissions, or by the maiesty of our Kings, the Defenders of our liberties, or by the authoritie of our Parliaments vnder them, to which the maintenaunce of the Ecclesiasticall discipline apperraines. And much lesse would I aduise, to appeale to a generall Councell to be held hereafter, as our ancient French were wont to doe in such affayres. Neither would I stir vp the faithfull care of all generall Proctors of Parliaments to appeale, as from abuses, from the thundring of this Bull : which were the shortest way.

God forbid that I should furnish the world with presidents that might be preiudiciall to the holy Sea. But if this great Pope were aliue, I would cast my selfe at his feete, and appeale from him to himselfe, & beseech him in all humilitie, that it would please him to cōsider, whether by his absolute power, he be able to make two contraries agree in the same subiect; that cōtrarie to the law of God, a man should lodge riches in pouertie : so that, in this article it should seeme, that both Gods law, and cōmon sence is forgotten. I would farder beseech him to consider, whether it were his meaning to giue such a permission, as he giues not to himselfe, and to graunt without exception, that thing to the Generall of the Iesuits, in which the Popes neuer dispence with thēselues : and that without regard of the vow of Pouertie, Chastitie, & Obedience, to which the religious are bound, the Generall of their order, might absolue them when it pleased him ?

Moreouer, I would shew him, that the Monasticall vowes, which one makes to God, ought to be simple : but not according to the new learning of the Iesuits, but to the auncient doctrine of Christians. And that as whē of old time in Rome, one past from one Familie to another by adoption, it was to be pure, simple, and without any condition ; so by greater reason, when wee forsake our carnall Fathers, to be adopted a new into the

family

familie of our spirituall Father, the Father of Fathers, we
ought to enter purely and simply, & not to bring in the
Foxe-like craftines of the Iesuits simple vow. Manie o-
ther particularities I could shewe him, which I remit to
the examination of our Diuinitie, both scholasticall &
morrall. I will content my selfe onely for the present, to
say, that all these demonstrations, should be superfluous,
because Pope *Gregory* neuer consented to this vow, but
was deceiued and coozned by the Iesuits false information : whereas nothing is so contrary to consent as error.

CHAP. 12.

¶ That besides the heresie which is in the Iesuits simple
vow, there is also in it a manifest
cooznage.

I Cannot stay my selfe heere, when I see
these hypocrits raigne in our Church, &
seeke to giue lawes to all faithful Christians : and yet sometimes it is not necessarie to make a generall change, but a reformation from good to better. And therefore, when it
was demaunded of the Oracle, which was the best Religion, hee aunswered, The auncientest. Beeing asked a-
gaine which was the auncientest, he answered, The best.
Intending to teach vs, that we are not to reiect all newe
things, when they are warranted by good & strong reasons.

The Iesuit *Montaignes*, to shew that there is no cause
why we should feare the noueltie of theyr simple vow,
tells vs, that 1600. yeeres hence, it wil be more auncient
then the Canons of the Apostles are now. Wherein hee
flouts both God and the world. For the same may be
alleaged, in defence of the erronious doctrine of *Luther*,
which is ancienter then that of *Ignace*, by three or foure
and twentie yeres : and of all the other, who in our time

E e   haue

haue gone aſtray from the auncient way of the Church. I finde not fault in the ſimple vowe, with the noueltie thereof, although that be much to be feared in matter of Religion, and eſpecially of the Catholique Apoſtolicke Romane religion; of which a man may truly ſay :

Moribus antiquis res ſtat Romana, viriſq;
Romes ſtate doth ſtand on ancient men & manners.

I onely finde fault with the hereſie that is in this noueltie, which cannot be amended by length of time. *Veritati præſcribere nemo poteſt, non ſpatium temporum, non patrocinia perſonarum, non priuilegium regionum.* No bodie (ſaith *Tertullian*) can poſſibly preſcribe vnto the truth, neither diſtance of times, nor patronage of perſons, nor priuiledge of Countries. Let vs then conſider the reaſons, by which the Ieſuits would giue a paſport to the noueltie of theyr ſimple vow. *Montaignes* rendering the reaſon, for which it is permitted the Ieſuit religious to enherit and enioy goods, for all the vow of pouertie made by him, ſaith thus; Becauſe it may come to paſſe, that, after ten or twentie yeres, the Ieſuit that ſhall be found incorrigible, may be diſmiſt by the Generall of our Order, and beeing ſent home againe, wee are deſirous ſo to deale by chriſtian charity, that he may haue no occaſion to beg. Beſides, wee vſe not this chaſtiſement but very ſildome, and almoſt alwaies with the liking of them that are diſmiſt. And truly this is a very charitable reuenge.

In other Orders of Religion, if any religious perſon behaue himſelfe diſorderly, ſometimes he is diſciplind openly in the Chapter-houſe, ſometimes he is made to faſt with bread & water in a darke priſon, more or leſſe, according to his deſerts, that he may ſerue for an example to his Brethren. By ſo dooing; without ouerthrowing the auncient vow of our Catholique religion, and making things ſcandalous, that is drawne frō the Munk

by

Tertul. de virg. velan.

by rigour, which by faire meanes could not be obtaind.
But in the holy order of the Iesuits, in sted of chastising
their disorderly religious, they are honestlie inuited to
ill dooing, and to make themselues incorrigible when
they are wearie of staying there; to the end, that theyr
Generall may haue occasion to send them home againe
to their owne houses, there to end theyr dayes, fat, fayre,
and rich.

What newe Idea of a Common-wealth or religion is
this, sith they seldome vse this punishment, which I
call a recompencing and reward of lewdnes? Is it meete
to turne vpside-downe the ancient constitutions of our
Church, and to damne an infinite sort of soules infected
with this new fayth, to the end that three or foure lewd
Iesuits may liue at theyr ease?

Let vs speake plaine, this is not the matter. For *Mon-taignes* himselfe, acknowlegeth in the end of his chapter,
that their Generall may send them home to their hou-
ses, not onely when they haue offended, but vpon euerie other occasion. But hee (saith *Montaignes*) that departs, with the aduise and good liking of his Generall,
who thinks it meet, that for some necessitie of minde or
body, or of his kindred, or of the publique good, or som
other iust reason, hee should be dismist, is absolued by
this meanes from his vow. Whereby you may see, that
it is not vnder the colourable pretence of chastizing
them, that they are suffred to enter vppon inheritances,
(which yet were a ridiculous and impious chastisement)
but to fauour their Generalls power, which is greater &
more absolute, then euer the Popes was ouer the Vniuersall Church.

But I pray forsooth, why doe not you practise that
which other religious persons doe, without innouating
any thing in our Catholike Romane Church? You
would be very sorry to doe so. It is not Christian charitie that leades you to that course, but Iesuitish charitie.

Your whole profession, is nothing els, but a particular coozning of our priuate Families, and a generall villanie of all the countries where you inhabite. I wil make it plaine, that both these are vndoubtedly found in this simple vow. You looke not after any thing but worldly goods, riches, & possessions, though you make a shew to ayme at no other mrak but heauen. If you know that your Nouice, after his two yeres of probation are expired, is capable of inheriting, vvherefore doe you coniure him with such circumstances and deuises during his Nouiceship, to giue away his goods before hee be admitted to the simple vowe? Surely, hee must needes be a man of weake capacitie, that will not imagin, that after this first assay, when you haue made him (for your behoofe) dispossesse himselfe of his goods, before hee become one of your Order, you holde him still in a lease, tenne, twentie, or thirtie yeeres : that is to say, so long as there is any likeli-hood of his comming to any inheritance, that afterward, when all hope of his inheritance fayles, you may make him enter into the second vowe, which is your first solemne vowe : which beeing once made, hee may not afterward possesse any temporall goods, nor be dismist by his Generall, though he be neuer so incorrigible ; and frō that time forward, you take such courses with him, as they doe in other Monasteries with their religious persons that offend.

But before he make this vow, the goods must eyther fal to him that first catcheth thē, or the Iesuit must again dispose of them to the benefit of the poore. I leaue it to you Gentlemen, to thinke who shall be these poore. For, if before he was taken in their nets, hee could not rid himselfe, without gratifying them with his goods, what may one hope for of him whē he is intangled, but the same liberalitie? As if it were to be presumed; that hauing beene brought vp a long time in the midst of them, and farder, beeing desirous to marry himselfe to
the

the second vow,which is a solemn one,he neither durst, would,or could, diftribute his goods otherwife, then to their profit, vnder whofe power he makes account to end his life, wihout any hope of releafe.

But to fay the truth, this queftion is idle. For *Montaignes* hath anfwered roundly, when he faith. That this referuing of the goods,is not for them, who haue renounced this right, but to helpe them afterward, if happily they fhould be difmift. Therefore, if they bee not difinift,thefe goods appertaine to their order. Was there euer more notorions cooznage then this? Alas, I wonder not indeed, that they very feldom difmiffe their diforderly Iefuit: for in fo doing, this fat morfell would fall out of their mouth. Chap. 50.

But why is the Iefuit during this fimple vow, kept away from his kinred, why is he fent out of one countrey into another, but to the end,that if any new inheritance fhould fall vnto him, no man might certainely know what his condition is, nor know how to call in queftion the right he pretends? Well, in the end he is freed from his vow, that he may be out of daunger of all empeachments, and hindrances. Which done, he fhall prooue himfelfe to be the right heire, and yet by a watch-word betwixt him and them, he fhall returne afterward to the Iefuits,to beftow his goods in almes vpon them. Adde hereunto,that this is a point,that toucheth the eftate,that by this meanes it is eafie for the Iefuit to make himfelfe in time, maifter and head of many Cities, Townes, Villages, and Caftles, according to the qualitie of them, whom he hath drawne vnto him. Let vs put cafe, that there are a doozen Gentlemen of good houfes, that haue made themfelues Iefuits, and that fome ciuill or forraigne warres, hath taken away all their brethren: who now, but the Iefuits of the fimple vow fhall fucceed in their inheritance, and fo being admitted to their firft folemne vow, fhall enrich their order there-

E e 3.   withall?

withall? And in time they will become Monarches.

But let vs leaue this point of goods: I am content that it be permitted their Generall to difmiffe them, and to beleeue that he will not enrich himfelfe with the fpoiles of great houfes. See I pray you of what confequence this difmiffing is, to fend into the midft of vs a man, that hath beene trained vp 1 0. or 20. yeeres, in the hypocrifie & doctrine of the Iefuits; or to fpeake more truly, in their more then barbarous impieties, fuch as that I will declare to you in their place. Is not this by indirect meanes to infect our countrey of Fraunce, as we fee by the effect? For how many are there in this Realme, that onely by hauing beene their Schollers and Difciples, fofter opinions, of murthers, maffacres, watch-words, and rebellions againft their Prince? What may you then looke for of them, that hauing bin brought vp 10. or 20. yeeres in their houfes, returne againe to vs, in their owne countrey? Further I would note vnto you, that in this fimple vow, there is lodged a race of men, which make expreffe profeffion of ignorance, whom they call temporall Coadiutors, by whofe meanes they may people a Towne, and make it full of Iefuits. I conclude, that this fimple vow contains vnder it, Herefie, Machiauelifme, Cooznage, and aboue all, a groffe deceiuing of the Sea Apoftolique. All which, tend to the ruine of the Familes, and commonwealths, where the Iefuits inhabit.

CHAP.

CHAP. 13.

¶ That the Iesuits Prouincials, take vpon them to dis-
charge their inferiours of the simple vow, in
the same sort that their Gene-
rall doth.

N all that I haue hitherto discoursed
vnto you, I see not that the Iesuits
haue any thing at all to alleadge in
excuse of their simple vow. And yet
that no man may thinke that I am
stirred against them vpon any particular quarrell, I shall be very wil-
ling to excuse them, if none but the Generall of their
Society may grant dismission, especially, when he is constrained to doe it, by some great & vrgent necessitie. Let
vs grant him this omnipotency ouer them of his order,
which our holy Father the Pope, dooth not giue to
himselfe, ouer any other religious of our Catholique
Church. But to permit a Prouinciall to doe it, for and
in his prouince: not vpon necessity, which hath no law,
but to pleasure him, that requires absolution from his
vow; I beleeue, that how much soeuer we can be content to winke at their doings, there is no good Catholique, that in any sort can beare it. This was practised in
the yeare 1 5 9 4. in the Iesuits Colledge in Paris. There
was in that Colledge, a Iesuit of the simple vow, promoted by them to the holy orders of Priesthood, and who
for many yeeres had ruled at Bourgesse, Neuers, Pont-
á-Mousson, and then had their first forme at Paris. This
man, being wearie of the hypocrisies, and other euill
fashions, which he saw raigned in all this Societie, not
able to beare this water any longer in his stomacke,
presented himselfe to Father *Clement du Puits*, Prouici-
all of Paris, and besought him that he might be dismist,
becaause

because it was not his intent to abide any longer with them. Father *du Puits*, perswaded him to the contrarie, shewing him, that although he had not made profession by the great vow, yet hauing made the simple vow, of Pouertie, Chastitie, and Obedience, he was bound to the keeping of that, so long as he liued there, as well as the religious of other Monasteries; and that he might not go from it, without the consent of his Superiour. Hereto the Iesuit replied. That he neither meant, nor would goe from it, of his owne authoritie, but that his Superiour might not denie him leaue, as long as hee requested it. That herein, there ought to be a mutuall consent of will and power, and that as the Superiour might dismisse the inferiour, without his liking, so the inferiour might compel the Superior to discharge him, though he were not well disposed to do it : that there was as much irrigularitie in the the first proposition, as in the second, and that if there were iustice in the one, there was like in the other. This question, surely was one of the hardest that belongs to their Societie, and if the obedience, that they all vow to their Generall bee such, as I will shew in this place, this doubt had need to to haue beene cleered by him, and his assistants. Notwithstanding, Father *du Puits* being long practised, and throughly instructed in the statutes of his order, without sending to Rome, gaue him of his owne priuate authoritie, his Letters Pattents of such tenour as followeth.

Clemens Puteanus Præpositus Societatis Iesu in Prouincia Franciæ, omnibus quorum interest & in quorũ manus ha littera venerint, S. in Domino nostro Iesu Christo. Fidē facio N. quamuis in Societate nostra aliquandiu vixerit, professionem tamen in ea non emisisse, quin potius ex causis rationi consonis, ipso petente, liberum ab omni, erga ipsam, obligatione esse dimissum. Testamur etiam eum ad omneis sacros ordines in eadem fuisse legitimè promotum, nec vllum scimus impedimentum

dimentum quò minus eis Domino ministrare possit. In cuius rei testimonium, eidem N. has litteras manu nostra scriptas, sigillo Societatis nostræ obsignatas dedimus. Parisiis vigesimo quarto Augusti, 1594. That is to say, *Clement Puteanus,* Prouost of the company of Iesus, in the prouince of Fraunce, to all persons to whom it may appertaine, and to whom these presents shall come, greeting in our Lord Iesus Christ. I giue you to vnderstand, that although the bearer hereof, haue liued a certaine time in our companie, yet was he not professed, but vpon some good considerations mouing him to request it, we haue franke and free dismist, and set him at libertie, from any thing that might tie him to our Societie. Furthermore we certifie, that he hath with vs beene promoted to all holy orders, and that we know no impediment why he may not exercise his function. In witnes whereof, we haue made him this Pasport vnder our own hand writing, and sealed it with the Seale of our Societie. Giuen at Paris the 24. and 25. of August. 1594.

I name him not to you, in fauour of whom these letters were graunted. He is a man of excellent learning, and knowne for such a one in the Vniuersitie of Paris. A man (I say) that had spent not onely some, but many yeeres among the Iesuits, and had taken holy orders, and read in diuers Colledges of their Societie. Yet not being one of the profest fathers, but onely of the simple vow, he procured letters dimissorie as you haue heard, wherein, though it be said (for iust cause) yet if you talke with him, he will tell you, that there was no other but onely this, hee would continue with them no longer, as I haue learned of himselfe; and you see it was at his owne request, that he came away, and not at the motion of the Superiour. And surely, sith *Clemēt du Puits,* vsed the matter thus, I assure my selfe, he might doe it by some mysterie, that is kept secret amongst them, without seeking the authoritie of the Gene-

rall:

rall: and if he might, I doubt not but the like authority is graunted to all the other Prouincials. Good God, what a discipline is this? What respect and obedience sheweth it to the holy Sea? The General may now defend himselfe by the Gregorian Bull, of 1 5 9 4. but in what Buls will the Prouincials find, that this power is graunted them? If that vpon the importunitie of an inferiour, he may dismisse him, to the preiudice of the 3. religious & ordinary vowes of all substantial orders, Pouertie, Chastitie, and Obedience? What a Religion is this, wherein all things are permitted him against our Religion? Are not all these iolly Maisters verie coozners, liuing in the midst of vs? But you shall find other manner of stuffe in the rest of their vowes, if it please you to giue me audience, as hitherto you haue done.

CHAP. 14.

How the Fathers Iesuits, vowing pouertie, by their
great and third vow, make a mocke of God.

Ou haue vnderstood of the Father Iesuit here present, that after the simple vow, they make a solemne vow, by which they adde nothing to the former, but onely that by making this second, they cannot any more inherit, nor be dismist by their Generall. There remaines now the third, which is the vowe of three steps, by which, besides Pouertie, Chastitie, and Obedience vowed by them, they make a particular vow of Mission to our holy Father the Pope, which is to goe to the Indies, and Turkie, for the winning of soules, if they be commanded by his holines. But aboue all, I make great account of that precise Pouertie, which is enioyned them by their constitutions. Runne through all the orders of religion, there is not one of them, in which Pouertie is so recommended,

ded, as among the Capuchins, which liue from hand
to mouth, and put ouer the care for to morrow, to the
onely goodnes of God. The foundation of the pro-
feſt, which are the Ieſuits of the great vow, is to vow yeere,1540,
pouertie, as well in generall, as in particular, as it is in all and 1550.
the orders of begging Friers. But becauſe their pouer-
tie had need to be expounded, let vs ſee the commentaries they bring vs by their conſtitutions. They haue Part.3.
three ſorts of houſes, one for their Nouices; another, conſtit.ca.1.
for their religious bound by their ſolemne vowes, which Art.27.
they call the houſe where there Church is; and another,
which they call a Colledge, for the religious, that are
bound only by the ſimple vow: wherof ſome are ſchollers probationers, others coadiutors, ſome ſpiritual, ſome
temporall.

In domibus vel ecclesiis quæ à Societate, ad auxilium ani-
marum admittentur, redditus nulli, ne Sacristiæ quidem, aut
fabricæ applicati, haberi possunt, sed nec vlla alia ratione, ita Part.6.
vt penes Societatem, eorum sit vlla dispensatio, sed in solo conſtit.ca.1.
Deo, cui per ipsius gratiam, ea inseruit, fiducia constituatur, Art.2.
sine reditibus vllis, ipsum nobis profecturum de rebus omnibus
conuenientibus; ad ipsius maiorem laudem & gloriam.

Professi viuant ex eleemosynis, in domibus, cum aliquò non Art.3
mittuntur, nec officium Rectorum, ordinarium, in Collegiis,
vel vniuersitatibus Societatis habeant, nisi ipsarum necessitas,
vel magna vtilitas exigeret, nec reditibus eorum in Domibus
vtantur.

Parati sint ad mendicandum ostiatim, quando vel obedi- Art.10.
entia, vel necessitas id exiget. Et sit vnus, vel plures, ad elee-
mosinas petendas, quibus personæ societatis sustententur, de-
stinati, quas eleemosinas simpliciter, amore Domini nostri
petent.

Non solum redditus, sed nec possessiones habeant in par- Art.5.
ticulari, nec in communi, Domus vel Ecclesiæ.

That is to ſay, In thoſe houſes and Churches, which
the Societie ſhall accept of, for the ſaluation of ſoules,
Ff 2. there

there shall be no reuenewes proper, eyther to be applied to the vestrie, or to the frame and buildings, or for any other purpose whatsoeuer. That the Societie may haue nothing to dispose of, but onely depend vpon God, whom by his grace they serue, trusting that without reuenewes he will prouide things necessarie for vs, to his praise and honour.

They that are professed (that is, men of the last great & solemne vow) shal liue by almes in their houses, when they are not sent forth to any countrey, nor take the ordinarie charge of Rectors of Colledges, or Vniuersities, except it be vpon necessitie, or vrgent vtilitie require it, neither shall they vse the Colledges reuenewes in their houses.

They shall be readie to begge from doore to doore, when obedience or necessitie requires it. And to this purpose let there be one, or two, or more appointed, to craue almes for the sustenance of the Societie, which shal begge the almes simply : For the loue of our Sauiour Iesus.

The houses and Churches of the Societie shall not onely haue no rents, or reuenewes, but no possessions or inheritance, in generall or particular.

Gather all these particulars together, was there euer pouertie more obstinately vowed then this? And therefore it was, that first *Pius* 5. and after *Gregorie* 13. ordained, that this Societie should be placed among the orders of Mendicants. If they would obserue that which heere is enioyned them, I would excuse them with all my heart, of the heresie of their first vow. And that, because that after they had a long time enioyed goods, during the time of theyr simple vowe, at the last to make satisfaction to G O D for it, being come to the period of their great vow, by reason whereof, they haue the name of Fathers aboue the other religious, yet not onely they vow from thence forwards a beggery, but al-

so

so themselues to become treasurers thereof. I would honour them, as the true followers of S. *Peters* repentance, after he had denied his maister, & would esteeme them aboue all the other orders of Mendicants : But when saw you thē goe with a wallet vp and down the towne? For all this they liue richly and plentifully, not with the Manna of God, (for they are not children of Israel) but by a notable poynt of Sophistrie, & see how. The houses, where these holy Fathers dwell, are not permitted to haue any goods, but onely their Colledges are.

By the Bul of Pau. 3. 1540. and that of Iulius, 1550.

Nowe so it is, that vnder theyr Generalls authoritie, they haue all the care and gouernment of their Colledges. These are the old *Cincinnati* of Rome, that bosted they had no gold, but commaunded them that had. In like sort these Maisters, though they may haue no proper reuenews but theyr wallet, yet doe they gouerne them that haue good store.

This foundation presupposed, you may easily iudge what will follow. For it is reason, that being fathers, they should be fed and maintained by their chyldren : and it is more honestie for thē to aske almes of their Colledges where they cōmaund, then to straggle vp & downe the Townes to craue it. See howe carefully they make sheaues of Fearne for God, as *Caine* did. And yet heerein they are the true & lawfull children of their good Father *Ignatius*, who in all his actions, reserud for himselfe the principall care of his Kitchen.

Rib. dinere teacheth vs, that he, *Iames Lainez*, & *Peter Faure*, soiourning in the Venetians territorie, while the other two went about the Towne to begge for theyr liuing, *Ignatius* tarried at home, to make ready dinner of that little they had gotten : And that afterward, when he was created Generall of his Order, hee began first of all with this charge, *Atque vt quò altiùs ascenderat, eò se gereret submissius, exemploq́, suo omneis ad pietatis studium prouocaret, culinam statim est ingressus, in eaq́; per multos dies,*

Ribad. ca.9 lib. 2.

Ribad. c.11. lib. 3.

F f. 3.

dies, & coquum agens, & alia vilia ministeria obire cœpit.
And to shewe (saith *Ribadiner*) that the higher *Ignace*
was aduaunced, the more he would debase himselfe, to
prouoke all to pietie by his example, hee betooke him
presently to the Kitchin, where he playd the Cooke, &
spent many daies in meane and homly offices.

Well, among these matters, you see the Kitchen goes
first. This was to teach his Disciples, that in the house of
godlines, which he was desirous to build, aboue al things
they must begin with the Kitchen: a lesson which they
haue learned, and obserued very well. Nothing is more
familiar to them by their Bulls and Constitutions, then
beggerie, & yet neuer had any men better skill to scrape
vp coyne, that they might liue at their ease. In this occupation, they played more tricks of legier du maine, then
Maister *Peter Patelin*, or *Frances de Villon*, or *Panurge de
Rabelais*: for all that these three worshipfull Doctors
did, was but in matters of trifles. But to doe as our reuerend Fathers the Iesuits doe, is to fish for Whales, not
for Gudgins; for which purpose they haue, first the instructing of youth, which is their first hooke, viz. the
allurements they vse to the, theyr auriculer confessions,
which they know how to employ to the benefit of their
house: the visiting of the sicke, the wayting vpon them
to the very last gaspe, that they may neuer bee out of
sight; the extraordinarie absolutions, which they say
they can giue them, wherewith they feede their humor,
that they may drawe some rich legacie from them; the
deuises of their simple vowe, and a thousand other hypocriticall shyfts, which they call charitie; but with this
condition, that their charitie begin at them selues: because the Predicament, *Ad aliquid*, is not an accident to
them, but wholly the substance of their Sect.

So that one may iustly call them, not the Order of Iesuits, but the ordure of Iesuits: onely by taking one letter from the one word, and putting it to the other. For
although

although they make shewe, not to meddle with retay-
ling, yet they sell by whole sale the administration of the
holy Sacrament, deerer then *Giesie, Elizeus* man, would
haue solde the spirituall gifts to *Naaman*. And I neuer
read so braue a passage as this notable sentence of *Mon-
taignés* the Iesuit.

If God (saith he) loue to be importund by them that
pray vnto him, rich men, which haue a desire to good,
and to imitate so good an example, must haue patience,
when the poore doe to them, as he that giues riches, desires that one should doe to him. The blessing of God
light on thee, thou Iesuitish soule. For my part, I find this
short instruction so worthy of a Iesuit, a Maister proceeded in the Art of beging, that falling frō his mouth
into the eare of a poore patient, it may bring forth meruailous effects, to the behoofe of this holy Order. At
once, so it is, that within these threescore yeres, they haue
raked together more treasure, by this their sophisticall
beggerie, then all the Monasteries of France haue done
in two or three hundred yeeres.

Chap. 58. de
la verite de-
fenduc.

CHAP. 15.

*That the Iesuits vow of Chastitie, containes a newe here-
sie: and withall, a briefe discourse of the title of Father, which the Iesuits of the graund
vow giue themselues.*

 Erusing ouer all the vowes of our Iesuits,
I found something to be reprooued, as
you haue perceiued by my former discourse, and shall by that which followes
in due place. But in the vow of Chastity,
me thought there was nothing new: at the least, I found
no new thing, either in their Bulls, or in their constitutions. Yet, reading *Montaignes* in his 50. chapter of his
booke called, *Truth defended*, I perceiue they haue a misterie;

sterie, that is not yet come to the knowledge of the holie Sea, or of the Church, no more thē their simple vow,
which they vsed by the space of fortie yeeres without a-
nie lycence. For, see I pray you, what *Montaignes* saith
when hee would excuse the simple vowe. It is a newe
Lawe, as well as the vow of Chastitie, which they of
this Societie make, which hinders marriage not yet contracted, and dissolues it being contracted.

Sith *Montaignes* affirmes it, I holde it for very true.
For although it be not so thought, yet so it is, that the authour of this booke, the Prouinciall of Paris, was a bot-
bomlesse Fountaine of the Iesuits doctrine. At the first,
I thought that his meaning had been, that after the vow
of Chastitie made by them, none might marry, vnder
paine of hauing his marriage disanuld, and the children
that shall come thereof, declared to be incestuous : But
afterward, when I had bethought my selfe, that this law
was not new, but very ancient, and that this Iesuit calld
their vow of Chastitie a newe one, by which, marriages
alreadie made were dissolued and disanuld, I assured my
selfe, that by this new vow, a married man becomming
a Iesuit, breakes the holy bond of mariage, which cannot
be dissolued but by naturall death.

VVas there euer any heresie more preiudiciall to
Christendome thē this ? It is Gods law, that they which
are married by him, that is to say by his Church, may
not be seuerd & put asunder by man, except in the case
of adulterie. Which ordinaunce hath been so strictly obserued in all times of old, that when the woman for her
fault, is shut vp in a Monasterie, though there bee no
fault at all on her husbands part, yet is it not permitted
him to marry againe, in our Catho. Apostlick Romane
Church, but he must beare his part of penaunce, for the
sinne cōmitted by his wife. So hath our Church thought
these two bodies indiuisible. I wot well, that som think,
that the wife beeing conuinced of adulterie in court of
iustice,

iuftice, the husband may marry another wife: But in
whether of the two is there greater error, them that fo
thinke, or the Iefuit? They cleauing onely to the letter,
imagine, that God hath giuen libertie to marry againe,
becaufe that in all other cafes, faue adulterie, he hath forbidden the feuering of man & wife: & yet the Church
neuer thought, that the breach of mariage was intended
in thefe words; for marriage is a Sacrament that cannot
be diffolued but by death: onely there may be a fepara-
tion of bodies. Wherein the Auncients were fo refolute,
that they thought, fome, as *Tertullian*, vppon cōmaundement, fome, as *Ierome*, vppon counfaile, that neither
of the married parties, might make any fecond marriage, as if their marriage had not beene diffolued by the
death of the former wife or husband.

I fpeake this, not to approoue their oppinions, for
Tertullians was condemned by the Church, and *Ieroms*
contrould by many great perfonages: but to fhew you,
that at the leaft, as long as we liue, the facrament of marriage may not be diffolued, no not for adulterie. What
new monfter then is that, which our Iefuits bring into
the Church, that he which becomes one of theyr order,
may breake off his marriage, without finning thereby
againft his wife? So that vppon a bare difcontentment
of the husband, the poore defolate wife fhall remaine
vnmarried, according to the lawes of Iefuitifme, & yet
may not marry another husband, becaufe the Lawes of
Chriftianitie forbids it. I haue heard it faid of other Orders & Monafteries, that it hath faln out fometimes, that
fome intemperate and ill aduifed men, haue become
Munks, rather by defpaire then deuotion, becaufe they
could not obtaine that folly which they fought for of
theyr Miftreffes; but to the breach of marriage, faue for
adulterie, vppon the onely difcontentment of the huf-
band, poffeffed with a fottifh deuotion, there neuer was
any that opend a gappe, but the Iefuits, men without

Gg   Chrift

Chriſt ſince firſt our Chriſtian Religion began. If they ſo much abhorre marriage, whence comes it, that hauing attain'd to their laſt vow, they call themſelues Fathers? A title indeed not ſo arrogant as that of Ieſuit, but yet full of ambition & pride: At the leaſt I am ſure, that S. *Ierome* would not haue thought well of it, who vpon the fourth to the Galathians, ſaith, that the word *Abba*, ſignifieth Father in Hebrue, and that our Sauiour hath declared, that the name of Father, appertaines not to any but to G O D his Father, therefore it was not to be liked, that in ſome Monaſteries, there were that were called Abbats, or Fathers. I thinke his meaning was, to ſpeake to the heads of the Munks, which were call'd Abbats: what would he ſay now, if he ſhould ſee the Ieſuits of the great vow take this title of Fathers? For in other Orders, we call theyr Superiour, Abbat, as him whom the Religious perſons muſt acknowledge for their Father; and as for them, they are called Brothers, as if they were all his chyldren.

This name, Father, appertaines not but to the principall dignities of the Church, as Pope, Patriarck, and Abbat: and whereas euery Ieſuit of the great vow, takes it as his portion, they ſhewe thereby, that vnder the feyned ſimplicitie of theyr Friers weede, they couer meruailous arrogancie. I know they will tell mee, that the Capuchins, who ſeeme to be an order not to be reproued, doe the like: and I will aunſwere them, that this fault of the Capuchins, may not ſerue them for a warrant. *Diogenes* the Cynick, making a ſhew of deſpiſing the world, was as proud as *Plato*, when he vaunted in his beggerie, that he trode *Platos* pride vnder his feete: and I will not ſay, that there is no ambition vnder a Capuchins gray patcht gowne. But yet there may be ſome excuſe for him: For hee among them, that firſt thought to bring ſom reformation into S. *Fraunces* order, meant to make them Munks like the good old Hermits, whom of old

they

they called Fathers. As in deede, when we reade theyr
liues, we call them the liues of the Fathers; and when I
see the Iesuits beggerie brought to that passe the Capuchins is, I shall easily be perswaded to excuse this title
of Fathers in them. But a man may see in them, a verie
manifest ambition; because, that beeing not content to
call themselues so, they make the worde (Reuerend) to
be added thereto, which belongs not to any but to Cardinalls and Bishops. Looke vppon *Bellarmins* works,
printed before hee was a Cardinall, for example, his
booke of Pardons, their title is, *R.P. Roberti Bellarmi-
ni, &c.* which is by abridgement, that which we call Reuerend father. Looke on the life of *Frauncis Borgia,* (the
third Generall of their Order,) translated out of Spanish into Latine, by *Andrew Scot,* a Iesuit. The priuiledge to *Troguse,* the Printer at Antwerp imports, that
hee had leaue to print, *Vitam Francisci Borgiæ,* ter-
tij Societ. Iesu Generalis, à Reuerendo Patre. Andrea Shot-
to Latinè scriptam.* The life of *Frauncis Borgia,* the third
Generall of the Societie, written in Latine by the Reue-
uerend Father, *Andrew Scot.*

   And truly I am sorry, for the loue I beare them, that
they haue so ambitiously desired this name of father, because it hath been a cause, that certaine curious fellowes,
haue employed their time in writing Anagrams vppon
these two wordes, *SECTA IESVITARVM,*
wherein they haue found matter of shame and reproch.
As it fell out the other day, when I was in cōpany where
there was speech of that title which they haue taken, a
good fellow said, that there was no reason we should enuie them that title of fathers, sith they tooke so good order to be so. To which another replied, that it was not
so, because the conceit that ariseth from these vvordes,
SECTA IESVITARVM, refutes that slauder,
whereunto he for his part gaue great credit. For if the
prognostication of our fortunes and manners (said he)

depend vppon names, according to the rule that *Ierom
Cardan* hath giuen in his booke *De Subtilitate*, there is as
much and more reason, to iudge the like of Anagrams,
which a man may finde in the names without loosing a-
ny one letter; as we say in that of king *Frauncis*, the first
of that name, *FRANÇOIS DE VALOIS,
DE FAÇON SVIS ROYAL*. And in that of
Estienne Iodelle, a great Poet, *Io le Delien est né*. And if
that which is to be found in these two words, *SECTA
IESVITARV M* be true, it is an absolute impossi-
bilitie for them to be Fathers.

*TVTE MARES VICIAS, non scortum,
non tibi coniunx,
Dic Iesita mihi qui Pater esse potes ?*

With women you lie not, but with males rather,
Speake Iesuit, how canst thou be a Father ?

To which I aunswerd him, that it was meere follie to
giue any credit to names, or Anagrams, as *Iulius Scali-
ger* hath very elegantly proued against *Cardan*. Besides,
I am out of doubt, that your Anagram is a lyer, as I will
proue by another, that is contrarie to it.

*TV MATRES VICIAS, thorosǵ, sacros,
Antistes pie, virginesǵ, sanctas:
Hoc qui martyrio fidem propagat,
Hoc qui consilio propagat orbem,
Is verè est pater, & pater beatus:
O tuam veneror beatitatem,
Amplectorǵ, piam paternitatem,
Iesuita Patrum Pater supreme.*

Thou stainest Mothers, and the marriage bed,
Prelate, by thee are holy Virgins sped.

Who

Who by this martyrdome graceth the steeple,
Who by this skill begets faith in the people :
He is a father, and a father blest,
Thy happines I honour with the rest :
Iesuit, I bow to thy paternitee,
Father of Fathers in the highest degree.

The diuersitie of these two Anagrams, which is a plaine contrariety, of doing & vndoing, teacheth vs, that there is no credit to be giuen to them. And I hold it for certaine, and an Article of faith, if you will giue me leaue to say so, that the Iesuits keepe their vow of chastitie, as strictly, holily, and religiously, as they do that of beggerie, wherefore let vs not trouble our talke with this ordure.

You are verie desirous (quoth the other) to fauour them without ground, and you consider not that your Anagram lackes one letter, E. whereas mine fits all. That which I haue said to you of them, is an inseparable accident, which the Logicians call, *Poprium quarto modò*. Remember the Templers, who were allowed heretofore, vnder the cloake of Religion, to wander ouer the world, to enlarge our faith by their swords, and what was one of the principall points, for which they were condemned. See if the Iesuits now adaies doe not follow their steps : the actiōs of a man, that rogues about the world, as the Iesuits doe, are to me meruailous suspicious. I beleeue no part of that you say, (quoth I) it is all but lies and slaunders.

Gg 3. CHAP.

CHAP. 16.

¶ Of the vow of Miſſion, and that by it the Ieſuits mocke vs all, and eſpecially our holy Father the Pope.

IN all other orders, they that are admitted make three vowes. In this of *Ignace* to enthrall the good liking of Pope *Paule* the third, that of Miſſion is added : not for his fellowes, but for them, which are of the laſt, and great vow. The words of their Buls are, that they promiſe without ſhifting, to go whether ſoeuer the Pope ſhall commaund them. *Ad profectum animarum & fidei propagationem, ſiue miſerit nos ad Turcas, ſiue ad quoſcumque alios infideles, etiam in partibus quas Indias vocant, exiſtentes, &c.* He that cauſed the defence of the Colledge of Clairmont againſt the Vniuerſity of of Paris to be printed 1594. ſaith thus, ſpeaking of the greatnes and excellencie of his new vow. The defendants haue a particular vow of obedience to the Pope, but *circa Miſſiones tantùm*, which is grounded vpon this, that they being called by God to ayde the Church, and to defend it againſt the enemies thereof, ſuch as the Infidels and heretiques are, muſt of neceſſitie be ſent abroad. And a little after : And they cannot be more rightly ſent then by him, that is ſet in Saint *Peters* chaire, and gouerns the whole Church : who as the Pilot in the ſterne, ſticking to the helme, appoints ſome to the fore-ſhip, ſome to the ancor, ſome to the ſailes and tackles, and other, to other offices in the ſhip. Let vs dwell a little vppon this goodly ſentence, ere we paſſe any further.

The firſt promiſe of this vow, is for the conuerſion of the Turks, which follow Mahometiſme, then, of all other infidels, yea euen of them that inhabit certaine

countries

countries vnknowne to vs, which they call the Indies.
I pray you tel me, if euer you vnderstood that they went
either to the country of the great Turke the Emperour
of Constantinople, or of *Sophy*, the Emperour of Persia,
to acquit themselues of this promise. They were neuer
commaunded to goe thither by our holy Father, will
some man say to me ; I grant, becaule those places were
too hot for them. Whither then haue they gone ? Into
those countries that are farre from vs, *quas Indias vocant*,
which *Ignace* cunningly added, as a thing harder to performe, then the conuersion of Turkie: and yet he knew,
being a Spaniard, that nothing was so easie, as to vndertake this charge, as you haue vnderstood by me, when I
recouted to you the Embassages of the Iesuits into Por- *Maff.lib.2,*
tugall, & the Indies, which were vnder the subiection of *chap.10.*
Iohn the third, King of Portugall. Do yoe thinke, Gen- *chap.16.*
tlemen, that if it had pleased the Pope to send thither
any of the foure orders of the Mendicants, they would
haue drawne backe from this seruice, permitting them
to goe in a secular habite, as the Iesuit dooth ? In
steed of one *Xauier*, that was sent thither by *Ignace*, there
would haue beene found, 500. men full of deuotion
and learning to performe this holy voiage. And why so?
Becaule it was a deuotion without daunger, for going
thither vnder the banner of a Christian king, who had
power of life and death ouer them, whom by faire
meanes he would bring to our Christian Religion, it
was a voyage without feare. But as for all Turky, which
is vnder Princes, enemies to Christianitie, I see not that
eyther the Pope would giue them commaundement, or
these worldly-wise Iesuits be any thing hastie to goe
thither : and yet read the first bull, and it appeares that
Ignace set downe the voyage of Turky, as the more easie
to be vndertaken. I would to God it had come into the
head of one of the Popes that succeeded *Paule* the third,
to commaund our Iesuits, to go to Constantinople, to
conuert

conuert the Mahumetans, to trie in good earneſt what obedience they would yeeld to this vow of Miſſion; we ſhould haue ſeene what miracles they would haue wrought there. Heare notwithſtanding, not a new Currier, but a diſcourſer of his moſt humble ſupplication & requeſt preſented to the king. We liue not vnder chriſtian princes only, but vnder heathē Potētates, & thoſe that are ignorant of the law & feare of God. We haue Colledges euen in Iappon, ſcituated to the Eaſt of our Hemiſphere; we haue to the Weſt, in Braſil, which is the beginning of America : in Lima, & Cucham, which is the end of Peru, and the vtmoſt part of the Weſt : in Mexico, which is in the middle of the two countries . To the Northward, we haue in Goa, a City & country that lies by ⅔ as far from Iappon, as Iappon from Lisbon, ſome 6000. leagues . We haue Colledges in many places of the eaſt & weſt Indies. That I may ſay nothing of thoſe we haue in Europe, which are a great many more then our enemies would, & fewer by a great many then the godly & zealous of our faith deſire. Beſides, the labourers of this Societie, without hauing Colledges prepared for thē, for the conſeruation of Chriſtians, & conuerſion of the heathen, frequent the countries of Mount Libanus, of Ægypt, of Africa, & of China. When I read this paſſage with a friend of mine, I told him that this Ieſuit without name, played in the dark ; and the verie lyer. As of old, *Apollonius Tianneus* the coozner did, alleaging to the Greekes for witneſſe of his miracles, the Gymnoſophiſts, that were in India. Whereupon *Æneas Goſeus*, in his Theophraſt, ſaith, that it was not without reaſon, that this impudent coozner, tooke for warrant of his cooznages, them that were a farre of, and dwelt as it were in an other world. I ſaid, that our Ieſuits Theatins, did the like at this day; who to feed vs with toyes, ſend vs to the ſame Indies and other countries, whereof we ſcarſe know the names. But at this word my

friend

friend smiling, said, that there was some *Picrochole* in
their doing. What *Picrochole* (quoth I?) I think it is the
name of a diuel, as *Macrobe* is. I perceiue, quoth he a-
gain, that ye haue not studied our *Rabelais*, who discour-
sing of a great warre, that king *Picrochole* made vpon
Grandgosier, after that his foolish noule had reckned vpō
the whole coūtry of France, which he took to be already
conquered : his gallants that followed him, added therto;
And moreouer, you shall assault, the kingdomes of Tu-
nis, of Hippo, Argier, of Bone, of Corode, & valiantly
all Barbarie. Passing further, you shall take into your
hands, Maiorca, Minorca, Sardinia ; Corsu, and the o-
ther Islands of the Ligustick and Balearick Sea : and
in coasting on the left hand, you shall beare rule ouer
all Gallia Narbonensis, Prouence, the Allobroges, Sien-
na, Florence, Luca : you shall take Italy, euen Naples,
Calabria, Apulia, and Sicill and sacke them all, & Mal-
ta to. Afterward, we will take Candy, Cyprus, Rhodes,
and the Cyclades, & we will set vpon Moria. It seemes
that this wise foole *Rabelais*, meant then in the person
of *Picrochole*, to paint out the imaginarie victories of
our Iesuits with their wallets, though they were not then
hatcht. You are a merrie man (quoth I) but let vs leaue
these trickes for the Iesuit *Dé la Fon* : For I see nothing
in this matter, but to laugh at. If the Iesuit had taken
Munsters Cosmography, he might haue added many
other sauage countries, and it had beene hard for vs to
haue proued him a lier : I remember that the wise *Tule-
nus*, seeing vpon a time the lawyer *Balduin* walking with
Andrew Theuet the trauailer, said, that they took no care
to disproue one with another, because the one had been
alwaies in his chamber, wedded to his booke, and the
other, had employed his whole time in trauaile, without looking vpon a booke : That the one might quote
many false authorities without being reproued, & the
other, name many countryes where he had neuer beene,

H h.   without

without being contrould. The very same you shall find in this case of the Iesuits we haue in hand. It is aboue 40. yeere since they bragd, that they had made these great conquests in the most part of those countreyes. Their Statutes ordaine, that when their General is dead, all the fathers of our prouinces, that are in any estate or dignitie, must come to Rome, to proceed to the election of a new successor. After the decease of *Ignace*, in the yeere 1556. many came thither, where *Iames Lainez* was chosen, he dead, in the yeere 1565. *Fraunces Borgia* was chosen; in neither of these elections, though there was a great care had that the titles of all the fathers Prouincials might be sent thither, yet I find not any one of those farre countries : and yet the names and titles of all the fathers that were brought thither, were verie carefully set downe. They are bound to send letters to their Generall euery yeere from euerie Colledge, to certifie him how their matters stand. I haue runne ouer all that were sent to their Generall *Aquauiua*, in the yeere 1583. yet find no mention among them of any of these Colledges. It should seeme their winning of soules hath beene meruailous great since that time.

Let vs leaue things as they be, & let vs not speak vpon idle imaginatiõs, but agreeable to common sense : If they be scattred in so many barbarous countries, & haue there conuerted so many soules to our Christian faith, they must needs haue had the gift of tongues to conuert thē. It is in the power of our holy Father, to send them into these vnknown countries, but not to bestow vpon them the gift of tongues. That was a grace of the holy Ghost particularly reserud for the Apostles, for the spreading of our Christian faith. Consider I pray you whether there be not likelihood of reason in that I say. Besides, where are the sauage Kings, Princes, & Lords, which after their conuersion, haue come to kisse the feet of the holy father to receiue his blessing? I vnderstand that once in 60. yers

they

they haue had a Maske in Rome, of 3. beggers disguisd
like kings,& this is all. I place therfore their vow of Mif-
fion in the chapter of money counted, but not receiued:
It is a very cooznage,by which these honest felowes dal-
ly with vs. And yet this cooznage is nothing in comparifon of that,whereby they abuse our holy father. It muſt
be granted by euery man, that he only and none but he,
hath authority to fend into heathen countries , for their
conuerſion, ſo that no man in this cafe may be ioyned in
commiſſion with him. But for all this, there is nothing,
wherein the Iefuits defpife his authority more, then in
this: the leaſt part of this Miſſion depends vpon the
holy Sea , and the refidue is in their Genarall . *Pof-*
fit tamen ipfemet Præpofitus pro tempore exiftens,fuos quo-
cum�q locorum, etiam inter Infideles, cùm expedire in Do-
mino iudicabit,mittere ac reuocare : & per nos ac fucceffores
noftros, ad locũ aliquem miſſos fine temporis certi limitatione,
cùm id expedire ad Dei gloriam, & animarum auxilium vi-
fum fuerit (fuper quo confcientiam dicti Præpofiti oneramus)
ad alia loca tranfmittere liberè & licite valeat. Yet let their
Generall (faith the Bul) for the time being,whenfoeuer
he fhall thinke it expedient, fend them of his order into
any heathen country whatfoeuer, and when he liſt, call
them home againe: and if we,or our fucceffors fhal fend
any of them to any place without limitation of time, let
him,whenfoeuer he fhal fee it expedient for Gõds glory
& the good of foules(wherin we charge the faid General
vpon his confcience) remoue them from thence whither he fhall think meet . From hence you may gather,
that the Generall not only may fend them, as well as the
Pope, but, which is more, may alter, clippe, & curtall
the Popes letters Patents,as pleafe him.Befides,there are
none but the fathers of the laſt vow, bound to the Pope
in this Miſſion , & they make account that the holy Sea
is infinitely beholding to thē for it. There Generall can
do more. For he is permitted by their conftitutions, to

Bull of
Paule the 3.
the yeere
1549.

Hh 2.   fend

send, as well some of them of the great vow, as of the other, whither soeuer he will, without partialitie, or exception of any person.

9.Par.conft.
ca.3.art.9.

Idem Generalis in Missionibus omnē habebit potestatem, eis tamen nulla ratione repugnando, quæ à sede Apostolica (vt in septima parte dicitur) proficiscuntur. Mittere ergo poterit omnes sibi subditos, siue professionem emiserint, siue non emiserint, quos mittendos iudicauerit, ad quaslibet mundi partes, ad quoduis tempus, vel definitum, vel indefinitum, prout ei videbitur ad quamuis actionem, ex his quibus ad proximorū auxilium, Societas solet exercendam. Poterit etiam missos reuocare, & in omnibus denique, vt ad maiorem Dei gloriam fore senserit, procedere. The said Generall (saith the Latin) shall haue all authoritie in Missions, yet without derogating any way frō those, which are granted by the Sea Apostolick, as it is said in the seuenth part. It is lawful for him therfore, to send any of his inferiors, whether they haue made profession of the vow or not, (whom he shal think meet) to any part of the world, for what time he please, prefixed or not prefixed, for any purpose, in which the Society is wont to be employed, for the good of their neighbours. It is lawfull for him also, to call home them that are sent, and to doe in all things, as he shall thinke it most conuenient for Gods glory.

I doe not thinke it straunge, that their Generall may countermaund them that are sent by the Pope, because he had leaue to do it, by the Bull of 1549. But concerning that point, which depends only vpon their constitutions, that the Generall may send whither he will, not only the fathers profest, but all other inferiors of his order, I cannot choose, but be greatly offended at the matter. For to grant such libertie, is to giue too much to their Generall and too little to our holy Father the Pope. Therfore, as oft as they trumpet out to vs this vow of Mission, by which their fathers of the great vow are bound to the holy Sea, they mocke both him, & vs. For

this.

this vow is superfluous, their constitutions being such
for their Generall, as I haue shewed you. Of which
constitutions also, they haue no Pope for warrant, and
they are extraordinarily punishable, for hauing vsurped
this priuiledge vpon the holy Sea, of their owne priuate authoritie.

CHAP. 17.

¶ Of the blindfold obedience which the Iesuits owe the Pope,
which at this day they impudently denie
by theyr new bookes.

Asquier, pleading for the Vniuersitie of Paris against the Iesuits, obiected to them, that they yeelded a
certaine particuler submission to the
Pope, that was vtterly contrarie to
the liberties of our Ch. of Fraunce.
A submission, that first brought in
a schisme into the Church, betwixt the popish Iesuit, &
the true catholique French-man. Besides, of such consequence, that if any quarrell should happen betwixt the
Popes & our Kings, the Iesuits would be as sworne enemies to the Crowne of Fraunce, as any that we foster in
Fraunce.

When this obiection was made against them, *Verso-*
ris theyr Aduocate, answered neuer a word to it, as you
may see by his Plea. But as the time hath refined theyr
wits, so they haue bethought themselues of a buckler for
this blow, by a new kind of Sophistrie, saying, that they
make no other particular vow to the Pope, then that of
Mission, and that in all other poynts, they are conformable to vs. So they would haue defended themselues,
in the yeere 1594. when their cause was pleaded the
second time in the Parliament at Paris, as you may vnderstand by that which I alleaged out of their defences.

And

And *Montaignes* in his book of the *Truth defended,* faith, that their vow is contain'd in these wordes of their profession, after the three vowes of Religion, *Insuper promitto specialem obedientiam summo Pontifici circa Missiones.* Which signifieth nothing els, but that they which are profest, promise to obey their holy father the Pope specially, without delay or excuse, to goe into any part of the world, to the Indies, or to the Turks, among the Infidels and heretiques to conuert them, or to the Christians to ayde them.

But aboue all, he best pleaseth me, which made *The most humble supplication and request to the King, for the Societie of Iesus*: who after he had daub'd ouer his cause with many hypocriticall reasons, when he comes to this poynt of obedience to the Pope, his booke beeing shut vp, as if by ouer-sight he had forgot to aunswere it, adds by way of an appendix beside the Booke, about some twentie lines to this effect. *Addition to page. 56.* The same Author, hath taught our enemies to take vp matter of reproch, about a vow that the profest of our Societie make to the holy Sea, vppon which they haue glozed, that wee promise to obey it wholy in all thinges, whatsoeuer it shall commaund: and that if the Pope be a Spaniard, we will be so to if he please: which glosse, is not onely contrarie to the truth, but also beside the purpose and matter. This vow, (my Liege) containes nothing but a promise, readily to employ our selues when it shall please the holy Sea, among the Infidels, Pagans, and Hereticks, to conuert thē to the fayth. The words of the vow are. Further, I promise speciall obedience to our holy Father, in the matter of Mission.

This vow contains no other particular obligation, & cannot be but commendable, in a time wherein there is so great need of good labourers, to succor the church in danger. And it weakens not, nor hinders in any poynt the submission, obedience, & allegeance, which all subiects

iects owe to their Princes; the French to the King of
Fraunce, the Polanders to the King of Poland, and so of
others: What cause haue they then to cry out, that wee
make a vowe to obey wholy in all thinges, whatsoeuer
shall be commaunded? and that this vow will make vs
Spanyards, if the Pope please? What agreement is there
of such an antecedent, with such a consequent? Let the
word Spayne goe. I will make no aduantage of it, eyther for or against the Iesuit. Euery Prince playes his
part vpon this great stage of the world, as well as he can
for the aduauncement of his estate: A thing which is
not vnseemly for him, according to the rules of state
matters, which giue Princes leaue to loue treasons, and
hate Traytors. Some such a one, may haue ayded himselfe by the seruice of the Iesuits in our late troubles, who
shall one day find, that they are very dangerous officers
in his Country, & that by experience of that which hath
past in Fraunce.

Let vs speake onely of that which concernes our present question, but without Sophistrie, at least if I may
entreat so much of our Iesuit. I will assaile them with
none but theyr owne writings. In the third part of their
Constitutions, chap. 1. where theyr vow of obedience,
as well to the Pope, as to their Superiours, is at large described, you haue these words following; whereby euerie man may see, with what impudencie the Iesuits lye,
and that euen in their humble request which they presented to the King.

*Et quoniam quæ ad votũ castitatis pertinent, interpreta-
tione non indigent, cùm constet quàm sit perfectè obseruanda:
nempe enitendo Angelicam puritatem imitari, & mentis &
corporis mũditia. His suppositis, de sancta obedientia dicetur,
quam quidem omnes plurimum obseruare, & in ea excellere
studeant, NEC SOLVM IN REBVS OB-
LIGATORIIS, SED ETIAM in alijs, licet
nihil aliud quàm signum voluntatis Superioris, sine vllo præ-
cepto*

cepto videretur. Versari autem debet ob oculos, Deus creä-
tor, & Dominus noster, propter quē homini obedientia præ-
statur, & vt in spiritu amoris, & non cum perturbatione ti-
moris, procedatur, curandum est. Ita vt omnes constanti a-
animo incumbamus, vt nihil perfectionis cum diuina gratia
consequi possimus, in absoluta omnium constitutionum obser-
uatione, nostrique instituti peculiari ratione adimplenda, præ-
termittamus, & exactissimè omnes neruos virium nostrarum
ad hanc virtutē obedientiæ, imprimis SVMMO PON-
TIFICI, DEINDE SVPERIORIBVS
SOCIETATIS, exhibendam, intendamus. Ita vt om-
nibus in rebus ad quas potest se cum charitate obedientia ex-
tendere, ad eius vocem, perinde ac si à Christo Domino egre-
deretur (quando quidem ipsius loco est, ac pro ipsius amore ac
reuerentia, obedientiam præstamus) quàm promtissimi simus,
re quauis, atque adeo litera à nobis inchoata, nedum perfecta,
studio obediendi, relicta, ad eum scopum vires omnes ac in-
tentionem, in Domino conuertendo: vt sancta obedientia, tū
in exequutione, tum in voluntate, tum in intellectu, sit nobis
semper ex omni parte perfecta, cum magna celeritate, spiri-
tuali gaudeo & perseuerantia, quicquid nobis iniunctum
fuerit, obeundo, omnia iusta esse nobis persuadendò, om-
nem sententiam ac iudicium nostrum contrarium CÆ-
CA QVADAM OBEDIENTIA, abne-
gando: Et id quidem in omnibus quæ à Superiore disponun-
tur, vbi definiri non possit aliquod peccati genus intercedere.
Et sibi quisque persuadeat quod qui sub obedientia viuunt, se
ferri ac regi à diuina prouidentia per Superiores suos, sinere
debent, perinde ac si cadauer essent, quod quoque versus se fer-
ri, & quacunque ratione tractari se sinit. Vel similiter atque
senis baculus, qui vbicumque & quacunque in re velit, eo
vti, qui cum manu tenet, ei inseruit. Sic enim obediens rem
quamcunque cui eum Superior, ad auxilium totius Religio-
nis velit impendere, cum animi hilaritate debet exequi. Pro
certo habens quod ea ratione potius, quàm re alia quauis, quā
præstare possit, propriam voluntatem, ac iudicium diuersum

(ectando

fectando, diuinæ voluntati respondebit. Vppon which paſſage, the gloſſe hath theſe words, *Obedientia quod ad exe-cutionem attinet, tunc præstatur, cum res iuſſa completur: quod ad voluntatem, cùm ille qui obedit idipſum vult, quod ille qui iubet: Quod ad intellectum, cum id ipſum ſentit quod ille, & quod iubetur, benè iuberi exiſtimat: Et eſt im-perfecta, ea obedientia, in qua præter executionem, non eſt hæc eiuſdem voluntatis & ſententiæ, inter cum qui iubet, & cui iubetur, conſenſio.* I will recite it vnto you in French, as neere as poſſibly I can. And becauſe thoſe things which belong to the vow of Chaſtitie, need no inter-pretation, for that it is certaine that it muſt be perfectly kept; namely, by labouring to imitate the puritie of Angels, in cleannes both of mind & bodie. Theſe things graunted, we will ſpeake of Obedience, which all muſt labour ſtrictly to obſerue, and to excell therein *And that not onely in thoſe things which they are bound,* but in other alſo, though they ſaw no commaundement for it, but only a ſigne of your Superiours will. God the Crea-tor, and our Lord Ieſus Chriſt, for whoſe ſake Obedi-ence is performed to man, muſt alwaies be before their eies, and they muſt prouide, that they ſtil proceed in the ſpirit of loue, and not with perturbation of feare. So that all of vs with reſolute mindes, frame our ſelues in ſuch ſort, that we omit not any of that perfection, which by Gods grace we may attaine to, by the abſolute fulfil-ling of all the conſtitutions; and particularly, by fulfil-ling our purpoſed intent, and that we bend our whole ſtrength to the performance of the vertue of obedi-ence, *Firſt to the ſupreme Biſhop, and then to the Superi-ours of the Societie.* So that we be readie at his call in all things, to which obedièce with charity maybe extended as if it were our Sauiour Chriſts owne voice, ſith he is in his place, and we yeeld obedience for loue & reuerence of him: And ſuch muſt our care and obedience be, as that if we haue begunne to make a letter, we ſhould

I i. leaue

leaue in the midſt of it, beeing called, and apply in the Lord, all our ſtrength and intention to obey. That our holy obedience may be perfit in euery part, in the execution, in the will, and in the vnderſtanding; that with great haſt, ſpirituall ioy and perſeuerance, wee accompliſh whatſoeuer ſhall be enioynd vs: perſwading our ſelues that all things are iuſt, denying by a certaine blindfold obedience, all opinion and iudgement of our own to the contrarie; and this muſt be obſerud in all thinges which are decreed by our Superiour, where it is not certainly knowne that there is ſome kind of ſin.

And let euery one perſwade himſelfe, that all they which liue vnder obedience, ought to ſuffer themſelues to be carried and gouernd, according to the prouidence of GOD by their Superiours, euen as if they were dead carkaſſes, which ſuffer themſelues to be turned & tumbled, how ſoeuer, and which way ſocuer a man will: or as an old mans ſtaffe, which ſerues him that holds it in his hand, to whatſoeuer he will vſe it, where and how he liſt. For ſo muſt he, that is obedient, with cheerefulnes of mind execute, whatſoeuer his Superior will employ him in, to the benefit of all Religion. Aſſuring himſelfe, that he ſhall fulfill the wil of God better by that meanes, then by any other thing that he can doe, following his owne will and iudgement differing from it. Vpon this paſſage, the gloſſe hath theſe words.

Obedience, concerning the execution of it, is then performed, when that which is commaunded, is done: concerning the will, when he that obeyes, wills the ſame thing that he doth which commaunds: concerning the vnderſtanding, when hee is of the ſame iudgment with him, and thinks that which is cōmaunded, to be rightly commaunded. And that obedience is vnperfeƈt, wherin beſides the execution, there is not this conſent of the ſame will and iudgement, betwixt him that cōmaunds, and him that is cōmaunded. Doe you not ſee, that the

Ieſuits

Iesuits are impudent lyers, when they say, that their particular vow to the Pope, is tied to nothing but Miſſion,
and when they call them ſlaunderers that ſpeake otherwiſe of it? For this which I haue here ſhewed you, makes
it manifeſt, that they are bound to obedience, not onely
in matters of their order which bindes them, but alſo in
all other things; and that with as ſtraight and abſolute
commaundement, as any poſſibly can be. But before
whom are they lyers? Before the maieſty of their King:
becauſe the humble ſupplication & declaration before
mentioned, was addreſt to him onely.

The Ieſuit thinks he ſinnes not at all by lying impudently before his Kings face, yea, and confirming his lie
with periurie, by laying his hand on the holy Goſpells.
And why ſo? Becauſe, hauing recciued a commaundement from his Generall to lie, his vow of obedience is ſo
preciſe, that he thinks hee is freed from all ſin, and that
hee had faulted much more, if by telling the truth, hee
had not obeyed him. I cannot ſtay my ſelfe from being
angry. For if this vowe of blindfold obedience be euill,
howe is it that theſe wicked men obſerue it? If it be
good, howe chaunce they diſclaime it, eſpecially, in ſo
high a poynt, and of ſuch importance as this is? As for
my ſelfe, who meane to liue and die in that fayth, which
at the day of my Baptiſme, my God-fathers and ſureties
promiſed to God for me, I will neuer doubt to acknowledge my ſelfe, in the midſt of all our aduerſaries, a Catholick, Apoſtolick Romane, as my predeceſſors haue
beene.

They muſt needes vnderſtand one thing in this theyr
diſclaime, which I am conſtraind to tell them. Doe not
think, that the Ieſuits are ſuch men as we are. They haue
two ſoules in theyr bodies, the one, a Romane ſoule in
Rome, the other, a French in Fraunce. That they may
be welcome to Rome, they ſpeake there of nothing ſo
much, as this abſolute obedience, in all things that may

be commaunded them by the Pope. In Fraunce they flatly denie it, for feare of beeing banisht from thence. For, that you may know how the case stands, our church of Fraunce, liues vnder the obedience of the Church of Rome, but with certaine liberties, by meanes whereof, it is preseru'd against the practises of the court of Rome, as well in temporall things as spirituall. The Popes are men, made of such parts as all other men are, so that in their holinesses, there is somtimes a little of humane corruption. If a Pope, wunne thereto by deuises, and false informations of them that are about him, should make warre vppon our Kings, assure your selues, the Iesuits would be as great enemies to them.

The Pope smites with his principall sword, which is his censures; a declaration of heresie followes quicklie after them, & then a publishing of the Croysade. Mingle with this, the factions and preachings of the Iesuits, and this vow of blindfold obedience, vnknowne to all antiquitie, and assure your selfe, this were to bring our Realme into a meruailous disorder. Call to minde in what sort Pope *Sixtus* the fourth fayled to surprize the estate of Florence, from the house of *Medices*, where *Iulian* was slaine in the church as he was hearing Masse. Imagin how it had beene possible for those Lordes to haue saued themselues from that vnlookt for conspiracie, if there had beene a band of Iesuits in their towne. Call to minde that which past of late memorie in thys Country of Fraunce, vnder Pope *Sixtus* the fift, and how we were at the first afflicted, by his winking at, and furthering our troubles. Both these had beene begging Fryers, and afterward became Popes.

The one set himselfe against the pettie Commonwealth of Florence, but at such time, when as yet there were no Iesuits in the world. The other, led by the Iesuits hand, was brought against the florishing Realme of Fraunce. You shall find, that it is not without great reason,

fon, that they difclaime their Particular vow of blindfold obedience to the Popedome : becaufe they know
in their confciences, that no ftate can euer be fecure
from the Popes anger, fo long as they continue there.

❡ *What fhifts the Iefuits vfe, to couer the impieties of
theyr blindfold obedience.*

S the Aduocate ended this difcourfe, the
Iefuit thinking that hee had a newe aduantage againft him, fpake thus to him.
You trim vs heere after a ftrange fafhion, and are fo blind, that you fee not in
the meane while, that the paffage, which
you haue alleaged againft vs, brings with it the folution
of all that which you vpbrayd vs with. For what precife
obedience fo euer be enioynd vs, yet is it with this condition, *Vbi definiri non poſsit aliquod peccati genus*, there,
and in fuch cafe, as that a man can perceiue no kinde of
finne therein. And this is that which *Montaignes*, one
of our Order, alleaged ere-while by you, hath very wifely aunfwered.

    Chap. 25. &
29. of Truth
defended.

    You teach mee no new thing (quoth the Aduocate)
and I would not haue fayld to tuch this ftring, though
you had not interrupted me. But it is wel, that you haue
had fome pittie of mee, that by this little pause, I might
take my breath awhile. For indeed, to tel you the truth,
I begin to wexe wearie, yet ere I make an end, I will acknowledge, that this claufe alleaged by you, is interlaced. For you gallants, neuer want fhifts to couer your
fhame. Make thefe foure or fiue words, agree with the
reft of the article, and I will yeeld you the caufe. Your
vow conftraines and bindes you to belieue, that when
our holy Father the Pope, or your Superiours enioyne

I i. 3.   you.

you any thing, though it bee not such as by your Order is obligatorie, you are to thinke that G O D is in theyr mouthes, and that as soone as you are commaunded, in the twinckling of an eye, without gain-saying, all worke set apart, yea, if it be a Letter begun, you must of necessitie obey. That in your obedience, you must bring the hand, the hart, & the iudgement all together. That you are in this matter, as a dead carkasse, or a staffe, which receiue no motion, but as they are thrust by him that guides them; and to conclude, that the obedience, you must performe is blindfold. This in short, is your vow, which you make a shew to limit by these words (so that a man find no apperance of sin in it;) can it possibly be, that I should iudge that he commaunds me any sinne, in whom you will haue the presence of God acknowledged in commaunding? Besides, doe you giue me leasure to thinke on it, though I might perhaps doe it, when as in the twinkling of an eye I must obey? More, you ordaine, that my will and iudgement assist the execution of this commaundement. Whereby you take from me all examination, meaning that I should be like a staffe in the hand of an old man. And for conclusion, this obedience, which you wil haue to be blindfold, should haue eyes, if it were permitted me to settle my iudgement vpon the goodnes or badnes of the commaundement. And indeed a man must haue neither eye nor iudgement, no more then you haue in your blind obedience; or else he must needs say, that these foure or fiue words, which haue beene foysted by *Ignace* into this Article, are void, and to no purpose. If I had nothing but this to say, yet it were inough to make your Sophistry appear: but I wil not tarry in this broad way. It was *Ignace* that made this constitution. For *Ribadiner* acknowledges; that all your constitutions came from him. There is not then any more faithfull interpreter of *Ignace* intent, then himselfe. *Peter Maffee*, a
Priest

Prieſt of your Societie, hath written his life, and that
with the approbation of your Generall *Aquauiua*; for
to him the booke is dedicated. I doe not thinke that he
would haue ſuffered it to be printed, and much leſſe de-
dedicated to him, if he had not thought that it made
much for their order. Marke now what a commentary
we may draw out of this booke, to ſhew that *Ignace*
meant, that the obedience of them of his order ſhould
be blind.

Obedientiæ ſtudium, quibuſcumq́, rebus potuit ſemper oſ-   Maff. lib.3,
tendit : Romano quidem Pontifici, cuius in verba præcipuo cap.7.
quodam ſacramento iurauerat, ita erat præſto, vt ad ipſius
nutum ſeſe paratum exhiberet. Confecta iam ætate, vnius
baculi adminiculo, pedibus, quocunque opus eſſet, peregre pro-
ficiſci, vel etiam nauigium aſcendere planè exarmatum, ſeque
eodem pontifice iubente, mari ventiſque, ſine vlla dubitatione
committere. Quem ipſius animum vir quidam primarius
cum haud ſatis probaret, & in eiuſmodi re, conſilium pru-
dentiamq́, requireret, Prudentiam quidem non obedientis,
verùm imperantis eſſe reſpondit Ignatius. Et ſane cum in ſo-
cietate noſtra, virtutem hanc, cæteris virtutibus anteferret,
tum nihil huic laudi tam contrarium dicebat eſſe, quàm in
Superiorūiuſſis & conſilio examinando, moram, vel potius ar-
rogantiam, negabatq́ obediētis nomine dignū haberi oportere,
qui legitimo Superiori, non, cum voluntate, iudicium quoq́,
ſubmitteret. Id enim gratiſſimum eſſe Deo holocauſtum, cum
omnes animi vires, ac præſertim intelligentia & mens, quæ
ſummum in homine obtinent locum, in obſequium Chriſti co-
guntur. Qui verò inuiti ac diſſentientes, actu exteriore dum-
taxat, iuſſa præpoſitorum exequerentur, hos inter viliſſima
mancipia, vel pecudes potius numerandos aiebat. And a little
after. *Quinetiam in ſermone quotidiano vſurpare ſæpe con-*
ſueuerat, qui ad Superioris nutum, voluntatis propenſionem
ſolummodo, non etiam iudicij conſenſionem accommodarent,
eos, altero tantum pede intra Religionis ſepta verſari.

Hee alwaies ſhewed his care and obedience, by all
meanes

means he could : He was at the Bishop of Romes beck, to whom he was sworne by an especiall oath. When he was verie old, he went a foot on pilgrimage, whither soeuer it was needful, hauing nothing but his staffe to rest on. Neyther did he refuse to goe by Sea, whensoeuer the said Bishop commaunded him, though in a ship neuer so ill prouided. Which mind of his; when a certaine principall man mislikt, as finding therein want of wisedome & discretion, *Ignace* aunswered, that wisdom was not for him that must obey, but for him that commands. And as in our Societie he preferrs this vertue before other, so he was wont to say, that nothing was so contrary to the commendation of obedience, as delay, or rather arrogancie, in examining the reason of our Superiours commaundements, and he denied that he was worthie to be called obedient, that did not submit both his wil, & his iudgement also, to his lawfull Superiour. For that, said he, is a most acceptable Sacrifice to God, when all the powers of a mans mind, and especially the iudgement and vnderstanding, which are the most principall, are brought to the obedience of Christ. As for them that vnwillingly, and with mislike performd the commaundements of their Superiour, onely in outward act, he made no more account of them, but as of most base Vassals, or rather brute beasts. And a little after. Moreouer, he was wont to say in his common speech, that they which brought onely a readie will, and not a consent of their iudgement to the fulfilling of their Superiours will, had but one foot within the cloyster of their order.

You see what obedience *Ignace* would haue performed, first to the Popes, & then the superiors of his order. Let vs gather the chiefe points of it. Behold a man, that hath one foot in the graue; he must go trauaile. Behold a broken Barke in the midst of a tempestuous Sea, this poore man must go aboord her, if the Pope command.

God

God forbids mee very expresly to be a murtherer of my
selfe, vpon paine of euerlasting damnation. In these two
commaundements, I see my death present before mine
eies, was there euer any greater reason to say, that a man
is not bound to obey? And yet by this obedience enioyned by *Ignace*, not onely we are bound to obey, but if
we doe not, we commit a great and grieuous sinne. O-
bey, and you sinne against the expresse law of God.
Refuse to obey, and you sinne against *Ignace* law, which
the Iesuits take to be greater then Gods. If *Tertulian*
were reproued by our auncestors, because he forbad a
Christian to flee from one Citie to another, to saue himselfe from persecution for religion, as if therby he would
haue vs become murtherers of our selues, what shal we at
this day say of this cruell proposition of *Ignace*? Once
you see our Iesuits are but mockers, when as to excuse
the impietie of their blind obedience, they adde : *There,
where they discerne not that there is any sinne* . For *Ignace* did not only not suffer them of his order to discern
that there was any, but contrariwise, accouted the worse
then slaues or brute beasts, if they withstood that which
was commaunded them. And that you may see better
and better, what the intent of this great Law-giuer was,
see what *Maffee* addes. *Atque ad sapientem hanc sanc-
tamque stultitiam cæcæ (vt ipse aiebat) Obedientiæ, suos vt
essent ad subita & seria promptiores, interdum etiam fictis in
rebus erudiebat.* And that they of his Order, might be
the redier vpon a sodaine in earnest matters, by this wise
and holy foolishnes of blind Obedience, as he called it,
he did sometimes put them to it in iest, by occasions deuised for the nonce. And vpon this proposition, he tels
a tale, that one day a Priest of their Societie, being attired in his Vestments, comming out of the Vestrie with
the Challice in his hand, as he went to say Masse, receiued a message from *Ignace* to come to him presently ;
The Iesuit obeied him and left his Vestments and Cha-

K k.   lice.

lice, *Ignace* askt him, if he did not miſlike this commaundement. No (quoth he) I hold it for verie good, ſith it came from you. Know then, quoth *Ignace*, that I ſent not for thee, becauſe I had any thing to ſay to thee, but onely of purpoſe to make triall of thy obedience. And thou haſt done a more meritorious worke, in leauing the Sacrifice thou waſt about to offer, then if thou hadſt offered it. So that although the Sacrament of the Altar of God, be of ſuch importance, as it is, yet Obedience is better then Sacrifice, as it is writtē. Another time, as a Ieſuit prieſt was hearing the cōfeſſion of a yong gentleman, *Ignace* ſent for him, to whō when the Prieſt had anſwered, that he would not faile to come to him, as ſoon as he had giue abſolution to the penitēt, *Ignace* not content with this anſwer, ſent for him the ſecōd time. Which this Confeſſor ſeeing, intreated the Gentleman to haue patiēce & went preſently to *Ignace*, who at the firſt word ſpake thus to him. What? Muſt I ſend twice for thee? And ſharpely rebukt the man with verie bitter words: not becauſe he had any thing for him to do, but to make him know, what obedience he muſt vſe in things that are ſeriouſly enioyned him. If he might haue entred into an examination, and conſideration of the ſinne, the honour, dignitie, good order, and dutie to the Church, forbad theſe two Ieſuit Prieſts to obey their Generall. But he would not take this for payment, becauſe it appertaind not to the inferiour, to enter into conſideration, whether there were ſinne in the matter or no; neither is wiſedome to be lookt for, at his hands that is commaunded, but at his that commandeth. Theſe are then indeed very dallyings, theſe are mockeries, theſe are illuſions and fancies, by which the Ieſuit would abuſe vs, when hee alleages, that he is not boūd to obey, if he find any apparence of euill in the commaundement. For contrariwiſe all ſinnes are couered, and blotted out, when he obeyes. This is that (Gentlemen) which I had to ſay this mor-

ning

ning: and becaufe after we haue fed our mindes with
difcourfe, it feemes to me high time to refrefh our bodies with fome nourifhment, I pray you hold me excufed, if I proceed no further : yet with proteftation that
after dinner I will declare to you at larg, all that feemes
to me to be behind of this matter.

CHAP. 19.

¶ Of the wifedome of Ignace, and the fottifhnes of the newe
Iefuits. A Dialogue betwixt the Iefuit, and the
author of this difcourfe.

He companie not onely yeelded to the
Aduocates motion, but alfo thankt him
for the paines he had taken, and promift
to take : all of vs being refolued to heare
him as fauourably after dinner, as we had
doone in the morning. But the Gentleman faid, If I
be King in my houfe, as the Collier is in his, I appoint
this afternoone be fpent in walking, and efpecially you
particularly my good friend, quoth he, to the Aduocate, are permitted to giue your thoughts leaue to play,
till to morrow morning, when, if it pleafe God, we will
make an end of our difcourfe. As he appointed, fo it
was done.

Dinner was brought in, the cloth taken away, euerie
man rofe vp to go whither it pleafed him, into the Garden, into the walks, into the Parke, into the fields, mea-
dowes or woods : For our hofts houfe had all this varietie. For my part I went to the Iefuit, whom I found
reafonable wel difpofed, after we had walkt two or three
turnes togither, I faid to him; What thinke you of our
Aduocate? For in my opinion, though much of his
fpeech were to verie good purpofe, yet he went fome-
what too far in reproaching the of your order. It is not
for me to iudge of him, quoth he. For if I fay, he fpake
well, I fhall wrong our Societie: if ill, you will thinke

Kk 2.

it

it is to flatter my felowes. In fine, which way so euer you
take it, I may well be accepted against.

Away with these points of Rhetorick (quoth I) you
and I are heere in a place of truth, where wee are not to
dissemble. Do you not remember you haue read in *He-
rodotus*, that when the wife puts off her smock in bed, by
her husband, shee puts of shame to ? Sith you haue cast
off the habite of your Order, I suppose it is very easie
for you to cast off also that hypocrisie, which your il-
willers say lodges in your Houses. You are a trauailer,
and *Homer* could not tell how to represent the wisedom
of men better, then in an *Vlysses*, that had seene diuers
Countries. Sith you were chosen by your Generall to
passe from countrey to countrey, to sound the diuersity
of our behauiours and opinions, that you might make
report thereof to him, it is not likely, but that at one
time or other, when you are alone in the fieldes, you
vvill finde leysure to play the Phylosopher, in considering the carriage of your Societie. Therefore I hartilie pray you, tell me plainly and trulie, what your opinion is of them, and withall, of this discourse of our Aduocate. For although you are meruailously kept vnder
by your Constitutions, yet your thoughts are free. The
Law-maker of your Order, was not able to take any order for them.

Then said the Iesuit, sith you coniure me in so friendlie
a manner, I should be very discurteous if I should not
satisfie you. The Aduocate is too blame, but not so
much as some man would thinke. If he haue spoken ill
of our Societie, wee are the cause of it. No man is hurt
but by himselfe. The greatest secret that I finde in matter of religion, is, that the secrets of them be not made
commonly knowne, & that euerie religious person, according to the profession he makes, liues in peace of cō-
science. I see, that amongst the olde Priests of the Heathen law, greatest account was made of the Druides, &
there

there was nothing that got them so much credit, as an auncient policie, of not leauing theyr doctrine in wryting, but to keepe it secret, and deliuer it from hand to hand, by a long tradition from their auncesters to their successours. If wee had followed the wisedome of our great and wise *Ignatius,* wee had neuer faln into this inconuenience. For it was his opinion, that wee should keepe our selues close and hidden, so that the people might haue no knowledge of our gouernment. To the end, that our ceremonies, or to speake better, our deuotions might be seene of the people, but not read.

Our enemies then spake of vs (if I may so say) but by gesse. Now our Bulls and Constitutions are suffered to come to this and that mans handling, I doubt mee wee shall be vndone, and whereas many in former time honoured vs, heereafter they will abhorre vs. And this is a poynt wherein I can not sufficiently praise our *Ignatius* his wisedom. For although he had not onely deuisd, but put in practise his Constitutions for the gouernment of our Order, along while in his life time, yet would he neuer publish them, neither came they abroad till after his death; namely, till after the assembly that wee held in Rome in the yeere 1 5 5 8. We made account then, that we shewed our selues worthy men, but indeed, there was neuer any thing doone more foolishly, as the euent beareth witnesse.

He had besides, another very wise rule, that he would neuer at any hand, suffer that any of our Order, should set pen to paper to defend or iustifie vs when wee were accused. It may be he did it in Christian chaiitie, it may be also in worldly wisedom. *Spreta* (saith the wise *Tacitus*) *exolescunt : Si irascare, agnita videntur.* There neuer was any thing that seemed to be so preiudiciall to our Societie, as the censure of the Diuines of Paris, in the yeere 1 5 5 4. Some whose fingers itcht at it, woulde needes haue aunswered it, and those of the most woorthy

Kk 3. thy

thy and sufficient of our Order, who perswaded themselues, that they should get the better of them: But *Ignace*, more subtile and wise then they, forbad them very expresly. And it is not to be doubted, but that by this aduise, he got more aduantage by silence, then all our blotters and scriblers of paper since, haue done by wryting. For it is certaine, that this censure by length of time, was buried in the graue of forgetfulnes, if we had not giuen occasion to renew it, by pushing as wel at the generall estate, as at some particuler men in Fraunce.

While *Ignace* liued (as I told you) wee were not permitted to set out our conceits lightly to the view of the world, how well so euer wee were perswaded of them. Now adaies, there is none of our Societie so meane, but abuseth both his pen and his wit, without considering what good or hurt may redound to the whole order by his writings. They please themselues in their own conceit, by a certaine itching desire to write, which afterward costs vs deere, while they set abroch many false & erroneous propositions, squared by the rule of their owne follies. And God wot, our ill-willers knowe too well how to make theyr aduantage of them.

One *Iohn Peter Maffee*, first, in the yeere 1 5 8 7. and after him, one *Peter Ribadinere*, in 1 5 9 2. did set out the life of our good founder *Ignatius*, and *Horace Turcelline*, the life of *Fraunces Xauier*, with so many flatteries, (I must needs say so to my great griefe) absurdities, and contrarieties, that I assure my selfe, I shall see some man or other ere long, that is full of leysure and spight, make an Anotomie thereof, to the disgrace of the memorie of those two holy Fathers, and the confusion of our Order. You may thinke he is as wise a Priest as our *Emanuell Sa*, who entiteld himselfe Doctor of Diuinitie of our Societie, vvhen hee caused his Aphorismes of confession to be printed, wherein he bragges hee had labourd fortie whole yeeres.

How

How many Articles find you among them, that tend not to the defolation of Kings & kingdoms ? If hee had beene as wife as our firft Fathers, thefe had beene good leffons to whifper into the eares of thefe Idiots, that take vs to be the great Penitentiaries of the holy Sea, and to fuch as ordinarily come to vs to confeffe theyr great finnes : but by blowing abroade all thefe circumftances of finnes ouer all his Booke, it teacheth vs, that this *Emanuell Sa*, hath labourd fortie whole yeres, to make all the world in the end perceiue, that hee is none of the wifeft.

As for our reuerend Father *Robert Bellarmin*, I acknowledge him to be a very fufficient man, as one that by his writings, hath found meanes to purchafe a Cardinalls hat. But I may fay to you, as a thing too true, that he marrs our market in making his owne, as you may perceiue by his bookes of the *Tranflation of the Empire*, & *Of the Indulgences of Rome*. In the latter of which, he hath toucht many particulars, which concerne not pardons, and for which he had need aske pardon of Kings & Bifhops. It is not my meaning to offend him by thys fpeech, but if euer he and I meete together alone, I will fpeake two or three words to him in his eare, & requeft him to write a little more modeftly heereafter, as I affure my felfe hee will doe, hauing now attayned to that which made him write fo; were it not, that perhaps he hopes to be Pope one day. But I thinke him fo wife, that hee will not tie his thoughts to fuch an impoffibilitie. For the wife Confiftorie of Rome, will neuer fuffer a Iefuit to come to that high degree of the Popedome, for an infinite number of reafons, which I had rather conceale then vtter.

Since the fentence pronounced againft vs, 1494. in Paris, I find fiue bookes fet out by our men, the titles whereof are thefe : 1. *The Plea of Maifter* Peter Verforis, *Aduocate in the Parliament for the Priefts and Schol-*
lers.

lers of the Colledge of Clairmont, founded in the Vniuersitie of Paris, plaintiues against the said vniuersity being defendant. 2. *The defence of the Colledge of Clairmōt, against the Complaints & Pleas printed against them heretofore.* 3. *A most humble remonstrance & supplication, of the religious of the Societie of Iesus, to the most Christian King of Fraunce and Nauarre,* Henrie *the fourth of that name.* 4. *The truth defended for the Catholique Religion, in the case of the Iesuits, against the Plea,* of Anthonie Arnault, *by* Frances Montaignes. 5. *An aunswere made by* Rene de la Fon, *for the religious of the Societie of Iesus, against the Plea of* Simon Marion, *made against them, the* 16. *of October.* 1597. With other notes vpon the Plea, and other matters concerning *Stephen Pasquiers* Researches.

Assure your selfe, there is neuer a one of these gentle Writers, that in defending vs, accuseth vs. And although you shall find some tough points here and there in others, yet I cannot tell how, euerie where they sauour of a Scholler. When I haue said this, I haue said all. Our company pleaseth not all. No not many French Catholiques. It is a misfortune that accompanies vs in the midst of the blessings we receiue of God. But such a misfortune, as we make well the worse by an other. For if we find any man, that doth not like vs, by and by we pronounce him an heretique. It is a new Priuiledge. that we haue giuen our selues to turne cursing into religion, and we thinke our selues acquitted of it, if we father our iniuries vpon some counterfait name. *Benet Arias,* a Spaniard, a man that neuer erred from our Catholique Religion, caused the Bible to be printed in Antwerpe, 1584. with some points of importance, wherein hee complaines of great wrong that was done to him by our Society, *Qui cùm sibi soli sapere* (saith he, speaking of vs) *soli benè viuere, Iesumque propius insequi & comitari videantur, atque id palam professi iactitent, me qui minimum atque adeo inutilem Iesu Christi discipulum*

discipulum ago, odio habuerunt gratis. Atque hi quod
neminem qui alias bene audiat, improbare audent, alio-
rum quos ad eam rem occulte inducere possint, ingenijs
& nominibus abutuntur. Who, thinking themselues
onely wise (saith he, speaking of vs) that they onely liue
well, and seeme to follow Iesus verie neere and strictly, and openly make profession thereof with boasting,
hated me without any cause, that am a poore & vnprofitable seruant of Iesus Christ. And these men, because they dare not mislike any man, that is otherwise
wel spoken of, abuse the names & wits of other, whomsoeuer they can vnder hand perswade to such a course.
His meaning is, that we abuse other mens pens against
him, not daring to deale with him, by our owne. That
was our our practise at that time, but since, wee haue
found a new course, to make bookes vnder supposed
names, such as those two bookes that goe vnder the
name of *Frances Montaignes* and *Rene de la Fon,* which
I was not able to read without choller. And touching
that book, that is said, to be made by *Montaignes,* I find,
that the author made choise of a name fit for his booke.

Parturient montes, nascetur ridiculus mus.

See what a goodly peece of worke he hath made, by
discouering the secrets both of our simple vow, and that
of chastitie, and into what daunger he hath brought vs
amongst Kings, by committing their Crownes, to the ful
and bare disposition of the holy Sea. I will adde here-
vnto, that as our fingers are still itching, this booke is
translated into Latine by one of our order, who hath
called *Montaignes, Montanus,* which was the name of a
notorious old heretique, that he might still giue our e-
nemies occasion to speake euill of vs. As for *la Fon,*
he that deuised that name, should rather haue termed
him Foole, so many follies, and flatteries are there in that
booke. *Stephen Pasquier* hath written many bookes
which are wel liked, both in Fraunce and in other coun-

L l. tries.

tries. *Montaignes* in his booke *Of Truth defended,* maketh fauourable mention of him. This little foole, *la Fon,* to supply his companions default, breaks out with rayling on him, worſe thē a ſtrumpet out of the ſtewes : And I am afraid, *Paſquier* that hath not the gout in his hand, will not let him be long without an aunſwere. And ſo there will be one good turne for another.

Thinke not ſo, (quoth I) to the Ieſuit, for when I ſpake with him of it, he aunſwered me thus. Sir, my good friend, this diſguiſed Ieſuit, is like one of the Shrouetueſday Maskers, who by the libertie of the day, carry blacking about them, with which they markè euery one that comes in their way ; who ſhould be but a laughing-ſtocke to the people, if they would be angrie at it. My collections of Fraunce, amongſt which my Plea is, carrie their ſafe conduct in their faces ; If a man will read them, they wil anſwer for me. If any man will not read them, let him come to me, & I will anſwer for them. If any man of learning, finde any obſcuritie in them, I will thinke my ſelfe honoured by him, if it will pleaſe him, to let mee cleere the doubt to him. For in few words, I perſwade my ſelfe, that this Mountebank, thinking to accuſe me, accuſeth ſometime Saint *Paule,* ſometime Saint *Luke,* one while *Lactantius Firmianus,* an other while, Saint *Bernard,* and venerable *Bede :* and which is more, their owne fellow *Bellarmine,* whoſe authoritie is of greater worth with them, then Saint *Pauls.* It is a ſingular vertue that Ieſuits haue, that the further they goe, the more fooles thy proue.

Would you know the reaſon of it ? The firſt leſſon, that is taught thē when they enter into their nouiceſhip, is abſolutely to acknowledge Ieſus Chriſt, not onely in the perſon of their Generall, but alſo in all other their Superiors. Now, as ſoone as euer any of them commeth to any degree, he maketh account, that he is to other, ſuch as his Superiours were to him. Inſomuch that hee

beleeues

beleeues,that his fantafticall imaginations are articles of
our faith : and vpon this vaine beliefe, he powreth out
himfelfe into a thoufand fooleries. Let it fuffice you,that
I meane not to giue life to this abortiue booke by my
anfwer . When their Librarie was fold at Paris , they
had my Latin Epigrams,in the fixt booke wherof, they
fhall find thefe foure verfes,which I giue for a full aunfwere to this foole.

Carmine nefcio quis nos corrodente laceffit,
   Refpondere fibi me cupit, haud faciam.
Rurfus at ecce magis, magis infectatur & vrget,
   Refpondere fciat me fibi, dum taceo.

VVith biting verfe I know not who prouokes,
   Me to make aunfwere, but I meane to ceafe.
Yet more and more, he followes me with ftrokes,
   I make him aunfwer, when I hold my peace.

You fee (quoth I to the Iefuit) what I can report
to you of *Pafquiers* aunfwere , whereby you may perceiue,that he defpifeth your *la Fon.* Whereunto the Iefuit anfwered.He may deceiue himfelf,For do not think
that our Societie is engaged in all the bookes that I named. The pollicie wee obferue in publifhing our
bookes, is this. The Author is like the Quirifters
in Cathedrall Churches, which carrie the bookes before others, and after that one of them hath fung a
verfe, he is followed by the whole bodie of the Quire.
So is it with our company. He that is the bearer of his
booke, fings firft, imparting it to the Prouinciall , the
Rector, Fathers, and Regents,as well of the houfe, as of
the Colledge where they abide. All which by a common confent,contribute thereto particularly : fo that the
generall frame is the Authors, but the moft part of the
feuerall peeces are many other mens. This is the firft
fhape we giue to this matter, after which followes ano-

ther. For we are expreſly forbiddē by the conſtitutions, to ſet out any booke without our Generals leaue. The booke is viewed by him, or by his foure Aſſiſtants, or by other deputed by him. In briefe, hold it for a moſt certaine ground, that all the bookes mentioned by me, hauing had this courſe, are approued by our whole order. If it be ſo (quoth I) your order is meruailous ignorant, to ſuffer all theſe furious bookes to run vp & downe the ſtreets : And there need but a few of theſe to make your order come backe to the wallet, whence your Hiſtoriographers ſay it had the beginning. That is the thing (quoth he) that greeues me moſt of all, to ſee that our Superiours, ſhould be ſo ſet vppon a blind reuenge, that thereby they became fooles with fooles. But in the meane while, what ſaid *Paſquier* to that noble Epitaph, which our *De la Fon* makes of him, in theſe words ?

Well, let him liue yet ioyfully, and write and raue if he will againſt the Ieſuits, hee ſhall doate at laſt in his old age, vntil ſome one of this Societie, or if they diſdain it, ſome other, for the publique good, take a generall ſuruey of that which he hath printed, and a collection of his follies, rauings, aſſeheadnes, ſpightfulnes, hereſies, and Machiaueliſmes, to erect a Tombe of balefull memorie, wherein he ſhall be coffind aliue, whither the Rauens and Vultures may come a hundred leagues by the ſent, and to which, no man may dare to approch by a hundred paces, without ſtopping his noſe by reaſon of the ſtinck : where brambles & bryers may grow, where Vipers and Cockatrices may neſtle, where the Skriechhowle and Bitter may ſing; that by ſuch a Monument, they that now liue, and they that ſhall liue hereafter, may know, that the Ieſuits had for their accuſer and ſlaunderer, a notorious lyer, a capitall enemie to all vertue, and all that are vertuous ; and that al ſlaunderers may learne, by the loſſe of one proude ignorant fellow, to bethinke theſelues better of that which they write againſt religious orders,

Orders, & not impudently to slaunder the holy church of God, by their infamous & blasphemous writings.

Doe you aske mee (quoth I to the Iesuit) what *Pasquier* saide of it? I will tell you. Hee said to mee in fewe words, that this Pasport did well beseeme a Iesuits soule: and he was desirous it might be engrauen ouer the gates of all theyr Colledges, as a true portraict of theyr charitie: that euery man might know, that they did not name themselues the Societie of Iesus without great reason, who vppon the Crosse, prayed to God his Father for them that crucified him.

I and the Iesuit, past the afternoone in these & such like discourses, by which I perceiued that this honest man had many good parts in him, not common to other Iesuits. Also I found, that there is great difference betwixt him that being shut vp in his chamber, hath all his wisedome from his bookes, and him, that besides his bookes, pertakes of wise mens discourses by word of mouth. The studie of the former, hath his times of breathing, but the latter, that studies without studying, hath great aduantage ouer the other. For my part, I was willing to be in his company, and I think I had spent the rest of the day with him, but that ill hap (enuious of my content) depriued me of it, by the comming of two or three foolish fellowes, who began to iest at mee, saying, they saw well my intent was to become a Iesuit. You may be sure of that (quoth I) if all Iesuits were of thys mans temper. So wee walkt, and talkt one thing or another, till supper time: during which there was nothing but iesting and merry talke, all earnest matters beeing layd aside till next morning: when all of vs beeing met together in the Hall, euery one cast his eyes vppon the Aduocate, whom the Gentleman requested to make an end of his carriere, which hee did in such sort as you shal presently vnderstand.

The end of the second Booke.

Ll 3.   The

The third Booke of the Iesuits *Catechisme*.
(∵)

CHAP. 1.

⸿ Touching the Anabaptiſtrie which is found in the vowe that the Ieſuits make, concerning their blinde obedience to theyr Superiors: alſo, that by the meanes thereof, there is not any King or Prince that can defend himſelfe from theyr ſtings.

Haue (ſaith the Aduocate) diſcourſed vnto you, touching the Ieſuits doctrine and theyr coggings, as alſo, how that obtayning theyr priuiledges, they haue maliciouſly circumuented the holy Sea Apoſtolick. But I haue reſerued this morning time, to treat of the affaires of the ſtate, which they haue adioyned to theyr doctrine, within which, (by meanes of their abounding pietie that raigneth amongſt them) they haue alſo intermingled that leſſon which we learne out of *Machiauell*, in his Treatiſe touching a Prince, & in the Chapter of wickednes. For the murthers and killings of Kings & Princes, are as common among them in their conſultations, as amongſt the moſt vvicked murtherers that are in the world. Beſides, they haue giuen themſelues libertie, to trouble thoſe Realmes and Kingdoms, wherein they haue once had anie footing.

It may be euery one amongſt vs, will much meruaile at it, but if you will examine, (and that without paſſion) that

that blinde obedience which they vowe vnto their Superiors, it shall be an easie matter for you, cleerely to see the truth thereof. And marke I pray you, that I doe expresly say, (vnto theyr Superiors,) because, though they likewise vow the same vnto the Pope, yet it is not with so precise a declaration. And that it is so, you may well perceiue by this, that in the Article which yesterday I read vnto you, they speake but once of the Pope, and many times of their Superiours : So great a desire had *Ignatius Loyola* (their first founder and Law-maker) to teach, how much this obedience ought to be esteemed of, in regard of themselues, and their owne respects.

Concerning which poynt, I wil freely say thus much, that though in Fraunce wee admit not this particular obedience of the Iesuits towards the Pope, yet is it without comparison much more tollerable then the other. For in respect of my selfe, I will easily belieue this, that the opinions of these great Prelats, are so well ruled and grounded, that though one should vow vnto them, the most exact obedience that can be, yet they would not abuse it. Those Prelats are the men (the greatest number whereof, comming from meane place) which were for their vertues, merrits, and sufficiencies, at the first made Bishops, afterwards Cardinalls, and at the last aduaunced to that high throne of the supreme Pastor. In so much that theyr faithfulnes, holines, great experiences and auncientie, haue (as it should seeme) drayned and dryed vp in them, all those foolish passions, which commonly transport and carry vs away. But to speake the truth, I cannot, I dare not, I will not giue the like iudgement, touching the Superiors of the Iesuits order, because the honour, reuerence, and respect that I beare to the holy Sea, forbid me so to doe.

Yet notwithstanding, in their Chapter of obedience, as I haue alreadie said, after that they haue once mentioned the Pope, they speake of nothing but theyr Superiours

riours, that is to say, of their Generall, their Prouincials, their Rectors: for these are they, who euerie one of them in regard of their Order, beare the
name of Superiours ouer others. And you haue alreadie heard, that by the obedience that the inferiour oweth them, they are enioyned to beleeue, that by
their meanes, the commaundement floweth from Iesus
Christ himselfe, and that therefore they ought, euen
at the twinkling of an eye, not onely to obey in such
things of their Order, as binde them, but in all others:
yea, that without loauing or bidding, as wee say, they
should obey, and tie the will to the execution, and the
iudgement to the will, to the end, that the inferiour may
beleeue, that the commaundement is verie iust, seeing
that it was giuen vnto him. And who seeth not, that this
may well be resembled to a dead bodie, or to staffe, that
receiueth no motion, but by an other mans hand: yea
to be short, that this commaundement or law is without eies. And that therefore, to commit this absolute comaunmdement, to an Vsher or vnder offi-
cer, and that vnder the maske of Gods supposed presence, is properly to put a sword into a madde mans
hand.

And when I consider this vow, me thinkes I see the
Anabaptists, who said, that they were sent from God,
to reforme all things from good to better, and so to
reestablish them. And as men that hammer such matters in their heads, they caused a booke of reformation
to be published and dispersed. And they had for their
king, *Iohn Leyden,* and vnder him, certaine false Prophets
who were their Superiours, who made the people beleeue, that they talked and conferred with God, sometimes by dreames, sometimes by lies and forgeries, and
that they vndertooke nothing, but by Reuelation from
him. Afterwards, they breathed their holy Ghost, into
the mouthes of those whom they found best fitted, for

their

their furious opinions, diſtributing and diuiding them thorow their Prouinces, as their Apoſtles, to draw and bring vnto them, the moſt ſimple, and eaſie to beleeue. By meanes whereof, they brought to their lure and whiſtle, almoſt all Germanie, eſpecially within the town of Munſter, where they had eſtabliſhed, and ſet vp their monſtrous gouernment, one while commaunding murthers and maſſacrings, and an other while, executing them with their owne hands, in which they pretended nothing, but inſpiration from God. And going about to make as a pray vnto themſelues, all the Kings, Princes, and Potentates of that part of the world, they publiſhed, that they were expreſly ſent from G O D, to driue them away. Wherupon, they made account to murther them, if men had not preuented their purpoſes and practiſes. Now then tell me, I pray you, what doth the great vowe of the Ieſuites towarde their Superiours, elſe import, but the obedience of the Anabaptiſts? For further proofe whereof, let vs ſet before vs a General of their Order, who eyther thorow a certaine vnruly paſſion, or particular ignoraunce, went (but verie ill fauouredly) to make himſelfe a Reformer, as well of our religion, as of all politique ſtates: who alſo being in the middle of his companions, ſpake vnto them after this manner.

My little children, you know, that I being here preſent with you to commaund you, our Lord Ieſus Chriſt is in my mouth, and therefore that you ought thorowly, and in euerie reſpect to yeeld obedience. God powred out his holy Spirit, vpon our good Father *Ignace*, the better therby to ſuſtaine & vpholde his Church, which was readie to fall, by reaſon of the errours of the Lutherans; errors, I ſay, which are ſpred thorow al Europe to the great griefe of al good Catholicks. Now then, ſith it hath pleaſed God, to make vs the Succeſſors of that holy man, ſo it behooueth vs, that as

he

he himfelfe, fo we alfo, fhould be the firft workemen,
vtterly to root out the fame. Wee fee herefies raigne in
many Realmes, where alfo the fubiect armeth himfelfe
againft his King. In fome other places we behold Princes tyrannizing ouer their Subiects. Here a Queene
altogither hereticall : not farre from her : A King pro-
feffing the fame thing : and other fome feeding vs,
with faire fhewes & allurements,the more deeply to deceiue vs. It belongeth to vs, yea, to vs I fay,to defend the
caufe of God and of poore fubiects, not in fome fmall
femblance, as our forefathers haue done, but in good
earneft.

They that in former time occupied themfelues therein, haue drawen a falfe skinne ouer the wound, and by
confequent haue marred all. But we fhall doe a meritorious work,to vnburthen countries,& kingdomes therof. We muft needs become executioners of the foueraigne iuftice of Almightie God, which will neuer be
grieued or offended,with any thing that we,as Arbitrers
and Executors of his good will and pleafure fhall doe,
to the preiudice of fuch Kings as rule wickedly, and
fuffer their kingdomes to fall vnto them, whom in our
confciences we fhal know to be worthie thereof. How
beit, you thinke not your felues ftrong inough in your
felues, to execute my commaundements, yet at leaft, let
this be a leffon vnto you, that you may teach in the
midft of Gods Church. Wherein alfo,you muft imploy all the beft meanes you haue,leaft the danger, dif-
eafe, and Gangrene, get fo deepe a roote, that it will
not eafily be remooued. Wee fhall at the length finde
good ftore of workemen and Surgions, to helpe vs forward herein. But aboue al things, apply & refer to this,
all holy and neceffarie prouifion of Confeffiõ,of Maffe,
& of Cõmunicating,to the end,that we may with greater
affurance of their confciences, proceed on in this holy
worke and bufines. The neceffitie of the affaires of

Mm 2. Chriften-

Chriftendome commaundeth it, and the dutie of our charge, bindeth vs thereto. Thefe are the aduices and councels, that I haue receiued, from our Sauiour and Redeemer Iefus Chrift, who fuffered his death and paffion for vs, and for whofe fake, as it were in counterchaunge, we ought rather to die, then not to ridde our feluesof thefe wicked Princes. And thefe, euen thefe I fay, are the aduifes which I haue from God, whofe Vicegerencie I exercife and execute ouer you, though I be vnworthie.

I leaue heere to your owne confiderations, the places, examples, and authorities of holy Scripture, which are miftaken, and this Monfiure might alleage. For of this affure your felues, thefe Atheologians, or maimed Diuines, will no more faile therein, then the Negromancers do, in the inuocation of their fpirits, and diuels, or in their healing of difeafes. And yet all thefe matters tend but to Anabaptiftrie : or elfe, to the commaundements of that old dotard of the Mountaine, (mentioned in our Chroniclers) and called the Prince of the Affafines, who charmed and charged his fubiects, to kill handfmooth our Princes that went into the Eaft to recouer the holy Land. Whereupon alfo, there hath remayned amongft vs, and that euen to this day, the word Affafine, as proper againft all murthering Traitors.

But is not all this found in our Iefuits ? And is not this doctrine fcattered in the midft of that holy Order ? Haue we not feene the fplintors & fhiuers of it ? When the laft Prince of Orange was not at the firft time flaine in Antwerpe, was not this by the inftigation of the Iefuits ? And when at the fecond time he was flaine, in the yeere 1584. by *Balthazar Girrard*, borne in the countie of Burgundie ? And where alfo *Peter Pan* a Cooper, dwelling at Ipres, vvas fent to kill *Maurice* Prince of Orange and Earle of Naffaw, the other princes

ces

ces sonne, of whom I pray you did they take counsell ?
As for *Girrard*, before hee was examined he confessed,
that he went to a Iesuit, whose name hee knew not, but
that he was of a red haire, & Regent in the Colledge of
Trers, who also assured him, that hee had conferd touching that enterprise with three of his companions, who
tooke it wholy to be from God; assuring him, that if he
died in that quarrell, he should be enroled and registred
in the Kalender of the Martirs.

And the second confessed, that the Iesuits of Doway,
hauing promised him, to procure a Prebend for one of
his chyldren, the Prouinciall gaue him his blessing before he went about it, & said vnto him, Friend, goe thy
wayes in peace, for thou goest as an Angell vnder Gods
safegard and protection. And vpon this confession, he
was put to death in the Towne of Leyden, by solemne
sentence giuen the twentie-two of Iune, in the yeere
1598. Neither am I ignorant of this, that the Iesuits will
say, that they gaue that councell to kill two Princes, who
had armed theselues against their King. But I tell them,
that then the King himselfe must put them to death, be
they neuer so many, because they were the first enter-
prisers and attempters of our last troubles in Fraunce, as
well against the King that dead is, as against the King
that presently raigneth.

But their murthers haue a further reach then that. For
minding to stirre vp *Robert Bruse*, a Scottish Gentleman, either himselfe to kill, or to cause to bee killed by
some other, my Lord *Iohn Metellinus*, Chauncellour to
the King of Scots, euen of hatred towards him, because
hee was the Kings very faithfull subiect, they caused the
said *Bruse*, because hee would not condiscend & yeelde
vnto them, to be summoned, and sore troubled at Brux-
elles. And were they not pertakers with the Iacobin, in
the assault and murther that was committed against the
last French King ? And haue they not at sundry times,

Mm 3   and

and by fundry meanes, attempted to take away the life, of the Lady *Elizabeth*, Queene of England? And to be fhort, haue they not doone the like againft our King, both by the meanes of *Peter Barrier*, and *Iohn Caſtell*? frō which, God hath miraculoufly preferued him. To euerie of which particularities, I will allow his proper difcourfe, and begin the ſtorie of their aſſaults and mur-thers, that ſhould haue been committed by the Scottiſh Gentleman.

CHAP. 2.

¶ Touching an extraordinarie proceſſe and courfe, that was held in the Low-countries, againſt Robert Bruſe, *Gentle-man of Scotland, vpon the accuſation and information of Fa-ther* William Chrichton, *Ieſuit, becauſe he would not cauſe the Chauncellour of Scotland to be murthered.*

En ordinarily giue out, and grant extra-ordinarie proceſſe, againſt ſuch as mur-ther, or confent to murther, but to pro-cure it, or make it againſt one that would not confent thereto, this is the firſt of that qualitie that euer was heard of. And this is the very ar-gument of this preſent chapter.

A little after the death of *Mary* Queene of Scots, the late King of Spaine, cōmaunded the Duke of Par-ma, (who was then Gouernour for him in the Low-countries) to ſend *Robert Bruſe*, a Gentleman of Scot-land, to the Scottiſh King with Letters, in the which he promiſed him, men & money enough, to reuenge him-ſelfe, for the death of the Queene his Mother, vnto whō he proteſted, that hee bare alwaies a finguler affection, becauſe ſhe had vowed, and ſo declared herſelfe, to the laſt gaſpe of her life, to be of our Catholique Religion: which affection, hee would continue to the King her ſonne

fonne by fucceffiue right : but yet fo, as hee fhould promife, to become the inheritour, of the vertues and religion, of that good and worthy Princeffe.

My purpofe is not largely and by peece-meale, as we
fay, to treat and declare, howe this matter proceeded,
though I haue good and faithfull Intelligences of it.
This onely I will tell you, that the faid Gentleman, had
at the fame time, charge of certaine great fums of money, for the fraight of threefcore fhipps, to the end, that
they might firft ferue, for tranfporting of victualls and
munitions into the Low-countries, and afterwards, for
men of war, which the Spanyard refolued to fend into
England, hoping that the Queene of England, fhould
be affaulted on both fides.

A fhort time after *Brufes* arriuall in Scotland (he hauing beene all his young dayes brought vp and nouri-
fhed with the Iefuits) there came thother, Father *William
Crichton*, a Scottifh man, who fome-time had beene
Rector of the Colledge of the Iefuits at Lyons. And he
was in the company of the Bifhop of Dumblaine, who
was fent by Pope *Sixtus* the 5. to the King of Scotland,
to make him offer of a marriage with the Infant of
Spaine, fo that hee would become a Catholique, and
ioyne with them againft the Englifh.

My Lord *Iohn Metellenus*, fet himfelfe againft thys
negotiation, and for fundry good and weighty reafons,
councelled his Maifter not to regard it. Infomuch, that
the Bifhop returned thence, without effecting any
thing, leauing *Crichton* in Scotland, who ioyned himfelfe with *Brufe*, and was his companion. And becaufe
hee conceiued, that *Metellenus* alone had turned the
King from accepting the offers made him, he purpofed
to fhew him a Iefuits trick indeed. And that was this. A
catholick Lord, had inuited the King & his Chauncellour to a banquet. *Crichton* folicited *Brufe*, if it would
pleafe him to lende him fome mony, to compaffe thys
Lord,

Lord, that should giue order for procuring the slaughter of the Chauncellor, asturing himselfe, that by means
of the mony, he should make him doe whatsoeuer hee
would.

Bruse flatly refused, and that not onely because hee
was sent to another end, as hee made it appeare to him,
by the instructions and memorials which hee had from
he Duke of Parma; but also, and that much the rather,
by reason of the shame that would fall out vpon the execution of that enterprise: especially, he hauing before,
made shew of friendship & familiarity with the Chauncellor. Yea that, that murther, would neuer be thought
good and lawfull, beeing committed in the midst of a
banquet, and in the Kings presence, against whom the
iniurie should specially be performed, as well by reason
of the small account they made of his Maiestie, as for
the slaughter they should commit, vpon a person, who
he entirely affected for his fidelitie and wisedome. And
that if he did this deede, they should minister matter to
the King, to exasperate him against the Catholicks, as
murtherous, infamous, and trayterous persons to God
and the world, who to that present houre, had receiued
all bountifull kindnesses & curtesies from their King.

Crichton, seeing he had missed of this his match, went
to moue him to another, and to perswade *Bruse* to giue
fisteene hundred crownes to three Gentlemen, that did
offer to kill the Chauncellor, after some other lesse slan-
derous and offensiue manner. But *Bruse* answered him,
that, as in respect of the fault or sin, it was all one, to kill
a man with his owne handes, and to giue money to
procure such a purpose and act to be doone. And that
for his part, hee was a priuate person, that had not anie
authoritie ouer the life of any man, & lesse ouer the life
of the Chauncellour, who was a chiefe man, in the execution of the iustice of the Land. Furthermore hee added, that besides, hee had no charge from the Prince of
Parma,

Parma, to employ his money in such trade and Merchandize.

Metellinus, beeing welbeloued of the King his Maister, had two offices, to wit, the Chauncellours, & the chiefe Secretaries of estate: & that after his death, there were two great Lords, worse then he to the Catholicks, who beeing fauoured of the King, would part between them the spoyle of the other. To be short, that for an vncertaine good thing, which a man might promise vnto himselfe, hee should not accomplish a certaine euill thing, no, though a man were assured of good to come therby. And seeing the question was, touching the aduancing of Christian religion, this should be the meanes wholie to ruinate the same, in as much as men went about to promote it, by slaughter and murther, and that to the great scandale of all in generall, & the perpetuall dishonour of the holy order of the Iesuits in speciall.

And thus spake *Bruse* in his conscience, as one that hauing spent all his youth in theyr Colledges, bare them all manner of reuerence. And yet Father *Crichton,* would not yeeld for all this: for hee & his companions, haue theyr common places of antiquitie (but yet euil alleaged) to prooue, that murthers and such like wicked practizes are permitted. By meanes whereof, *Bruse* beeing more importuned then before, demaunded of him, whether in a good conscience hee might consent to that enterprise, or whether he could dispence there-withall? To which the Iesuit replyed, that hee could not: but this, that the murther beeing commited by him, and hee comming to confesse himselfe vnto him, hee would absolue him of it.

Then *Bruse* replyed in these termes; Sith your reuerence acknowledgeth, that I must confesse my selfe of it, you also, thereby acknowledge, that I should commit a sinne: and I for my part know not, whether, when I haue done it, God would giue me grace, and inable me

N n.   to

to confesse it. And thereto I verilie belieue, that the cō-
fession of an euill, that a man hath done of set purpose,
vnder an intent to confesse himselfe thereof, & to haue
absolution of it, is not greatly auailable, and therefore
the surest way for mee, is not to put my selfe into such
hazard and danger.

And so my Maister Iesuit missed at that time of his
purpose. But afterwards, hee knew verie well, to haue
his reuenge for it. For the Duke of Parma being dead,
and the Countie Fuentes a Spaniard, and Nephew to
the Duke of Alua, comming in his place, *Crichton* accused *Bruse* of two crimes before the said Countie. The
one, that he had ill managed the Kings treasure: The
other, that he was a Traytor, because he would not dis-
burse money, to cause *Metellinus* to be slaine: and thys
was the principall marke, at which the Accuser aymed.
A great fault certainly in the Iesuits common-wealth, &
for which, hee was worthily kept prisoner in Bruxells,
full fourteene months together. For as concerning the
first point, *Crichton* made no great account of that: but
touching the second, he to the vttermost stood vpon it:
and that so much the more, because the prisoner denied
not the crime.

The processe had his course. At the last, after that
Bruse had beene a long time troubled and afflicted, the
prisons were opened to him, and he was set free, but not
with any commaund to that holy Father the Iesuit, no
not so much as to repayre his good name, or to pay his
costs, dammages, or losses whatsoeuer. The reason
whereof was, (as a man may easily belieue it) that hauing
attempted this deuout accusation, he did nothing at all
therein, but that which might be directly referd to the
holy propositions of his owne Order.

CHAP.

CHAP. 3.

❡ *Concerning the murther, which* William Parry *an En-lishman (thrust on thereto by the Iesuits) meant to execute, against* Elizabeth, *Queene of England, in the yeere* 1584.

H E that writ the humble remon-strance & petition to the King, (minding to make it appeare, that men slaunderously accused the Iesuits, of hauing a purpose, to attempt any thing, against the Queene of England, sayth thus. In respect of English peo-ple, those that truly write of these matters, can witnes our faithfulnesse, and neuer yet durst accuse vs of attempting any thing against the Queene in her estate; & those that meant to calumniat & charge vs there-withall, could neuer fasten their lies and lealings vpon our behauiours and carriages of our selues, by any probable or likely reason of truth.

But now I will shew, that this Iesuit, is a second *Hero-dotus.* And let him not thinke but I doe him great ho-nor, when I resemble him to that great personage, whō men say, was the first Father of a lying historie.

William Parry, Doctor in the Lawes, a man full of vnderstanding, but yet more full of his pleasures & de-lights, after that he had consumed all his owne stocke & substance, and the greatest part of his wiues also, yea, & charged with a great controuersie and question, against *Hugh Hare,* Gentleman of the Temple, purposed in the yeere 1582. to take the wind and to saile into Fraunce, whore being arriued, and come particularly to the cittie of Paris, and purposing to be familiar with certaine En-lish Gentlemen, that were fled out of theyr Country for theyr religion, they doubted to be familiar with him, thinking that he came expresly to them to spy out their actions. By meanes whereof, hee tooke his iourney to Lyons, and from thence to Venice, where, euen at his first entrance, because hee was an Englishman, hee was put into the Inquisition: but he yeelded so good an account touching Catholique religion, that his Iudges found he had a desire and dutie to returne: beeing welbeloued of all the Catholiques, and particulatly, of Father *Bennet Palmeo*, a Iesuit of great reputation amongst his owne brotherhood. Afterwards, he tooke a conceit, to do such an act, as he once did that in old time burned the Temple of *Diana* at Ephesus; that so hee might be spoken of for it. Hee plotted to kill the Queene, his naturall Ladie and Soueraigne, & by the same meanes, to set fire on and in the foure corners and quarters of England, making thys the ground-vvorke of his practise and enterprise, and that as well to deliuer his Countrie, from tyrannie and oppression, as to aduaunce to the Crowne, *Marie* the Queene of Scots, vvho vvas a Catholick Princesse, & neerest of the blood to succeed. An oponion and conceit, that came from his owne instinct and motion, without acquainting the Scottish Queene any whit at all before his departure, as hee afterwards confessed, when hee was in prison. But because, this enterprise and attempt was verie hawtie, and that he vndertooke it with a great blow to his conscience before God, he conferred hereof with *Palmio* the Iesuit, (who according to the ordinarie Maxim and principle of that Sect) did not onely, not discourage or turne him there-from, but greatly confirmed him, and prouoked thereto: affirming, that there was nothing in that buisines, that could hinder him, vnlesse it were protracting and delay. After this, hee tooke againe the way to Lions, where, discouering himselfe to the Iesuits, he was greatly praysed and honoured of them. A

little

little while after, he returned to Paris, where certaine English Gentlemen, that were fugitiues out of their countrie, vnderstanding of his purpose and practise, began to embrace him : and by name, *Thomas Morgan,* who assured him, that so soone as he should be in England, and should haue executed his enteprise, hee would take order, that a puissant armie should passe out of Scotland, to assure the kingdome to the Queene of Scotland.

Now, though that *Parrie* seemed altogither resolute, yet was he in some sort hindred by sundrie remorses of his conscience : And indeed, he communicated the same, to certaine Englishmen, that were Ecclesiasticall persons, who all laboured to remoue him from it, and particularly a learned Priest, named *Watell*, who wisely declared & shewed vnto him, that all the rules of God, and the world, were directly contrarie to his deliberation and purpose. In this his irresolution and want of staiednes, he purposed to conferre with the Iesuits of Paris : amongst whom he addressed himselfe to father *Hanniball Coldretto,* to whom also in confession he discouered his first aduice and councell, and the vncertainty into which *Watell* had brought him. But the Iesuit, that lacked not perswasiue reasons, maintained vnto him, that *Watell,* and all the other, that put these scruples into his minde, were heretiques. And hauing againe set him in his former course, caused him (according to their ordinarie custome in such cases) to receiue the Sacrament, with diuers other Lords and Gentlemen. The English man being thus perswaded, tooke his leaue of them, and returned into England, fully purposed to bring his treason to effect and issue, whereunto the better to attaine, he sought all the meanes he might, to kisse the Queenes Maiesties hand, saying that he had certaine things of verie great importance, to acquaint her withall. And this was about the moneth of Februaris

Nn 3.

arie, in the yeere 1 5 8 5. At the laft, being brought before her Maiftie, he largely difcourfed vnto her the hiftorie of his trauaile, and how, that counterfaiting the
fugitiue, he had difcouered all the practifes and plots,
that the Englifh Catholiques had brewed or deuifed a-
gainft her Maieftie; yea, that he had promifed them, that
he would be the firft that fhould attempt her death,
which had purchafed him verie great credit amongft
them. And yet notwithftanding, that he would rather
choofe a hundred deaths, then to defile his foule with fo
damnable a thought.

He was a well fpoken man, of a good countenaunce,
& fuch a one, as had prepared himfelfe to play his part,
not vpon the fodaine, but wel prouided. The Queene
(who wanteth not her fpies) knew, that one part of that
which he had fpoken, was verie true : which alfo caufed her to credit the reft : and gracioufly accepting of
that honeft libertie and freedome, which he pretended,
charged him not to depart farre from the Court : and
that in the meane feafon, he fhould by letters, found the
affections of her enemies: which thing he promifed, and
vndertooke to do : and vpon this promife, feeding the
Princeffe with goodly fhewes, he did many times talke
verie priuately with her. And amongft other, fhe going
one day to hunt the fallow Deere, he followed her,
neuer fuffering her out of his eye. At laft, being a good
way, from her owne people, and difmounted from her
horfe, to refrefh her felfe at the foote of a tree in the
wood, *Parry* being nigh vnto her, twife had a defire to
kill her; but he was with-held there-from, by that gracious familiaritie which her Maieftie vfed towards him.
At another time, he walking after Supper with her, in
the garden of her Pallace, called white Hall, which ftan-
deth vpon the Thames fide, (where alfo he had a boate
readie, with the greater fpeed to faue him, and to carrie
him away, when he had giuen the blow, as alfo he fought
opportunitie

opportunitie for it) the Queene escaped from him in this manner.

He supposed, to draw her some-what farre from the the house, and that then he would kill her, at the gardens end. But she returned towards her Pallace, and said vnto him, that it was time to betake her to her chamber, being troubled with heat, and the rather, because she was the next day, to take a bath by the appointment of her Phisitions : And thereupon laughing, she withall added, that they should not drawe so much bloud from her, as many people desired. And with this speech she with drew her selfe, leauing *Parrie* much amazed at this, namely, that hee had fayled, in that his so worthie an enterprise.

Now as he behaued himselfe after this manner about the Q. he supposed, that he wanted a trusty friend to second him in his attempt, & therupon he addressed himselfe to his friend *Edmond Neuill*, an English Gentleman, who for his Religion and conscience sake, had his part amongst the afflictions & troubles of England, whom also he diuers times visited: and after that he had sworne him vpon the Euangelistes, not to reueale or discouer that which he should tell him, did particularly, and by peace-meale discourse to him, his whole intention, & prouoked him to take part with him therein, as one that had great reason, liuely to feele the iniuries that had bin committed against him : And that this was the time and onely meane to reestablish the Catholique Religion in England, and to set vp there the Queene of Scotland : and that in doing this, both of them should haue a good portion in the bootie that should be deuided. But *Neuill*, could at no hand well sauour or like of this new counsell. Wherupon, *Parrie* demaunded of him, whether he had Father *Allens* booke, which would stand him in steed of a continuall spurre, to prouoke him to this enterprise, though that of himselfe, he were not well

disposed

diſpoſed and prepared thereto, that by that booke, it was permitted to excommunicate Kings, & to depoſe them, yea, and to conſtraine and enforce them: and that ciuill warres for the cauſe of Religion were honourable and lawfull. I haue verie good and readie acceſſe to the Queene, ſaid he, as you alſo may haue, after that you are once knowne in Court. After that we haue giuen the blow, and done the deed, we will get into a boate, which ſhal be readie for vs, to go downe the Riuer withall, and from thence, we will be imbarked vnto the Sea, which you and I may eaſily doe, ypon my credit, without trouble or hindrance. *Neuill*, entertaining him with goodly words, & faire promiſes, yet neuer giuing him an abſolute yea, or nay, at the laſt reſolued with himſelfe, no longer to delay the matter, but to aduertiſe the Queene thereof: vnto whom ypon the eight of Februarie 1584, he related all that had paſſed betweene him and *Parrie*, who that night ſupped with the Earle of Leiceſter. The Queene being much amazed thereat, commaunded *Walſingham*, her chiefe Secretarie of eſtate, to apprehend both the one and the other, and yet notwithſtanding, to deale gently with *Parrie*, the better to draw the truth from him. Which alſo he did, declaring vnto him, that the Queene had receiued ſome new intelligence, of a conſpiracie againſt her. And becauſe the diſcontented Sect, had ſome good opinion of him, he prayed him to tell him, whether he had heard any thing thereof. And being twiſe or thrice asked, touching the matter, he ſaid, that he vnderſtood nothing of it at all.

If he had confeſſed the ſtorie, touching himſelfe and *Neuill*, and for excuſe had ioyned this vnto it, that what he had done therein, was done colourably, and that ſo he vſed it, the better to ſound the opinions of them, that hatched ſome diſcontentment in their minds. *Walſingham* ſaid afterward to ſundrie perſons, that they had

ſent

sent him away, fully cleared and absolued. But hauing
stoutly denied it, he set before his eyes *Neuils* deposition, which greatly astonished him; and so for that night
became his host, to hold him fast. On the morrow
morning, *Parrie* went to him in his chamber : and
told him, that he remembred, that he had held some
discourse with *Neuill*, touching a poynt of doctrine,
contayned in the aunswere that was made, to the booke
intituled, *The execution of Iustice in England:* by which
aunswere it was proued, that for the aduauncement of
the Catholique Religion, it was lawfull to take away a
Princes life: But for his owne part, he neuer spake word
touching any enterprize against the Queene. *Parrie*
and *Neuill*, were sent to diuers prisons, the latter, because he concealed that conspiracie sixe moneths and
more, the former, for the treason whereof he was accused: both the one and the other were examined, and
afterwards vppon charge giuen vnto them, they put
downe their confessions in writing. *Neuill* did it the
10. of Februarie, and *Parrie* the 11. and the 13. *Neuils*
contained the subornations, pursuits, and procurements,
that *Parrie* had made in respect of him : *Parrie* his,
that he had first plotted this Treason at Venice, being
heartned thereto, by the exhortations of *Palmio* the Iesuit: and that he was afterwards confirmed therein, by
the Iesuits of Lyons: and at the last he was wholly setled in it, by *Hanniball Coldretto,* & other Iesuits of Paris:
where, vpon this deuotion, he had beene first confessed,
and afterwards receiued the Sacrament. And this is
one poynt, that me thinketh should not be kept in silence, that being demaunded and examined by his
Iudges, he acknowledged, that when he first discoursed
with, and discouered vnto the Queene, the conspiracies, that the fugitiue Catholiques practised against her,
that so they might be brought againe to their houses,
she aunswered him, that it was neuer her mind, to deale

hardly

hardly with any for religion, but becaufe that vnder the colour & fhadow therof, they had purpofed to attempt mifchieuous matter, againft her & her ftate: and that for the time to come, none fhould be punifhed for the Popes Supremacie, fo long onely, and fo farre forth, as they carried themfelues, like good and faithfull fubiects. *Neuill* being called againe, & confronted before *Parrie*, perfifted in his depofition, and yet it was of no great weight whether he had done fo or no, but fruftratiue rather and needlefle. For *Parrie* had confeffed inough, yea, there was found in his houfe, fundrie letters, inftructions, and memorials, which condemned him. Befides, whiles he was in prifon, he wrote letters to the Queene, by which he verie humbly befought her, to abfolue him from the fault, but not from the punifhment which it deferued.

There were appointed vnto him for his Iudges, Sir *Chriftopher Wray*, Knight, Lord chiefe Iuftice of England, and diuers other great Lords of note and marke, who caufed him to be brought from the prifon to Weftminfter, and there againe being asked and examined, in the prefence of all the people, he confeffed his treafons: yea, there were read vnto him, his former confeffions, and the letters that he had fent to that purpofe, and other writings, tending to verifie vpon him the offence wherewith he was charged; all which, he confeffed to containe truth in them: adding withall, that there had not beene any confpiracie, for the matter of Religion, from the firft yeere of the raigne of the Queene, till then, whereof he was not partaker, excepting that touching the *Agnus Dei*, or Bull rather: and that befides all this, hee had put downe his opinion in writing, touching the Succeffour to the Crowne, that fo hee might the better ftirre the people to rebellion. This criminall caufe, was in handling, from the eight day of Februarie, in 84. vntil the 25. of the fame moneth. Vpon which

which day, *Parrie* was condemned to behanged by the
necke, and that the rope prefently fhould be cut in two,
and that he fhould be ripped vp, and his bowels taken
out, and caft into the fire, and burned before his eyes,
and that afterwards his head fhould be cut off, and his
bodie hewen into foure quarters, and that he fhould
be drawen vpon a hurdle, from the prifon, all along
the Citie of London, till he came to the place of execution. This fentence was then pronounced againft
him, but yet it was not prefently executed. But the fecond of March, *Parrie* was committed to the power
of fuch as execute foueraigne Iuftice: whereof being
aduertifed by the Sherieffes of London and Middlefex,
he arrayed himfelfe (as if a man had beene going to a
mourning) with a faire long gowne of blacke Damask,
and fet vpon the ftocke of his fhirt a great cuffe curiouf-
ly fet, fuch as was neuer at that time in the land. And taking his leaue of other prifoners, he did with a gallant
countenance, offer for a prefent, to the Lieutenant of
the Tower, a Ring: In which there was fet, a rich Diamond, deliuering it with this fpeech, that he was greatly
grieued, that he was not able to pleafure him more.
From thence he was drawen vpon a hurdle to the place
of execution, and being vpon the ladder, fome fay, that
he prayed the hangman that affayed to put the rope a-
bout his necke, that he would not diforder or marre his
cuffe: and thus died this great Martyr of the Iefuits,
promifing to himfelfe nothing leffe then Paradife, for
this his deteftable enterprife.

And thus haue I related vnto you a hiftorie, of 14.
or 15. moneths, for he returned into England, in the
moneth of Ianuary 83. and he was executed in March
84. Maifter *Anthonie Arnauld,* in his pleading, obiec-
teth againft the Iefuits this attempt and wicked facte
whereunto *Montaignes,* that wrote againft him, hath
aunfwered nothing at all, acknowledging by his filence,

that

that the obiection was verie true. For in obiections of leſſe conſequence and waight, he aunſwereth, and ſpareth him not. He that made *The defence of the Colledge of Clairmont*, confeſſeth, that *Parrie* was put to death for that pretended treaſon: but yet it was a charitable worke done to him, by the deadly enemies of the Ieſuits: which indeed is nothing elſe but to couer himſelfe with a wet ſacke. The proceſſe againſt him, is kept in the Records and Roles of Iuſtice: And particular enmitie or hatred, could not eaſily preuaile ſo farre, that there he ſhould be condemned to death, who by his diſſimulations and hypocriſies, had in ſome ſort gotten the Queenes fauour. But now ye ſhall heare an other tragedie, played againſt the verie ſelfe ſame Princeſſe and Queene.

CHAP. 4.

§ Of an other aſſault and murther, procured in the yeere 1597. by the Ieſuits againſt the Queene of England.

He Ieſuits miracle, when they conuerted *Parrie*, was great, but yet not ſo great, nor yet of ſo good ſtuffe, as that which I will now declare vnto you: for *Parrie* in his laſt confeſſions acknowledged, that he had had, part in all the conſpiracies, that for religion were directed againſt the Queene, except it were one. But this man, of whom I will preſently ſpeak, alwaies was and had bin, of the religion of England, and yet notwithſtanding, he was by an Engliſh Ieſuit, not only happily turned to our religion, but alſo induced to kill his owne Queene. Inſomuch, that if his enterpriſe had taken good effect, it had deſerued, to be ioyned to the booke of miracles that *Lewes Richeome*, of the Societie of Ieſus, made and publiſhed.

Edward

Edward Squire, Englishman, who had som acquaintance
& place in the Queenes stable, did in the yere 1595. embarque himselfe in the Fleete with *Drake* to the New-
found world. The Vessell wherein *Squire* was, beeing
by the fortune of the Sea scattered frō the rest, hee was
taken at Gadolup, & was brought as a prisoner or cap-
tiue into Spayne : where beeing breathed vpon and fauoured by Father *Richard Wallpole,* a man of great authoritie there, he was set at full libertie, by the intercessi-
on and sute of that Iesuit, who began to dog and watch
him, and to deale with him : notwithstanding, finding
him firme in his English religion, hee procured another
prison for him, which went to, or touched the conscience. And beeing committed to the Inquisition by in-
terposed persons, hee knew so well and skilfully to handle him, that at the last he became Catholicke, perhaps
vppon no other respect or denotion, but that hee might
get out of prison. Whatsoeuer the matter or manner
were, there is nothing in all this but praise woorthie to
the Iesuit.

Now, hauing gotten this first aduantage against him,
he suffered him not to breathe ; but sought out all sorts
of cunning, to make him fall into his Nets, declaring vnto him the afflictions of the English Catholickes that
were in that Country; and more particulerly, of them
that had forsaken it, and all their goods, to the end they
might liue in the libertie of their consciences : and that
the Earle of Essex (then great Marshall of England, and
afterwards Viceroy of Ireland) was the chiefe Author
of all these euils and miseries : that he must rid the coūtry of him by poyson, and that hee would giue him the
meanes to atchiue thereto, without hazard or danger.

Whereunto, hauing in some sort perswaded him, hee
proceeded further, and treated with him concerning the
Queenes life, which also he might as easily bring to an
end as the Earles. That this also shold be a goodly sacri-

fice to God : and that *Squire* need not feare the danger
of his life or person, by reason of the meanes which hee
had opened vnto him . And though this his enterprise
might fall out otherwise then hee might desire, yet hee
should assure himselfe, that he should change his present condition, into the state of a glorious Saint & martyr in Paradise.

And he persued him in such earnest & cōtinuall manner with his perswasions, that in the end, hee made him
to yeelde to his will and pleasure . And seeing him now
and then to wauer, hee oftentimes confessed or shroue
him, to confirme him therein : declaring further vnto
him, that he should no more admit any cōsultation with
himselfe, touching this poynt, because he was quiet in
his conscience, and that he should no more make question of it whether it were good or ill, but stand vppon
the maintenaunce & vpholding of his vow : wherein if
he failed, he should commit an vnpardonable sinne before God, and throw himselfe headlong into the deepe
pit of hell ; alleaging for that purpose vnto him, the example of *Iephtha*, who liked rather to kill his daughter,
then to infringe the vow he had made.

This poore miserable man, beeing thus dealt withall,
passed at the last his setled resolution to the Iesuits, who
caused him yet once againe to come to confession or
shrift, as the perfection of that theyr holy plot ; he gaue
him his blessing, comforted him, and put his left arme
about his necke, and with the right hande making the
signe of the crosse, after that hee had mumbled betwixt
his teeth certaine words in Latine, hee said distinctlie in
Englishe : My sonne, God blesse thee, and make thee
strong ; bee of good courage , I pawne my soule for
thine : and beeing either dead or aliue, assure thy selfe
thou shalt haue part of my prayers. Vppon thys embracing , *Squire* tooke leaue of *Wallpole*, and returned
into England.

Now,

Now the inſtruction that the Ieſuit had giuen him, was touching a ſecret poyſon , betweene two hogs bladders,which he gaue him for a preſent : with charge, that he ſhould not touch it, but gloued, leaſt he poyſoned himſelfe : and that when the Queene would goe to horſeback,he ſhould make ſundrie ſmal holes in the firſt bladder, with which he ſhould rubbe the pummell of her ſaddle,aſſuring himſelfe,that of neceſſity the Queen laying her hand thereupon, and bringing it to her face, this poyſon ſhould be of ſuch power, that ſhe ſhould die thereof. And that hee muſt doe the like to the Earle of Eſſex, who prepared himſelfe to ſet ſayle for the Ilands of Terſeras, and had gathered great troups when *Squier* arriued : who preſenting himſelfe to the counſel of eſtate, and ſeeing he was verie fauourably receiued at his arriuall, he purpoſed to put in execution, his deſigne and practiſe againſt the Queene, before the Earle ſhould take ſhipping,whom alſo he meant to follow in that voyage : ſuppoſing,that if the poyſon did not worke, but with length of time, and brought forth the effects thereof whiles he was abſent, he ſhould be altogither free from ſuſpition . Vpon this conceit , he watched all the meanes to worke his enterpriſe : he vnderſtood that the Queene would goe abroad on horſebacke, and entred thereupon into the ſtable, where alſo he found the horſe ſadled . Then making ſhew to ſee all things fit and neat, he rubbed the pummell with the bladder, that was hid vnder his hand , which alſo was couered with a gloue, all according to the inſtruction that the father his Confeſſor had giuen him ; and as he was occupied about this worke, he ſung and ſaid aloud, God giue the Queene long life , repeating that word ſundrie times . But God would not that the poyſon ſhould work. But for all this,the wicked man let not his hope goe, but ſuppoſed it would declare the working of it in ſome time afterwards.. Vpon which opinion he
embarqued

embarqued himselfe six daies after. And as the Earle was at the Sea, betweene Fayall and Saint Michaell, and was readie to go to dinner, *Squier* rubbed the leaning places of his chaire with the same poyson. And it so fel out, that at supper time, the Earle found loathsomenes, and distaste in himselfe : whereupon *Squier* supposed that he had gotten the goale, but he was deceiued in this, euen as he was in the first attempt.

Moreouer, many moneths passed away, and *Walepole* receiued no newes touching the Queens death : wherfore supposing that *Squier* had mocked him, he resolued to reuenge himselfe vpon him therefore : and did expresly send an other English man, who affirming that he was escaped out of the Spanish Inquisition, related particularly, and laid open all this conspiracie : and that hee was of purpose come from thence, to aduertize the Queene thereof. And though at the first, some supposed, that this was but some stuffe, or scout-hole inuented, by some one or other of *Squiers* enemies, yet (as in a matter of such consequence, men may not countenance any thing) plaine processe was made thereof, and vpon this returne, he was taken, and men were thereby better informed, touching the truth of this point. And perceiuing himselfe conuicted, by such as held and determined truth against him, and being also inforced by his owne conscience, he confessed all the matter euen as it was. And in the end, was by sentence condemned to death, and executed in the yeere, 1598. A punishment indeed fit and meet for a Iesuit, and yet verie admirable also, that the Queene of England, had not intelligence of this treason by any other, then by him that had giuen the first counsell touching the same. And if *Richeome* would credit me, he shall adde this miracle to his booke.

CHAP.

CAAP. 5.

¶ *That the Iesuits doe at this day make shew to condemne*
their wicked doctrine, in all things concerning eyther
the murthering of Princes, or rebellion
against their States.

Efore the comming of Iesuits into our
countrey, we knew not what it was, hand-
smoth, as we say, to kill Kings and Soueraigne Princes. This is a certaine kind
of Merchandize and ware, that hath
come out of their ships, by reason of that wicked vow
of blind obedience, which they make to their Superiours. Insomuch, as Princes lawes depend at this day,
vpon the good minde of these honest people. And
though their profession bee, as you haue heard, yet
doe they at this day in their bookes disaduance the same
with many goodly speeches, of which they are neuer
without store. And because amongst all manslaugh-
ters and murthers, there is none more plaine and euident, then these that *Barriere*, and afterwards *Chastell*,
meant to commit against our Kings, I will first deale
with that of *Barriere*, concerning which *Montaignes*
speaking, saith that it was a deceit or coozning, and that
the Iesuits are altogether cleare of it.

The truth is (saith he aunswering *Arnault*) that *Bar-*
riere deposed, that he had asked councel of a Iesuit, concerning his purpose and practise, that is true indeed:
for he came to *Varade* a Iesuit of Paris, from whom,
he was sent away, and sharpely reproued : he declaring
by his countenance and speech, that he was so farre carried against him in it, that hee would not heare it in
confession or shrift. This also is true (which you made
no account to deliuer) that this man *Barriere*, asked
aduice of all the world touching his enterprize, and that

Chap. 59. in
his booke
of Truth
defended.

P p,   long

long time before he did it, caufed to affemble at Lyons, the Diuines on the other fide of Saon, there to haue their aduice therein, where there was not one Iefuit prefent. Alfo, that in the Church of Saint *Paule* in the fame Citie, he caufed his funerals on the fecond day of Auguft to be folemnly kept, leauing there his blacke fcarfe, and armes, as the badges and pledges of the fore-pretended victory that would follow. Againe, that he depofed, that a Iefuit of Lyons, diffwaded him from that enterprife. All which things declare in that act, the vanitie of this man, and the innocencie of them, whom thou haft accufed, with fo cruell amplifications, and ex-aggerations, all tending to manifeft the ouer-running of of thy lying tongue. And though there were fuch a dif-pofition (as indeed there was not) and that it were as forcible againft the Iefuits, as any thing in the world could be, yet being wrung from them by torture and torments, it was not any matter of importance forcible, foundly to proue it.

This Iefuit *Montaignes*, denieth the fact: the rea-fon is, becaufe euerie villanous and foule fact, muft be denied. And he reproueth *Arnauld* of lying, though in all that, which I haue alreadie laid downe out of him, there is not fo much as one word of truth. Let vs goe forward to the fentence of condemnation, which the fecond Iefuit giueth againft his owne Order, in the verie humble petition which he prefented to the king.

The fecond crime (faith hee) concerning your Ma-ieftie in particular, is more tedious and troublefome, and indeed had more need to be confuted, for to fay that we are enemies to Kings and ftates, without mentioning particular or fpeciall poynts, is to forme a propofition of too large a reach, and which cannot eafily be defen-ded : but to affirme it in the fpeciall, will draw the point into a narrow roome. And therefore our ene-mies haue endeuoured, to bring vs within the limits

and

and liftes of the particular, faying, that we are the enemies of your Maiefty in particular, and of the ftate. The
generall porpofition, would ferue for hound and horne
to fet the game on foot: But the particular propofition,
would blow the fall of the Deere, and finifh the chafe.
Sir, before in this place we declare our innocencie, we
humbly befeech your Maieftie, that that which is alreadie paft, fpecially if you hold an opinion, that you haue
forgotten and forgiuen it, may not be preiudiciall to our
iuftification.

May it pleafe your Maieftie to remember, the aunfwere full of magnanimitie of one of your aunceftors,
which is in euerie mans mouth, by reafon that it is worthie to be noted. It behooueth not a King of Fraunce
to purfue the quarrels of a Duke of Orleans. Sir, you
are no leffe couragious then this King was, neither
fhall you haue leffe praife, but rather greater, if you
vouchfafe to fay: It behooueth not the King of France
to reuenge the quarrels of the King of Nauarre, nor
the eldeft fonne of the Church, to be incenfed againft
all, by reafon of one mans opinion repugnant to the
fame Church.

May it pleafe your Maieftie then, to fhew vs that
wonted fauour which you haue extended vnto all your
fubiects, and to burie in euerlafting forgetfulnes, euery
thing which hapned in that feafon. May it pleafe your
Highnes, here to be informed, that we neuer intended
any thing againft your Royall perfon in perticular, as
our aduerfaries haue fought often times to prooue a-
gainft vs, and yet could neuer doe it: And that amongft
all things whatfoeuer, which the Clergie, the Preachers and others, haue done or faid, wee haue faid or
done farre leffe then they reported of vs vnto you; and
that they alwaies carried a tange rather of a bad gloffe,
then of a true text in whatfoeuer they did or faid. For
if they now dare at high noone, and in the bright Sun-

shine of our peace, charge truth with a thousand inuentions contrarie to truth indeed: what might they haue done then, when as amidst all the rumours and foggie clouds of warre, lying had his full course without encounter? and where truth durst not shew it selfe. For the time of warre, is the time of lying, saith the old prouerbe.

If happily wee may obtaine that of your Maiestie, we doe thereby obtaine the vpper hand, and the second accusation will be without force: for it hath nothing to vphold it from falling to the ground with the least touch. For by what argument can they prooue, that we in particular are enemies against your Maiestie? From what spring doe they meane this hatred must proceede? And from what premises doe they inferre this conclusion? Is it by reason that you are a King? Why, our Societie honoureth Kings: and this is approued by witnesses, by experience, and by reason. Is it because that you are the eldest sonne of the Church? We respect this qualitie as much, yea and rather more then the first. Is it by reason that you are King of Fraunce? Fraunce is our natiue countrey, and you as King are our Father. Whom shall wee loue, if we loue not our Father and mother? Is it by reason that you are a worthie warrier, and Captayne of Kniges, and King of Captaynes? This vertue maketh it selfe at all times to be beloued both of frends and foes. Is it by reason that you are milde in your conuersation, wise in your sentences, free in your manners, stedfast in your promises, prompt in your actions, ready to labour, bold in daunger, forward in combat, moderate in victorie, and in euery thing royall? These qualities cannot ingender or bring forth hatred, but on the contrary, they are amiable in all, but admirable in the person of a King.

This speech was appropriated in particular, to the Kings

Kings owne royall perfon ; and a little before, neere the fame place, is another fentence, by which this honeft man the Iefuit vpheld, that men had wronged them, in imputing vnto them, to haue as it were wraftled againft the ftate. To thefe witneffes, dread Soueraigne, we adde a fecond argument taken from the caufe. Whereupon we building, doe demaund, what true likelihoode there is in our profeffion, that we fhould bee enemies of Kings and of their States. Are wee fo ignorant of the law of God, that we know not, that it is God that giueth them ? that by him kings doe gouerne, and by him Legifers make and giue good lawes ? That both the name & action of a king is a right of patronage proper to the Diuine and Supreme Maieftie ? and that kings beare in their royaltie the image of God ; and in this calling God willeth vs to obey them, to honour and ferue them for the fafetie of their perfons and the State. And if wee know thefe things, hauing both preached and written them, and againe doe preach and write them : how may it be that we haue fo little confcience, as to hate that, which we beleeue that God loueth : to difpife that, which he alloweth ; to deftroy that which he maintaineth ; to haue fo little iudgement, as to publifh one thing and doe another ? Are we to be reputed religious ? Nay, rather more heathenifh then the heathens themfelues, then Canibals and Mamelues, who though they can do nothing, but fhew hatred and reuenge, yet doe they notwithftanding loue their Princes.

I praife thofe two fentences, (Iefuit be thou whatfoeuer thou art) and wifh, I to God, that thy foule were as cleane, as thy wit is fine, and as I perceiue thy words to be fmoothly couched together. I cannot but loue thee, in feeing thee draw to the life, the counterfait of thofe fingular and admirable vertues of foule & bodie, which fhine in our King : and with all I muft honour thee, in feeing thee fet out the picture of Obedience, which the

fubiect

subiect oweth vnto King . And sure if thy heart and
my penne agree, I know thou wilt condemne them all
that would haue attempted any thing against the person
of this great Prince, who hath not yet met with his pa-
ragon, as one who in martial prowesse, hath far surpas-
sed all others. Thou carriest too noble a mind (were
it not that thou art a Iesuit) to Iudge of it any otherwise. Go to now, I will shew thee, that all that which thy
fellow hath said, in his *Truth defended*, is but a starke lie:
for that which toucheth the deed of *Barrier* when he
came to murther this king, whom thou so much exaltest,
was contriued by the expresse counsel of thy fellowes, &
copartners. Not only then, when he was but simply king
of Nauarre, but since he was called to the Crowne of
Fraunce, & reduced into the bosome of our Catholique
Apostolique and Romane Church. If againe I shew
vnto thee, the generall rebellion of Fraunce, enterprized
vnder the title of the holy League, which was first begun
after conducted by your holy religious persons, against
one *Henrie* the third, King of Fraunce, one of the most
Catholique kings that euer France enioyed, what iudgement wilt thou passe against thy owne party ? I remit it
euen to thy owne conscience, yea to the conscience of
any good Catholique, that is not a cloaked Iesuit : Nay
further I say, that these two parties, are the onely vphol-
ders of your condemnation, and vpon them grounding
my opiniõ, I take vpon me directly to shew, that to establish you again in France, were great lack of iudgement
& experience. I wil therfore lay down these two points
in order, and first I will begin wrac *Barriere* : afterwards
with *Chastell* : then with the Vniuersall reuolt , of the
which you Iesuits (take it amongst you) were the first
authors within this Realme.

CHAP.

CHAP. 6.

¶ *A prodigious historie of the detestable paricide attemp-*
ted against King Henry *the fourth of that name, the most*
Christian King of Fraunce and Nauarre, by Peter
Barriere, *for the raysing vp of*
Iesuits.

 Will recite vnto you faithfully this
historie of *Barriere*, and that you
may beleeue mee, I will speake it
vpon perill of my goods, of my
bodie, and of mine honour : for I
haue learned it of a friend of mine
whom I esteem of as my selfe, which
was then present at Melun, when this deed was done :
and who spake twice vnto *Barriere* in the presence of
Lugoly his Iudge, who saw him executed to death, heard
all that he maintained during the time of his tortures,
vntill the last breathing of his life, who handled the knife
of the which I will hereafter speake, who since drew out
the Copie of his triall, and who by posts sent it with
speed, by commaundement of the King, to make it manifestly knowen through all this Realme ; and lastly, being drawen forth, he made me partaker of a Copie
thereof which I haue kept vnto my selfe : and thus it is.

The King, hauing made peace with God, and truce
with those that were his enemies, tooke his progresse
from the cittie of S. *Denys,* to come to Fountane-bleau,
and as he entred Melun, hee was aduertised by *Lodowic*
Brancaleon, an Italian Gentleman, vnto him vnknown,
that a souldier departed purposely from Lyons to kill
him : He told the King, that he had not onely seene the
partie, but that he had drunke twice with him in the Iacobins Couent. And besides he said, that this man was
of a tall stature, mightie and strong of his ioynts : his
beard

beard was of an abrun cullour : hee had on a Spanish leather Ierkin, and a paire of Oringe-tawney culloured stockings vppon his leggs. The King not easily astoni-shed, yet full of prudence, sent for *Lugoly* , beeing then Lieftenant general of the long gownes in the Prouostie of the Altar. To whom when he had recited that which he had vnderstood, commaunded him to make a priuie search through the Cittie , for this man who had beene thus set forth and thus described vnto him.

The same day, the reporter saw this fellow whom he looked for in the Kings house; but as hee was in the midst of many people, so lost hee the sight of him vn-wares, as God would , to the end the partie should be remitted vntill the next day. Which Traytor, hauing lodged in a Hamlet, a part of the ruinated suburbs of *S. Liene* , as hee would haue entred the Cittie by *S. Iohns* gate, he was taken vpon presumption of the fore-saide marks. This was the 27. of August, 1593. *Lugoly* cau-sed him to be put in prison, where hee examined him : and finding him some-what variable, caused yrons to be put on his hands and feet, as the importance of the mat-ter did require.

Presently after his departure, *Anna Rousse* the Iaylors wife, asked the prisoner what he would haue to dinner : He answered her, that he would neither eate nor drink, vnlesse that hee might haue poyson brought him. This aunswere being well noted of the assistants, caused him more to be suspected, and his actions more narrowly to be looked into. Amongst the rest , there was a Priest prisoner, called Maister *Peter* the Ermite, who accor-ding to the loosenes of the time , became a souldier de-termined for the League. *Barriere*, hauing learned of him, that they were both of one Societie, acquainted himselfe with him. So, after some conference, the priest enquired of him if he had not a knife; the other think-ing to haue met with his mate, aunswered him yea, and

at that inftant time drewe foorth from his hofe a knife,
whereof the making was thus, the blade thereof very
ftrong about two ynches neer vnto the handle, hauing a
backe as other kniues haue, and the reft of the knife being fiue ynches long, did cut on both fides like a two ed-
ged fword, the poynt was made in manner of a Barly
corne, or poynard : the knife of a right murtherer, as one
who would not fayle of his ftroake. The Prieft in a fmi-
ling manner told him, it was a fit knife to payre nayles,
but if it were feene it would be his death. *Barriere* now
requefted him to lay it vp for him, the which the other
did promife him. But at the fame inftant, he fent for
Lugoly, vnto whom he difcourfed what had hapned betweeene them, and deliuering the knife into his hands,
Lugoly informed and examined the *Iailors* wife, touching the poyfon, the Prieft touching the knife, and the I-
talian Gentleman of that which had paft at Lyons the
2 8. of Auguft. The prifoner being diuers times examined, you fhall vnderftand, that in all his examinations, hee named himfelfe *Peter Barriere*, *alias*, *La
Barre*, borne at Orleans : by his firft trade, a Basket-ma-
ker, and fince that, inticed by one Captaine *De la Cour*,
being in a Ladies feruice, whom he forfook & became a
fouldier of the cõpany of the Lord of *Albigny*, the fpace
of one whole yeere making warres for the League, vntil
he was taken by the Lord *De la Gueft*, Gouernour of If-
foire, where he remayned fome certayne daies. And
from the time that he ferued this great Lady, he had purpofed to kill the king, eyther with knife or piftoll, in the
midft of his Guards. By which act, he thought, to haue
made a great facrifice to God, in killing a King of a
contrarie religion to his owne. Vpon which motion,
being fent backe againe by the Lord *De la Gueft*, he intended to paffe by Lyons, where he would inquire of
fome religious, if he might iuftly kill the King, being
conuerted to our religion : to whom was aunfwered, no.

Q q.   And

And beeing conftrained in the fame place to fell his cloake, and a paire of filke ftockings to get him victuals, from Lyons he paffed by Burgonie, then to Paris, and in the ende, arriued at Melun, where hee had lien in a barne neere Saint *Liens* Church. Neere which place, a little before he had receiued the blefled Sacrament at Bricontre-robert vpon a working day, and that he was come to the kings Court to feeke a mafter. And that if he were put to death, thofe of his confederacie would find themfelues grieued. He faid alfo, that the knife had coft him 18. pence in Paris, and that he bought it to no other purpofe but to vfe at the Table.

The next day being the 29. he was examined the 4. time vpon the fame articles: and amongft other points whereof he was examined, he affirmed, that being at Lions, he might haue had the Lieutenantfhip of the Marques of S. Surlin, or vnder him, the leading of a company of light-horfemen, if he had beene willing. Then *Lugoly* preffed him, and asked him, why he held for the League, and parting thence, came to feeke feruice in the kings Court. At thefe words he remayned dumbe for a time, and at laft faid, that he had aunfwered alreadie as the truth was. Foure witneffes were examined againft him. *Brancaleon*, who gaue information of *Barriers* counfel takē at Lyons to flay the King, & who had kept nothing hid from the Commiffioners that he knew: the Iaylors wife, examined of the poyfon: Maifter *Peter* the Ermite, concerning the knife: and Maifter *Thomas Bowcher*, the Curate of Bricontre-robert being called for, declared to haue confeffed him eight daies before, and the next day after communicated with him, and further, that he had told him how he had confeffed himfelfe 4. daies before in the Citie of S. *Dennis*, but not a word of any thing concerning his attempt againft the king. All thefe witneffes, who of him were imbraced as coadiutors, and

coun-

councellers,are not onely not reproued, but withall,they
atteſt their depoſitions to containe the verie truth of all
they knew ; *Brancaleon* excepted,who affirming, that he
had coinmuned with him of this enterpriſe againſt the
King,acknowledged therewith,that he had eat & drunk
twiſe with him in the Iacobins houſe. The matter after
this manner examined by *Lugoly*, the king cauſed by his
Letters-patents,ſix Counſellers of the councel of State,
accompanied with two Preſidents of ſoueraign Courts,
to adiudge and giue ſentence of him as he had deſerued.

Heere needed no doubt to be put of the lawfull proceeding againſt him. For was it not ſufficient,yea and by
too too many proofs,to declare him guiltie and conuinced of that crime,in the execution wherof he was preuented? Was it not ynough to conuince him of the fact,
who had confeſſed he had a mind to kill the King before his conuerſion ; and miſſing of his purpoſe then,
had ſince deliberated with 4.Munks at Lyons about the
ſame act, to wit , whether he might iuſtly kill him or
no. In witnes whereof,he that drunke with him at that
time as he pretended to come to the Court for that purpoſe,had pointed him forth to the King by euery particular marke to make him known. Was there not matter
ynough to iudge him guiltie, who had iudged himſelfe
euen by his owne conſcience from his firſt committing
into priſon,as wel by demaunding for poiſon, as alſo,for
the murtherers knife , whereof hee was found ſeazed ?
Was there not euident proofe to condemne him, who
confeſſed,he had left the League of purpoſe,to come to
the Court only to ſeeke a Maiſter ? Queſtionles, he was
iuſtly iudged to die : And therefore by decree the 31.of
Auguſt he was condemned to be drawne vpon a ſledge
or tumbrell,& as he paſt through the ſtreets,his fleſh to
be pulled of with hot irons.This being done,to be led to
the great market place,and there to haue his right hand
burnt off with the knife in it : after that,to be laid vpon

a scaffold, and so to haue his armes, legs, and thighes broken by the Executioner, and after his death, his body first to be consumed to ashes, and then to be cast into the Riuer: his house razed, his goods confiscated to the King. Moreouer, before his execution, he should be plied with questions, aswell ordinarie as extraordinarie, to learne by his owne mouth, who had induced him to this wicked enterprise. This was the summe of the sentence denounced against him.

Hitherto you haue seene nothing in this prisoner which chargeth the Iesuits of Paris, neither likewise that he was distracted in mind, as *Montaignes* would describe him, but rather a man aduised, who bare off euery blow in the best maner that he could: and from whom the Iudges drew by foure seueral examinatiōs, what they could for searching out the truth. The sentence the same day being pronounced against him, the Interrogatories were committed to two of his Iudges, and *Lugoly* to see them propounded vnto him, and to examine him. This poore wretch being there brought forth, requested them, that he might not be quartered quick, but rather giue him leaue, and he would to the vttermost, confesse the truth of euery particular poynt for that matter.

First then he began to lay open euery particuler concerning the passage at Lyons, from poynt to poynt, as *Brancaleon* had deliuered of him to the King, and acknowledged, that in the said Citie, he had conferred with foure religious persons, to wit, a Carmelite, a Iacobin, a Capuchin, and a Iesuit: with whom he agreed to commit this murther, and thereupon departed the next day after the Assumptiō of our Lady, to this intēt arriued he in Paris, and lodged himselfe in the street, called *De la Huchet*, where he inquired who was the most zealous of Gods Church and honour in Paris. Whereunto one answered him, saying, the Curate of S. Andrewes of Arts.

Hereupon

Hereupon, he presently went to visite him, and recited vnto him his whole determination; where-with the Curate seemed well pleased, and made him drinke : saying, hee should gaine by that act, both great glory and Paradise. But before hee proceeded any further, it were very coüenient, that he should first goe visit the Rector of the Iesuits, of whom he might take more certaine resolution.

Whereupon, he went to the Iesuits Colledge, spake with their chiefe Commaunder, & vnderstood by him, that he had beene chosen Rector not past three weekes before. Marry after many faire speeches, and friendlie entertainment, hee concluded, that his enterprise vvas most holy, and that with good constancie and courage he should confesse himselfe, and receiue the blessed Sacrament; and so led him into his Chamber, and gaue him his blessing. And the next day following, hee was confessed by an other Iesuit, to whom hee would not discouer himselfe by his confession, but afterwards receiued the Sacrament in the Colledge of the Iesuits. Hee likewise spake of it to another Iesuit, a preacher of Paris, who spake often against the King, & adiudged this counsell most holy, & most merritorious : And for this act intended by him, bought the knife that was deliuered into the Iustices hand, the poynt whereof he caused to be made sharpe like a dagger poynt, as heeretofore hath beene recited.

But to returne, he thus parting from Paris, went to S. *Denys*, where the King was, with a firme resolution to kill him in the Church. But seeing the King so deuoutly at Masse, as appaid with feare, hee stayed his hand from that fact, euen as if he had lost the vse of his armes, or beene lame of his lymmes. From thence hee followed him to the Fort of *Gourney*, afterwards, to *Bricontre-robert*, where, after that he had beene confessed & communicated againe, the King passed by, & so

escaped

escaped him, while he was drawing the knife out of his hose. Thus to be briefe, he arriued at Melun, where he was taken. And nowe when these Iudges came to instruct him, and told him that it was ill done, to haue receiued twice the holy Sacrament, hauing this bad intention in his minde, knowing (as hee could not be ignorant thereof) that it was to his damnation.

Then began he to lament, and said, that hee was vnhappie, and gaue thanks vnto God, in that he had preuented him from such a wicked stroake. His confessions were read vnto him, to the which he stood, without deniall of one word. His confessions (I say) made ere euer he felt one twitch of the rope. So being frō thence drawne to the place of execution, as hee was vppon the Scaffold, *Lugoly* willed him to tell the truth, warning him to take heede that hee should not charge any one wrongfully. Vnto which he aunswered, that all which he had said in the place of examination was true. Of which hee asked God, the King, and the Iustices forgiuenes.

This done, he had his right hand burned in flaming fire, afterwards, his armes, legs, and thighes broken, & he was put vppon the wheele, where the Iudges meant to haue left him languishing, till hee had giuen vp the ghost. But there againe examined, if hee would say any thing for the discharge of his conscience? Hee aunswered, that whatsoeuer he had said, was true, and no more but the truth: and that there were two blacke Friers, which went from Lyons to the same intent, but hee tooke vpon him to be most forward to atchiue the act, for the honour of the enterprise. Thus most humbly requesting the Iudges to ridde him out of his paine, that his soule by despaire might not be lost with his bodie. Vpon these words, *Lugoly*, by the commaundement of other Iudges, caused him to be strangled: and the next day, his body was consumed into ashes, and the ashes

cast

caſt into the Riuer. After the execution doone, which was vppon Tueſday, the 31. of Auguſt, newes vvas brought by a Cittizen of Melun to Paris, (for the paſſages were free wherſoeuer, by reaſon of a truce made :) And vpon the Sonday following, one *Commolet*, a Ieſuit, made a ſermon, about the end whereof, he requeſted his audients to haue patience, for you ſhall ſee (quoth he) within fewe dayes, a wonderfull miracle of God, which is at hand, you ſhall ſee it, yea, eſteeme it as alreadie come. Theſe words vttered openly in the preſence of an innumerable multitude, cauſed the Iudges to be moſt aſſured, that what ſoeuer *Barriere* had ſpoken, was moſt true.

CHAP. 7.

How the heatheniſh impietie of the Ieſuits, had been preiudiciall in our Church, if their execrable counſell had come to an effect.

 Haue moſt faithfully diſcourſed vnto you, what was the proceedings of *Barriere*, now ye may well gather, that what-ſoeuer is penned downe by the Pleader of Clairmont Colledge, and againe by *Montaignes*, within his fabulous truths, are as it were old womens fables, ſuch as we read in the moſt part of their anuall Epiſtles, ſent amongſt their friends. And moreouer, that *Barriere* was not a plaine ſimple and innocent man, but rather one moſt reſolute, and ſtoute, who ſtoode vppon his garde as much as in him lay : yea, before the Magiſtrate, and who after his condemnation, had his memory ſo perfect, as he could intreat that he might not be committed to the mercie of the Wheele, or other torture. And therfore moſt falſe is that which *Montaignes* giueth out of him; that he was frighted, and his memorie paſt him, by

meanes

meanes of the torments hee suffered. This (I say) vvas false; for he was neuer tortured, vntill his confessions of the fact were all ended, as is before set down at large.

Before the sentence of death was denounced, the Iudges shewed no great suspition had of the Iesuits, but hauing found sufficient matter to condemne the malefactor to death, then they all gaue consent (by reason of his fact) that he should be plyed with questions, whereby he might reueale his pretences. So that without being put to the tortures, (seeing it was in vaine to delay) hee declared each thing in particuler of that which was past. And thereupon, as you haue heard, he accused 4. religious persons of Lyons, & amongst others, a Iesuit, without naming him. But the Gentlemen, by his deposition haue informed vs, that it was one *Petrus Maiorius*. Afterwards he recited what had beene done with him at Paris, in the Iesuits Colledge there, by him that held the first place, to wit, the Rector, whose name also hee knewe not. But *Montaignes* hath discouered him vnto vs by the name of *Varade*.

As indeede it was a thing easily knowne, for that he then commaunded in the Colledge : adding thereunto, that the King beeing since entred into Paris, *Varade* saued himselfe by agilitie of body, taking himselfe to flight; as one that knew full well, there was no surer witnes against him then his owne conscience.

As touching *Commolet*, there needed no other vvitnesses then those which were at his sermon. Moreouer, passages on each side were free and at liberty, by reason of the truce made : so that many honest persons, which had with-drawn themselues by flight into Melun, being now come backe againe into Paris, vnderstood this great miracle of which he prophecied. Concerning the rest, the prisoner before hee was put to death, persisted vpon the Scaffold in all that hee had said and spoken in the place of examination : & againe after that, vpon the

wheele, beeing full of good memory and vnderstanding; for they had medled with no part about him, but
onely the breaking of his armes, thighes, and legs. And
after he had perseuered a while in that paine, he requested *Lugoly* not to occasionate his fall into despaire, and
that loosing his body, hee might not also there-with
loose his soule. Vppon which wordes, the saide *Lugoly*
caused him to be strangled, after that he had giuen his
last report vnto the Iustices of all, and had receiued permission to doe it.

Therefore, it is a most shamefull lie, to publish it a-
broade, that *Varade* found him so weake of vnderstanding, that hee could not in any wise giue credite vnto
him. It was a most notorious lie to say, that the confessions of *Barriere*, were forceably taken from him at his
examination, notwithstanding that he was not questio-
ned withall but twice at seuerall times vppon the Scaffold, where he persisted vpon those poynts which hee
had confessed in other places, as I here haue said. As
touching other matters, of the meeting of the Diuines,
& the Scarffe which was hung at S. *Paules*, if there had
beene any such thing, no question but hee would haue
confessed it as willingly as he did the rest. I come again
to those flattering speeches, which the second Iesuit fee-
deth the King withall, to the end that his Societie might
be reestablished. Where are now these faire speeches?

It behoueth not (saith he) the King of Fraunce to reuenge the quarrels of the King of Nauar, neither the eldest son of the Church, to be mooued with an opinion
contrary to the Church. Is not this a shamelesse Piper,
who would againe vnawares ouercome our king by the
sound of his pipe? I haue here from the beginning recited the plausible persuasions of the Iesuits, to the end
euery one might know, that there is no better to be looked for, to come frō such lying lips as they haue. I haue
here frō the beginning, set down the history of *Barriere*,

R r.   to

to the end, that each one might know, that it is impoſſible to doe worſe , and that there is not in the world any
beaſt more cruell, ſubtile and fierce , then is the Ieſuit :
wherefore, all men ought by all meanes poſſible to beware of his treaſons. But I pray you , howe were theſe
Nets ſpred, & of what ſtuffe were they ? Marry ſo long
as the King was of another religion then ours is, the Ieſuits neuer made ſhew of any willingneſſe or intent to
haue him murdered ; no not in the greateſt broyles of
our troubles : And now, being recōciled to our church,
vppon ſome feare which was reſident in them , as they
fayned, leaſt that the King made himſelfe a Catholicke
vpon diſſimulation, this (ſaid they) was cauſe of offering
vnto his Maieſtie ſuch cruell warres . But when ? in the
midſt of the ſworne truce , when euery man eſteemed
himſelfe to be at reſt whereſoeuer he liued, by the publique and mutuall fayth which euery one had ginen one
towards another, then began this newe counſell to proceede.

This *Iudas* had neuer any purpoſe to kill the King
before hee became a Catholicke : becauſe they deemed,
that as long as hee was plunged in his error, the people
whom they helde in theyr rebellion , would neuer be
drawne to liue ſubiected vnder his obedience . But as
ſoone as he was conuerted, they doubting of theyr fortunes, fearing leaſt his reconciliation might reduce them
beeing his ſubiects, to theyr accuſtomed dutie , they
hereuppon endeuoured with all their power to preuent
it , and thought by one meanes or other hee ſhould be
ſlaine, to enioy afterwards that priuiledge which they
vſe, and likewiſe to place ſuch a Monarch in the kingdome, as eſteemed himſelfe moſt ſtrong , and one that
ſhould ſtand to theyr deuotion.

My intent & meaning is, that this matter be handled,
not onely before our holy Father the Pope, & his Conſiſtorie, but alſo, that it ſhould come before the meaneſt
perſon

person in the world, if he haue any sparke of religion &
iudgement. For was there euer impietie more abhominable then this ? That our Iesuits should haue charmed
such a weake spirit as this was, by the holy Sacraments
of the Church,& haue inticed him to murder the king ?
Not because that he was an heretick, but by reason that
they suspected there was dissimulation in his conuersion.

Be it that they suspected hee was but dissemblinglie
conuerted, which I beleeue not . But admit that they
had suspected it , yet is it therefore of necessitie , that
the life of so great a King, should depend vppon theyr
vaine imagination ? and that vppon this pretence, they
should counsell such a detestable murther ? and barter
likewise to haue compacted with those, that would vndertake it, to giue them Paradise for a counterchange ?
Besides, in giuing more scope to theyr wickednes , they
haue abused the holy Sacrament of the Altar. O God,
was there euer a wickeder Atheisme since the world was
a world ?

It was not onely a simple King of Nauarre whom
they shot at , but the greatest King that euer Fraunce
enioyed . It was not a Prince of a contrary fayth to
ours , but rather him , vvho vvith all humble submission , had reduced himselfe into the bosome of the
Church. Now will we giue eare to this cogging Iesuit,
I deceiue my selfe : but wee will heare him to the end,
that, that which hee hath handled, may serue for a condemnation against him, and all his.

But behold, what fruite had our Catholick Apostolick and Romaine Church brought forth, if this hateful
counsell had come to an effect . Doubt you not , but
that the conuersion of our King , was vnto the Hugonots a great cut in their harts . So that if any mischance
had hapned vnto him, as touching his life, by the Clergie, good God, how would they haue set vp their ban-

ners againſt vs in their aſſemblies ? What ſubiect might their Miniſters haue had to haue thundred out, yea, euen in their Pulpets, bringing heauen and earth together, and to haue ſaid, that it was a blowe come from heauen: by reaſon that the King hauing forſaken their Church, (theſe be the wordes which they would haue vſed) God had permitted it that hee ſhould be ſo ſoone taken out of the world, yea,& by thoſe religious Prieſts vnto whom hee yeelded himſelfe. Might they not haue had great occaſion to haue ſaid vnto them ; Our Preachers in theyr Pulpits, handle a thouſand matters with leſſe loſſe then that was ?

Had it not beene a meanes to maintaine them in their errours in ſtedde of preuenting them ? Did not all thys turne to the ruine and deſolation of the holy Apoſtolicall Sea of Rome, of which our Ieſuits ſay they are Protectors. Theyr propoſition is not Catholicke, but rather Anabaptiſticall, the which they reuiue againe, in minding to take away the life of Kings.

CHAP. 8.

¶ *Of the murther which* Iohn Chaſtell *(brought vp at*
Paris, in the Ieſuits Schoole,) ſought to at-
tempt againſt the King, in the
yeere 1594.

IT happened vpon Saint *Iohn* Euangeliſts day, beeing the 27. of December, 1594. after the reducing of Paris vnder obedience to their Soueraigne, that the King going to his Chamber, accompanied with many Princes and Lords, founde himſelfe vnlookt for ſuddenly ſtrooken in the mouth with a knife, ſo that neither he,nor thoſe that were with him, could perceiue it : for aſſoone as *Iohn Chaſtell* who was the Traytor, &
but

but nineteene yeeres of age, had giuen the stroke, he dropped downe the knife, and sette himselfe in the midst of the prease. He was but young, and none would haue deemed this furious enterprise to haue beene in so tender yeeres.

Euerie one was in a maze, and busie to thinke who had done that traiterous deed, and it wanted not much, but that this yong youth had made an escape. Notwith-standing, God would not permit, that this detestable act should remain vnpunished. By chance it was, that some one casting his eyes vpon him, he became as one sore affrighted and appald with feare. But as he promised himselfe to haue the Paradice of Iesuits if he died one of their maytyrs, so also he confessed this fact more readily and promptly then was looked for at his hands. Whereupon, by decree of the Court of Parliament in Paris, he was condemned to die. Now here the Iesuits make a great boasting of their innocencie, saying, that in his examination, and out of it also, he neuer charged any one of them : but all that he had done proceeded of his owne will, and that in this confession he perseuered vn-till the last gaspe of his life. As for my part, I haue no greater argument then this, to shew that the trade of murthering was lodged within their Colledges. And where there was any exercise of good education and studie, no scholler would haue vndertaken such a dam-nable determination, but such a one as was brought vp vnder them. Wherefore we remayne all in one minde, that he had there studied and passed his course in Philo-sophie. True it is, that it was reported, that he had not beene conuersant there for the space of eight moneths past.

The reason of this diuersitie is most easie, for in the other Colledges, they know not what it meant to in-struct schollers how to murther Kings, and specially in ours. But in the Iesuits Colledges, it is contrarie, and

preached

preached in their owne affemblies nothing fo much as that alone. Of the which indeed they were but too pro-digall in their Sermons: fo as this young boy, hauing as yet his foule infected with their poyfon, being newly departed from their fchooles, was not altogether healed.

Quo femel eft imbuta recens, feruabit odorem Tefta diu.

Behold how that vpon the auncient inftructions and memories of the Iefuits, their Difciples fuppofe to of-fer a holy facrifice vnto God in committing murther, yea, and that of Princes. The fame hapned fometime in Italy, where there was one *Cola Mentouan*, who taught the youths of Millan in ftudies of humanitie, and amongft the chiefeft difcourfes of his Dictates, he trea-ted ordinarily of no other thing, but happie is he who with the price of his blood, redeemeth a commō-wealth from the bondage of a Tyrant. Thefe difcourfes tooke fuch hold with three Gentlemen of a Towne named Cafes, and of the families of the Empoignane, Vifcont, and Olgiate, that hauing attained to ripenes of yeeres, they cofulted together to put in execution the inftructi-ons of their Maifter. And in conclufion, vpon S. *Ste-phens* day in Chriftmas, as *Iohn Galeas*, Duke of Mil-lan, went into the great Church to heare Maffe, they doubted not but to murther him in open fight of all the people : though they were affured, that hardly they fhould efcape the furies of the Dukes guard, as it hap-ned vnto them. For in the fame place there were two of them flaine, and the third who had efcaped, was taken fome few dayes after; and led to the gallowes, where he confeffed, none but himfelfe and his fellowes, as *Chaftell* did. And neuertheleffe, the truth is fo well noted and knowen by the Hiftoriographers of Italy, that the in-ftructions of *Cola* their Maifter, had been their firft ftir-rer or prouoker. By thefe meanes, our Iefuits are verie fcoffers, when they think to excufe themfelues vpon the anfwers of *Chaftell*. I know not whether they were fuch

as

as they affirme, but wel I wot, that al their Lectures and
Sermons, tend to no other but bloodshed, exhorting
men to murther : therby yeelding themselues sole pledges and sureties, for their Paradice that will vndertake
this great maister-peece of worke.

CHAP. 9.

¶ That it is an heresie to approoue the killing of Prin-
ces, though they be heretiques.

Ith what hypocrisie soeuer the Iesuits
now disguise themselues in their moderne writings, yet without doubt they
haue both made profession of, & taken
a glory in, the murther of Kings and
soueraigne Princes. Besides an infinite
number of examples which I could alleadge, there is
one *Peter Mathew,* a Doctor of both lawes, who in the
yeere 1 5 8 7. made a collection of many Latin Poems,
written by Italians; and the yeere following, heaped together sundrie decrees of Popes, frõ the time of *Gregory*
the 9. vnto *Sextus Quintus.* Now, euen as among those
Poems, the fayrest peeces are the most shamelesse ones,
as the *Priapus* of *Bembus*, wherein he suffers his wit
to play vpon the resemblance there is between the word
Mints, an hearbe, and the Latin *Mentula*; and the *Siphi-*
lis of *Fracaſtor*, wherin he describeth the beginning, and
and proceedings of the Poxe; so in this second collection, among all the Orders of Religion, allowed by those
Pontificall decrees, he commendeth none so highly as
that of the Iesuits : who valewe greatly the iudgement
so honeſt a man giues of them, and often bring him on
their ſtage. Now marke his discourse vpon the Pauline
inſtitution of the yeere 1 5 4 5. *Dum super seminat ini-*
micus homo Zizania, adsunt diuino Pneumate acciti Patres
societatis Iesu, qui Petri sedem illuſtrant, in Lutherum arma
diuini

diuini eloquij parant , TYRANNOS AGRE-
DIVNTVR , *Lollium ab agro Dominico euellunt , &*
fidei Christianæ præclarissimi buccinatores , verbo & exem-
plo cunctis prælucent. This passage copied out word for
word by *Montaignes,* is withall , translated in this sort;
Whilest that the enemie of mankind, soweth Tares, behold,the fathers of the Societie of Iesus,called by the holy Ghost, who adorne S. *Peters* chaire,vse the weapons
of Gods word against *Luther,* Assaile Tyrants,pluck vp
those Tares out of their Maisters field, & as most excellent Trumpets of the Christian faith, excell all others
both in doctrine, & example. *Montaignes* saith, hee was
not a Iesuit that writ this ; and I am of his mind : but this
Peter Mathew was a man(I know not whither he be now
aliue or no) whose spirit was altogether Iesuited, and
vnto whom the whole Sect is very much beholding : for
besides the Elegie, which he hath made in their behalfe
vpon the Bull of *Paulus* 3. he addeth vnto that of *Grego-*
rie 1 5 8 4. a catalogue of all their Colledges,and houses,
(though there be many of them in it,but imaginary) and
vnderstands their busines no lesse then he , who vnder
the disguised name of *Montaignes,*hath falcified the truth
it selfe. Now were it as naturall,and familiar to Iesuits to
assaile Tyrants, as Lutherans, I perswade me , that who
should offer to exempt murther from their order,would
resemble a foolish Phisition , that finding a body haife
taken, and benumbd with a palsie,cuts off that halfe to
saue the other ; for so he might be sure to ruine both together. Here *Montaignes,*by a sophistical quidditie,saith
in the same Chapter, that the name of a Tyrant,hath no
affinitie with that of a king : a good meanes to make one
kill a Prince, and after to fall into dispute whether hee
were to be held a King, or a Tyrant : for to what purpose; if not to this end maketh he such a distinction ?

This question hath beene long agoe resolued, and it
displeaseth me, that I must now bring it in doubt gaine.

After

After that *Iohn* Duke of Burgundie,had caused *Lewes*
Duke of Orleans, son and brother of a king,to be slaine
at the gate Barbets,he produced a yong Doctor of Diuinity,named *Iohn Petit*,whom he had maintaind at studie . This fellow came vnto the porch of our Ladies
Church in Paris, and there preached before an infinite
number of people this doctrine, that the murther was
iustly committed, as vpon the person of a Tyrant, and
proued by many false reasons, & wrested authorities the
action to haue bin most tollerable.Thus got the Burgonian Duke his sute in the common opinion of the base
valgar:and therupon,the same error crept into the harts
of many young Diuines,who stifly maintained , that it
was lawful to kill a Tyrant: vntil that Maister *Iohn Gerson*,Chancellor of the Vniuersitie of Paris (and one of
the greatest Diuines that euer were in the Church) not
enduring that this damnable opinion,should win more
ground, got him to the Towne of Constance,where a
general Counsel was then held, and there procured this
proposition to be denounced hereticall , as we learne by
the 15.Session.*Præcipua sollicitudine volens hæc sacrosancta
Synodus ad extirpationē errorū & hæresum in diuersis mundi
partibus inualescentiũ prouidere,sicut tenetur,& ad hoc collec-
ta est, nuper accepit quod nonnullæ erroneæ assertiones in fide
& bonis moribus,ac multipliciter scandalosæ, totius Reipubli-
cæ statũ & ordinem subuertere molientes,dogmatizata sunt :
Inter quas hæc assertio delata est. QVILIBET TY-
RANNVS potest & debet licitè & meritoriè occidi per
quemcunq, Vasalum suũ & subditum, etiam per insidias, vel
blanditias, vel adulationes,non obstante quocunq, iuramento,
seu confœderatione, factis cum eo,non expectata sententia,vel
mandato iudicis cuiuscunq. Aduersus hunc errorē satagens
hæc sancta Synodus insurgere,& ipsum funditus tollere,decer-
nit,& definit huiusmodi doctrinam erroneam esse in fide & in
moribus,ipsamq, tanquam scandalosam, & ad fraudes,decep-
siones, mendacia, proditiones,periuria vias dantem , repro-*

S L   *bac*

bat & condemnat. Which is to fay: This holy Councell chiefly defiring (as it is bound, & therfore affembled) to prouide for the rooting out of errors, & herefies, which now begin to fpread abroad in diuers parts of the world, hath lately beene enformed, that fome divulge opinions, erronious in faith, againft good manners, and verie fcandalous, tending to the fubuerfion of the whole State, and order in States, among which this affertion paffeth for currant. Euery Tyrant may, and ought lawfully and meritorioufly to be killed by any his Vaffal, & fubiect, euen by ambufhments or flatteries, or faire allurements : notwithftanding any oath paffed vnto him, or League made with him, and without attending the fentence, or commaund of any Iudge whatfoeuer. Which this holy Counfel endeauouring to refift, and wholly to root out, decrees, ordaines, and iudgeth, to be erronious both in matters of faith, and manners : and reprooues and condemnes it as a point moft fcandalous, opening the way vnto all manner of guiles, deceits, lies, treafons, and periuries. An ordinance which I refpect, and reuerence, not only becaufe it was enacted in that great counfel of *Conftance*, wherby the abufes of the Church, and herefie, were rooted vp, but in that it was deriued from our Fraunce, *Gerfon* being the firft, and principall Solicitor againft the new Diuines, who then had intertained this opinion ; which fince that time, our Iefuits haue reuiued in the death of good king *Heny*, whom they called a Tyrant, & had done the like to our great King now liuing, if God by his holy grace had not preferued him. But becaufe the Iefuits would feem to deny their *Peter Mathew*, as not being of their Sect, what fay they to father *Emanuel Sa*, terming himfelfe a Doctor of Diuinitie, and of their Societie ; who by two artcles in his Aphorifmes of confeffion, hath maintained, that it is lawfull for fubiects to kill the Tyrant, and to expell a misbeleeuing Prince out of his Realme : as if the people could, or
                                                                    fhould

should giue lawes vnto their King, whom God hath giuen them to be their soueraigne Magistrate.

I am ashamed that I must prooue, no subiect ought to
attatch his Prince, what part soeuer he doth play : but
hauing vndertaken to combate an heresy which Iesuits
haue practized by deeds, & now would faine go from it
in words, I purpose to giue thē a fulsome gorge therof.
Learne therefore of me this lesson, Iesuit, (for I owe this
duty to al Christians) we ought to obey our kings whatsoeuer they be, (I will say) good or badde, this is that the
wise man teacheth vs in his Prouerbs, S. *Peter* in his Epistles, S. *Paule* vnto the Romans, to *Titus*, & to *Timothie*,
the Prophet *Baruch*, speaking of *Nabuchodonozer*, whō
God, of all other Princes, had made to fall into a repro-
bate sense ; the goodly example of *Dauid* persecuted by
Saul. Such Kings as God bestoweth on vs, such are we to
receiue without examining, as thou dost, whither they be
Kings, or Tyrants. The hearts of Kings are in the hands
of God ; they execute his iustice euen as it pleaseth him
to punish vs, or more, or lesse, whereto we are not to oppose our selues, but by our humble praiers vnto him : if
we deale otherwise, we resemble those ouerweening Gi-
ants described by ancient Poets, who offring to skale the
heauens, there to sit cheek by iowle with Gods, were in
a moment tumbled down to hel by their god *Iupiter*. Yet
ought not a King abuse his power, but know he is a father, not to prouoke his subiects, his children, vpō euery
sleight occasion ; for if he do, God the father of Fathers,
& king of Kings, wil (when he least thinks of it) dart his
vengeance against him with a most dreadful & horrible
arme. To conclude, seeing that thou Iesuit, yeeldest a
blind obediēce to thy superiors, who are but thy adopted
Lords, thou owest it in greater measure a hundred-fold
vnto thy King, thy true, lawfull, naturall Lord, & father.
Therfore art thou a most dangerous yonker, to propose
vnto vs in thy writings, this distinction of a King & Ty-

rant; not that I know not the great difference which is
betweene the one & the other ; but we are to blindfold
our eyes vnder their obedience, otherwise we shroud a
rebellion of subiects against their Prince ; Rebellion
which produceth much more euell then the tyrannie
whereunto we were subiect.

CHAP. 10.

§ *A memorable act of* Ignace, *whereupon the Iesuits haue
learnt to kill, or cause to be killed, all such as stand
not to their opinions.*

THere remained in the confines of Spain, certaine
dregs of the Marranes, whom king *Ferdinand* had
chased out of that realme, & therfore got the title
of Catholique, a surname wherwith his successors
haue since adornd themselues. One of these rascals,
mounted on a Mule accoasted *Ignace* on the high
way (somwhat after he had changed his former life:) ha-
ning told one another to what place they were bent,
they entred into sundry discourses, & at length fell into
talke of the blessed Virgin *Mary*, whom the Moore acknowledged for a true Virgin before her Conception,
but not after : grounding his opiniō on natural reasons,
the which haue no affinity with our faith. *Ignace* vrged
the contrary, with good deuotion, that she was a Virgin
both before, & at, and after her deliuery, & searched euery cornerof his braine to make it good. But being then a
simple nouice, & if you wil needs know it, but an a. b. c.
man in points of religiō, it was not for him to manage so
high misteries: so that supplying the want of arguments
(wherof he had none left) with a iust choller, the Moore
who laughed at him in his mind, spurring his Mule, and
giuing him a ful carriere, left *Ignace* all alone, who cha-
fingthat he was not able to get the victory at the blunt of
the tongue, went yet to win it at the sharp with thesword;
and so resolued to pursue him amaine, & presently to kil
him,

him. Notwithstanding, like a man of a good conscience, he found himselfe extreamly perplexed. For on the one side, it vexed him to see a monster fraught with impiety and blasphemie, goe vpon the ground; on the other, he weighed his owne feare of offending the Virgin, in sted of defending her. In this cōtention, suspended between yea and no, at length hee determined to take his Mules aduise. Hee sawe the fellowe passe into a crosse way, and knew whether it led: wherefore, in admirable wisdome he resolued, not to slacken the reynes of his choller, but to giue his beast the bridle; on condition, that if of her owne instinct she followed the tract of that Infidell along the crosse-way, he would dispatch him without all remission: but, as God would haue it, she chose another path, by meanes whereof, *Ignatius* suddenly appeased himselfe, supposing the matter happened to his Mule by diuine inspiration.

God sometimes giues aduise vnto false Prophets by their beasts; as we read of *Balaams* Asse, and this *Ignatius* his Mule, without the which he had most furiously executed his disseignment. Therefore I finde no whit strange the resignation he hath made of the same furie vnto his successors, with whom I list not dispute whether it be fit or no, but send them, after his example, vnto a Mule for resolution.

At this word, the Iesuit woulde needes lay himselfe open: Excuse me, I pray you, quoth he, me thinks you deliuer not the vvhole matter: For *Ribadinere*, one of them of whom you borrowed this historie, sayth, that *Ignatius* at that time, was surprised with a remembrance of his old Adam. *Homo quippe militaris fallaci veri honoris imitatione olim elusus:* he was falne into this foolish opinion of reuenge, but that afterwards, arriuing at our Ladies Church of Mountserrat, hee hung before her alter all his weapons, after hee had confessed himselfe, by writing, of all his sinnes, three dayes together. *Ibi optimo*

fario, totius vitæ suæ crimina per triduum ex scripto confes-
sus est, illique homini omnium primo, animi sui propositum
aperuit, iumentum reliquit, gladium pugionemq́, quibus
Mundo meruerat, ante aram beatissimæ Matris Dei apen-
di iussit : which was in the yeere 1 5 2 2.

Truly, replyed the Aduocate, I heeded not those 4. or 5. lines when I perused *Ribadinere,* and I thank you hartilie for putting mee in minde of them; for I will vse but this one poynt, to shewe your Sect to be most wicked, and most vnhappy, that hauing this faire, & goodlie mirror of your Father and Author before your eyes, your heads haue entertaind no other obiects but the disquiet of the Realmes you liue in, especially of our countrey of Fraunce, as I will proue immediatly.

CHAP. 11.

Of the holy League, brought by the Iesuits the yere 1 5 8 5.
into Fraunce : and that they are the cause of the
Hugonots new-footing a-
mong vs.

Etherto I haue discoursed vnto you, of the murders, paricids, and massacres of Kings & princes; now I will shewe you the ruine, and desolation of kingdoms, procured by them, and beginne first with our owne. It is not for a King of Fraunce, (saith the Iesuit in his *Most humble Request*) to reuenge the quarrell of a King of Nauarre; nor fits it the Churches eldest sonne, to be sencible of what was done against an opinion contrarie to the Church.

Goodly words, which I remember often, so wel they please mee: as though the Iesuits had onely warred against

againſt the King now liuing, and no way touched the laſt, *Henry* the third, not onely adorned with the title of *Moſt Chriſtian*, a title long agoe beſtowed on our kings, but who among the moſt Chriſtian, was in particuler the moſt Catholick. We ſaw him in the beginning of his raigne follow the Ieſuits, beeing charmed by them, and holding them the ſoundeſt Catholicks : afterwards, the Friers Minims of Nigeon, hard by Paris, where hee had his chamber for his priuate prayers by night, on feſtiuall dayes, and for his deuotion at theyr Mattins at certaine other ſeaſons; then haunted hee the Capuchins and Feuillants : and with a like zeale inſtituted the brotherhood of the Penitentiaries, & Whippers ; and after all this, the congregation of the Hieronimits at our Ladies of Vincennes, where hee and his companions, changed theyr habits, as Munks, on thoſe dayes and feaſts, whereon they were confined thether.

I know well that his enemies, imputed all this to hypocriſie, for his ill hap, or to ſay more truly, their vnhappie ſhifts, would haue led men to turne all his actions to the worſt. If you ſay, that the greateſt part of ſuch as ioyned with him, did it for hypocriſie, onely to pleaſe him, I belieue you ſay moſt truly, but as for him, I doubt not but he did it onely to pleaſe God. It were a want of common ſence to auerre, that a King, nouriſhed in the midſt of delights, and fulnes of all pleaſures, would haue choſen this painfull courſe, had hee not beene drawne vnto it by true zeale and deuotion : hee who otherwiſe had tenne thouſand means to credit himſelfe by : ſuch leud hypocriſies may fall into the harts of meane companions, who by religions maske ſtriue to ſeaze on new greatnes, but not into theirs, whoſe auncient right aſſures it them alreadie.

Then muſt the Ieſuite, the hypocrite, raze this clauſe out of his paper, that the warre, whereof I will hereafter speake, was vndertaken against a King of any other opinion then the cōmon : it resteth to know, by whom the warre was vndertaken. Some charge Princes and great Lords with it, & therein altogether are deceiued. I will deliuer it at large vnto you.

After the decree of the yeere 1 5 6 4. had passed, we liued in some rest throughout all Fraunce, vntil the yere 1 5 6 7. about which time, the enteruiew had at Bayon betweene vs and the Spanyard, vndid vs. For it put iealousies (perhaps not without cause) into the harts of such as were not thorowly setled. Ielousies that bred in Fraunce tenne thousand mischiefes, which to remember, makes my haire to stare. Nowe let vs examine the Iesuits carriage during this loose & generall corruption. A surceasing from Armes being appointed in councel, the yeere 64, they thought also to haue had leysure e-nough for the venting their ambition. Whē their cause was pleaded, that irregular profession of theirs was one-lie dealt against : the wiser sort foresaw, as in a clowde, that this Impostume could not chuse in time, but yeelde a malignant and lothsome matter, though to poynt at it in particuler, none either could, or durst; because that outward simplicitie wherewith they shadowed their in-ward thoughts, surprised euen such as wished thē most euill; for they imagined the Iesuits would haue forwar-ded our Religion, by good examples, zealous prayers, wholesome manners, holy exhortations, and not by Armes.

But stayed they in these termes ? nothing lesse, they brought into their houses, the knowledge of State matters; they made themselues Iudges of Princes actions, disposing them at their owne pleasure; they contriued warres thereby to compasse their dessignes : and the Pulpits out of which they preached, were to no other vse, but as Drums, Fifes, and Trumpets, to incense our Princes in theyr combats one against another. And

especi-

especially, we are not to doubt of their beeing the Authors, solicitors, and cherishers of our last troubles, a
thing which not onely they denie not, but make theyr
boast of in their bookes, as you may find in that of the
Iesuit *La Fon.* I vndertake not in this place to recite at
large the storie of these troubles, this only I wil tel you,
that before the yere 1576, wee neuer had put the word
League in vse: it was onely familiar in Italie, the chiefe
harbor of Iesuits. VVhen the Parliament was held at
Blois, a Lord of some note in Paris, (whom I will not
name) whose hart was wholly Iesuited, and who on fe-
stiuall dayes, left his own Parish-church to be present at
their Masses, sent to the Deputies of Paris these instructions following.

In this assembly, some laboured harde to make immortall & mercilesse war, against the Hugonots, & yet
demaunded an abatement of Subsidies: a proposition
ill sorting with the former, those Subsidies hauing heen
introduced of purpose to further the warres. By means
whereof, the man of whom I speake, taking first aduise
of the Iesuits, propounded a third course, to league theselues against the Hugonots, and that such as willinglie
enroled themselues vnder the League, should be bound
to contribute vnto the charge of this new warre. These
instructions receiued and published, the Deputies did
nominate a certaine Prince to be their head. The last
King, knowing of what consequence this practise was,
and that succeeding, it would make 3. parties in France,
his owne, (which was not one properly) that of the
League, another of the Hugonots: to breake this blow,
discreetly affirmed, that he approued well this League,
but that he would be chiefe thereof : which was to the
end the League should flie no further then he was pleased to giue it wings.

The first stone of our ruine beeing cast in this manner, the Prouosts of the Merchants, and the Sheriffes

Tt.   of of Paris, returning home, and loath that thys opinion of a League (which they held moſt holy) ſhould miſcarie, ſent theyr Commiſſions throughout all the Wards, to to the end, that ſuch as would contribute, ſhould ſubſcribe their names. The Conſtables bare them vnto euerie houſe, ſome hardier then the reſt, oppoſed themſelues, the greater number, fearing worſe, ſubſcribed. The Commiſſion was brought to *Chriſtopher le Tou,* chiefe Iuſtice, whoſe memorie vvee cannot honour too much: this good Lord, refuſed not onely to ſubſcribe, but detayned the Commiſſion it ſelfe, and the next day, in open Court deteſted this vnhappy innouation, as an aſſured deſolation to our ſtate. His authoritie, his honeſtie, his reaſons, wrought ſo great effect, that euery one allowed, and followed his aduiſe. From thence-foorth, this opinion of the League did weare away, or rather vvas remitted to another ſeaſon, that better might befit the purpoſes of ſuch as broached it.

Suddainly, after the Parliament was ended, Father *Aimon Auger,* a Ieſuit, got the King to giue eare vnto him through his plauſible hypocriſies : And after him, Father *(laudius Matthew* of Lorraine; both the which had ſo great part in his good fauour, that (as *Montaignes* teſtifieth) hee ſome-times cauſed them to ride along with him in his owne Coach. At length, this good King, founde that theſe coozeners, were deſirous to incroach vppon the managing of State-matters about him, *Auger* eſpecially; whom for that cauſe, hee gaue order to his Embaſſadour at Rome, to get him remooued out of Fraunce, by Letters of obedience from his Generall.

The King departing from the Parliament, pacified his ſubiects by an Edict of the yeere 1577. the which hee ſayd was vvholly his owne; and yet had by his wiſedome, cleane daſhed the reformed Religion without
bloodſhed :

bloodshed, if the Iesuits would haue vouchsafed him the leisure to finish what he had begun: Wageing in the midst of peace, a gentle warre against the Hugonots: gentle, but more forcible in great mens oppinions then any weapons could haue made it. For although that the Edict of 77. gaue some libertie vnto them, yet the king neither called them to places of iudgement, nor vnto offices in his Exchequer, nor to the gouernments of Prouinces and Townes.

Hee had moreouer deuised the order of the holie Ghost, reserued wholly for Catholicke Princes and Lords, as also, that of the Hieronimitans of our Lady of Vincennes, where none were to appeare, but Apostolicall Romane Catholiques, and with whom (laying aside his most high authoritie) he fraternized in all kind of deuotion. Nowe, the presence of these, causing the others absence, belieue it was no small meanes to force them into the right way. For there is nothing which the French Nobilitie affect so much, as to be necre theyr King, nor any thing that afflicts the common people more, then to be kept from Offices : this is a disease of minde that spoyles the Frenchman.

As soone as a Lawyer, or Marchant, haue by theyr endeuours, stuffed theyr Closets and Storehouses with siluer, the thing they chiefely ayme at, is to bestowe it on places of Iudgement, or roomes in the Exchequer for theyr Children : so that the newe Religion beganne alreadie to dissolue, and it grieued not the Aunciens thereof (vvho for shame, and to auoyde the imputation of lightnes, stucke vnto it) to suffer their chyldren to be instructed in our Schooles, and consequently to learne there the principles of our Religion.

All matters in this sort proceeded, from ill to well, from well to better ; the Countriman plyed harde his plough ; the Artificer his trade ; the Merchant his traffique ; the Lawyer his practise ; the Cittizen enioyed his reuenew; the Magiftrate his ftipend; the Catholick his owne religion throughout all Fraunce, without impeachment. The remainder of thofe Hugonots that liued, being fequeftred into a backe corner of the kingdome; when our Iefuits feeing themfelues remoued frō theyr Princes fauour, beganne to lay this fnare to intrap him.

Euen as the Societie of Iefuits, is compofed of all forts. of people, fome for the pen, others for practife; fo had they amongft them, one Father *Henry Sammier* of Luxembourge, a man difpofed for all affayes, and refolued vnto any hazard. This fellow was fent by them in the yeere 1581, towards diuers Catholicke Princes to founde the Foorde: And to fay truly, they could not haue chofen one more fit; for he difguifed himfelfe into as many formes as obiects, one while attired like a foldiour, another while like a Prieft, by and by like a country Swaine: Dice, cardes, and women, were as ordinarie with him, as his prefixed houres of prayer; faying, he did not thinke he finned in this, becaufe it was done to the furtherance of a good worke, to the exaltation of Gods glorie, and that hee might not be difcouered: changing his name together with his habite, according to the Countries wherein he purpofed to negotiate. He parted from Lorraine, and thence went into Germany, Italie, and Spaine. The fumme of his inftructions were, that forefeeing the eminent danger of our Catholick religion, the feeming conniuence which the King gaue to it, and fecret fauour hee yeelded on the other fide to the Hugonots, whereof the Duke his brother had made himfelfe an open Protector in the Lowe-Countries, their holie focietie had refolued to vndertake this quarrell vnder the leading of a great Prince, making fure account of Gods affiftance, feeing that it was directed to the aduauncement of his holy Name, and good of his Church.

Thus

Thus *Sammier* got intelligence from each part, and tooke aſſurance on all hands: but preſently to manifeſt their proiects, the ſeaſon fitted not; becauſe the Duke was aliue, and the two brothers forces once vnited, were ſufficient to ſwallow all ſuch as had made head againſt them. And this was but the preamble vnto our Troubles. In the yeere 83. he died. That let remoued, the Ieſuits imbarqued in their quarrell ſuch Lords as they thought good: and from thence forward, Father *Claudius Mathew* Prouinciall of Paris, deales in the matter more earneſtly then before; ſits and aſſiſts in all delibe rations, and counſels, takes vpon him a iourney vnto Rome, & Father *Henry Sammier*, another into Spayne; where they ſo wel acquitted themſelues in their Embaſ- ſages, that Pope *Gregorie* the 13. and the Spaniſh King promiſed, each for his part, a great ſumme of money towards the maintenance of this warre. The Embaſſa- dors being once returned, we beheld Enſignes diſplaid, Fraunce couered with ſouldiers, and many Townes ſur- priſed, wherein there neuer had beene any exerciſe of new Religion.

Now might you ſee three parties on foot, the Kings, very much entangled; that of the holy League; (ſo was the Ieſuits warre intituled) & that of the Religion; for ſo the Hugonots did terme their faction. Pope *Gregorie* died: then feared the Ieſuit he ſhould looſe halfe of his credit, for which cauſe father *Mathew* returned backe to Rome, where he found Pope *Sixtus* choſen, of whom to his exceeding great contentment he obtained the like promiſe his predeceſſor had made him before. In his re- turn he died at Ancona, the yere 1588. by means wherof a new ſuit is begun by Father *Odon Pigenat* a Burgonian (the elected Prouincial of France by deceaſe of *Mathew*) which was not reiected by *Sixtus*. This gaue occaſion to certaine Catholiques not onely to propound a peace, but euen to wiſh it in their ſoules. Yet notwithſtanding

T t 3. ſome

some there were, that would haue bridled our thoughts: for this proposition disliked our Iesuits. There be two sorts of Catholiques, the one called Pollititians, of worse condition then Hugonots, because they wisht for peace; the other zealous Catholiques, or Leaguers, beloued of the commmon people, because they desired an endlesse warre : a distinction that planted a Nurserie of warres betweeene Catholique and Catholique, and withal, procured a peace with our common enemy. What say I, a peace ? we put hereby a sword into his hands to beat vs with, we opened him the way to raunge in, to come forward, to thriue, to increase without our resistance, we who had enfeebled our selues by this same new diuision.

Armes were taken on all hands, and yet was it not a ciuill warre only, it was a general throat-cutting all France ouer : which to remedy, our two Kings had successiuely need of all their peeces : and so the Hugonot came by a good part in their quarrell, for the maintenance, & support of the State. And the Iesuits Colledges were manifestly the places whereto the other side vsually resorted. There were forged their Gospells in Cyphers, which they sent into diuers countries : there were their Apostles bestowed into sundry Prouinces, some to vpholde the troubles by their preaching, as their father *Iames Commolet* within Paris, and their father *Bernard Rouillet* within Bourges, others to commit murther, and bloud-shed, as *Varade*, & the same *Commolet*. Not so much but father *Odon Pigenot* seased in all credit, prerogatiue, and authoritie among the Sixteene of Paris, (dregs of the vulgar, and entertainers of sedition:) A thing all Iesuits agree on, in the bookes which they haue published since the yeere, 9 4.

I haue said (and truly said) that Iesuitisme, argeeth with the Anabaptists opinion in two propositions : In medling with State matters; and in causing Princes

and

and Kings to be murthered, accordingly to the conue-
niencie of their affaires. I will adde, that in the carriage
of this Iesuiticall warre within Fraunce, there was some
conformitie of names betweene, this, and that the Ana-
baptifts vndertooke in Germanie the yeere 1535. For
they had one *Iohn Mathew* their chiefe Prophet, vnder *Iohn Leydon* their king, and one *Bernard Rotman*,
and *Bernard Cniperdolin*, principal actors in their faction
for the seducing of simple people : euen as our Iesuits
had their father *Claudius Mathew*, & *Bernard Rouillet*. I
will not here recite the other particulars of our troubles,
being contented plainely to haue shewed vnto you, that
our Iesuits were the firſt Seminaries thereof : onely I
will diſcourse what fruit we haue reaped by them. God
withdrawing his anger from vs, would in the ende ap-
peaſe all matters. In this reeſtabliſhment, the Hugonots,
who during our troubles thinke they haue beene some
inſtruments of keeping the Crowne on the Kings head,
as well as other Subiectes, which were Catholiques,
haue also thought, that after the peace was made, they
ought not to bee accounted as outcaſtes from among
vs : therefore haue they importuned the King by sundry requeſts, to reſtore them to their auncient Priuiledge, graunted them by the Edicts of Pacification,
from which, ſince the peace of the yeere 77. they
haue beene almoſt wholly driuen.

Wee haue, said they, followed yours, and the laſt
Kings fortunes during your troubles, we haue expo-
ſed our liues and goods for the vpholding of your
royall eſtate, againſt the Iesuiticall faction, which called in a Sraunger to make him Lord, and Maiſter
of your Kingdome. Is it meete, that wee, for our
good ſeruice to you, ſhould looſe our part in your common-wealth and gouernment, and that the Iesuits, for
hauing vſed all the badde practiſes they could againſt
you, ſhould beare ſway, rule, and triumph in your
Realme

Realme of Fraunce? What could a wife and prudent King doe in this cafe, being preft with fo iuft a Petition as this was? What? but affent thereunto: to auoid of two mifchiefes the greater, and not to fall backe into that gulph, out of which we were newly but efcaped. Tell me, I befeech you, to whom are we beholding for this laft Alarum in Fraunce, but onely to our Iefuits, the firebrands of our lateft troubles? Which troubles had they not beene, the Hugonots credit had beene vtterly ouer-throwne. This is one bond amongft other, wherein we ftand obliged to that holy Societie of Iefus.

CHAP. 12.

¶ That Auriculer confeffion hath beene vfed by the Iefuits, as a chiefe weapon for the rebellion, and in what fort they are wont to manage it.

IN vaine doe wee leuell our courfe to the works of pietie, vnleffe confeffion leade the way, and a due & worthy repentance follow. This is the Iefuit licenced, to exercife vppon all in generall that prefent themfelues before him, (to the preiudice of Ordinaries) but by a meruailous priuiledge, fuch as vvas neuer graunted to any Munk, no not to Curats themfelues, who of all Ecclefiafticall perfons, next vnto Bifhops, are moft authorifed that way. The tenor of the Bull, graunted by *Paulus tertius*, in the yeere 1545. is thus. After he hath giuen them permiffion to preach in all places, where they pleafed, he addes: *Nec non illis ex vobis qui prefbyteri fuerint, quorumcunq; vtriufque fexus Chrifti fidelium ad vos vndecunq; accedentium confeffiones audiendi, & confeffionibus eorum diligenter auditis, ipfos & eorum fingulos ab omnibus & fingulis eorum peccatis, criminibus,*

*criminibus, excessibus & delictis quantumcunque grauibus
& enormibus, etiam sedi Apostolicæ reseruatis, & à quibusuis ex ipsis casibus, resultantibus, sententijs, censuris &
pœnis Ecclesiasticis (exceptis contentis in Bulla quæ in die
Cœnæ Domini solita est legi) ac eis pro commissis, pœniten-
tiam salutarem iniungendis .* That is, we giue leaue,
and permission, to as many of you, as are Priests, to
heare the Confessions of the faithfull of the one, and
the other Sexe , from what part soeuer they come
vnto you, and them, being diligently heard, to absolue
from all and singuler their sinnes , crimes , excesses,
and offences, how great and enormous soeuer : yea, e-
uen those, that are reserued to the Sea Apostolique,
and all circumstances thence arising, by sentence, censure or paines Ecclesiasticall, (those excepted, which are
contayned in the Bull, accustomed to be read on Maun-
die Thursday) and to ordayne to the Penitents, for
the faults by them committed, wholesome and profitable
penaunce .

As the priuiledges, which they perswade themselues
haue beene graunted them for the Catechising, and instructing of youth , haue peruerted all the auncient
order of famous Vniuersities : so this large and extraordinarie licence, permitted them in matter of Confession, hath beene the cause , that the greatest part of
the people, haue in great and haynous sinnes, forsaken
the auncient custome, of resorting to the Penitentiaries of Cathedrall Churches, and had recourse to the
Iesuits, whom wee see by vertue of this Bull, to be all of
them authorized for Penitentiaries . And God knowes
how farre these holy and blessed Fathers haue abused it.
The first breaking forth of our troubles, was in the
yeere 1585. at which time all that resorted to them to
be confessed, if they affirmed themselues to be good
subiects, and loyall seruators to the King (for they were

queſtioned vpon that article) they were ſent backe by the Ieſuits without receiuing abſolution. Which beeing obiected againſt them by *Arnauldus*, marke I beſeech you, the cold aunſwere which they make in their defence againſt his accuſations. For in the 17. article it is obiected (ſaith *Arnauldus*) that the ſaid Defendants, haue at diuers & ſundry times, denied abſolutiō to them that ſtoode for the late King, from the yeere 1585. The ſaid Defendaunts aunſwere, that the article is vntrue, although themſelues know, that it hath beene often by ſundrie perſons auouched, yea and depoſed againſt them in the preſence of the late King in his cloſet: and what witneſſe could there be produced againſt them in this caſe, ſaue only thoſe, who had been by them denied abſolutiō? There is no ſmoak without ſome fire.

Read their annuall letters of the yeere 1589. when griefe, rage, and furie of the laſt troubles beganne, you ſhall find, that the number of their confeſſions was infinitely encreaſed, and ſpecially in the Colledge of the Ieſuits at Paris. *Totius vitæ confeſſiones auditæ trecentæ.* Wee haue heare 300. totall confeſſions, wrote the Subſtitutes of the Colledge to their Generall *Aquauina*. If you aske me whence this new deuotion of the common people to them proceeded, I wil tell you. Our Kings repreſent the true image of God: Againſt whom this yeere there hapned three ſtraunge and vnuſuall accidents; firſt, the rebellion againſt the late king, which they coloured with the title, and pretext of tyrannie: for the faireſt title they could affoord him, was the name of Tyrant: ſecondly, the parricide committed vppon his perſon by a Munke: and laſtly, the continuance of that rebellion, againſt the King that now is, for his religion.

Be you aſſured, that all ſuch, as did not hold their conſciences at as low a rate, as many of the Cleargie doe,

doe, found themselues much difquieted vpon thefe accidents. Which was the caufe, that during thefe troubles, they went to be confeft by thefe vpftart Penitentiaries, fome were to be refolued by them, whether it were fin not to yeeld obedience to their King, others to be abfolued for the fame. But this was to commit the Lambe to the Wooluas cuftodie : for their confeffions were as many inftructions, or rather deftructions, to teach Rebellion : refufing to abfolue them, which eyther were not in their confciences fully confirmed in their reuolt from the two Kings, or had any inclination to acknowledge them for their Soueraignes. And, (which is full of horrour and deteftation) their ordinarie courfe was, before they would abfolue them, to make them fweare by the holy Gofpell contayned in their breuiaries, neuer to take thefe two Kings for their lawfull Soueraignes.

That which I fpeake, I haue by good information from many, that were fayne to paffe through that ftrait, and I know one amongft the reft, more neere mee then the reft, who rather then hee would giue credit to their doctrine, departed from his Confeffour, without receiuing abfolution. This reacheth to the whole bodie of the Realme. But as concerning priuate Families, the Iefuits make a double vfe of miniftring Confeffion : One is, to take information from the Penitent, not onely of his owne finnes, but of their demeanour likewife that dwell with him, or with whom hee dwelleth; nay of the whole neighbourhoode : as if it were a finne in him, not to difcouer an other mans finne in confeffion, eyther if hee know it, or fuppofe that he knowes it. Which is as much in effect, as to make fo many fpies and carrie-tales in a Towne, as there be Iefuits Confeffors. The fecond vfe, which toucheth them in a neerer refpect, is,

V v 2.   of

that in fucking by the eare the foule of a timorous confcience , they fucke or rather fwallow there-withall his goods, and poffeffions : by promifing abundance of Spirituall goods in the world to come after their death, to thofe that fhall, in their life time, be charitable to them out of their temporall goods . A courfe whereby they haue carried away an infinite maffe of wealth, if you beleeue thofe, that haue taken vppon them to write their Legend; for I know not by what other name to intitle the liues of thefe holy Fathers.

One point more I will adde (whereof I defire to be refolued by our auucient Doctors in Diuinitie) they haue a rule in practife, that men are bound to accufe themfelues to their Confeffour, and not themfelues onely , but all their confederates likewife, and (as for the Magiftrate) the malefactor being condemned to die, after he hath once made confeffion of his finnes to his ghoftly father, is not tyed to reueale it to his Iudges nay it is lawfull for him to ftand in ftiffe deniall thereof, at the time of his execution, as being cleere before God (although he perfift in a lie) after he hath once difcharged the depth of his confcience to his Confeffor. A thing that breedeth much fcruple in the minde of a Iudge, who otherwife is greatly quieted in confcience, when an offender adiudged to die, howfoeuer he haue before time ftood in deniall of the fact , yet at the time of his death confeffeth the truth.

CHAP.

CHAP. 13.

¶ Of a generall assemblie of the Iesuits, holden in Rome
in the yeere 1593. wherein they are prohibited
to entermedle in matters of
state.

 Haue formarly in this discourse, charged the Iesuits to haue beene both the
first sparkes and the chiefest flames of
our last troubles: for proofe whereof
I wil seeke no more assured testimonie
then this. *Aquauiua* their Generall,
perceiuing that he could not make so good aduantage
of these troubles, as hee had at the beginning promised
vnto himselfe, caused the Prouincialls, Rectors, & most
auncient Fathers of theyr Societie, to be summoned to
meete at a generall Synode, which he appointed to be
holden in Rome. This depended some sixe months, in
which meane time, the King raunged himselfe into the
bosome of the Church, in Iuly 1593. From that time
forward, euery man bent his studie to mediate a good
peace through Fraunce, and to make way thereunto;
were concluded two or three seuerall truces, the vsuall
Kalender of a peace to ensue.

During these cessations, men had safe entercourse frō
one partie to the other. This opportunitie doe the Iesuits lay hold on, (as being sent them frō heauen) to worke
an attempt vpon the Kings person. *Barriere* is the man
that freely offers himselfe to this seruice, but without
successe. These honest Fathers, perceiuing that all their
practises, as well in generall as in particuler, fell short of
their dessignes, made shewe, as if they would by theyr
Synode make a finall end of the warres betweene the
Princes.

In

In the month of Nouemb. 1593 was this decree made,

This decree is at large set down in the accusation of the Iesuits, in the yeere 1594.

Vt ab omni specie mali abstineatur, & querelis etiam ex falsis suspicionibus, prouenientibus, præcipitur nostris omnibus, in virtute sanctæ obediëtiæ, & sub pœna inhabilitatis ad quænis officia & dignitates, seu prælationes, vocisque tam actiuæ quã passiuæ priuationes, ñe quispiam publicis & seculariũ Principum negotijs, vlla ratione se immiscere, nec etiam quantumuis, per quoscumq̃, requisitus, aut rogatus, eiusmodi res tractandi curam suscipere audeat, vel presumat. Idq̃, serio commendatur Superioribus ne permittant nostros ijs rebus vllo modo implicari, & si quos ad ea propensos animaduerterent, eos loco mutandos quam primum commutent, si alicubi sit occasio, vel periculum se eiusmodi implicationibus irretiendi.

That there may bee an abstinence (sayth hee) from all appearance of euill, and to meete vvith all complaints, howsoeuer grounded vppon wrongfull surmises, be it enioyned to our Collegiats, in vertue of the holy obedience, and vpon paine of beeing made vncapable of any office, dignitie, or promotion, & to loose their voice or suffrage, as wel actiue as passiue, that none of thē presume (be he neuer so much therevnto praied, and required by whomsoeuer) to entermeddle in matters publique, and belonging to secular Princes. And be it straightly commaunded to the Superiours, not to suffer those of our Societie, to entangle themseles by anie meanes in such affaires : and in case they shall obserue any of them to be thereunto enclined, that they remoue them to another country out of hand, if in that place there be opportunitie, or danger, to wrap themselues into such intangles.

The Iesuits make great vse of this Article, in pretending that by vertue of this Decree, they are restrayned from entermedling in those matters, and I as great, in affirming, that notwithstanding this Decree, they haue intermedled. But ô holy blinded obedience, vvhere doost thou now reside ? If thou be of the first & principall

pall essence of their vowes, it must needes followe, that
all the chiefe Fathers of that Order, are hereticks in their
sect. For, since this great and holy decree, Father *Iames
Commolet*, did notwithstanding intermeddle in those affaires: who in a Sermon, taking his text out of the third
chapter of the Iudges, wherein was mention of one *E-
hud*, that murdred *Eglon*, and saued himselfe by flight.
After he had long time thundred, touching the death of
Henry the third, and placed the Iacobin, that accursed
Iudas, amongst the soules of the blessed, at last, exclay-
ming with open throate, he said: *We stand in neede of an*
Ehud, *be he Munke, or souldier, or souldiers boy, or shep-
heard, it skills not, but wee neede an* Ehud. *Wee want but
that feate, to bring our matters to the passe which our soules
desire.* This was strogly enforced against the by *Arnault*,
but neither he that wrote the Defence against his Accusation, nor *Montaignes*, haue toucht it in their aunswer:
which perswades mee, that they are agreed vppon that
poynt. *Wallpole* the Iesuit, in the yeere 97. deliuered a
poysonous confection to *Squire*, there-with to make a-
way the Queene of England his Soueraigne. The Iesuits at Doway, in 98 sent the Cooper of Iper to kill
Graue *Maurice* of Nassaw: haue all these performed
obedience to this synodall decree?

Adiew religion of the Iesuits, (as I said to a friend of
mine of that Societie) seeing your obedience hath broken rank. For you doe not onely disobey your particuler Superiors, but that also which hath beene decreed in
full chapter by your whole Order. Whereunto he wisely made aunswer, that I did much misinterprete the Article, which did not beare an absolute, and simple restraint from medling in those affaires, but in case, the
Superior perceiued, there might danger growe by in-
termedling therein, *Si alicubi sit occasio vel periculum se
eiusmodi implicationibus irretiendi.* This decree then is
but meerly to blind the eyes of Princes, that they may
                                                    stand

stand leſſe vppon their guard then heretofore they haue done. And to ſpeake truth, to deale in ſtate matters, and to praƈtiſe the death of Princes, are as eſſentiall parts of their funƈtion, as their Confeſſion it ſelfe.

CHAP. 14.

¶ Whether the Ieſuits haue Spaniſh harts, as their enemies charge them to haue, or if they be, for Who giues moſt.

Heare many thunder againſt the Ieſuits, charging them to be Spaniſh in hart and affeƈtion; they on the otherſide, ſeeme to feare nothing more, then to incurre thys opinion in Fraunce. I purpoſe preſentlie to deliuer them of this feare, and for a neede to become their Aduocate in this poynt, not ſo much for the good affeƈtion I beare them, as that the truth enioynes mee thereunto. It's true they fauoured the Spaniſh procee-dings, about the middle and end of our troubles, (which makes them feare leaſt the memorie thereof ſhould be reuiued) but that their harts are Spaniſh, I vtterly deny. It proceeded not of any eſpeciall deuotion, which they had to the late King of Spayne, more then to any other Prince, but for that (following the courſe of Ieſuits, who meaſure the right and iuſtice of a cauſe, by the aduaun-tage of theyr owne affaires) they deuote themſelues v-ſually to him, whom they ſuppoſe to haue the ſtrongeſt partie, and from whom they ſtand in expeƈtation of greateſt commoditie, which is no ſmall ſecret in matters of ſtate, for them which in their harts ſtand neutrall, & indifferent.

The ſame leſſon was likewiſe put in praƈtiſe in time of our laſt troubles, by Pope *Sixtus* the fiſt, a man of as great wiſedome & gouernment, as euer came in Rome. Such was the contagion of thoſe times, after the death

of

of the two Brothers at Blois, that certaine young Diuines, infected with the poyfon of the Iefuits, loofed the
reines to fubiects againft their King, in the yeere 1589.
notwithftanding, themfelues confeffed at that time, that
their aduife in this poynt ought not to take place, without the formall confirmation of the Sea Apoftolicke.
Neuertheleffe, *Commolet* the Iefuit, and his adherents,
the day following, founded the Trumpet of warre in
their Pulpets, againft the King deceafed, affirming withall, that it was confirmed by Decree. Whereupon infu-
ed thofe outragious diforders, which wee haue feene in
Fraunce fince that time. To take Armes againft his Soueraigne, was herefie, but much greater herefie was it,
not to tarrie for the allowance, or difallowance of the
holy Sea. So that this was to offer violence to two Soueraigne powers at once, the fpirituall power of the A-
poftolicall Sea, and the temporall power of the King.
And Pope *Sixtus*, if hee had pleafed, might with one
ftroake of his pen haue extinguifht all our troubles, by
excōmunicating all thofe, who without his knowledge
& authoritie, had prefumed to arme themfelues againft
their King, whom hee knewe to be a moft deuout Catholique. But he kept himfelfe well enough from that,
for in fo dooing, he fhould haue excōmunicated them,
who at that time had all the ftrength on their part, in
fauour of a poore King, againft whom, heauen & earth
feemed to confpire. Contrariwife, he conuented him to
Rome, to anfwer that he had done, againft al the lawes,
cuftoms, liberties, and priuiledges of our Countrie of
Fraunce.

Our King now raigning, was at his firft comming to
the Crowne, of a contrarie religion to ours, and it pleafed the Pope at the firft to cenfure him for fuch a one :
but when hee once came to knowe his valour, and that
his enemies did but feede his holineffe with falfe bruits
of imaginarie victories, he began to fhrink his head out

of

of the coller, and would neuer after haue any hand in the matter. And from that day forward, vfed the King vnderhand with all the curtefie that coulde be defired. Neither doe you thinke for all this, that *Sixtus* ftood the worfe affected to the King that dead is, or the better to him that now raigneth, but he thereby out of his vvifedom, fauoured the more his owne proceedings. Albeit certaine foolifh Schollers charged him a little before his death, that hee was inclined to the Kings partie: And vppon this challenge, fome rafh fpirits haue not fpared to fay, that he was poyfoned: whereunto I will giue no credite, although it were true.

The like may be faid of our Iefuits, who ayme at nothing elfe but the aduauncement of theyr Commonwealth, which they entitle, *The Societie of Iefus*: which as it hath taken his originall and increafe from nothing but from the Troubles; fo doe they fhoote at nothing, but to difturbe thofe countries wherein they remaine, & in that difturbance, they euer encline to thofe which are able to maifter the weaker part, as I will make good by an ocular demonftration.

After they had fet fire to the foure corners and midft of Fraunce, and that the late King was brought to a narrow ftraight, they deuoted themfelues to him aboue the reft that was the Captaine generall of the League, becaufe all things fell happilie on his fide. And as long as Fortune fmiled vppon him, all theyr Sermons vvere of nothing but his greatnes and merrits. But when they once perceiued that hee beganne to decline, and that he was forced to call to the King of Spayne for affiftance, then beganne they likewife to turne theyr face from the Duke, wedding themfelues to the partie of a King, whom they efteemed to be exceeding mightie.

There is at this day a new King in Spayne, what his good or ill fortune fhall be, is knowne to G O D onelie. For my part, it fhall neuer grieue me, to fee as many

Crownes

Crownes on his heade, as were on his Fathers, the late deceased King. Imagine, that for a new opinion of war, (vvhich is eafily harboured in the braine of a young Prince) he fhould breake with vs, and that our affaires fhould haue profperous fucceffe in his dominions, bee affured you fhould fee our Iefuits altogether French, albeit they were Spaniards by birth. Thefe are true birds of pray, that houer in the ayre.

It was wel befitting the perfon of a foueraigne prince, to play that part which *Sixtus* did, but for a fubiect it is an ill prefident, & a matter of dangerous confequence. This is to prooue, that which way foeuer you turne your thoughts, you fhall finde no reafon, why the Iefuits fhould be nourifht within a kingdome, who are as many (I will not fay efpialls, but) enemies to theyr Prince, if he fortune to prooue the weaker. And for a neede, if there fhould happen newe factions in Rome, and that the Pope were put to the worft, hee himfelfe fhould feele the effects thereof, notwithftanding the particuler homage, which they fweare vnto him at euerie change of the Sea.

Scarcely had the Aduocate finifht this difcourfe, but the Gentleman replyed, Take heede you be not deceiued, and that this your pofition doe not imply a contradiction. For if the Iefuit bee naturallie addicted to him, that is, moft beneficiall to him, as you hold, then muft it of confequence followe, that hee is naturally Spanifh, and not French. VVill you know the caufe? hee is fure, that what trouble foeuer hee may breede in the confciences of thefe, and thefe priuate men, by his nevve kinde of confeffions, yet fhall hee neuer be able to get fuch footing in the whole Realme of Fraunce, as hee hath alreadie in Spayne, wherein the fupreame Magiftrate is fallen from one extremitie into another. For the Spaniards, beeing of olde accufed to be halfe Pagans, as holding a mungrell Religion, and not wholie

Chri-

Chriſtian, doe novve in theſe dayes, to purge themſelues of that calumnious accuſation, (for ſo I will ſuppoſe it to be) they ſpeciallie, and aboue all others, embrace the Ieſuits, eſteeming them vaſſales to the Papacie, without all clauſe or exception. And vpon thys
opinion, they graunt them in theyr Citties, an infinite
number of prerogatiues, aboue the common people,
yea, euen aboue the Magiſtrates themſelues, whom
they rule at their pleaſures.

And albeit antiquitie haue giuen vs in Fraunce, the
title of the eldeſt ſonnes to the Catholique Apoſtolick
Romane Church, yet is it with certaine qualifications,
vvhich the Ieſuits ſhall neuer be able to remoue out of
our heads, what ſoeuer ſhewe of continuation they
bring to the contrarie. And that is the cauſe, why they,
ſuppoſing their commoditie vvould be greater, if the
Spaniard were Maiſter of all Fraunce, then at this preſent it is, will euermore leane to that ſide, rather then to
ours, albeit they were naturally French. Theſe are pollititians, which cleaue rather to the certaine, then to the
vncertaine.

Thinke not your ſelfe interrupted by thys ſhort
Parentheſis, but if you pleaſe, fall againe into your diſcourſe. I will doe ſoe (aunſwered the Aduocate) and
I vvill tell you a ſtrange thing, which I haue obſerued
in all their practiſes.

CHAP.

CHAP. 15.

¶ *That the Iesuits were the cause of the death of* Mary *the Queene of Scots, together with a briefe discourse, what mischiefes they haue wrought in England.*

Auing hitherto discoursed of our countrey of Fraunce, it will not bee amisse to cut o-uer into England , where *Ma-rie* the Scottish Queene was sometimes detayned as a pri-soner to the State, for the space of 19. yeeres. This Princesse was a most zealous Catho-lique, and was mightily bent, to take an order with the Puritans of England , their Queene being once gone, who had none neerer of blood to succeede her, then the Queene of Scots. As then the Iesuits in the yeere 1582. stirred the minds of great personages, inciting them to take Armes , so did Father *Henrie Sammier* their Embassadour, goe ouer into England, to trouble the State there. He was then in the habite of a souldier, in a doublet of Orenge tawny Satten, cut and drawne out with greene Taffata, a case of pistols at his saddle bow, his sword by his side, and a Scarfe about his necke. I haue it from them, that were not farre from his company. Thus attired as he was, hee practised a secret reuolt with certain Catholique Lords, against their Queene, which afterwards cost them deere by the wisedome of the Lord Treasurer.

After that, he fell in with the Queene of Scots, bearing her in hand, that hee, and those of his Societie, treated with all the Catholique Princes, as well for the reesta-blishing of Catholique Religion in England, as also for the libertie of this poore desolate Princesse, coniuring her by all manner of obtestations to listen thereunto, and to dispose all her seruants and subiects to the accomplishing of so high an enterprise, assuring her for his part, to make good to her the Realme of England. This proiect he laid with her, but (as these Iesuits haue naturally two hearts) he plotted farre otherwise with the aforesaid Noble men of England, in the behalfe of a more puissant Prince, to defeat his poore Ladie of her future right, both he and his adherents diuerting the principall Catholiques from the seruice, which they had vowed to this Princesse, signifying vnto them, that her meanes was too weake and feeble, for them to build any hope of rising thereupon. And accordingly about the same time, did the Iesuits publish in print, the title which that other Prince pretended to the Crowne of England. Which libel they dispersed in sundrie places of Christendome.

And albeit this was the principall marke they shot at, yet did not *Sammier* desist to follow the said Queene tooth and nayle. At the first hearing whereof, she seemed to pause, foreseeing the mischiefe that might ensue: whereupon the audacious Iesuit said vnto her, that if she were so cold in the matter, he knew a meanes, how to cut off both her, and the King of Scotland her sonne from all hope of England for euer: and that it was a clause in his instructions : *quod si molesta fuisset, nec illa, nec filius eius regnarent*. Insomuch as she was constrayned to yeeld thereunto. And at that time the late Duke of Guise, not knowing of the factions and partialities which these men wrought vnder hand in behalfe of the other Prince, promised to be wholly for the Queene his Coosen. And certainely I make no question, but hee as a noble and valiant Prince, would haue gone thorow withall, had not the Iesuits engaged him in another new quarrell : which he embracing

embracing on the one fide, and on the other forfaking his Coofens, was left in the lurch in the end. The Queene vpon the firft intelligence of this new defigne, fhedding aboundant teares, and falling vpon her knees, cried out : Wo is me, for both my coofen, and my felfe are affurdly vndone. In this meane time the troubles fet footing in England by the practifes of the Iefuit : the Scottifh Queenes confpiracies were difcouered, wherein fhe wanted a head : the law proceeded againft diuers : the poore Catholiques, which till that time were not molefted for their confciences, were forced to forfake their wiues and children, and to leaue their houfes, to auoid the Magiftrates feueritie. Moreouer, *William Parrie*, who was executed in 84. confeft, that the murther of the Queene of England, which he had confpired, was to eftablifh the Scottifh Queene in her throne, albeit fhe were not priuie to this plot : which confeffion of his, made the Queene and Counfell of England to ftart, and to ftand better vpon their guards.

In conclufion the Scottifh Queens proceffe was commenced & profecuted to effect, fhe was adiudged by Parliament, to lofe her head, & not long after died a Catholick with meruailous refolution. By this you may collect, that the Iefuits were the fole contriuers of her death : and that they are fo farre from hauing eftablifhed Catholique Religion in England, that contrariwife, by their meanes, both it hath beene quite banifht, and a number of great and worfhipfull houfes brought to vtter ruine and deftruction. By reafon whereof they haue confirmed the erronious doctrine of the Puritans, and depriued thofe of our religion, of all hope, to fet in foote againe, vnleffe it be by fpeciall miracle from heauen.

CAAP.

CHAP. 16.

¶ That the Iesuits entermedling in matters of State, af-
ter they haue troubled whole Realmes, yet doe
all things fall out quite contrarie to
their expectation.

Hen our Sauiour Chriſt taught vs, that we ſhould giue vnto God, that which belonged vnto him, and to the Empe-rour of Rome, his right likewiſe, his meaning was, that paying the Empe-rour his tribute, we ought alſo to giue God his, and in regard of him not to exceed the limits of our calling. By which reaſon, the good and true re-ligious perſon, ought to giue himſelfe wholly to faſting, prayer, and hearing of Sermons. I know, that the kings of this land, doe ſometimes call Prelates to be of their Councell, according as their owne diſpoſition leads them, or as they finde thoſe perſons meet and able for the place, yet doth it not therefore follow, that they ſhould make that a generall rule, and preſident for the whole Clergie.

Were not the ſpirit of Diuiſion, otherwiſe called the Diuell, ſeated within the breaſts of Ieſuits, I would ſay, that there was neuer wiſer Decree made, then that of their Synode, in the yeere 1593. whereby they were prohibited to meddle in State affaires: not only becauſe it is forbidden by God (for that is the leaſt part of their care) but for that in reaſoning the matter, as a Stateſ-man, I cannot ſee that euer they brought their practiſes to thoſe ends which they aymed at. They are like a March Sunne, which ſtirreth humors in our bodies, but is to weake to diſpatch and diſſolue them. I will goe further, ſuch is their ill fortune, that if they fauour any partie, af-ter they haue ſhuffled the cards al they can, yet when the

game

game is at an end, he whose part they take, euermore prooues the looser. Insomuch, as albeit to humane reason the Iesuit may seeme to be an enemie of some value, yet so it is, that by Gods secret iudgement, it is more for our profit to haue him our enemie, then our friend. I will prooue it by fiue or sixe notable examples.

They went about to make alteration in the State of England, and to that end bent all their strength : what followed of that their enterprise ? the ruine of a number of poore Catholiques misse-led by them, which before time liued at ease in their owne houses : the death of the Scottish Queene, the establishing of the Queene of England for a long time both in her Religiō & estate.

I come next vnto Scotland, as being next in place to England, where Father *William Crichton*, and *Iames Gourdon*, both Scots by birth, had their residence, *Crichton* tooke a conceit, vpon some discontentment, to depart the land : he takes his course directly into Spayne, by the licence, and permission of his Generall. Whether he is no sooner come, but he practiseth to insinuate himselfe into the Kings fauour : and to that effect, drawes a tree of the descent, and petigree of the *Infanta* his daughter, shewing therein that the Crownes of England and Scotland, did by right appertain vnto her : and to incite him the rather to take armes against the Scottish King, he scattred abroad diffamatorie libels against him. Whereunto the King of Spayne giuing no eare, *Crichton* determined with himselfe, by letters to sollicite the Catholick nobility of Scotland to the same purpose; and to that end, wrote letters in the yeere 1592. to *Gourdon*, and other Iesuits remayning in Scotland, whereby he gaue them to vnderstand, in what grace he was with the King, who by his incitement was resolued, aswell for the inuasion of England, as for the restoring of the ancient religion in Scotland, But this mightie Prince, desired to haue assurance before hand from the Catholique

Lords of their good affection towards him, from whom he willed them to procure blanks readie signed, to be supplied afterwards by himselfe with deputations in their names, which being obtained, he had the Kings promise for two hundred, and fiftie thousand crownes, which should be sent ouer to be distributed amongst them. The Iesuits of Scotland, vpon this aduertisement, drew many blanks from diuers persons, which they deliuered to *George Ker* to carrie, who being discouered by the folly and indiscretion of *Robert Albercromi* a Iesuit, was apprehended with his letters and blanks : and the Scottish King, supposing this aduertisement giuen by *Crichton* to be true indeed, caused the Baron of Fentree, a Gentleman endued with many good parts, to be beheaded. The like had hapned to the Earle of Anguis, the chiefe Earle of that country, if he had not cunningly escaped out of prison. After, in continuance of the troubles, his Castles were ruinated, as also the Earle of Huntlies, a man of the greatest power of them all, & the Earle of Arrols, the Constable of Scotland. All which, since that time, haue made profession of the pretended reformed religion, as wel to returne into fauor with the king, as to liue within their owne countrey in securitie of their goods, & persons. Insomuch, as in conclusion, Scotland hath lost that small remainder of our Catholique Religion in the yeere 1596.

The like fell out as well in the Realme of Portugall, as of Arragon; I will first speake of Portugall. To say that the Iesuits procured the death of King *Sebastian*, as some in their writings haue charged them, is hard to beleeue : for as *Montaignes* hath very well declared, they were too highly in his fauour. But marke the proceedings: among all the nations of Spaine, there is none so superstitious, as the Portugall, and of all the kings of Portugall, there was neuer any more superstitious then *Sebastian*. The Iesuits being cunning, and subtle headed, thought this

to be a fit foyle for them to plant their vineyard in. And
to win the more credit, they caufed themfelues at their
firft comming, to be called, not Iefuits, but Apoftles, putting themfelues in rank with thofe, that followed our Sauiour Chrift in perfon. A title thich they hold as yet in
that place, as being generally affented to. The kingdome
being fallen to *Sebaftian*, thefe holy Apoftles conceiued
a hope, that by his means it might defcend vnto their family, & dealt with him many times, that no man might
from thence forward, be capable of the Crown of Por-
tugal, except he were a Iefuit, & chofen by their Society,
as at Rome the Pope is by the Colledge of Cardinals.
And for as much as he (although as fuperftitious, as fu-
perftition it felfe) could not, or rather durft not condefcend thereunto, they perfwaded him, that God had appointed it fhould be fo, as himfelfe fhould vnderftand
by a voice from heauen neere the Sea fide. Infomuch as
this poore Prince, thus caried away, reforted to the place
two or three feuerall times, but they could not play their
parts fo well, as to make him heare this voice. They had
not as yet got into their côpany, their impoftor *Iuftinian*,
who in Rome fained himfelfe to be infeĉted with a lea-
profie. Thefe Iefuits feeing thy could not that way attaine to the marke they fhot at, yet would they not fo
leaue it. This King being in heart a Iefuit, determined
to lead a fingle life. Therefore to bring themfelues into
neerer employment about him, they councelled him to
vndertake a iourny for the conqueft of the kingdom of
Feffe, where he was flaine in a pitcht field, lofing both his
life and his kingdome together. This then is the fruite
which King *Sebaftian* reapt by giuing credit to the Iefuits. And this which I haue here difcourfed vnto you: I
had frô the late Marques of Pifani, an earneft Catholick,
who was then Embaffador for the king of France in the
Spanifh kings Court. I omit all that hath fince paffed in
that Realme, as being impertinent to my difcourfe.

I come vnto that which hath since hapned within the Realme of Arragon: wherein you shall see the like accidents by the indiscreet dooing of the Iesuits. The people of Arragon, had in their foundation from all antiquitie, verie great priuiledges against the absolute power of their kings: and the oath of fealty, which they tendered their King at his Coronation ranne thus. *Nos qui valemos tanto come vos, y podemos mas que vos, vos elegemos Rëy, con estas y estas conditiones intra vos y nos, que el à vn que manda mas que vos.* That is: We that are as great in dignitie as you, and of greater power then you, doe elect you our King, with this and this condition between you and vs, that there shal be one amongst vs, who shall commaund aboue you. And vnder that, they specified all their priuiledges, which the King promised by oath to obserue most exactly.

These liberties hauing beene infringed in the person of *Antonio de Peréz*, their countriman, and Secretary of Estate to the late King of Spayne; he escaping out of prison, wherein he had beene long detayned in Castile, takes his way to Arragon, where hee recounts the wrongs that had beene done him, to the preiudice of the auncient priuiledges, and liberties of their countrey. His complaint was generally applauded by all, and especially by the Iesuits, who inwardly reioyce at any occasion of trouble and commotion. They begin by their confessions, (one of their chiefe weapons) to winne the hearts of diuers subiects, against their King, in Sarragossa, the mother Citie of the Realme, giuing the counsell to rise vp in armes, & in this heat euerie man betakes himselfe to his weapons: The king of Spayne on his part, armeth himselfe in like manner. The Iesuits seeing the forces of the Arragonians on foot, readie to put themselues into the field, to encounter the kings power, they turning their coates, began by their sermons, and confessions to runne a new course.

There

There was no more talking of priuiledges, they made no reckoning of the world, but of their consciences towards God, who commaunded them precisely to liue in obedience to their King: that if they would submit themselues vnto him, he would take them to mercie: a thing whereof they were well assured, hauing Letters signed by him to that effect.

Vpon this promise of theyrs, some particuler persons retyre themselues to the Kings Lieutenant generall, and obtaine their pardon. By whose example manie others doe the like. By this meanes, the Armie of the Arragonians is dissolued of it selfe. The King of Spaynes forces enter Sarragossa, without any stroake strooken, where they beginne to play theyr parts, they pull downe diuers houses to the ground; as well of the Cittie as of the Countrie, put the chiefe of the Nobility to death, raise a Citadell within the Towre, and put a garrison into it. And since that time, the King of Spaine hath commaunded there absolutely, as hee doth in the rest of his dominions.

Those that are ill affected to the Iesuits, giue out, that they sowed the first feedes of this rebellion, by a double carriage of the matter vnderhand, which kinde of dealing is very common and familiar with them. If that be true, they are the more to be condemned. I, for my part, who am enclined to iudge the best, impute it wholy to theyr simplicitie, and that in medling in matters of state, wherein (God wot) they are but Nouices, they ouerthrow those, that fondly giue eare vnto them. Wherunto the gentleman replying; I am not (saith he) of their number, that wish them ill, for they neuer deserued ill of me, yet I make no question, but when they incited the Arragonians to reuolt; it was but a iugling trick, to further the King of Spaines intendments. For, as you know much better then my selfe, Kings are manie times well pleased with such rebellions, that they

Yy 3. may

may thereby take occasion to suppresse, and restraine the auncient priuiledges of theyr subiects, and to reduce them into euen ranke with theyr fellowes. And this leades me, persisting in my former opinion, to conceiue more and more, that the Iesuit beares a Spanish hart, that is, a hart naturally deuoted to the King of Spaine. Besides, if you take this Arragonian historie euen in that sence, yet should your rule fall short: for this practise of theirs, fell out most successfully vnto them.

The Aduocate made aunswere to the Gentleman, saying: The matter is not great, you may conceiue of it as please your selfe: as for mee, I am of another minde, & I am perswaded my opinion comes neerer the truth. But not to digresse from the matter in hand, you shall finde no historie more strange, as touching the argument in question, then that which of late memorie hath happened to the King of Poland, *Stephen Batori*, beeing also King of Sweden. This Prince being altogether Iesuited, and hauing beene mightily importuned by them, to be admitted into his Realme of Sweden, at last resolued to satisfie their desire. His ordinarie residence is in Poland, and for Sweden, Duke *Charles* his Vncle, is his Lieutenant generall. The King, desirous to accomplish what the Iesuits requested, signified his pleasure directly to his vncle: *Charles* made him aunswere, that the people would neuer be brought to like of that Societie, and besought the King his nephew, not to grow into termes with his subiects, to whom he had giuen his promise, at the time of his coronation, neuer to receiue the Iesuits into his Realme; wherunto the chiefe States of the Land had likewise subscribed.

But he, that saw not, but by their eyes, & heard not, but by their eares, resolued to goe thorow withall, (notwithstanding these humble admonitions) and to enter his realme with an Armie, to make his subiects belieue that

he

He meant good earneſt : for preuenting whereof, they arme themſelues likewiſe on their part. The matter was ſo carried, that the Prince was firſt ouerthrowne by ſea, afterwards diſcomfited by Land, and taken priſoner : within a while after, he was ſet at libertie, and reſtored to his Crowne, vnder promiſe to call a Parliament, and to obſerue, what ſhould therein be concluded and agreed vpon.

The States were ſummoned, he in time of the Parliament, conueyed himſelfe away, leauing garriſons in certaine places, which were at his deuotion . Beeing returned backe againe to Polande, by the inſtigation of the Ieſuits, who wholy poſſeſt him, hee gathered together the ſcattered boordes of his ſhipwrackt Armie, & implores ayde of the States of Poland, to reuenge the wrong which he ſayd was done him.

In the meane time, while hee was about his preparations, (as yet he is, the Polanders lending a deafe eare to the matter) his vncle tooke frō him thoſe places, which were remaining in his ſubiection within Sweden, and is at the poynt, to put him quite beſides his kingdome, which was gotten by the proweſſe of *Guſtaue* his grandfather, and kept by the wiſedome of his Father ; Poland beeing not very firme to him withall. And for all thys his fall and ouerthrow, he may thanke none but the Ieſuits, whoſe protection he would needs vndertake.

After I haue trauāiled into all theſe farre Countries, I will returne to mine owne. The Ieſuits raiſed troubles in the ſtate of Fraunce, vnder pretence to roote Caluiniſme out of the land. In this quarrell the Spaniard was called to for aſſiſtance, who entertained no meane hopes, ſeeing himſelfe commaund within Paris with open armes, and aboue all other, fauoured by the Ieſuits, who had the whole rule and ſuperintendencie ouer that Anarchie, or confuſed gouernment of the ſixteene Tyrants, ſet vp by the multitude.

I will not say what the departure of the Spaniard was, this I will say, that the Kings entrance into Paris was so tryumphant, as the Spaniard thought himselfe happie, that he might hold his life of him by fealtie & homage. Moreouer, the trayterous practises of the Iesuits, which vanished into smoake, were the occasion, that by a decree made in the high court of Paris, themselues were banisht and expelled, as well out of the good Cittie of Paris, as out of the iurisdiction of that Court.

To conclude, I see not after they haue raised tumults in all Countries, that theyr designements sort to effect.

CHAP. 17.

¶ That the Pope hath not power to translate the Crowne of Fraunce from one to another, against the dangerous position of the Iesuits : and some other discourse tending to the same effect.

He Iesuits, not content to haue offered violence to our King in time of the troubles, doe at this day in the time of peace, by theyr pennes, offer violence to the Royaltie it selfe. Hee that maintaines in Rome, that the Pope may transfer Empires and Kingdomes from hand to hand at his pleasure, deserueth a Cardinals hat, as Father *Robert Bellarmine* the Iesuite : he that maintaines the same position in Fraunce, is worthie of a hat of that colour, but not of that kinde as the Cardinals. Kings die whē it pleaseth God to call them, the Roialtie neuer dies. Which is the cause that the Parliament Court of Paris, when they accompanie the funerall obsequies of our Kinges, are not in mourning weedes, but in Scarlet, the true marke and ensigne of the neuer dying maiestie of the Crowne or Royaltie. One of the chiefe flowers of our Crowne is, that our Kings, cannot incurre the censures of the Church of Rome,

Rome, nor their realme be interdicted, nor conſequently tranſpoſed. It is a law not made, but bred with
vs, which we haue not learned, receiued, or by long inſtruction imprinted, but a law, which is drawne, inſpired, and deriued into vs out of the very breaſts of our
Mother Fraunce,wherein we are not nurtured,but nur-
ſed, that if any thunderbolts fortuned to be ſent from
Rome againſt the maieſtie of our Kings , ſo as in conſequence thereof, the realme might fall vnder the ſentence of Interditement, we are not bound to yeeld obedience thereunto. Neither yet for all this , did our kings
euer looſe the title of *Moſt Chriſtian*, nor wee of the *Eldeſt ſonnes of the Church.*

The Ieſuit hath beene condemned by a decree of the
Court, he drawes his chaine after him ſtill , yet will hee
not ceaſe to be a Ieſuit : that is, a Seminarie of diuiſions,
factions,and diſſentions within our country. Let vs then
heare what he ſaith, who vnder the name of *Montaignes,* hath publiſht the booke of the *Truth,* as hee intitles
it, but of the forged and lying *Truth.* After hee had diſcourſed, that the Temporall ſtate onely appertained to
the King,and the Spirituall to the holy Father,who clai-
med no intereſt in their ſouerainties,hee affirmes, that if
the king happē at any time to tranſgreſſe, God hath put
a rod into the Popes hand to chaſtiſe him, and depriue
him of his kingdome. And this is for the behoofe, & *Mont. cap.
15. of the
Truth de-
fended.*
for the good of Princes, (ſaith he) who moſt common-
lie are reclaimed, and brought to their duties, rather for
feare of their Temporall eſtate, which they euer-more
hold deer,(though otherwiſe ill giuen)then of their Spirituall, which they ſet not by,vnleſſe their conſcience be
the better, which is not generall to all of them.

But the Pope is no God : no more was *Samuell,* who
executed that ſentence againſt *Saul.* So as God had
annointed *Saul* King by the Prophet, ſo doth he ſend
the ſentence of his depoſition by him, and by him tranſ-

late the kingdome, & annoint Dauid king.

In the time of *Ofias* king of Iuda, the high prieſt (no more a GOD then *Samuell*,) gaue the kingdome from the father to the ſonne, he being ſtrooken with leproſie for his preſumption. This tranſpoſition of the Crowne, was doone by the appointment of the high Prieſt, (according as by the Law was ordained) and conſequently the depoſition of the Father.

Iehoiada was no God, but a prieſt, and Gods Lieutenaunt, when, after he had cauſed *Athalia* the Queene to be put to death for her tyrannous gouernment, hee put the ſcepter into the handes of *Ioas*, a prince of the blood, and lawfull ſucceſſor to the Crowne. All thoſe were but Gods miniſters to execute his decrees, as the Pope likewiſe is.

And ſeeing God hath infinite meanes to tranſlate a kingdome, by the force and weapons of Pagans, as of Moores, Turks, and other ſtrange Nations, making the Aſſyrians conquerours ouer the Greekes, the Greekes ouer the Aſſyrians, both of the Iewes, and the Romans of both, what milder courſe could he haue ordained among Chriſtians, what way more reaſonable, or more ſecure, then by the mediation and authoritie of the head of the Church, and the common Father of all Chriſtians, who beeing ſpecially aſſiſted by God, and by men both learned and religious, will in likelihood doe nothing preiudiciall to the right of the lawfull ſucceſſors, and will proceede without paſſion, and withall moderation and mildnes in a caſe of that importance, hauing an eye euermore to the honour of God, and vnto the publique and priuate good.

In concluſion, by this learned poſition, which our pernitious Ieſuit maintaines, the Pope hath authoritie to transferre kingdoms frō one hand to another, when he ſeeth cauſe ſo to doe, and dooing it, hee is ſubiect to no mans controule: inaſmuch as if God himſelfe may

doe

doe it, then is it lawfull for his Vicar to doe the like : the Pope hauing no lesse preheminence ouer Kings, in these times of Christianity, then the Prophets had in the time of Moses law.

This fond opinion of thine, brings mee to a meruailous straite, forcing mee to combate against the authoritie of the holie Sea. First, if you will argue this position morallie, where shall you finde that a King constituting his Lieuetenants generall in Prouinces, giueth them in all poynts as ample authoritie, as himselfe hath ouer his subiects ? And to say, that God hath transferred his omnipotent power into any man whatsoeuer, is a poynt of blaspemie against the Maiestie of G O D. Besides, tell mee Sophister, where finde you that you ought to beg such examples out of the old Testament, to transplant them into the new ?

But with such illusions doe you and your associats, surprise the consciences of the weake & ignorant multitude. For if that reason of yours were of any value, or consequence, we should by the same, bring Circumcision into vse againe at this day, because it was vsed vnder the Law of *Moses.* And by the same pretext, it shall be lawfull for the subiect, to lay violent handes vppon his Soueraigne, because *Ehud* murthered *Eglon* King of Moab, vnpunished. Iudges. 3.

Seeing you terme your selfe a Iesuit, let vs follow the footesteps of Iesus Christ ; for to this marke ought all our cogitations to leuell, whereunto restraining our discourse, I will make it appeare, that I am a true Cathotholicke liegeman to the Pope, and thou a true Catholique Impostor. VVee consider the power of our Sauiour Christ in two different times: one was, vvhen for our Redemption hee descended from heauen into the earth : the other, vvhen after his death and passion, hee ascended from earth into heauen. The first was the time of his humilitie, in respect whereof hee professed,

that

that his comming was not to be an vmpire of their con-
trouersies, which they would haue referred to him : at
what time he diftinguifht the power of God, from the
power of the Romane Emperour, faying ; That wee
muft yeeld vnto God, that which belonged vnto God,
and vnto *Cæſar*, that which was due vnto *Cæſar*. And
being demaunded of *Pilate*, whether he were a king or
no, he made him aunſwere, that his kingdome was not
of this inferiour world. The ſecond was the time of his
glorie, whereunto all thoſe excellent ſayings of the prophet Dauid are to be referred : as when he ſaid, that the
earth was the Lords : *Aske of mee , and I will giue thee
nations and heritages, and they ſhall be vnto thee for a poſſeſſion vnto the vttermoſt bounds of the earth.* And in another place, that hee was *Lorde of Lordes , and King of
Kings.*

Let vs not falſifie the holie Scripture : For the more
you ambitious Ieſuits apply out of it to the Pope, to au-
thoriſe, not his greatnes, but your owne, the more you
take from him. At what time did Chriſt aſſigne Saint
Peter to be his Vicar ? Surely while hee was yet on
earth, and at the poynt to finiſh his pilgrimage, that he
might repreſent his perſon heere below, in his eſtate of
humilitie : and ſo gaue him the keyes of heauen, & not
of earth, to ſignifie vnto vs, that he gaue him the charge
of ſpirituall matters, without mingling there-withall
temporall buſines.

And certainly our auncient Popes were very igno-
raunt, if giuing them-ſelues the title of *Seruus ſeruo-
rum*, they meant to repreſent Ieſus Chriſt, as hee is
in the fulneſſe of his glorie, and after hee aſcended into heauen, to ſit on the right hand of GOD his Father.
In like manner was it an hereſie in *Luther*, to teach his
folowers, that the Pope was wrongfully termed head of
the church, & Vicar general to Ieſus Chriſt : & no leſſe
hereſie was it in *Ignacius*, when to oppoſe *Luther*, hee
affirmed,

affirmed that the Pope was Chrifts Vicar, not onely in his eftate of humility, but euē in his eftate of glory like-wife. Hee then is a true Catholique liegeniān to the Pope, who doth acknowledge and approue his authori-tie, according to the originall inftitution thereof, with-out any augmentations, or additions from men.

Iefuit, I now come vnto thee : let vs weigh how ful of danger this pofition of thine is. Our Kings know beft, what is expedient for the maintenance & preferuation of their eftate : and like skilful Pilots, are faine fomtimes to ftrike fayle in a tempeft. This courfe the Pope being carried away with other refpeects, will not like of, & will perhaps fummō our kings to cōform their proceedings to his mind. After fome two, or three admonitiōs, if they obey not, he wil proceed to cenfure thē, & confequētly to make a diuorce between them & their fubieects: or if not fo, to interdite the Realm, & expofe it for a pray to any Prince, that fhal be firft able to poffeffe himfelfe of it. Good God ! into what a confufion doft thou bring our State ?

Iefuit, learne this leffon of me; for I wil not fuffer, either our countrimē to be infeected with thy poyfonous propofitions, or ftraungers that fhal read this booke of thine, to conceiue, that the Maieftie of our kings is, by thy comming, any whit empayred. Firft we maintayne, and vphold it for an article inuiolable in Fraunce, that the Pope hath no authority, to be liberal of our Realme, for any mans aduantage whatfoeuer, what fault foeuer our king fhall be found culpable of, none excepted. The Pope hath no power, but what is giuen him by commiffion from God; he is neither that *Samuel,* nor that *Iehoiada,* who were commaunded by God to doe, what they did vnder the olde law : for vnder the new, which we call the new Teftament, there is no mention of any fuch matter. The Pope cannot by the power of his fpirituall fword, controule the temporall. I fay not

Zz 3.   therefore

therefore, that any king of Fraunce should forget him-selfe, eyther in the Catholique Religion, or in the go-uernment of his subiects, to whom he ought to be a second father : for if he doe, let him be assured, that God will sooner, or later forget him, and auenge himselfe by some meanes vnexpected, and vnthought of, but that we are to seeke this redresse at Rome, I flatly denie.

For this first position, I hold it to be cleere : that which now I will deliuer, may seeme more questionable. We hold it for another article firme and indubitable in this Realme of Fraunce, that our kings are not subiect to the Popes excommunication. A thing, which we haue re-ceiued from all antiquitie. I remember I haue read that *Lothaire* king of Austracia deceasing, left *Lewes* his bro-ther, who was Emperour, and King of Italy, to be his successor. King *(Charles, the Bald,* vncle to them both, seazed on it by right of occupation, as lying fit for his hand. *Lewes* had recourse to Pope *Adrian,* who vnder-tooke the quarrel for him, and summoned *Charles* to do his nephew right, vpon payne of excommunication : but *Charles* would giue no eare to him. By reason wher-of, the Pope went on to interpose his censures with bit-ter curses and comminations : and knowing the high authoritie, which rested in *Hingmare,* Archbishoppe of Reims, he enioyned him not to admit the king, to com-municate with him, vpon paine, himselfe to be depri-ued of his Holinesse his communion.

There was neuer Popes Iniunction, more iust, & holy then this. For what colour could there be for an vncle to intercept his nephewes right in succeeding his owne brother ? Yet neuer was Iniunction worse entertayned then this. For *Hisgmare* after he had imparted the let-ters Apostolical to diuers Prelats and Barons of France, to be aduised by them, how to carry himselfe in the mat-ter, he wrote backe to Pope *Adrian,* what he had drawn and collected out of their aunsweres; namely, that all

of

of them were much offended, & agreeued with that his
Decree, alledging, that the like proceedings had not
beene seene, no not when the kings were Heretiques,
Scismatiques, or Tyrants : and maintayning that kingdomes were purchased by the edge of the sword, and
not by the excommunications, or censures of the Sea
Apostolique, or of Prelates. And when I vrge them
(said *Hingmare*) with the authoritie, which was dele-
gate by our Sauiour to Saint *Peter*, and from him deriued by succession to the Popes of Rome ; they aunswere me. *Petite Dominum Apostolicum vt : quia Rex
& Episcopus simul esse non potest : Et sui antecessores Eccle-
siasticum ordinem (quod suum est) & non Rempublicam
(quod regum est) disposuerunt. Non præcipiat nobis habere
regem,qui nos in sic longinquis partibus adiuuare non possit,
contra subitaneos & frequentes Paganorum impetus: & nos
Francos iubeat seruire, cui nolumus seruire. Qua istud iugū
sui antecessores,nostris antecessoribus non imposuerūt. Quia
scriptum in sanctis libris audimus,vt pro libertate & hæreditate nostra vsque ad mortem certare debeamus* . That is,
Tell our Apostolicall Lord, that he cannot at once be
a King and a Prelate, and that his predecessors ordered
the Ecclesiasticall State (which belongeth vnto him) and
not the temporall, (which pertaines only to kings.) Let
him not inioyne vs to receiue a King, who remayning
in a countrie so farre distant, cannot ayde vs, against the
sodain, & ofte incursions of the Infidels. Neither let him
commaund vs (who of our Franchise and Freedome
beare the name of Franks) to serue him, whom we list
not to serue : which yoake his predecessors neuer imposed vppon our Auncestors. And we finde it written in holy Scripture, that we ought to fight to the
death,for our libertie and inheritance. *And a little after,
Propterea si Dominus Apostolicus vult pacem quære-
re,sic quærat vt rixam non moueat.* That is; Therefore if
our Apostolicall Lord seeke after peace,let him so seeke
it,

it, as he be not an occaſiõ of war. And in concluſiõ, *Hing-*
mare ſhuts vp his letter with theſe words. *Et vt mihi expe-*
rimento videtur, propter meam interdiɛtionem, vel propter
linguæ humanæ gladium, niſi aliud obſtiterit, Rex noſter, vel
eius Regni primores non dimittent, vt quod cœperunt, quantũ
potuerint, nõ exequantur. That is; And as I find by proofe,
our King, or the Peeres of his Realme, are not minded,
eyther for my excommunication, or the ſword of mans
tongue (vnleſſe ſome other matter come to ſtop them)
to deſiſt from proſecuting what they haue begun.

By which letters you may vnderſtand, that the Pope
tooke vpon him, not onely to cenſure King *Charles, the*
Bald, for his diſobedience in ſo iuſt and rightfull a cauſe,
but to make himſelfe Iudge alſo of Empyres and Kingdomes: wherevnto neither the king, nor his ſubieɛts
would euer aſſent: auouching, that the Pope could not
confound Religion with State, and that they were reſolued to withſtand him, whatſoeuer it coſt them: as being a new law, which he meant to obtrude vpon the
land, to the preiudice of our kings.

It may be, ſome honeſt meaning man will ſay: How
doth this hang together? You allow the Pope all primacie, and ſuperioritie in ſpirituall cauſes, and yet limite
his general power in your owne king, though he ſhould
runne aſtray out of the right way. For in reſpeɛt of temporall matters, I grant it; but as for this high point of
ſpirituall authority, all things make againſt that poſition.
Whom I aunſwere thus. We acknowledge in Fraunce,
that the Pope is ſupreame head of the Catholique and
Vniuerſall Church, yet is it not therefore abſurd, or in-
conſequent, that our Kings ſhould be exempted from
his cenſures.

We ſee that all auncient Monaſteries, are naturallie
ſubieɛt to the iuriſdiɛtion of theyr Dioceſans, yet are
many of them by ſpeciall priuiledge exempted from
the ſame. Our auncient Kings haue beene the firſt protectors

tectors of the holy Sea , as well againſt the tyrannie of
the Emperous of Conſtantinople , as againſt the incur-
ſions, and inuaſions of the Lombards, which were dailie at the gates of Rome. One king alone , *Pepin*, conquered the whole ſtate, or Herarchie of Rauenna, which
he freely gaue to the Pope, deliuering their Cittie from
the long ſiege, which *Aſtolpho* king of the Lombards
had held about it. And *Charlemaine* the ſonne of *Pepin*,
chaſed out of Lombardie , *Didier* their king, and his
whole race : making himſelfe Maiſter , as well of the
Cittie of Rome, as of all Italie, where he was afterwards
acknowledged, and crowned Emperour of the Weſt
by Pope *Leo*, whom he reſtored fully and wholly to his
auncient libertie, againſt the inſolencie of the people of
Rome, who repined and mutined againſt him. And at
that time was it concluded, that the Popes elect, might
not enter vpon the exerciſe , or adminiſtration of theyr
functions, vntill they were firſt confirmed by him or his
ſucceſſors.

I am certainly perſwaded, that hee and his poſterity,
were at that time freed, and exempted from all cenſures
and excommunications of the holy Sea. And albeit we
haue not the expreſſe Conſtitution to ſhew , yet may it
be extracted out of the Ordinaunces of the ſaid Emperour, recorded by *Iuon* , Biſhop of Chartres : *Si quos* Epiſt. 123.
& 195.
culpatores Regia poteſtas, aut in gratiam benignitatis rece-
perit, aut menſæ ſuæ participes fecerit, hos & ſacerdotum,
& populorum conuentus ſuſcipere Eccleſiaſtica communione
debebit, vt quod principalis pietas recepit , nec à Sacerdoti-
bus Dei extraneum habeatur. If the king ſhall receiue a-
ny ſinner into the fauour of his clemencie, or make him
partaker of his owne table, the whole companie of the
Prieſts and people, ſhall likewiſe receiue him into the
cōmunion of the Church : that, that which the princes
pietie hath admitted, be not by the prieſts , held as caſt
off or reiected.

If then the table, or the fauour of our Kings, did ac-quite and abſolue the excommunicated perſon, from the Eccleſiaſticall cenſures, wee may well ſay, that our kings themſelues were exempt from all excommunications. Our kings had right to confirme the Popes after their elections, a right which the Popes alledge, to haue beene by them remitted; then why ſhould we be more enuied then they, if the auncient Prelacie of Rome, haue priuiledged our kings from all excommunications and cenſures whatſoeuer?

Sure I am that Pope *Gregorie* the fourth, going a-bout to infringe that prerogatiue, to gratifie the ſonnes of king *Lewes the Milde*, the ſonne of *Charlemaine*, the good Biſhops and Prelats of Fraunce, ſent him vvord, that if he came in perſon to excommunicate their king, himſelfe ſhould returne excommunicated to Rome. A peremtorie ſpeech I muſt confeſſe, but it wrought ſo, as the Pope, to couer his packing, pretended hee came into Fraunce for no other intent, but to mediate a peace betweene the Father and the ſonnes, as indeede he did: and had he ſtood vppon other termes, hee would haue gone out of Fraunce greatly diſpleaſed.

So much doe wee embrace this priuiledge of our kings, as wee dare affirme, that it had his beginning ey-ther with the Crowne it ſelfe, at what time *Clouis* be-came a Chriſtian, or at leaſt in the ſecond line, within a while after our kings had taken in hand, the defence & protection of the Church of Rome: for ſo doe we find it to haue beene obſerued ſucceſſiuely in *Charlemaine*, *Lewes the Milde*, his ſonne, and *Charles the Balde*, his grand-child. And ſince in the third line, when our kings ſeemed ſome-what to forget the right way, and that it was requiſite to extend the authoritie of the Church to-wards them, the Pope, or his Legates, were fayne to ioyne the Clergie of Fraunce with them. In briefe, as long as all thinges were quiet and peaceable betweene
the

the King and his subiects, the censures of Rome were neuer receiued against our Kings.

In our auncient Records, wee finde a Bull bearing date from Pope *Boniface* the eyght, the tenor whereof is, *Vt nec Rex Franciæ, nec Regina, nec liberi eorum ex communicari possint*: That neyther the King nor the Queene of Fraunce, nor theyr chyldren can be excommunicated.

It fell so out after that time, that the same Pope, falling at variance with king *Phillip the fayre*, hee needes would excommunicate him, but there was neuer excommunication cost Pope so deere, as that did him. For his *Nuncios* weare committed prisoners, his Buls burnt, and *Boniface* himselfe, being taken by *Naugeret*, Chauncelor of Fraunce, presently after died, for very sorrow & despight that he had receiued so foule a disgrace at the hands of his enemie. Wherein *Phillip* did nothing, but by the counsell and consent of the whole Cleargie of Fraunce. So farre was this excommunication, from falling to the preiudice of the King and his Realme, that contrariwise, it turned to his shame and confusion, by whom it was decreed.

Benet the 13. otherwise called *Peter de Luna*, keeping his sea or residence in Auignon, hauing interdited *Charles* the sixt and his realme, the king sitting in the throne of iustice in the Parliament, or high Court of Paris, the 21. of May, 1408. gaue sentence that the Bull should be rent in peeces, and that *Gonsalue* & *Confeloux*, the bearers thereof, should be set vpon a pillorie, and publiquely notified, and traduced in the pulpit: the meaning wherof was, that the people should be taught and informed, that the king was not liable to any excommunication. Which decree was accordingly put in execution in the month of August, with the greatest scorne that could be deuised, the two *Nuncios* or Legats hauing this inscription vppon their Miters: *These men* are disloyall to the Church, and to the King. *Iulius* the second, offered the like to king *Lewes* the twelfth, & his censures were censured by a Conuocation of the Clergie of Fraunce, holden at Tours, 1510.

Not to goe too farre from our owne times, the like censures came from Rome in time of our last troubles, in the yeere 1591. & by the sentence aswel of the Court of Parliament of Paris, then remoued to Tours, as of the soueraine or high chamber, holden at Chalons in Champagnie, it was ordered, that the Bulls should be burnt by the publique Executioner, as accordingly they were. A Maxime so grounded in the realme of France, that in the treatie of peace, which was made in the towne of Arras, in the yeere 1481, between king *Lewes* the 11, and *Maximilian* the Arch-duke of Austria, and the States of the Low-countries, the Deputies for *Maximilian* and the States, treated with ours, that the King should promise to keepe & obserue this agreement, and to that end he and his sonnes should submit themselues to all Ecclesiasticall censures: Notwithstanding the priuiledge of the Kings of Fraunce, *Whereby, neither hee nor his Realme, might bee compeld by Ecclesiasticall censures.* Which treatie, was afterward confirmed by king *Lewes* the same yeere at Plessi, neere vnto Tours, the confirmation carrieth these words: *Wee haue submitted vs, and our said sonne, and our Realme, to all Ecclesiasticall censures, for the keeping and obseruing of the saide treatie: notwithstanding the priuiledge which we haue, that wee, nor our successours, nor our Realme, ought not to be subiect, nor liable to censures.* VVhich thing hath beene since that time confirmed, by a decree made in the yeere 1549. *Charles* Cardinall of Lorraine, Archbishop of Reims, to make his memory immortall, by a most honourable action, founded an Vniuersitie in Reims, with manie great priuiledges, hauing first obtained leaue and permission of the King, *Henry* the second, and next of the
Pope

Pope, *Paule* the third, for fo much as concerned the
fpiritualties: who graunted forth his Buls verie large,
and ample, contayning amongft other claufes, this
one.

Nos igitur piū & laudabile Henrici *Regis, &* Caroli *Cardinalis defiderium, plurimū commendantes, præfatūm* Hen-
ricum *Regē à quibufuis excommunicationis, fufpenfionis &
interdicti, alijfque Ecclefiafticis fententijs & cenfuris, pœnis
à iure vel ab homine, quauis occafione vel caufa latis, fi quibus quomodolibet innodatus exiftat, ad effectum prefentium
duntaxat confequendum, harum ferie abfoluentes.* What
greater fauour, or courtefie could we expect from
Rome, then that our king without any fuit of his, fhould
be abfolued from all cenfures, which he could incurre
de iure, or *de facto?* Neuerthelefle, this courtefie was by
the Court of Parliament at Paris, as frankly refufed, as it
was offered. Becaufe in the verification afwell of the
Buls, as of the kings Letters-patents, it was enacted by a
decree in Court, giuē the laft faue one of Ianuary 1549,
with this prouifo, that notwithftanding this pretended
abfolution, it be not inferd, that the king hath beene, or
hereafter may be, any way, or for any caufe whatfoeuer,
fubiect to the excommunications, or cenfures Apofto-
licall, or thereby preiudice the rights, priuiledges, or
preheminences of the king, and of his Realme. As alfo
the fentence giuen againft *Iohn Chaftell,* the 29. of December 1594. contained this peculiar claufe, that amon-
geft other things, he was condemned, for hauing maintayned, that our king *Henry* the fourth, raigning at this
prefent, was not in the Church, vntill he had the approbation of the Pope: whereof he did repent, and aske
forgiuenes of God, the king, and the Court.

This that I haue deliuered in this prefent difcourfe, doth not proceed of any finifter affection,
which I beare to the holy Sea (fooner let GOD
bereaue me of my life) but onely to make it appeare,

Aaa. 3.   that

that our kings carrie together with their Crowne, their
safe conduct in all places, and are not subiect to the
trecherous practises of their enemies neere the Pope.
Notwithstanding you see, how these accursed Iesuits,
enemies of our peace, instruct vs in the contrarie, that is,
kindle and prepare vs to reuolt, in case our kings should
stand in ill termes with the Pope: which prooues, that it
is not without iust cause, that by a Decree of the Parliament of Paris, they haue beene banisht out of
Fraunce.

CHAP. 18.

⸹ The Decree of the Parliament of Paris, against the
Iesuits, in the yeere 1 5 9 4. and a Chapter taken out
of the third booke des Recerches de la
Farunce, by Stephen
Pasquier.

Lib.3.des
Recer, ca.3 2

 Auing dedicated this booke,
(saith *Pasquier*) to the liberties
of our Church of Fraunce, I
hope I shall not digresse from
my purpose, if I entreat some-
what of the Sect of the Iesuits,
which, to the subuersion of our
State, maintayneth principles
quite contrarie to ours. The Ie-
suits hauing got into their hands the great legacies,
giuen and bequeathed them by Maister *William du*
Part, Bishop of Clairmont, they bought *Langres* place
lying in Saint Iaques street in the Citie of Paris, where
they, after their manner, established the forme of a Colledge, and of a Monasterie in diuers tenements : and taking vpon them to instruct youth without the authoritie of the Rector, they made sute sundrie times to be
incorporated into the Vniuersitie. Which when they
could

could not obtayne, they exhibited a petition to the same
effect, to the Court of Parliament in the yeere 1 5 6 4.
The Vniuersitie did me the honour, to choose me in
a full congregation for their Aduocate. Hauing prepared my selfe for the cause, (being armed with that sacred
Decree, which the facultie of Diuinity had pronounced
against them in the yeere 1 5 5 4. where those two great
pillers of our Catholique Religion, *Monsieur Picard,*
and *Monsieur Maillard* were assistants) I was perswaded, that I was able with a free and vncontrouled conscience, to encounter hand to hand, with this monster,
which being neyther Secular, nor Regular, was both togither, and therefore brought into our Church an am-
biguous, or mungrell profession. We pleaded this case
two whole forenoones, Maister *Peter Versoris,* and I,
he for the Iesuits, I for the Vniuersitie, before an infinite
multitude of people, who attended, to see the issue
thereof: Maister *Baptist du Menill,* the Kings Aduocate, a man of great sufficiencie, was for me. In
my declaration, I alledged the irrigularitie of their profession; the iudgement, and determination of the whole
facultie of Diuinitie, pronounced against them tenne
yeeres before: the obiection made by *Monsieur Bruslard,*
the Kings Attorney Generall against their admittance,
for that their vow was cleane contrarie to ours, that if we
should harbour them in our bosome, we should bring
in a Schisme amongst vs; and besides, so many espials
for Spayne, and sworne enemies to Fraunce, the effects whereof wee were like to feele, vpon the first
chaunge that the iniquitie of time might bring vpon vs.

Notwithstanding for the conclusion, we were referred to Counsell. Eyther partie both got, and lost the
day. For neither were they incorporated into the Vniuersity, nor yet prohibited to continue their accustomed
readings. When God hath a purpose to afflict a realme,

he

he planteth the roots thereof long time before hand.
These new-come guests, blind and bewitch the people
by shewes of holines, and fayre promises. For, as if they
had the gift of tongues, which the holy Ghost infused
into the Apostles, they made their boasts, that they (forsooth) went to preach the Gospel in the midst of barbarous, and sauage people, they that (God knowes) had
ynough to do, to speake their mother tongue. With
these pleasant baits did they inueigle and draw the multitude into their snares. But as they had brought in a
motly religion of Secular and Regular, disturbing by
meanes thereof all the Hierarchie of our Church, so
did they intend, to trouble thence-forward, all the
politique states in Christendome. In as much, as by
a newe inuented rule, they beganne to mingle and
confound the State with their religion. And as it is
easie, to fall from liberty to vnbridled licence, so
did they, vpon this irriguler rule of theirs, ground the
most detestable heresie, that can be deuised : affirming,
that it is lawfull to murther any Prince, that should not
conforme himselfe to their principles : treading vnder
foot both the checke, which our Sauiour gaue to Saint
Peter, when he drew his sword in his defence, and the
Canon of the Councell of Constance, whereby they
were pronounced accurst, that set abroach this position.

When I pleaded the cause, I mentioned not these two
propositions against them. For though they bred them
in their hearts, yet had they not as yet hatched them : only I said, that there was no good to be hoped for of this
monster : but that they would euer put in practise eyther that principle, which was broched by the old Moū-
tainer, who in time of our wars beyond the Seas, dispersed
his subiects, called cut-throats, or murtherers, through the
the Prouinces, to slay the Christian Princes : or that horrible Anabaptisme, which sprung vp in Germanie, when
we were young : this should I neuer haue imagined.

Notwith-

Notwithstanding, both the one and the other Maxime, hath beene by them put in execution, in the sight and knowledge of all Christendome. For as concerning the first, there is no man but knowes, that they, hauing set foot in Portugall, not vnder the title of Iesuits, but of Apostles, they sollicited King *Sebastian* by all maner of illusions, to make an vniuersall law, that none might be called to the Crowne, vnlesse he were of their Societie: and moreouer, elected by the consent, & suffrages of the same. VVhereunto they could not attayne, albeit they met with the most deuout and superstitious Prince that could be. And not to lead you out of our owne countrie of Fraunce; they were the men, that kindled the first coales of that accursed League, which hath beene the vtter ruine and subuersion of the land. It was first of all debated amongst them, and being concluded, they constituted their Fathers, *Claudius Matthæus* a Lorrain, and *Claudius Sammier* of Luxembourg, (for so are their Priests of greatest antiquitie called) to be their trumpets for the proclayming thereof ouer all forraine nations. And after that time, did they with open face, declare themselues to be Spaniards, as well in their Sermons, as publique Lectures. In fauour of whom, they attempted to bring their second principle into practise, not all the while that the King was diuided from vs in religion (for they knew, that was a barre sufficient to keepe him from the Crowne) but as soone as they saw him reclaymed into the bosome of the Church, they set on worke one *Peter Barriere*, a man resolute for execution, but weake and tender in conscience: whom they caused to be confessed in their Colledge at Paris, afterwards to receiue the Sacrament, and hauing confirmed him by an assured promise of Paradise, as a true Martyr, if he died in that quarrell, set forward this valiant Champion, who was thrise at the the verie point to execute his accursed enterprise; and

Bbb. God

God as often miraculoufly ftayed his hand, vntill at length being apprehended at Melun, he receiued the iuft hyre of his trayterous intention, in the yeere, 1593.

I fpeake nothing, but what mine eyes can witneffe, and what I had from his owne mouth when he was prifoner. View, & perufe all the impieties, that you will, you fhall find none fo barbarous as this. To perfwade an impietie, and then to couer it with fuch a feeming maske of pietie : In a word, to deftroy a foule, a King, Paradife, and our Church, all at a blow, to make way for their Spanifh and halfe-Pagan defignements. All thefe new allegations, caufed the Vniuerfitie of Paris, the Citie being brought vnder the Kings obedience, to renew their former fuit againft them, which had beene ftayed before time by the Counfels appoyntment. The caufe was pleaded effectually and learnedly, by Maifter *Anthonie Arnald*: but when the proceffe was brought to the verie poynt of Iudgement, there fell out another accident, which made them proceed roundly thereunto. *Iohn Chaftell*, a Paritian of the age of 19. yeeres, a graft of this accurfed Seminarie, ftroke our king *Henrie* the fourth with a knife in his Royall Pallace of the Louvre, in the midft of his Nobilitie. He is taken, his proceffe being commenced and finifhed, fentēce enfueth, dated the 29. of December, 1594. the tenour whereof followeth.

Being viewed by the Court, the great Chamber, and the Tournel being affembled, the arraignement, or proceffe criminall, begun by the Controller of the kings houfehold, and fince finifhed at the requifition and demaund of the Kings Atturney generall, plaintife againft *Iohn Chaftell* of the Citie of Paris ftudent, hauing made the courfe of his ftudies in the Colledge of Clairmont, prifoner in the prifon called the Conciergerie of the Pallace, by reafon of the moft execrable and abhominable parricide attempted vpon the perfon of the King : The examinations and confeffions of the

said

said *Iohn Chaſtell*: the said *Iohn Chaſtell* being heard and examined in the said Court touching the said parricide: therebeing heard also in the same, *Iohn Gueret* Prieſt, calling himſelfe of the Companie and Society of the name of Ieſus, abiding, & continuing in the said Colledge, and ſometimes Schoolemaiſter of the said *Iohn Chaſtell*, *Peter Chaſtell*, and *Deniſe Hazard*, the father and mother of the said *Iohn Chaſtell*: the concluſions of the Atturney generall, all waighed and conſidered. BE IT KNOWNE, that the said Court hath declared, and doth declare, the said *Iohn Chaſtell*, attaynted and conuicted of the crime of treaſon, againſt God and man in the higheſt degree, by the moſt wicked and deteſtable parricide, or murther attempted vpon the perſon of the King. For repayring of the which crime, it hath condēned, and doth condemne the said *Iohn Chaſtell*, to make an honourable amends, before the gate of the principall Church of Paris, naked in his ſhirt, holding a Torch of waxe burning of the waight of two pounds, and there on his knees, to ſay and declare, that accurſedly & traiterouſly, he hath attempted the said moſt barbarous and abhominable parricide, and wounded the King in the face with a knife; and through falſe and damnable inſtruƈtions, he hath said in his said triall or proceſſe, that it was lawfull to murther Kings, and that the King, *Henrie* the fourth, now raigning, is not in the Church, vntill he haue the approbation of the Pope: whereof he is heartily ſory, and asketh forgiuenes of God, the King, & the Court. This done, to be drawn in a doungcart to the place of execution called the Greue; there to be pinched with hotte pincers, on his armes, & thighs, and his right hand, holding in it the knife, wherewith he attempted, to commit the said murther or parricide, to be cut off: after that, his bodie to be diſmembred, and drawen in peeces with foure horſes: and his quarters & bodie to be caſt into the fire, and conſumed to aſhes.

and

and the ashes to be cast into the winde, and it hath declared, all his goods to be forfeyted, and confiscate to the King. Before which execution shall the said *Iohn Chastell* be brought to the racke or torture, as well ordinary, as extraordinary, to know the truth of his confederates, and of certaine cases arising out of the processe: Hath made and doth make inhibition, and restraint to any persons, of what qualitie or condition soeuer, vpon paine of being guiltie of high Treason, not to speake or vtter the said speeches, which the said Court hath pronounced, & doth pronounce to be scandalous, seditious, and contrarie to the word of God, and condemned as heretical by the sacred decrees: It doth ordaine, that the Priests and students of the Colledge of Clairmont, and all other, calling themselues of that Society, as corrupters of youth, and disturbers of common quiet, enemies of the King, and State, shall auoid within three daies after the publication of this present sentence, out of Paris, and other Cities, and places where their Colledges are; and fifteene daies after, out of the Realme, vpon paine, wheresoeuer they shall be found, the said terme expired, to be punished, as guiltie and culpable of the said crime of high Treason. The goods aswell moueable, as immoueable, to them belonging, shal be employed to charitable vses, and the distribution and disposing thereof to be, as shal be ordained by the Court. Moreouer, it forbiddeth al the kings subiects, to send any schollers to the Colledges of the said Societie, being out of the Realme, there to be instructed, vpon the like payne to incurre the crime of high Treason. The Court doth ordaine, that the copies of this present sentence, shall be sent abroad to the Bayliages, & Shriualties of this iurisdiction, to be executed according to the forme & tenor therof. It is enioind to the Baylifs & Shriefs, their deputies general and particular, to proceed to the execution therof after the terme, or respite thereni contained, & to the deputies

of

of the Atturny generall, to further the said execution, to giue information of all lets or hinderances thereof, and to certifie the Court of their dilligence heerein performed, vppon paine to be depriued of theyr seuerall places and offices . Signed by *Tillet.* Pronounced to the said *Iohn Chastell,* executed the 29. of December, 1594.

During these proceedings, whereupon this sentence ensued, certaine Barons of the Court, were appointed to goe vnto the Colledge of Clairmont, who hauing caused diuers papers to be seazed, they found amongst others, certaine bookes written by the hand of Maister *Iohn Guignard,* a Iesuit priest, containing many false & seditious arguments, to proue, that it was lawful to murder the late king *Henry* the third; and instructions for the murdering of King *Henry* the fourth his successor. In conclusion, this was the end both of the Iesuits, beeing the Schoolemaisters, and theyr vnhappy schollar.

¶ *Another sentence against* Iohn Guignard, *Priest: Regent in the Colledge of the Iesuits, in the Cittie of Paris.*

BEeing viewed by the Court, the great Chamber & the Tournell assembled, the triall or processe criminall, commenced by one of the Councellors of the said Court, at the requisition or demaunde of the Kings Atturny generall, against *Iohn Guignard,* priest, Regent in the Colledge of Clairmont, of the Cittie of Paris, prisoner in the prison of the Conciergerie of the Pallace, for hauing beene found seazed of diuers bookes, containing amongst other matters, the approbation of the most cruell and barbarous parricide of the late King, whom God pardon; and inductions to cause the King nowe raigning, to be murdered: Examinations and confessions of the sayd *Guygnard,* the said bookes openly shewed, acknowledged to be framed &

com-

composed by himselfe, and written with his own hand : conclusions of the Kings Atturny generall: the sayd *Guignard* being heard and examined vppon the matters to him obiected, and contained in the said booke: and all weighed & considered: BE IT KNOWNE, that the said Court hath declared, and doth declare, the said *Guignard* attainted, and conuicted of the crime of high treason, and to haue composed and written the sayd bookes, contayning many erroneous and seditious arguments, to proue, that it was lawfull, to commit the said parricide, and was allowable to kill the King nowe raigning, *Henry* the fourth: For repayring whereof, it hath condemned, and doth condemne, the said *Guignard*, to make an honourable amends, naked in his shirt, a haltar about his neck, before the gate of the principall Church of Paris, & there kneeling, holding in his hands a Torch of wax burning, of the weight of two pounds, to say and declare; *That wickedly, accursedly, & against the truth, hee hath written: that the late King was iustlie slaine by* Iaques Clement, *and that if the King nowe raigning, should not die in the warres, he ought to be killed*: For the which he is hartily sorrie, and asketh forginenesse of God, the King, and the Court. This done, to be led to the place of the Greue, there to bee hanged vntill hee be dead, vppon a Gibbet, which shall be there erected for the same purpose. And afterwards, the dead bodie to be consumed to ashes in a fire, which shal be made at the foote of the said Gibbet : it hath declared & doth declare, all and singuler his goods to be forfeited and confiscate to the King. Pronounced to the saide *Iohn Guignard*, and executed the seauenth day of Ianuarie, 1595.

¶ *Another sentence against* Peter Chaſtel, *Father of* Iohn
Chaſtell, *and* Iohn Gueret *Prieſt, naming himſelfe
of the Companie and Societie of the
Name of Ieſus.*

BEing viewed by the Court, the great Chamber, &
the Tournell aſſembled, the triall, or proceſſe criminall, cōmenced by the Controuler of the Kings
houſhold, and ſince finiſhed at the requiſition and
demaund of the Kings Atturny generall, plaintife a-
gainſt *Iohn Gueret*, prieſt, naming himſelfe of the Cōpanie, and Societie of the Name of Ieſus, abiding in the
Colledge of Clairmont, and heretofore Schoolemaiſter to *Iohn Chaſtell*, lately executed by ſentence of the
ſaid Court, *Peter Chaſtell* Cittizen and Draper of the
cittie of Paris, *Deniſe Hazard* his wife, the Father & mother of the ſaid *Iohn Chaſtell*: *Iohn le Comte*, and *Katherine Chaſtell* his wife: *Magdelan Chaſtell*, the daughter
of the ſaid *Peter Chaſtell*, and *Deniſe Hazard*, *Anthonie
Villiers, Peter Ruſſell, Simona Turin, Louiſa Camus*, theyr
man and maid-ſeruaunts, Maiſter *Claudius l' Allemant*,
prieſt, Curat of Saint *Peters* of Arcis, Maiſter *Iaquet
Bernard*, prieſt, Clarke of the ſaid charge, and Maiſter
Lucas Morin, prieſt, qualefied in the ſame, priſoners in
the priſons of the Conciergerie of the Pallace: examinations, confeſſions, and deniall of the ſaide priſoners,
confrontation being made of the ſaid *Iohn Chaſtell*, to
the ſaide *Peter Chaſtell* his Father, information beeing
giuen againſt the ſaid *Peter Chaſtell*, the witnes therein
heard, produced face to face, the proceſſe criminall intended againſt the ſaide *Iohn Chaſtell*, by reaſon of the
moſt execrable, and abhominable parricide, attempted
vppon the perſon of the King; the proceſſe verball of
the execution of the ſentence of death, giuen againſt the
ſaid *Iohn Chaſtell*, the 29. of December laſt paſt : The
conclu-

conclusions of the Kings Atturny generall: the said *Gueret*, *Peter Chastell*, *Hazard* being heard, and examined in the said Court, vpon the matters to them obiected, and contayned in the said processe: other examination, and denialls made by the sayd *Gueret* and *Peter Chastell*, on the rack or torture, to them applied by order of the said Court: and all weighed and considered: BE IT KNOWNE, that the sayd Court, for the causes contriued in the said processe, hath banished and doth banish, the sayd *Gueret* and *Peter Chastell*, out of the Realme of Fraunce, that is to say, the said *Gueret* for ewer, and the sayd *Chastell* for the terme & space of nine yeeres: and for euer out of the cittie & suburbs of Paris: it is enioyned them, to keepe, & obserue their sentence of banishment, vpon paine to be hanged without any other forme, or manner of processe: it hath declared and doth declare, all and singuler the goods of the said *Gueret* forfeited, and confiscate to the King: & hath condemned and dooth condemne, the said *Peter Chastell*, in two thousand crowns for a fine to the king, to be employed to the releasing and relieuing of prisoners in the Conciergerie, and to remaine in prison, vntill the full payment and satisfaction of the said sum: neyther shall the time of theyr banishment runne, but from the day that he shall haue fully paid the said sum.

The said Court doth ordaine, that the dwelling house of the said *Chastell*, shall be puld downe, ruinated, and raced, and the place made common, that no man may heereafter builde thereon. In which place, for euerlasting memorie of this most wicked and detestable parricide, attempted vppon the person of the King, there shall be set vp and erected, an eminent piller of Marble, together with a table, wherein shall be written, the causes of the said demolition, and erection of the said piller, which shall be made with the mony arising out of the demolition, or pulling downe of the said house.

And

And as touching the said *Hazard, le Comte, Katherine*
and *Magdalen Chastell, Villiers, Russell, Turin, Camus,*
l' Alemant, Bernard, and *Morin,* the sayd Court dooth
ordaine, that they shall be set at libertie. Pronounced to
the said *Hazard, le Comte, Katherine* and *Magdalen (Cha-*
stell, Villiers, Russell, Turin, Camus, l' Allemant, Beruard,
and *Morin,* the seuenth of Ianuarie, & to the said *Gue-*
rot and *Peter Chastell,* the tenth of the said month. 1595.

These are the three sentences of the Court of Parliament of Paris, whereby it appeares, what diligence, religion and iustice, was performed in the whole proceeding, how those that were accused, were punished more
or lesse, those that were onely suspected, freely discharged and released, in a case which concerned the vvhole
state of Fraunce. Let vs now take a view, if you please,
of the comments, which the Iesuits haue made and doe
make vpon these sentences: for of late they haue againe
recouered their speech.

CHAP. 19.

¶ The Iesuits vnder couert termes, chalenge the sentence
giuen against Iohn Chastell, *of iniustice: and how* GOD
suffered him to be punished, to make the punishment
of the Iesuits more notorious to all
posteritie.

Gainst this Sentence, touching *Iohn*
Chastell, doe our Iesuits outragiouslie
exclaime, and making shew, as if they
would excuse the Court, they accuse it
of vniustice, by it committed, in condemning them.

VVee are (saith the hypocriticall Iesuit in his most
humble petition presented to the King) enemies to
Kings, the state, and your person, & seducers of youth.
Against these generall accusations, we first oppose the
testi-

teſtimonie of the Court of Parliament of Paris. The Court had heard the Aduocates, which brought, and emptied their baggs, loden with theſe weightie accuſations: it had beene with all importunitie ſollicited to condemne vs: It had aboue 9. months reſpite to weigh and ballance the cauſe; that is, from the laſt of Aprill, vntill Chriſtmas following: It condemned vs not, but ſuffered vs to remaine in peaceable poſſeſſion of our rights, reſeruing it ſelfe to a fitter ſeaſon, to call them to account, which had moſt vncharitably ſuggeſted theſe calumnious accuſations againſt vs.

Thinke you, that this body of Iuſtice, compoſed of the moſt famous ornaments of the Lawe, vvhich the world yeelds, and of the ſtrongeſt & firmeſt members of the ſtate, if it had ſeene the leaſt of theſe crimes, as ſufficiently prooued, as they were maliciouſly obiected, thinke you, I ſay, that it would not haue proceeded, to condemne vs in the very inſtant? And hauing not condemned vs, hath it not, by his ſilence, condemned our Accuſers, and giuen moſt aſſured teſtimonie of our innocencie? If ſince that time it haue condemned vs, that proceeded not of the due and formall pleadings of the Aduocates, or of any aduantage of law, which our aduerſaries had againſt vs: it is an inconuenience vvhich hath condemned vs in coſts, but not ouer-throwne our cauſe.

And vvithin a fewe leaues after: In Iuly 1594, at what time the proceſſe was reuiued by two pleading Aduocates, they charged vs with *Barriere*, and framed many like imputatiõs, to agrauate this crime againſt our credite and reputation. But all theſe were but blunt aſſertions, not ſharpe proofes, proceeding frõ the tongue, and not from the truth, the Court made no reckoning of them, and by their ſilence cleered & acquited vs.

Rene de la Fon followeth his ſteppes, and goeth about to proue in like manner, that the cõdemning of *Chaſtell*,

is

is the acquiting of all their Societie: in as much as hee
being racked and tortured, appeached none of them.
But theyr intelligence was very bad in this matter: For
albeit this wretched fellow by his aunswers, and interrogatories to him miniftred, fpared the names of particulers, yet did he accufe the whole Order in generall, as
I wil verifie hereafter more at large. Moreouer, thefe Iefuits feeme to be both of them, altogether ignorant in
the courfe of Iudgements, pronounced by thofe high
Courts.

The Court (faith the firft) hath not forthwith proceeded to iudgemēt in this caufe, notwithftanding the fharp
accufations wherewith we were charged : *Ergo*, by his
filence it pronounced vs guiltleffe. Furthermore, *Barriere* his fact was laid to our charge, yet the Court would
not prefently condemne vs; *Ergo*, the Court intended
by filence to acquite vs thereof. I befeech you, feeing
you profeffe your felues to be Logicians, & to haue the
ftart of all men in fcholafticall Diuinitie, by what principles can you make good thefe conclufions ? Yet are
they not ftrange, to proceede from a Iefuits pen. For
thefe reuerent Fathers are in place and authoritie, to cō-
demne Kings without hearing them, and to abandon
their realmes, and lay thē open for a pray, to him that can
poffeffe himfelfe thereof, as they did to the laft King.

High and foueraigne Courts, obferue another manner of proceeding. They heare the Counfell on both
parties, yet reft not thereupon : but in fuch important
caufes as this efpecially, they remit their iudgement or
fentence, to their better leyfure, and to theyr fecond
thoughts. The like courfe was held in their caufe. *Arnauld* and *Dole*, vrged in their Declarations, the tragical
hiftorie of *Barriere*, the Court gaue no credite therevnto, and not without good confideration. In as much
as it was requifite for them to view *Barriere* his triall or
proceffe, which was made at Melun by *Lugoly*, that they

might

might be throughly informed of what had there paſſed.
But alas Ieſuit, what is become of thy wit ? Thou dooſt
acknowledge this Court to conſiſt of the greateſt ornaments of the Law, which the world yeeldeth : as elſe-
where alſo, that referring both parties to counſell, they
had proceeded without paſſion , or partialitie : and yet
in the inſtant, thou changeſt thy note, challenging it to
haue done iniuſtice, in grounding their ſentence againſt
you vpon *Chaſtell,* who had not accuſed you . Iudges
proceede indirectly , when eyther they want skill to
iudge, or that their iudgements are corrupted by hatred,
fauour, or other ſuch partiall affections. Neither of theſe
defects can be ſhewed in the managing of your cauſe, as
your ſelfe confeſſe : therefore it is preſumption in vs
both : in you to aſſay by Sophiſtrie , out of your ſhal-
lowe braine to elude this ſentence : in mee, to endeuour
by reaſons and arguments, to maintaine and vphold the
ſame.

Let it ſuffice vs, that it is a Decree, or Arreſt, and it is
our part therefore to reſt our iudgements there-vppon.
In all cauſes, eſpecially in thoſe of weight, and importance, like this, G O D is in the midſt of the Iudges to inſpire and direct them . Many times a man, that
hauing heard a caſe pleaded on both ſides , prepared
himſelfe in his minde, either to acquite, or condemne,
this or that partie, yet, when hee heares the firſt Iudge
deliuer his opinion, hee changeth his mind : yea, oftentimes it falleth out, that one word vttered by the firſt,
giueth new light to him that ſecondeth, when as happe-
ly he that ſpake it, dreamt not thereon : and when it cōmeth to the caſting of the Bell, (for by that by-word
doe the Lavvyers terme the vp-ſhot, or concluſion of
all) they gather and collect out of the precedent opinions, a generall ayre, or abſtract, whereuppon this ſentence is built.

Dooſt thou think, that *Chaſtells* fact was the ſole occaſion

caſion of your fall? thou art deceiued. The Court had
wiſely referred the cauſe to counſell, giuiuing thereby
to vnderſtand, that it meant not to proceed therein eyther with paſſion, or raſh haſtines, two great enemies
of iuſtice. In the meane time hapned this damnable
act, committed by one of your ſchollers: the principals
which were before diſpoſed to your condemning, were
taken in hand a freſh: in the handling of *Chaſtels* cauſe,
your cauſe is adiudged all vnder one.

The indignitie and deteſtation therof, awaked iuſtice
in the hearts of the Iudges, which in your cauſe might
peraduenture haue ſlept, had it not beene thereby ſtirred, and excited. And in all this, there is nothing
wrought by man, but by a ſpeciall iudgement of God,
which wee ought to proclayme through the whole
world. It is well knowne, that your Colledge was the
fountayne, and ſeminarie of all thoſe calamities, which
we endured, during the laſt troubles. There was the
rebellion plotted and contriued, there was it fully and
wholly nouriſhed and maintayned; your Prouincials,
your Rectors, your deuout Superiours, were the firſt
that troad that path, they that firſt and laſt dealt with
this merchandiſe. Your Colledge was the retreat, or
Randeuous, of all ſuch as had vowed, and ſold themſelues
aſwell to the deſtruction of the State, as to the murther of the King: in which your doings, you at that time
gloried, and triumpht, both in your Sermons and Lectures.

The true hearted ſubiects, who had the *Flower de
Luce* imprinted in their breaſts, beheld this tyranny, and
ſighed in their ſoules; for they durſt not giue breath to
their ſighes; all their recourſe was to God, that it would
pleaſe him to haue compaſſion on their miſerable e-
ſtate. God ſuffered you to raigne fiue yeeres and more;
(ſwaying both people, Magiſtrate, and Prince) to trie
whether there were any hope of your amendment in

time. The King was no sooner entred into Paris, but
the iust hatred of the people towards you, brake forth:
the Vniuersitie of Paris stirreth against you, and reui-
ueth their former suite, which had beene referred to
Counsell in the yeere 1 5 6 4. the occasion thereof was
founded vpon your owne fresh practises, and lewd mis-
demeanours: the cause is pleaded by two worthie Lawyers, *Arnauld* and *Dole*, heard with patience discreetly,
not iudged forthwith, by reason of the waightines: besides, the heat and choler of those which prosecuted
the cause against them, might in time coole, and asswage
(as the manner of French men is.) The Iudges neuer
stirre in any cause, but as they are vrged thereunto; o-
therwise they should doe themselues wrong, and men
might say, they were rather soliciters, then Iudges. In
this pause, the iudgement of your cause was likely to
haue beene forgotten, when on a sodain, beyond all imagination, this fact of *Chastels* came to passe, whereby the
humors both of the Iudges, and of the parties are stirred
a fresh.

This was the houre of Gods wrath, who hauing long
temporized with your sinnes, thought it good to make
Chastell a spurre in the hearts of the Iudges, to incite
them, to doe iustice aswell vpon you, as vpon him, and
that you might all serue for an example, for posteritie
to wonder at. To the accomplishing of this worke, he
permitted that *Chastell* (who had beene nurtured, and
brought vp in your schoole) should assay to put in practise your deuout Lectures, and exhortations against the
King, not in the countrie, but in the Citie of Paris, and
that his dwelling should be, not in any obscure corner of
the Town, but in the verie hart of the City, standing as it
were in the midst of two other Townes, & moreouer, in
a house right opposit to the gate of the Palace, the ancient habitation of our Kings, & of the supreme and soueraigne Iustice of Fraunce. This house belonged to the
father,

father, who was so infortunate, as not to reueale to the
Magistrate the damnable intention of his sonne, wherof
he had knowledge, as himselfe confessed. God made
speciall choise of that place, of purpose to make the punishment more notorious. For in like offences of high
Treason, the Iudges are in dutie bound to their Soueraigne, to cause the habitations of the malefactors to
be raced, and pulled downe, and there to be engrauen
a memoriall of the whole proceeding: for which cause
this house was ruinated, & raced by order, & in the place
thereof a Pyramis or piller raised, bearing the memoriall,
not onely of *Chastells* offence, but of the Iesuits also, and
this to stand in opposite view of this great and Royall Pallace. To the end, that our posteritie may know
hereafter, how highly Fraunce is beholding to this holy
Societie of Iesus. Was there euer, I say not in Fraunce,
but in the whole world, a more famous or notorious
punishment, then this?

CHAP. 20.

Of the Pyramis, which is raysed before the Pallace of
Paris, and of the sentence giuen in Rome, by the re-
nowmed Pasquill, *concerning the restau-*
ration of the Iesuits, sued for by
themselues.

Ell me, Marble, (saith the hypocriticall
Iesuit in his most humble petition, speaking of the *Pyramis*) to record, and testifie to posteritie, the happines of a
great King, and the misfortune of a
great offender, what hast thou to doe with a poore
guiltlesse Societie? hast thou not inough of thy iust
burthen, but thou must charge thy selfe with his
slaunder and defamation, that had no hand at all in
this fact? But sith thy backe hath a tongue to vtter
falshoode, let thy tongue aunswere me: and speake
the

the truth. Who hath engrauen vpon thy backe, that the Iesuits did prouoke, or perswade an vnhappie Frenchman, to murther the *most Christian* King of France? what witnes, what deposition, what confirmation hast thou hereof, seeing thou doest take vpon thee to witnesse it, to depose it, to confirme it so assuredly to all the world? Hast thou heard more without eares, & seen more without eyes, then fiue & twentie thousand eares, & as many eyes, were able to heare or see, at that executiō of iustice in the place of the Greue? Dost thou in a brauerie say more, then that offender durst say, being vrged therunto with such rigorous tortures? Assuredly, the force of a strong fancie or imagination is great, aud wonderfull: not only to cause these prodigious effects in our minds, but euen in our bodies themselues. For so we read, that *Crasus* his sonne beeing dumbe, recouered speech, seeing his father in daunger to be slaine: and *Cippus* a King of Italy, sitting to behold the fight of the Buls, with a fixt and stedfast apprehension, fell a sleepe, and when he awaked, he felt his forehead planted with a paire of hornes.

One *Lucius Cossitius*, greedily and furiously apprehending the pleasure, which he expected of his wife that should be, the first night of his mariage, was chaunged into a woman. Which makes me greatly feare, least this honest Iesuit, reading in this Pyramis, the generall condemnation of his brother-hood, should be transformed into a stone, as *Niobe* was, when she saw her children slaine. For I alreadie perceiue by him, that he hath lost the eyes both of his bodie and mind, setting forth with such eagernes, the innocencie of his Order, and bearing vs in hand, that this sentence was builded vpon no other ground, but *Chastels* offence. Seing therefore, that of a wilfull blindnes, thou art ignorant euen in that, which the walles themselues can testifie, and teach, and that thou framest thy speech to a stone,

I

I thinke it best that thou shouldest be aunswered by a stone, but a most auncient, and authentique stone, the great and venerable *Pasquill* of Rome, who suiteth and resembleth you in many poynts. For as you iudge Kings and Princes by certayne texts of Scripture, wrested and misunderstood, so hath *Pasquill* beene allowed from all memorie, to do the like by Popes and Cardinals, vpon the same texts, ordered after his owne liking, and appetite. And as you by meanes of confession, come to to the knowledge of a thousand secrets, as well of the publique State, as of priuate families, so is he priuiledged by aunciēt foundation, to receiue intelligence from all countries, whereby he layeth open to the world, that which men presumed to be hidden from all knowledge.

Considering which sympathie & argreement betwixt you & him, I make no doubt but you will be the rather inclined to beleeue him. For do not think, but this cause hath beene by him handled in Rome, and with mature deliberation adiudged, that for the interest you haue in him, he hath left nothing vndone, aswell to disanull the sentence, and deface the Pyramis, as to restore you into Fraunce, howsoeuer his endeuours haue wanted successe. Heare therefore, what he hath written to thee in Italian, which I haue translated into French, as faithfully as I could; it may bee thou wilt rest satisfied thereby.

Thrice reuerend Father, I haue perused at large the humble remonstrance and petition, preferred by you to the *Most Christian King*, *Henrie* the fourth of that name, as also the notes and instructions deliuered to Father *Magius*, to present vnto his Maiestie for your reestablishment: which wrought in me great pleasure, and displeasure both at one instant: Pleasure, to see the choise and varietie of good words, that abound in you, displeasure, to vnderstand in what euill manner your Fatherhoods haue beene entreated. If I mistake not, the

D d d.   chiefe

chiefe marke you ayme at, is to deſtroy and pull downe
the Pyramis : for what boote were it for you to be reſtored, vnleſſe this ſtone be taken away, whereby you
are charged with ſundry crimes,which you eſteeme falſe
and calumnious ?

Seeing therefore your intent was to commence ſuite
againſt a ſtone, I preſumed that the hearing of the cauſe,
belonged abſolutely to my ſelfe,and to none other. And
that you may vnderderſtand, with what diligence and
iuſtice I haue proceeded in the examination thereof, I
remembred that your cauſe had beene twiſe pleaded,
and twiſe referred to counſell : Firſt, in the yeere 1564.
wherein you were plantiues, ſuing to bee incorporated
into the Vniuerſitie of Paris : Secondly, in the yeere
1594.wherein the Vniuerſitie of Paris were plantiues,
requiring that you might be inſtantly baniſhed, and expelled the land. To be throughly informed of the firſt,
I required a Copie of *Paſquier* his declaration againſt
you, *Verſoris* his Plea for you , as alſo of the latter, by
Meſnill, the Kings Aduocate. By all which I found,that
the onely matter in queſtion at that time, was the noueltie, and ſtraunge rule of your Order, being contrarie to
the auncient liberties of the Church of Fraunce. And
being deſirous to be yet further inſtructed in the matter, behold certaine mutinous ſpirits, preſent me with
three bookes on your behalfe : In the firſt,were contained, the Buls by you obtayned for your commoditie
and aduantage : In the ſecond, were your orders or conſtitutions, diuided into tenne parts : In the third, the
Examen, or, if I may ſo terme it, the Abſtract, or a-
bridgement thereof. Out of which, I collected many poynts, which before time were to me altogether
vnknowne : a ſimple and abſolute vow, which your e-
nemies alleage to be full of ſubteltie, and hereſie ; many extraordinarie vſurpations vppon the Ordinaries,
and Vniuerſities : a rich kind of pouertie profeſſed by

VOW :

vow: a blinded obedience to your Superiors: (for as for that to the Pope, I meddle not therwithal,)your principall Buls, wherein it seemes you haue surprised, and abused the sanctitie of the holy Sea. Whereupon I said, that, that villaine, whatsoeuer he was, that brought these bookes out of your Colledges, deserued to be hanged for his paynes.

It is not meet the world should know the secrets of a profest Societie: It doth but open mens mouthes to scanne, and descant thereupon at their pleasures, to the discredit and disgrace of the whole Order. But seeing the offender cannot be discouered, I thinke it best, that these three bookes be sent backe into one of your Colledges, there to receiue open discipline for this offence. This is not the first time, that sencelesse things haue beene dealt withall. For in that manner doe we read, that the Sea hauing trespassed against *Zerxes*, that wise and prudent king of Persia, who had purposed to passe ouer into Greece vpon a bridge of cordes, was by him condemned to be whipt. As contrariwise, the Signiorie of Venice, to flatter and insinuate with the Sea, is wont yeerely vpon Ascension day, to espouse and wed it with a Ring, which they present vnto it. I assure you, when I compared the priuiledges of the Church of Fraunce, with yours, I stood greatly perplexed, what to thinke: holding this with my selfe for a law inuiolable, that howsoeuer all lawes were wauering and vncertaine, according to the chaunge and alteration of times, yet this stood firme, stedfast, and immutable, that we are to liue according to the lawes of that countrey, wherein we desire to liue. And finding your Buls, and constitutions, to goe flat against the liberties of the Church of Fraunce, it bred no small scruple in my mind, howsoeuer I was inclined or deuoted to fauour your cause.

Hauing viewed and reuiewed, the bookes and euidences, concerning the first cause, which was referred to counfel: I paffed ouer to the fecond inftance, of the yere 1594. wherin I employed all the powers of my braine. Herein you were not called in queftion for your doctrine, or profeffion any more, but for your attempts, and practifes, made afwell againft Princes and Princeffes, as againft the feuerall countries, wherein you are refident, and efpecially againft the Realme of Fraunce. A matter full of waight, difficultie, and of daungerous confequence: which caufed me, for the difcharge of my place and confcience, to interpofe my felfe in this caufe, contrarie to that cuftome which I haue hitherto learned and practifed. For in other cafes, I receiue fuch packets, as my Vaffels and Subiects lift to impart, giuing credit thereunto vpon their bare relations. But in this, I haue taken a farre other courfe. For hauing perufed your petitionarie booke, full of pittie and compaffion, I fent forth fummons to all quarters without exception, to come in, and fpeake their knowledge in the matter: I directed out Commiffions ouer all countries (according to the prerogatiue, which from all antiquitie hath beene graunted me through the whole ftate of Chriftendome) to informe me afwell by letters, as by witneffes, of what I thought requifite for your iuftification, commaunding all Iudges, of what qualitie foeuer, (vpon payne of a grieuous fine at my pleafure) to fend me the whole proceffe, afwell criminall, as extraordinarie, which had paffed in your caufe; being refolued, your innocence once verified, and confirmed, to caft downe this Pyramis, and to preferre this fentence into the Inquifition. As your felues fometimes caufed the cenfure and determination of the Sorbone, pronounced againft you in the yeere 1554. to be cenfured by the Inquifition of Spayne. For it is not for euerie man to iuftle with your holy Fatherhoods.

And that which prouoked mee the rather hereunto, was your booke, wherein reading, to my great difcomfort,

fort, the hard meafure which hath beene fhewen you, by the Court of Parliament of Paris, yet you acknowledge the faid Court, to excell all other in knowledge, iuftice, and religion. Vpon my fummons (I muft confefle the truth) there appeared at the firft dafh a great troope of French, Englifh, Scottifh, Arragonians, Portugalls, Polanders, Flemings, Swethlanders, who reported much more then I defired to heare. And albeit the peoples voyce be the voyce of God, (if you belieue the cõmon prouerbe) yet would not I for the fequell build my iudgment thereon.

Your owne booke, increafed my fcruple & doubt, much more then before, when for your iuftification you fay, that in the yeere 1593. by a generall Synode, holden by your Societie at Rome, thofe of your Order were forbidden to entermeddle henceforward in matters of State: which poynt I could not well conceiue. They are prohibited (faid I) to entermeddle hence-forward in State matters, therefore it is prefuppofed, that heretofore they haue medled therein. I cannot be perfwaded, that thefe deuout and holie men, did euer apply themfelues that way: becaufe fuch is the calamitie of our times, that in our State affaires, wee harbour commonly more impietie then Religion, to bring our defignements to paffe. And ftanding thus in fufpence, one rounded me in the eare, and bad mee be cleere of that poynt: for he that made *The Defence of the Colledge of Clairmont*, in 1594, hath inferted (faith he) the whole article in Latine. I called for the booke, & found it true, as he told me.

Another brought me *Montaignes* his booke: reade this place (faith he) heere you fhall find the foundation and originall of our laft troubles. In this booke I finde, that Father *Claudius Mathew*, and *Aimond Auger*, were fometimes in high fauour with *Henry* the third: in fomuch, as oftentimes hee tooke them into his Coach:

after

after hee addeth ; That fathan hauing caft into the Realme the Apple of ftrife, fufpicion, and ieloufie, all things changed their courfe, and then was brewed that vineger and gall of ciuile diffentions, which fince that time wee haue feene and tafted. As to all texts, there want no comments: fo in the reading of this place, thys fellow faid vnto me, that two words fufficed to a good vnderftander, and that this alteration fell out by meanes of the repulfe, which thefe two bleffed Fathers receiued of the King, when he faw them begin to fet their hands to matters of State: and that they played as did *Narfes* the Eunuch, whom the Empreffe commaunding to goe and fpin her diftaffe : he made aunfwere, that he would fpin her fuch a quill, as fhee, or her husband fhould ne-uer be able to vnwind. And indeed kept promife with her, by bringing the Lombards into Italie.

Euen fo, thefe two honeft Iefuits, beeing eftranged from the grace and fauour of the King, would let him know, they could skill of fomwhat elfe, then to fay ouer our Ladies Pfalter. And to fpeake freely what I think, I neuer knew men of a better confcience, then are thofe of your Societie, nor that leffe feared to incur the cen-fures of Rome. Firft Father *Henrie Sammiere*, (a ftir-ring pragmaticall fellow) confeffed, that about the yeere 1 5 8 0, or 81, (if I miftake not) he was fent by you in-to diuers Countries, to treate or commune about the generall reuolt, which you intended to ftirre vp againft the late King of Fraunce. And albeit I maintained, that it was neyther true nor probable, in as much as you had no caufe at that time to attempt it; he bad me, feeing I beleeued not his words, to looke but vpon the arraign-ment and triall of *William Parry* an Englifhman, vvho was executed the third of March, 1 5 8 4. that there I fhould finde at the latter end of a certaine Letter, which he wrote to the Queene during his imprifonment, *That fhee fhould finde, the King of Fraunce had enough to doe at home,*

home, when shee had neede of his helpe.

Parry(as *Sammiere* told me)departed out of England in 1582, and came into Fraunce, where hee was dealt withall by our Societie to destroy the Queene of England, and to make an innouation in the State, and when he obiected, that it would hardly be brought to passe, in as much as she were like to be ayded, and assisted by the King of Fraunce, we made him aunswer, that we would cut out the King of Fraunce so much worke, that his hands should be full of his owne busines, without stirring to ayde or succour another. Whereby it appeares, that euen in those daies our web was on the loome.

I had not at that time the acts of *Parry* his tryall, but hauing since procured them, I haue read the Letter, & haue found all true that *Sammiere* reported. Who in a good meaning proceeded further, and confessed, that himselfe, and *Roscieux*, were sent in 1584. to the King of Spaine, and Father *Claudius Mathew*, to Pope *Gregorie* the 13. to vnderstand, what summes of mony they were willing to contribute, towards the charges & maintenaunce of the holy League : whereunto *Roscieux* replyed; Yea, but this honest Munk telleth you not, what a cast of his office he shewed me. For hee and I riding post together, he, perceiuing one night, that I, beeing wearied with trauaile, was buried in a dead sleepe, caused fresh poast-horse to be brought him, and away hee went, leauing me in bed for a pawne : and such speede and diligence he vsed, as that our whole busines was by him, almost dispatched with the King of Spayne, before I could ouertake him.

To bring this processe to a conclusion, I caused to be brought vnto me the pleadings of *Arnauld*, Aduocate for the Vniuersitie, and *Dole*, who was retaind for the Curats of Paris. The aunswere to the same, vnder the name of the Colledge of Clairmont : *Fräncis de Montaignes* his booke *De la veritè Defendue*, against *Arnauld;*

nauld: and certaine other bookes, or euidences, seruing
to the state of the cause. I belieued *Sammier* for so much
as concerned himselfe: but as for Father *Claudius Matthew*, I would not the memorie of him should be touched vpon another mans confession. Wherefore I had
recourse to the litterall proofe, and read *Arnauldus* his
pleadings, wherein he toucheth him to the quick: and
the aunswere thereunto, contained in that Plea, which
is as followeth ; *And whereas* Arnauldus *alledgeth , that*
Claudius Matthew, *of the Order of the said Defendants,*
hath beene the Authour, and contriuer of the League : the
said Defendants aunswere, that Claudius Matthew *, ha-*
uing spent his whole time in their Colledges,& amongst chil-
dren, liuing euer in the course of a Scholler , could not haue
iudgement, policie, industrie, and authoritie requisite, for the
contriuing and knitting, of so great & strong a League. And
be it, that the saide Mathew, endeuoured to fortifie the sayd
League, as many others of all estates & coditions haue like-
wise doone, that prooues not therefore that he was the Au-
thour, or beginner thereof. Besides, this is but one particular.
And fiue or sixe lines after, *There was not one of them at*
the first acquainted with his actions , and had they beene, yet
could they not haue hindered them, inasmuch as hee was
their Superiour.

Comparing *Arnaulds* obiection with this colde and
faint solution , mee thought you were agreed, that
Fraunce should thinke her selfe beholding to none but
your selues for her last troubles. And desiring more ful-
lie to informe my conscience, as touching the Reuolt,
which happened in Paris, euen in the Sorbon it selfe, the
seauenth of Ianuarie, 1 5 8 9, there came a crew of Diuines, beeing men of credit and reputation, who certified me, that in truth, they were at that time assembled
to debate the matter, & that all the auncienter sort, were
of a cotrarie opinion, howsoeuer the younger were not,
the greater part whereof, had beene schollers to the Iesuits

suits of Paris. So as the voyces being numbred, and not weighed, it was carried away by pluralitie. Neuerthelesse, they did not as yet altogether loose the reynes to rebellion, but determined to suspend the effect of thys their conclusion, vntill such time as it were confirmed and ratified by the Sea Apostolick. But the day following, Father *Iames Commolet*, a Iesuit, sounded the drum within Paris. And that I might be assured, if not of the whole, yet of the greatest part of the premisses, by the annuall Letters of the Iesuits, of the yeere 1589, and moreouer, by their Pleas, I went directly to theyr Letters, and found in those; which were written from your Colledge of Paris, *Doctores Sorbonici, quorum magna pars descipuli nostri fuere:* The Doctours of the Sorbone, a great part whereof haue beene our Schollers. And by your Pleas: *It is certaine that for these fewe yeeres, a great part of the Bachelers of Diuinitie, & the better sort of them, haue spent the course of their studies in our Colledge.* Which caused mee somewhat to suspect, that thys conclusion, had been before handled from time to time in your Lectures.

I read in the same Letter, that notwithstanding you were inhibited by *Gregorie* the 13. to come at any Processions, yet as soone as the Reuolt was concluded on, one of your Societie, to stirre the people against theyr King, assembled three or foure thousand boyes, which he led in procession all ouer the cittie, with a rabble of all sorts of people at their heeles. I read in another place, that about that verie time, you instituted in Lyons, the Brotherhood of our Lady, and in Burges, of the Pænitents, vnder the name of Ieronomitans, not to appease the wrath of G O D, but to prouoke it against the late King.

And as I was turning ouer your Letters, there commeth in Father *Iames Commolet*, (whom I name with al due title of honor) who with teares standing in his eyes, (as one that at al times hath teares at commaundement) confeſſed vnto me, that the day following this determination of the Sorbone, hee in a Sermon made at the Church of Saint *Meri*, publiquely preached, that the whole Sorbone, was reſolued to take Armes againſt the King, & if any ſhould oppoſe themſelues, to withſtand it, they ought not to thinke it ſtrange, in aſmuch as in that number which followed our Sauiour, (the moſt perfit ſocietie that euer was) there was one *Iudas* found. And that thereuppon, the people ranne head-long to Armes. Wherein hee ingeniouſly confeſſed his fault, in concealing from the people, that this Reſolution, vvas referred to the pleaſure and arbitrement of the holie Sea.

Furthermore, that the 15. of the ſame Month, certaine of the chiefe and principall Iudges of the Court of Parliament, beeing committed pryſoners to the Baſtille, he went to viſite and comfort them: and for theyr conſolation, preached nothing elſe but of the tyrannie of King *Henrie* the third; thereby to ſtirre and excite them to rebelliou: & that he who had been their king, ſhould be ſo no longer.

Moreouer, that as long as the Troubles endured, hee was a Trumpet in all Churches, to rend and deface the reputation, as well of the late King, as of him that nowe raigneth: but that this was vſuall with all Preachers, and therefore the more excuſable in him. Which *Montaignes* did not denie, excuſing it by the heate and choller vvhich is incident to Preachers when they are in the Pulpit.

With that, a troubleſome fellow whiſpering mee in the eare, bad me, looke to my ſelfe: For (ſaith he) that which he termes choler, he would ſay it were the holie Spirit, if he durſt. I told him, hee was a buſie companion, and bad him hold his tongue, if hee could. All thys did *Commolet* côfeſſe he had done in Paris: but Father

Bernard

Bernard Rouillet proceeded on further, & acknowledged, that by his packing and preaching, hee had withdrawne the cittie of Bourges, from the obedience of the King. But aboue all, the Confession of Father *Alexander Hayes* did most satisfie me, who entertained me with these words.

Right honourable *Pasquill*, seeing you charge and coniure me in the name of God, and in vertue of the Apostolicall censures, I will deliuer my whole knowledge, as well concerning the proceedings of our Colledge at Paris, as mine owne particuler actions in thys busines. As touching the generall, I must confesse to you, that vppon the first breaking out of the Troubles, wee presently instituted within our Colledge of Paris a Brotherhoode, which we named a Congregation in the honour of our Lady, beeing for that cause, called the Congregation of the Chappelet, because the Brethren of that Companie, were bound to carry a Chappelet, or payre of Beades, and to say it ouer once a day. Into this Congregation, did all the zealous and deuout personages of our holy League, cause themselues to be enrolled, the Lord *Mendoza*, Embassadour for the Catholick King of Spayne, the Sixteene Gouernours of Paris, with their whole families, and diuers other holy & religious persons, whereof I haue kept no register, neither was it any part of my charge.

Our Congregation was kept euery Sonday in a certaine high Chappell, where all the brotherhood was bound to be present, if there were no necessarie cause of let or impediment. There were we all seuerally confessed on the Saturdayes, and on Sonday wee receiued the Sacrament. When Masse was done, one of our Fathers went into the Pulpet, and there exhorted all the Audience to continue stedfast in their holy deuotion, which at this day is in Fraunce called Rebellion, (sith it pleaseth the Magistrats to haue it so, I cannot be against

E e e. 2. it.)

it.) This done, all the common sort departed, and those of greatest place and authoritie stayed behind, to consult about the affayres of the holy League. Our good Father, *Odon Pigenat*, was long time President of that Counsell. And this briefely is the summe of what I am able to deliuer, as touching the generall proceedings of the whole Colledge.

As concering my selfe in particular, you must vnderstand, that those that know mee, call me Father *Alexander Hayes* the Scot, who, during the troubles, was Regent of the first Forme of our Colledge, for the space of 3. or 4. yeeres. Not to recapitulate the whole, but some of the principall, and most notable acts of my historie, which may peraduenture giue light to the residue : I read to mine Auditours, *Demosthenes* his Inuectiues against *Phillip* king of Macedonia, wherein I some-what suited with our good Father *Commolet* : for as hee wrested to his purpose, all the texts of Scripture against the * *Biarnois*, (giue me leaue to vse that terme before your Highnes, which was then currant in Paris,) so did I play by the *Philippica*, which to say truth, were not Lectures, but despightful inuectiues against him, which I amplified accordingly, as I was caried by a violent kind of deuotion, which I was neuer able to bridle or restraine. For it was an ordinary branch of my lectures, that he were a happy man whosoeuer could kill him; & if he fortuned to die in the execution of so blessed an enterprise, hee should goe directly into Paradise, and though his soule were stained with some veniall sinnes, yet should it be exempted from the paines of Purgatory. And if God should so much afflict the citie of Paris, as that the *Biarnois* should enter, & passe through S. *Iames* his gate, I made open protestation, that I would leape downe vpon him frō the highest window in our Colledge : being assuredly perswaded, that this fall, would serue me for a ladder, to clime vp into heauen.

That

That day, that hee first heard Masse at Saint *Den-nis*, vnderstanding that certaine of my Auditors had beene present thereat, I debarred them the day follow-ing from my Lecture, as persons excommunicated, for-bidding them to enter, vntill they were absolued for it by some of our Societie. When men began to mutter a-bout a peace, I commaunded one of my Auditors, the best scholler among them; to declaime in Greeke, touching the miseries of Fraunce, and the lamenta-ble gulph of ensuing calamities, whereinto she was a-bout desperately to plunge her sellfe : (this was, as I said, the time of the conference, when euerie man on both parties breathed nothing, but vnitie, and reconcilement) the scholler, forgetting those particulers, which I had prescribed him, onely propounding to himselfe the ge-nerall subiect of the miseries of Fraunce, declaimed and discoursed first of the miseries and calamities, which happen in a Realme, by the rebellion and disobedience of the subiects : which, he said, to be the gulph, wheinto God suffered a nation to fall, when after his long pa-tience, he would haue them feele his hand, for some transgressions, which he had long time suffered to go vnpunisht. Aterwards he declared, that the misgouer-nance of a Prince, could not exempt the subiects from their alleageance : which he likewise confirmed by an infinite number of examples, shewing what ill successe they euer had, who were of a contrarie minde. I seeing him forsake the path, that I had prescribed, and take a farre different course, grew mightily out of patience, and made him come downe out of the seat, calling him caytise, and heretique, with many other reprochfull termes. The first day that the Reading began, after the Citie of Paris was reduced to the obediēce of the *Biar-nois*, one of my schollers, cōming into the colledge before the houre, wrote all about my Forme, *God saue the King.* When I came in, and espied this shamefull act, my cho-

Ece 3. ler

ler turned into rage, and with a fell and terrible voyce, I exclaymed, *Quis ita infecit parietes nostros?* Who is it, that hath thus berayed our walles? If I knew what he were that hath made these scribble-scrabbles, (for that was my terme) I would cause the President of the Colledge to punish him openly: and after dinner, I made it to be wiped out, adding withall, that if I might know any man hereafter, that should bescribble the walles in that order, I would make him feele, how much I was displeased withall. I confesse freely, (right honourable *Pasquill*) what I haue done, neither doe I feare to speake it, seeing I am now in the Citie of Rome, and none of the *Biarnois* his Subiects, being a Scot by birth, and be it that I were a natural Frenchman, yet am I perswaded, that all these vnkindnesses, ought to be pardoned me, who haue alwaies carried so good a conscience, as in playing with my fellowes, or others, I neuer medled for money, but for *Pater noster*, and *Aue Maria* onely: and doe stedfastly beleeue, that this merite alone towards God, saued me from the Parliament of Paris, where I was in some perill: and I assure you, had I beene put to any torture eyther of bodie or mind: (of bodie, being laid on the rack, of mind, by any censure of the Church) I had beene quite vndone.

Thus much did I get out of father *Alexander*, whom I found to be another *Alexander* the great amongst you Iesuits, that is, a Prince of an inuincible spirit. After I had heard him, I examined the litterall proofes. By your Pleas I learned many things which me thought made very much against you. For *Arnauld* and *Dole* charging you, that your Colledge was the Spanyards *Randenous*, wherein they consulted of the affaires of the holy League: you confesse in your aunswere, that the Embassadour *Mendoza*, came thither indeed on holy-daies to heare Masse, and that afterward, you entreated

treated him, to refraine, for the auoyding of suspition. A friuolous excuse to my iudgement, for why should you pray him to forbeare that, which at that time, you tooke for a great honour done vnto you (if at least a man may beleeue the common report.) Furthermore, it being by your aduersaries obiected, that a Father of the Societie, *Odon Pigenat*, was Captaine, and Ringleader of the Sixteene, that commaunded within Paris, not onely ouer the ordinarie Magistrate, but ouer the chiefe and soueraigne, you confesse that article, as well in your Pleas, as in *Montaignes* his booke : marry you say withall, it was to temper and moderate their actions.

At the reading of which two places, all that were present fell on laughing, knowing *Pigenat*, euen in those daies when he had some sparke of wisedome, to bee euermore ouer-caried with heat and choller. Since which time he is growne so franticke, that he is kept within a Chamber bound and manacled. In the same Plea, I found these words. *They suppose they haue deserued well of the Citie of Paris, in as much as during the whole time of the troubles, they neuer ceased to teach their youth, there being at that time no other Colledge in the Vniuersitie, whereas those exercises were entirely kept.* Will you know the cause ? (saith a man of good sort standing by) the Principals of other Colledges, had let their hands fall, as bewayling in their soules, the miseries that grew by this rebellion : whereas these fellowes, lifted their hands vp to heauen, as thinking they had preuailed conquerers in the matter they had vndertaken. But nothing amazed me so much as a letter, which was sent into Spayne, but intercepted by *Monseur de Chaseron*, Gouernour of the Prouince of Bourbon, the bearer whereof was father *Matthew* the Iesuite. This letter was sent me to peruse, and the tenour of it, was as followeth.

Most

Most high and mightie Prince, your Catholique Maiestie hauing beene so gratious vnto vs, as to let vs vnderstand by the most godly, and reuerend father *Matthew*, not onely your holy intentions in the whole cause of religion, but also more especially the good affection, and fauour towards this Citie of Paris. &c. *And a little after.* We hope, that shortly the forces of his holines, and your Catholique Maiestie being vnited, shall free vs from the oppression of our enemies, who from before a yeere and a halfe vntill this present, haue so hemd vs in on all sides, as nothing can come into the Citie, but eyther by chaunce, or by strong hand: and would strayne themselues to go further, were it not that they feare those garrisons, which it hath pleased your Catholique Maiestie, to appoint vs. We can certainly assure your Catholique Maiestie, that all the Catholiques wish & desire, to see your Catholick Maiesty enioy the Scepter of this kingdom, and to raigne ouer vs, as we do most willingly offer our selues into your armes, as to our Father, &c. *And on the margent somewhat lower.* The Reuerend Father *Matthew*, this present bearer, by whom we haue receiued much côfort, being thorowly instructed in our minds, shall supply the defect of our letters, to your Catholique Maiestie, humbly beseeching you to giue credence to his report. This letter did mightily incense me against your iustifications, wherupon I desired to see the aunswer hereunto in your Pleas. Tenthly, *Arnauld* alledgeth, that the yeere 1 5 9 1. *Monsieur de Chaseron* intercepted certayne letters written to the king of Spayne, carried by Father *Mathew*, of the Order of the said defendants. We aunswere, that *Arnauld*, vnder correctiõ of the Court, is ill informed, for the said father *Mathew* died three yeers before at Ancona in Italy, that is, in the yeere 1 5 8 8. and by consequent could not, but by a greater miracle, then Saint *Dennis*, go and come into Spayne. *And addeth moreouer*, that that *Mathew* was

a Spanish Frier, of one of the four orders of the begging
Friers. I see the same aunswere to be likewise made by
Montaignes, one of the chiefe men of your Order, which
made me presently exclaime against *Arnauld*: O
straunge impudence of an Aduocate, against an innocent Societie! But one of the companie interrupting
me, prayed me to take better aduisement: for (saith he)
if there be any impudence herein, it is on the Iesuits
part; nay rather want of common sence. For *Arnauld*
was farre from saying, that father *Claudius Matthew*
was the bearer of those letters, but an other Iesuite,
whose Christen name iumpt with *Mathew* his surname. Let vs read his Plea. When King *Philip* (saith
he) by the Iesuits perswasion had sent a garrison of Spaniards into Paris, and desired to haue some colourable
title for that, which he held alreadie by force, whom sent
he thether but father *Mathew* the Iesuite, whose Christē
name was all one with the other *Mathewes* surname, the
Iesuit, that was the principall instrument of the League
in the yeere 1583. This *Mathew* in fewe daies, that
hee abode in this Citie, being lodged in the Colledge
of the Iesuits, caused this letter to be there written and
signed.

Marke (saith one of the companie, who against
my will insulted therupō) the foolish sophistrie of these
fellowes. For in their Pleas they make *Arnauld* say, that
which he neuer meant, hauing in plaine termes distin-
guished betweene the two *Mathewes*. Likewise to alledge, that it was a Spanish Frier, whose name was
Mathew, carieth lesse probabilitie: because the foure orders of the begging Friers are not called Fathers, but
Friers or brothers, and much lesse *Reuerend*: whereas in
this letter the bearer is stiled, *the Reuerend Father Mathew*. Which proueth palpably, and to the eye, that howsoeuer the letter were written in the name of the Sixteen
seditious Gouernours, and Tyrants of Paris, whereof

Pigenat was the Superintendent, yet came it out of the Iesuits shop, who were aswell the composers, as the bearers thereof. Compare the date of the letter, which is of the 2. of Nouember, 1591.with the sauage cruelty vsed the same month by those Sixteen, against him that was then chiefe President of the Parliament of Paris, and two other personages of name, who were attached, and executed all at one instant, it will appeare, that in all this buisines, there was nothing but proceeded from the Iesuits. If all these euidences in writing, and confessions by mouth, doe not yet satisfie you, read the booke of *René de la Fon*: you shall see, that he acknowledgeth the Iesuits to haue been the authors, & originals of our last troubles, and of the generall ruine of France. But forasmuch as this Pamphlet is of great consequence to our present purpose, you must vnderstand, that *Pasquier* in two or three places of his pleadings, fortuned to say, that the sect of the Iesuits, once taking root in France, would bring forth a Seminary of diuision, betweene the * Christian, and the Catholique: & in the end of his pleading, protesteth, that whē soeuer this misery should come to passe, yet at the least they that should liue in those daies, should acknowledge, that this age was not vnfurnisht of such, as had long before, as it were from a high Tower, foreseen the tempest to come.

In the yeere 1597. Monsieur Marion the Kings Aduocate in the court of Parliament of Paris, pleading against the Iesuits of Lions, recounting the mischiefes, which this sect had caused, added these words. Wherein appeareth a notable example of the true predictiōs, which God, when he pleaseth, inspireth into those whom he loueth. For the cause being solemnly pleaded aboue thirtie yeeres agoe, for the admittance, not of their Order, which was neuer approued in Fraunce, but of their Colledge into the bodie, & priuiledges of the Vniuesity, the wisest men of that time, hauing indeed a singular insight

* The French, and the Spayniard.

infight into the courfe of the world, forefaw euē in thofe daies, that in tract of time, they would kindle the flames of diffenfion in the midft of the Realme. *La Fon*, the Iefuit, fuppofing that he meant it fpecially by *Paf-quiers* Pleas, takes vpon him to aunfwere it, but in fo pleafant a manner, as I cannot but acquaint you withall. But what are thefe Diuine Diuiners (faith he) that pro-phecied, fo well, fo truly, fo effectually of the Iefuits? Is it not poffible for vs to diuine at their names, and Diuinations, although our breafts fwell not with the en-thufiafmes of thefe infpired fpirits? Is not *Pafquier* one of them? And *Marion* in the prophecies which he al-ledgeth, doth he not directly poynt at thofe which were vttered by *Pafquier?* If I prophecie truly, *Pafquier* his Pleas haue made me a Prophet. This Plea hauing lyen buried for thirtie yeeres, and digged vp againe within thefe three yeeres, like an old Image loaden with newe Pardons, hath like a ridiculous *Pafquill*, fpoken, and prophecied backward. That which in the yeere 1564. he neither could nor durft fay: returning out of hell in the yeere 1594. & 95. better inftructed in things, which were paft alredy, he hath pronoūced thē like an Oracle from the tripode: & from him haue I learnt them. But the mifchiefe wil be, whē thefe pleadings fhalbe one day brought forth in their originall forme, to difcouer the new Pardons that are pafted vpon this plaftred *Pafquin*, and when the reward of his prophecies fhal be branded vpon his backe.

O mightie and worthie champion, meriting to haue his ftatue fet vp in the mids of all your Colledges, for ha-uing fo valiantly hunted, not to couert, but to death, the auncient enemie of your Order; was there euer man, that behaued himfelfe better with his penne, and his wit? Onely this troubleth me, that giuing fuch a braue onfet vpon this poore old man, he chargeth him at laft to haue new forged his pleadings, and fet downe vnder the yeere 1 5 9 4. in manner of a prophecie thofe things which he had feene come to paffe through Fraunce, the yeere 1 5 6 4. whereby this honeft man doth confeffe, that all the miferies of Fraunce haue proceeded from the Iefuits: for this was the fcope of *Pafquier* his Plea. And my felfe alfo acknowledge, that the holy Ghoft was minded to fpeak by the mouth of this Iefuit.

O how great is the force of truth, which cannot but break forth, whatfoeuer fig-leaues of cunning, cloaking, or hypocrifie, we apply to couer, or difguife it withall. Then what need haue you, Right Reuerend *Pafquill*, to trouble your braynes, with fearching fo many records, to know whether the Iefuits were the authors, and contriuers of our troubles? There needeth no more, but this confeffion alone, which cannot be difauowed by the Generall, and other the Superiours of this Order: hauing fuch a ftatute in the 1 8. article of the firft Chapter of the third part of their conftitutions. *Libri edi non poterunt in lucem fine approbatione atque confenfu præpofiti Generalis, qui eorum examinationem tribus committat.* No bookes fhall be publifhed without the allowance, and confent of the Generall, who fhall commit the examination thereof, to three of the order. Be affured that in a matter of fo great importance, all the Iefuits bookes which haue beene produced before you, were by them publifhed, and fet forth by the authoritie and approbation of their Generall, or other Superiours by him authorifed, and affigned to that purpofe. Therefore you may hold for true, all the confeffions by them made, concerning our troubles, and in efpeciall, that of *René de la Fon.*

I beleeue as much (aunfwered I to this praring fellowe) neyther dooth that trouble mee, but that this lewde foole, *La Fon*, vnder the allufion of two names, fhould compare *Pafquier* to *Pafquin*. In as much as I doe not thinke there liueth that man

of

of what degree soeuer, which may enter comparison
with mine Excellencie. It is true that you say, (replied
the other) but when you once know what this *Pasquier*
is, it will not trouble you at all : for he is one, whom the
Iesuits feare more then they loue.

In conclusion, this was the course I tooke, to be thorowly informed in the first poynt of your Accusation,
which concerneth the last troubles of Fraunce. The second remaines, which toucheth your violent attempts
vpon the persons of Kings, princes, & other great personages, which are in dislike with your opinions. Setting my selfe to the enquirie of this poynt, I was presented with a booke of *Peter Mathew*, one of your Agents,
intituled, *Summa summorum Pontificum* : who speaking
of you (my Maisters) with all honour and respect vseth
these words; *Tyrannos aggrediuntur*, they encounter tyrants. VVhich some construed, as spoken in hatred of
the late King, *Henry* the third, who was slaine in 89. a-
bout which time, that booke was first printed at Lyons.
And your Aduersaries maintained, that these vvordes
were purposely inserted, after the parricide of the said
King, whom you were wont to entitle by the name of
Tyrant.

Contrariwise, your fellowes alledged, as well in their
Pleas, as in *Montagnes* his booke, that *Mathew* vvas
not of your Order, and that therefore his sayings ought
not to be preiudiciall vnto you. In this controuersie, I
commaunded Signior *Marforio*, to looke ouer the euidences fully, and wholly, and to make mee a true and
faithfull report thereof. His report was, that indeede
Mathew was not of the Order of the Iesuits, but that
he speaketh exceeding partially on their behalfe, wher-
soeuer he hath occasion to talke of them : marry it vvas
hard to iudge, whether his booke were published before, or after the death of *Henrie* the third.

That skilleth not: (saith another) for when he commendeth them for encountring Kings, he muſt needes meane it, either by the breaking forth of the Troubles, which were at that time wrought againſt the good King, or by the murder committed vppon his perſon. Take it whether way you pleaſe, they cannot cleere thēſelues of it, beeing for that poynt by name infinitelie commended by him, who through his whole Booke, dooth countenaunce and grace them all he may.

Beſides, the Ieſuits of Burdeaux, would neuer pray for the late King, as *Montaignes* alſo confeſſeth. And to prooue that *Mathew* maintaineth nothing, but the generall poſition of the Ieſuits, I referre you to *The Aphoriſmes of Confeſſion*, made by Father *Samuell Sa*, Doctor in Diuinitie, one of their Societie, who vnder the letter *Princeps*, affirmeth, that a King may be depoſed by his ſubieĉts from his Crowne and dignitie, if he doe not performe the dutie of a king. And vnder the letter *Tyrannus*: that the prince, who beareth himſelfe like a Tyrant, may be expelled by his ſubieĉts, albeit they haue ſworne perpetuall obedience and allegeance vnto him, in caſe, after he haue beene admoniſhed, he doe not reforme himſelfe.

By this meanes, bringing all ſoueraigne princes vnder the danger of theyr craftie confeſſions, for them to reſolue ignorant people, who they be, that beare themſelues vprightly in their gouernment; the reſt, that doe not ſo, beeing forthwith depriuable. Which poſition, agreeth with that of *Mathew*, by them ere-while diſauowed and diſclaimed.

To ſay truth, I wanted no ſycophants in this vvhole inquirie of the proceſſe againſt you: although I aſſure you, you had ſtout Champions, that very ſkilfully could ward their blowes. In this meane time, I had ſent mee out of diuers countries, the ſundry arraignments & trialls of ſeuerall perſons, who by the inſtigation of Ieſuits, had made, or conſpired to make, attempt vppon the

liues

liues of princes. Out of England, the triall of *William Parry*, in the yere 1584. and another of *Edward Squire*, in the yeere 1597. Out of the Low-countries, the try-alls of *Baltazar Girard*, in anno 84, and of *Peter de Pennes* in 98. Out of Fraunce, the trialls of *Peter Barriere*, in 93, and of *Iohn Chastell*, in 94. Aboue all the rest, I did most relie vpon *Peter Barriere* his processe, wherein I found the whole order to be deeply charged, & espe-cially the good Fathers, *Varade* and *Commolet*. Immedi-atlie after that, comes me in a huge traine of young fel-lowes, who, for discharge of their consciences doe con-fesse, that beeing schollers in the Iesuits Colledge, they had nothing else preached vnto them, but the murder of the *Biarnois*, (for so they termed the King of Fraunce that now raigneth.) In the end, I cast myne eye vppon *Chastells* processe, which did mightily confirme mee in all that the young youths had reported. For beeing de-maunded by the Court of the Parliament of Paris, as touching the murder which hee had attempted vppon the Kings person, marke the very words of the Interro-gatorie, and his aunswers.

Beeing demaunded, where hee had learnt this newe Diuinitie? (which was to kill Princes) He aunswered, it was by Philosophie.

Beeing demaunded, whether hee had studied Philo-sophie in the Colledge of the Iesuits? Hee aunswered, yea: and that vnder Father *Gueret*, with whom hee had beene two yeeres, and a halfe.

Being demaunded, whether he had not beene in the chamber of Meditations, into which the Iesuits vsed to bring the most enormous sinners, to the intent, that in that chamber they might behold the pictures of manie deuils, in diuers terrible shapes, vnder pretence to reduce them to a better life, thereby to affright theyr mindes, and incite them, to vndertake some great exploit? Hee aunswered, that hee had beene oftentimes in the sayd
chamber

chamber of Meditations.

Being demaunded, by whom he had beene perswaded to kill the King? He aunswered, that he had heard in many places, that it was to be held for a moſt true principle, that it was lawfull to kill the King, and that thoſe who ſaid ſo, called him Tyrant.

Being demaunded, whether that argument of killing the King, was not ordinarie with the Ieſuits? Hee aunſwered, that hee had heard them ſay, that it was lawfull to kill the King, and that he was out of the Church, and that they ought not to obey him, or hold him for theyr King, vntil ſuch time as he was abſolued by the Pope.

Againe, beeing demaunded in the great Chamber, (my Lords the Preſidents and Counſellours therof, and of the Tournel being aſſembled) he made the ſame aunſwers, and did in eſpeciall propound & maintaine, that Maxime, that it was lawfull to kill princes, & by name the king that now raigneth, who was not in the church, as he ſaid, becauſe he had not the Popes approbation.

The truth is, this poore ſeduced fellow, doth not particularly deſigne, or note any of your Societie, to haue taught him this damnable leſſon, yet doth hee not ſpare the whole bodie of your Order. And muſing ſomwhat thereat, this controller of your actions, that ſtood neere vnto me, told me, it was a thing not to be wondred at: becauſe the Ieſuits leſſon, when they would procure any prince to be murdered, conſiſted of two braunches: the firſt was, to giue an aſſured promiſe of Paradiſe, to whomſoeuer could atchiue this high peece of ſeruice, & that they ſhould not ſpare to kill him, though hee were in a Church, in the midſt of diuine ſeruice. The ſecond, that if the partie that ſhould attempt this, were intercepted, and deliuered into the hands of the Magiſtrate, to be made an example, he ought aboue all things to beware of diſcouering, or reuealing theyr names, by whō hee vvas ſet on worke, vppon paine of eternall damnation:

tion: & certainly, in *Barrieres* proceste it appeared, that
these instructions had beene giuen him, albeit, (not hauing beene bred vp in the schooles of the Iesuits, as
Chastell was) hee did not obserue them before his Iudges.

After I had examined this proceste, I lookt vpon the
triall of *Robert Bruce*, a Scottish gentleman, who was
appeacht, and accused by Father *William Crichton* a Iesuite, because he would not procure *Metellinus*, Chauncellor to the King of Scots to be murdered. I enquired
from whence all these tricks of Matchiauelisme, & A-
nabaptisme might arise. Whereupon they shewed mee
your Constitutions, which enioyne you a blinded obedience to your Superiours, and with as constant resolution to follow their commaundements, as if they had issued out of the mouth of our Sauiour Christ. And therwithall, they bring me *The Aphorismes of confession*, made
by your *Emanuell Sa*, & a booke composed by the Principall of the Seminarie at Reims, wherein they maintaine, that in certaine cases, it is lawfull for the subiect to
kill the King.

But aboue all, Father *Iohn Guignard* his Booke, one
of your Priests : wherein he laboureth to prooue, as well
that the late King, *Henry* the third, was iustly slaine, as
also that hee who now raigneth, ought to be serued in
the same manner. The wordes of his booke are these.
That cruell *Nero*, was slaine by one *Clement*, and that
counterfet Munke was dispatched by the hand of a true
Munk. This heroicall act, performed by *Iames Clement*,
as a gift of the holie Spirit, (so termed by our Diuines) is
worthilie commended by the Priour of the Iacobins,
Burgoin, a Confessor and Martyr. The Crowne of
Fraunce may, and ought to be transferred frō the house
of Bourbon, vnto some other : And the *Biarnois*, although conuerted to the Catholick fayth, shal be more
mildly dealt withall, then he deserues, if rewarded with

Ggg. a

a ſhauen crowne, he be ſhut vp into ſome ſtrict Couent, there to doe penance, for the miſchiefes which he hath brought vppon the Realme of Fraunce, and to thanke G O D, that he hath giuen him grace, to acknowledge him before his death. And if without Armes he cannot be depoſed, let men take Armes againſt him, if by war it cannot be accompliſht, let him be murthered.

Theſe are the ſcandalous, and if I durſt ſo call them, the blaſphemous words of a booke, ſprinckled with an infinite number of others. In concluſion, I read with all diligence, your Petition made to the King, full of pretie flouriſhes, whereby you condemne all thoſe attempts, as forbidden by all lawes both of God and man. While I was beating my braines about theſe euidences, meaning to reſt vpon the Sentence of the Parliament of Paris, pronounced as well againſt *Chaſtell*, as againſt the whole Societie, one of the companie ſaid vnto me; Remember that notwithſtanding this Sentence, the prints of rebellion remaine ſtill in their harts: And to prooue that this is ſo, you ſhall ſee *Montaignes* a Ieſuit, extoll *Iames Commolet*, *Claudius Mathew*, *Hanniball Coldretto*, *Bernard Rouiliet*, *Ambroſe Varade*. And after *Montaignes*, you ſhall ſee his Ape *La Fon*, increaſe that number by many more, which are notoriouſly knowne to haue proceeded Doctours in the profeſſion of murder and rebellion.

You ſhall ſee the booke of miracles compoſed by *Richeome*, their Generall of Aquitania, wherein amongſt other things, hee ſaith, that our Ladie of Buy, wrought many miracles, during the troubles, to preſerue the Cittie againſt her enemies, that is, againſt the King, for this Citty was of the contrary partie. But as for the miracles that S. *Geneuiefue* ſhewed for the King, hee is not too haſtie to recount them. Yet were they moſt euident in three caſes. The firſt: whē the League being to ſet forward towards Diepe, this Saints ſhrine

was

was taken downe, to carrie in solemne procession: the second, was when the *Cheualier d' Aumalle*, the night of this Saints feast, attempted to surprise the Towne of Saint *Denys:* the third, when the said shrine was againe taken downe in March, anno 1594, and generall procession made, for the withstanding of the Kings forces.

Notwithstanding, all these vowes, prayers, and purposes, turned to the côfusion of his enemies. For about Diepe he obtained a famous victorie, beyond all hope or expectation. The *Cheualier d' Aumalle* was slaine within the cittie of Saint *Denys*, vvhen hee thought himselfe Maister of it, and all his Companie put to flight. And in conclusion, Paris yeelded vp to the King, within two or three dayes after the taking downe of the said shrine. S. *Geneuiefue* is the holy Patronesse of Paris. The Cittie of Paris did in right appertaine to the king; and was therefore by her miraculously preserued, in the preuenting of these three chaunces. These miracles, this worthie reporter *Richeome* is far enough from mentioning: hee makes a conscience of that, seeing it is in fauour of the King.

Furthermore, read *Montaignes*, who maintaineth, that the Pope may translate kingdoms from one to another, in his booke *De la veritè Defendue.* A plausible, and true position in this Cittie of Rome, but scandalous in Fraunce, and subiect to corporall punishment. These three bookes were printed since the Sentence of the Court of Parliament: whereby you may gather, what deuotion, euen at this day, the Iesuits beare to their King.

All this was brought to my handes, and to say truth, the greatest part of these proofes came out of your own Colledges, a large Inuentorie framed as well for you, as against you. I thought it not good to trust mine owne iudgement in this processe, but rather in the determi-

ning

ning thereof to ioyne others with me, that were of long
experience, and practife in thefe matters. Signior *Mar-*
forio aduifed mee, to requeft two great perfonages of
Fraunce to be of the Commiffion : * Maifter *Pierre du*
Coignet, which of long hath held his feate & iurifdiction, within the Church of Paris: and another who hauing vowed perpetuall pouertie, hath from all antiquitie kept his refidence before the *Hostel-diu,* or Hofpitall
of Paris, and for his ftrange aufteritie of life, is called the
* *Faster.* I wrote my Letters to them, they at my fummons appeare. I deliuer the euidences to Signior *Mar-*
forio, to be diligently and exactly by him perufed. Wee
prefixed a day for iudgement. Being affembled, I made
it knowne to the companie, how mightily you founde
your felues agreeued with this piller, or Pyramis, as being a monument, to continue for euer the frefh memorie of that which had hapned in Fraunce. That the matter in queftion was, your Reftoring, and confequentlie
the defacing of this Pyramis. For which caufe, I entreated them to lay afide all affection, inafmuch as thys
iudgement by them pronounced, fhould be for euer
celebrated by all pofteritie.

Marforio reporteth the whole proceffe faithfully,
fhewing himfelfe to be no learner in this trade. Hauing
read, and pondered all the euidences on both parts, and
proffering in the end to deliuer his opinion firft, (as is
the manner of thofe, that make report of any caufe to
the Court) I entreated him to forbeare. Let vs giue thys
honour (quoth I) to the ftrangers. We are to fit in iudgment vppon a Stone, and in my opinion, thys honour
is moft due to Maifter * *Pierre,* whom I would requeft
to fpeake his opinion firft, & to remember, that we are
in queftion to reftore this worthy Order of the Societie
of Iefus, fo much honoured in Rome.

Maifter *Pierre* needed not much entreatie; for prefently he ftood vp, & with a rough kind of fpeech began:

* A ftone in
our Ladies
church at
Paris.

* Le Ieuf-
neur, a ftone
of great an-
tiquitie in
Paris.

* Stone.

gan in this manner. How long shall these lewde Impostors freely abuse our patience? how long shall we be so simple, to suffer our selues to be abused? can it be, that the Iesuits hauing giuen both fire, & fewell to our last troubles, their Colledge at Paris, hauing beene the common retreat of all such, as came into Fraunce, with a resolute determination to make themselues Maisters thereof: their Lectures so many trumpets, to encourage their schollers to the parricides of Kings, and their principall Agents hauing put weapons into the hands of many desperate soules, to murther our King, can they (I say) be so shameles, as at his hands to craue, that they may be restored? This were cunningly, and vnder-hand, to commence processe against the sacred Court of the Parliament of Paris, which neuer did or shal receiue, the least touch of imputation for any sentence passed by her, but onely herein, that in condemning this sect, she did not send all their adherents, which were within Paris, to the gallowes. For a farre lesse offence did that famous, and honourable Senate of Rome, long agoe adiudge sixe hundred slaues to death, because their maister was murthered in his owne house, it beeing not knowne by whom.

In this manner would Maister *Pierre* haue runne on, had not I interrupted him with these words: Haue patience Maister *Pierre*, haue patience. Little men, like you, are euermore subiect to choler. You must remember, that you are not Aduocate, but Iudge in this cause. Maister *Pierre* knowing that he had forgot himselfe, chaunged his tune: and turning to me, said in this manner. Right honourable *Pasquill*, I humbly entreat your excellencie, to excuse that iust griefe, wherby I am caried in behalfe of my countrey. Seeing then it pleaseth you to honour me so much, as to heare my opinion first in this matter, I must tell you, before you proceede further, that the cause belongeth properly to

your

your owne iurifdiction . For which way foeuer I turne
my felfe, I fee nothing but ftones . Your excellence,
Signior *Morforio*,the right reuerend *Fafter*,& my felfe,
are ftones, the Pyramis, a ftone, the Iefuits themfelues,
fuing to be reftored(as men altogether innocent)are vndoubtedly no better then fooles and innocents , or to
fpeake more properly very ftones : fay what you will,
they are as voyd of fenfe, as ftones,in ftriuing to reuoke
the fentence of the Court , pronounced againft them.
There was neuer fentence had more formall procee
ding then that : and though it had not, yet could it not
be retracted , but by the ordinarie? forme of lawe ,
which courfe they follow not . But admitte , that
treading vnder foot all the effentiall formes of law ,
we fhould reftore them to their former eftate, what
fortune could they expect hereafter , but worfe then
that before? we fhall need no other witneffe , but the
walles themfelues,to prooue that the people of Fraunce
hath worne haircloth, caried the skrip, and done pen-
nauance for their tranfgreffions during the fpace of fiue
yeeres. I paffe ouer all other proofes, their bookes,
wherunto onely I haue recourfe, wil ferue to condemne
them. Antiquitie teacheth vs, that *Mercurie* transformed *Battus* the fhepheard into a ftone, for a trecherous
part, which he plaid him.

Ouid. 2.lib.
Metamor.

> *Et me mihi perfide prodis,*
> *Me mihi prodis,aut,periuraq́, pectora vertit*
> *In durum filicem, qui nunc quoq́ dicitur Index.*

There was neuer Societie,that euer committed fo many trecheries, as this of the Iefuits againft the King, and
Countrey of Fraunce. *Mercurie* making fhew to fauour , and affect them, fometimes playeth with their
pens, and into them infufeth the gift of Battologie, or
Loquacitie ; but noting their trecherous practifes
hee

hee turneth all their bookes into a kind of Index, or Touchstone, making them the true touchstones or be-wrayers, & the assured proofes of their own lewdnes. I should wrong both the time, & your patience, to stand vpon particular recitall of all their doings. It shall content me, in briefe to say thus much, that the Iesuits are to be pronounced, *Not receiueable.*

And to this purpose doe I cite that sentence, which the Iesuit, author of *The most humble Remonstrance and request,* hath giuen against his owne order. But as concerning the generall state of the cause, seeing by auncient prerogatiue, you are the soueraigne of soueraigne Iudges in cases extraordinarie, my aduise is, that by vertue of your absolute authoritie, you adde this clause vnto that sentence. First, that their house, and Colledge at Paris, be raced and laid leuell with the ground, as sometimes was the Palace of *Bentiuolio* in Bologna in Italy, whereof there remaynes no memorie, but the rubbish, called at this day the ruines of *Bentiuolio.* Secondly, that there be sale made of all and singuler the temporall goods of the Iesuits of Fraunce, and the money thence arising, to be employed to the redeeming, or recouering of those demaines of the Crowne, which our King hath beene forced to alienate, and sell for the maintenance of the warres, whereof they were Authors.

At these words all the companie stood amazed: for he tooke the matter in a farre other sence, then we expected, and some muttering there was about this sale of their goods. Wherupon he said further: Let not this opinion of mine seem any whit straunge vnto you. If you had beene bred vp vnder the same law that I haue been, you would not thinke it so. The possessions wherewith they are indowed in Fraunce, is in respect eyther of their Monasteries, (which they call houses) or of their Colledges. In the first respect, they can enioy none: for
their

their owne ſtatutes forbid it : in the ſecond much leſſe, becauſe they were neuer receiued, or allowed in Fraunce for true and lawfull Colledges, capable of legacies, and charitable contributions, further then as they promiſed in the aſſembly at Poiſſi 1 5 6 1. to renounce all their vowes, & to raunge themſelues, (as all other Colledges did) vnder the obediēce of their Ordinaries : which they neyther haue, nor would performe ſince that time : and conſequently neyther may, nor ought to be reputed Colledges. If you will returne to the common & aunci-ent rules of the Roman law, which we are with all dili-gence to embrace, (the common lawes of a countrey, being not againſt it) there you ſhall finde, that if a Te-ſtator bequeath any Legacie to a Colledge, the Legacie is good and ſufficient, if the Colledge be approued by the Magiſtrates : if not, it is to be conuerted to the be-hoofe and benefit of ſome other Colledge which is au-thorized.

The Ieſuits cauſe was referred to Counſell, in the yeere 1 5 6 4. in which meane time their qualitie was ſuſpended, vntill in 1 5 9 4. it was adiudged flat againſt them, they being condemned to auoyde the Realme of Fraunce. Wherefore we may by the ſequell truly pro-nounce, that all the charitable deuotions, beſtowed vp-on thē, are to be conuerted to another vſe, for the benefit of the common-wealth. The Ieſuits were authors of the troubles, the troubles were the cauſes that ſome part of the Crowne-land was ſold, which conſequently ought by them to be made good : that they may be the Scorpi-ons of Fraunce, in whoſe death ſhe may find a medicine and remedie for their venemous bitings. Chriſtian cha-ritie, wherewith they abound (as themſelues boaſt) the pouerty of their order, which they proclaime quite tho-row their ſtatutes, the neceſſitie, wherein our State now is, the execution of iuſtice for example, will haue it ſo, for the diſcharge of their owne conſciences.

With

With this word Maifter *Pierre du Coignet* concluded, and was in fome fort feconded by the *Fafter* his companion : not for any deepe vnderstanding that was in him , but for that rule , which is common to men in miferie, who are much eafed, when they haue copartners in their affliction : he alfo would gladly haue feene the Iefuits kept poore, and *Fafting* like himfelfe. Wher-vnto *Signior Morforio*, and my felfe, would in no wife condefcend, in fo much as the proceffe was at the point to be broken off, we fuppofing it to be but a matter compacted betweene the two Doctors of Fraunce. By meanes whereof, *Morforio* after a little altercation began to fpeake.

To what purpofe (faith hee) are all thfee cenfures? *Recte quidem, fed quorfum quafo tam recte?* I fay not, but they are wifely handled, but to what end? Here is much good talke fpent to little purpofe . You argue the matter as if the Iefuits had now in their hands all thofe lands, or poffeffions, which haue beene by way of almes beftowed vpon them. I tell you, they are almoft all fold, and turned into money. Their money is in diuers banks out of your Realme, to relieue them in a rainie day , in cafe they fhould be forced to forgoe the countrey of Fraunce. And if at all they haue any certayne reuenew, that confifteth wholly in benefices , which they haue caufed to be vnited to their Colledges , and are not capable of alienation. Haue they fold them fay you ? (replied Maifter *Pierre*) by what right could they doe fo? By authoritie from their Generall onely, which we ney-ther approoue, nor receiue in Fraunce . Our lawes are farre other in that poynt of the fale, and alienation of poffeffions, belonging eyther to the Church, or to Societies in common. In a word all thefe pretended fales are void in law. Wherat I brake into thefe words. You open a gap, to an inconuenience that would fpread far, & at one blow, extend to the hurt of a number, who haue no

Hhh.   hand

hand at all in this quarrell. Whereby you fhould bring another Chaos, or confufion into the countrey of Fraunce, and therefore I referre you to the auncient law of the Romans : *Communis error facit ius*. A common error makes a right. Finally, after much wrangling and contention, it was concluded and agreed amongft vs, to leaue the matter as we found it, and that both the Pyrainis and the fentence of the Parliament, fhould ftand without any alteration in eyther. This was all I could obtayne of the companie, and that not without fome bitter words at litle Maifter *Pierre* his hand, who tolde me in mine eare, that he faw, I was at the poynt to turne Iefuit, to vphold mine ancient greatnes in the Citie of Rome, with men in higheft place and authoritie. Of all which proceeding I thought good to aduertife your Fatherhood (Right reuerend Father) as he that is wholy deuoted to your feruice. Befeeching you not to proclayme your innocency henceforward, becaufe fome turn it to a fcoffe, others to a fcorne. It is a puddle, which if you did well, you fhould let reft ; for the more you ftir it, the more wil your doings ftink. Your felfe are the firft, and laft iudge to giue fentence againft your Order. I fpeake to you by name, that are the author of the *Moft humble Petition to King Henry* the fourth : wherein you acknowledge, that he is more barbarous, then the Barbarians themfelues, who fetteth himfelfe againft his Soueraigne. And your *Montaignes* confeffeth, that to band himfelfe againft his Prince, is the humor of an heretique. Enter into your owne confciences, and tel me if this humor did not raigne in you (my Maifters) during the laft troubles of Fraunce. In conclufion, I would aduife you to giue order, that thofe of your Societie forbeare to write any more, or if they doe, that they be more difcreet hereafter, vpon paine of being expelled out of your number.

Mont.ca.34

CHAP.

CHAP. 21.

¶ *Of the diuision which seemes to be in the Parlia-*
ments, or iurisdictions of Fraunce, as concerning
the Iesuits, and what may be the
cause thereof.

 He Aduocate, hauing ended his long
discourse, paused a while, which gaue the
Gentleman occasion to say vnto him. I
assure you Sir, I cannot but much commend your inuention, in representing,
this matter in the person of Stones. For seeing men
will not speake, stones must: their dealinges beeing such as you haue shewed and prooued, not by
proofes at randon, and vncertaine, but most infallible,
and drawne out of their owne bookes. But how commeth it to passe, that this being so notoriously knowne,
and remayning of record, yet neuerthelesse there be certaine Courts of Parliament within the Realme, which
doe not onely receiue them, but honor, cherish and embrace them, within their Cities and iurisdictions. I did
expect, you should aske me that question (quoth the
Aduocate) and was about to haue entred thereinto of
my selfe, had you not preuented mee. Thinke it not
straunge it should be so: it is a mysterie hidden in the
secret counsell of God, who hath not wholy withdrawn
his wrath from vs, but intendeth one day to vse these, as
his instruments to bring more plagues vpon vs. Neuerthelesse, doe not you thinke, but that those other Parliaments, haue some great shew of reason for their
doings.

Did you neuer see a new Testament, wherein the
histories were drawne in pictures? In that place of the
Gospell, where our Sauiour is tempted in the desart,
Sathan is pictured in the habit of a Munke. Some *Lu-*

cianists flicke not to fay, that thereby is vnderſtood, that the life and conuerſation of Munks is Diabolicall. But I am of a contrarie opinion. For whoſoeuer the Painter was, that in this matter of the temptatiō, deuiſed to cloth the Diuell in thoſe weeds, he did it not without great conſideration : iudging, that this being the true habit of piety, there was no way more readie & certain to ſurpriſe the conſciences of well meaning men, then by it.

The Diuel, after he had ſet forth diuers mommeries of religious Orders, he meant, to ſet his reſt vpon this : and (transforming himſelfe into *Ignacius*, and his adherents) to pretend the holy name of Ieſus, and to promiſe by the mouth of the Ieſuits, not onely terreſtriall kingdomes to Princes, wherewith they would inueſt them, (as Sathan did to our Sauiour) but alſo the kingdome of heauen to ſuch as would execute their malice, againſt thoſe Kings, that were their enemies. Wherein the Diuell hath not much miſſed of his ayme. For vnder this glorious name hath he abuſed and ouerreached our Popes their holines, and conſequently a number of religious ſoules. And as himſelfe is the Spirit of Diuiſion, ſo is it no meruaile if the Ieſuits (his true and lawfull children) enioy the ſame priuiledge, that their father doth. They haue cauſed diuiſion between themſelues, and our Prelates of Fraunce, betweene themſelues and the Vniuerſities, betweene Popes, and Kings, betweene Popes and other Prelats, if now they cauſe a new diſſenſion, amongſt our Parliaments of Fraunce, they haue done that, which onely was wanting to the ful and abſolute accompliſhment of the Sorbones prophecie, when in her cenſure of the Ieſuits Sect, in the yeere 1554. ſhe ſaith: *Multas in populo querelas, multas lites, diſſidia, contentiones, æmulatioues, variaque ſchiſmata inducit* : It breadeth many quarrels, controuerſies, diſcords, contentions, emulations, and many diuiſions amongſt the people.

The

The Parliament of Paris, vpon mature & wise deliberation, hath banished thē out of their iurisdiction. Some
other Parliaments doe retaine them, albeit the attempts
of *Barriere* and *Chastell* vppon the person of the King,
be vnto them notoriously knowne, and that they were
the first plotters, and contriuers of our troubles. When
I thinke of these dissentions, I am put in minde of a dis-
creet aunswere made by King *Henry* the second, touching the case of *Pelisson*, President of the Parliament of
Chamberi, who by the sentence of the Parliament of
Digeon, was depriued of his office, besides sundry o-
ther disgraces, which he receiued, vpon the complaint,
and information of *Taboue* Atturny generall. Afterward, obtayning Letters for a second examination, and
and the cause being remoued to the Parliament of Paris, he was restored to his office, and *Taboue* condemned
to make him honourable amends, bare-headed, & in his
shirt, with a halter about his neck.

The King beeing informed of these proceedings
in both the Courts of parliament, wisely made aunswer,
that he esteemed all his Iudges to be men of honestie &
vprightnes : but that they of the parliament of Digeon,
had iudged according to their consciences, and they of
Paris, according to right and iustice . I make no doubt,
but that all the Iudges of other parliaments, are by their
consciences induced thereunto, but this I say, that there
was neuer any thing decreed in Court, more sufficiently and sincerely, then this was by the parliament of Paris.

The other, as I suppose, are swayed by the authority
of the holy Sea, supporting the Iesuits : which is no
small aduantage for them to leane vnto : notwithstanding, I will oppugne them by the same authoritie, beseeching them not to take in euill part this admonition,
which in all dutie & humilitie I offer vnto their côside-
rations, not doubting, but after they haue heard me, (if at

leaft they pleafe to giue me hearing) they will thēfelues condemne this their opinion.

You haue heeretofore vnderftood, how at two feue-rall times, our Iefuits had practifed the murder of the King, and not at that time when hee was deuided from vs in religion, but euen then when he was reconciled to our Church, in the time of a truce, defiring nothing elfe but a generall vnion, and reconcilement of all his fubiects throughout the Realme. They are highly fa-uoured at Rome, as the Iuie, which feemeth outwardly to fuccour the wall, when as inwardly it eateth into it: but if they had euer confpired any attempt againft the Popes perfon, I am out of doubt, that by the Decree of that great, and holy Confiftorie of Rome, theyr Order would haue beene put downe, and abolifhed for euer. At the leaft I haue feene the like practife in a cafe not vnlike, for a matter not fo dangerous for example, nor of fuch confequence as that, fhewed vppon the whole Order of the *Humiliati*. I will acquaint you with the hiftorie.

CHAP. 22.

¶ How the Order of Humiliatj *was fuppreffed by Decree of the Confiftorie of* Rome: *and that there is greater caufe to fuppreffe the* Iefuits, *then the* Humiliatj.

His Order in outward appearance, (like this of the Iefuits) promifed fo great fanc-titie, and deuotion, as Cardinall *Borrho-mæo*, the Archbifhop of Millan, vvould needes take vpon him the patronage and protection thereof. This good Prelate, perceiuing that the greateft part of them, gaue themfelues ouer to a voluptuous, and diffolute kinde of life, tooke in hand to reforme them: which fome of them tooke in fuch in-dignitie

dignitie, as that they vowed his death.

There was a Guardian of that Order resident in the Cittie of Versellis, his name was *Girolamo Lignana*, who with certaine other his confederats, vndertakes this execution. And to make way to their purpose, they resolued to kill Frier *Fabio Simonetta*, which had the treasure of their Monasterie at Millan in keeping, and vvas the head of theyr Order. Vppon this resolution they come with a stedfast purpose to strangle him, and finding him in the Church at prayer, God diuerted them from executing their malicious purpose, by meanes of a certaine iarre, that happened amongst them: but in sted thereof, they stole diuers peeces of gold, and siluer plate, whereof they made mony. This done, *Lignana* goeth to *Donato Facia*, a brother of their order, a desperate companion, and altogether set vppon mischiefe, whom he ouercommeth, and corrupteth with monie, to vndertake the murder of the Cardinall *Borrhomæo.* Hee beeing in this manner ouer-come, like an honest man wil not breake his word; but espying a time, when this great, & holy personage was at prayers in a chappel with his owne familie, he dischargeth a pistol vpon him, which by a great miracle, passed but through his gown. Within a while after, both hee and *Lignana* are apprehended, and beeing manifestly conuicted, they are executed, and therewithall, their Order wholie suppressed in a full Consistorie at Rome, by *Pius Quintus.*

The Iesuits (as I will heereafter declare) alledge that this was a general cospiracie of the whole Order against *Borrhomæo.* Wherein they lie impudently: for it cannot be found that euer any man had a hand in the plotting, or contriuing thereof, saue onely *Lignana*, Guardian of the Priorie of Saint *Christopher*, in Versellis, with certaine other priuate Munks. The Order was distributed into many other Monasteries, scattered heere and there throughout Italy, who were not of counsell with thys

catc-

enterprife. Yet neuerthelesse, this onely attempt against Cardinall *Borrhomæo*, though voyde of successe, was the chiefe cause, that the Order was finally suppressed.

Compare this historie, with that of the Iesuits (I speak to the Iudges of other Parliaments) are we not inwardlie ashamed, that at Rome there should be such an example of iustice shewen vpon the *Humiliati*, for that one of them made an attempt against the life of one onelie Cardinall, whose death could be no great preiudice to the whole Colledge of Cardinalls, and that wee should suffer this sect of Iesuits to liue amongst vs, which (as our selues knowe) hath procured two seuerall attempts vpon the person of the King, being but one in a whole kingdome, vpon whose life depend the generall quiet and welfare of all his subiects : beeing the worthiest prince, that euer raigned in Fraunce, any time these 5. hundred yeeres.

The dignitie of a Cardinall, hath beene very great in Rome, but yet inferiour to a King of Fraunce, especially in his owne kingdome. For in Rome there be many Cardinals, but in France there is but one King. Among all the Cardinalls, I haue euer honoured the memory of Cardinall *Borrhomæo*, but yet I cannot conceiue howe the losse of him should be of so fatall consequence to Italie, as the death of our great King to Fraunce. Nay further, (howe euer I may be censured ouer-partially preiudicate against the Iesuits) sith by the last confession of *Barriere*, there are challenged three other Religious persons of Lyons, one a Carmelite, another a Iacobin, and a third a Capuchin; notwithstanding (say our Iesuits, in their foure Bookes publisht since the last Arrest of Parliament) wee must punish the particuler offenders, and not censure the whole Order.

The punishment should be proportioned to the offence. The offence beeing personall, the punishment should be so to, and not inflicted vppon the Order. I

will

will not here say, that such proceedings, as else where are iniustice in affaires of State, may be auowed for iust, and that in the decimations which were anciently made among the souldiours, when there was question to punish a Regiment, as soone died the faultlesse as the offender: and yet was there neuer any exemplary iustice more agreeable to gouernment, nor more necessary for the maintenaunce of a Common-wealth . Much lesse will I say with the great *Tacitus* , *Habet aliquid ex iniquo omne magnum exemplum , quod in singulos vtilitate publica rependitur.*

I will not heere alledge the opinion of one of the greatest Lawyers in Rome, who was wont to say, That in cases of sedition, the first executions should be verie sharpe : Afterward , when thinges were well appeased, the Magistrate might slacke his hand, and growe more milde. I will not now heape vp all the rules & axiomes seruing to this purpose , although that which concerneth the life of a King, and the dependencie thereof, admitteth no example, nor cannot well be compared with any other. And howsoeuer some Romane *Manlius* may be of opinion, that a whole body or corporation, should be liable to the personal attempt of any of their companie, especially in an attempt against the life of theyr king; yet so it is, as hetherto Fraunce hath not receiued thys position. As it was manifest in *Iames Clement,* Iacobin, who although hee murdred our king , yet proceeded they not against the Order of the Iacobins, but onely against him and his Prior, who was torne in peeces with foure horses in Tours, after hee was discouered to haue beene his principall counseller.

Now, if there were but some few in the sect of the Iesuits, traded in this misterie of treason , it were happilie sufficient to punish the particuler offender : but the vow of treason is as familiar with them, as theyr other foure. That this is thus, we shall need no further proofe

then

then the tragedie of *Barriere*, wherein you shall finde such a packe, as besides the particulers mentioned in the Inditement, it cannot be auoyded but the whole bodie of theyr sect, was therein much engaged. I sawe of one side, a Iesuit in Lyons, verie deepe in the practise. I saw the murtherer, not well resolued in his attempt, come purposely to Paris to learne his lesson. But where dyd they bestow *Aubri*, Curat of Saint *Andrewes* of Arts, one of the most seditious of all their troope? Happilie they sent him to the Iacobins, in regard of the mischance which fell out vnder the other gouernment. Or to the Carmelites would they send him, or to the Capuchins rather? Nothing lesse, for hee was not assured, that in theyr Monasteries, murther, especially the murther of a King, would be approoued.

Whether then? Marrie he sendeth him to them, who were great Maisters in this Art: to the house of the Iesuits, where he knew the resort of the cursed crew to be. Iesuits, who knew by the modell of confessions framed, to make strange Geometricall proportions of sinnes & merrits. That to kill a king of Fraunce, there might bee a sinne *Ad quatuor*: But to kill him with an intention to inuest the king of Spayne in his kingdome, it were a merrit *Ad octo*. So as the merrit so much surpassing the sinne, the murther was not onely tollerable, but iust and lawfull.

This Curat, was he in this troope? No. For *Barriere* found one *Varade* Rector of their Colledge, who was of old acquainted with these courses. Hee found likewise one *Commolet*, who secretly subscribed to *Varades* counsell, and afterwards, by way of parable, in great iollitie before the people, maintained it in the pulpit. And yet were there but this sole example in this kinde, I should be verie iniurious to challenge theyr whole sect: but when wee see it is theyr continuall practise, what shall we say.

As

As for instance, theyr attempt against the deceased Prince of Orange, at Antwerpe: Afterwards, in the towne of Trierres, where he was murthered: At Doway likewise, against the Counte *Maurice* his sonne: At Venice, Lyons, Paris, against the Queene of England, in the yeere 1 5 8 4. Againe, against her in Spayne, in the yeere 1597. In Scotland, against the Chauncellor *Metellinus*. Againe in Fraunce, & that in Paris, against our King, in the yeere 1594, by one of theyr schollers, *Chastell*, who in open Court, before the face of the Iudges, was so shamelesse to maintaine, that in certaine cases, it was lawfull to kill his king.

Now if the rule of Logitians be true, that from manie particulers a generall may be concluded, I thinke I may truly affirme, that their axiom, whereuppon they ground theyr massacring of Kings, Princes, and great personages, is as naturall, and as familiar vnto them, as the rest of theyr vowes. It is most certaine, they consented to the death of the late king, and that *Guignard*, one of their order, since executed, made as I told you, a booke wherein hee maintaineth, that the death of such offenders is meritorious: and that the king now liuing, should be serued so to.

Hetherto you haue heard mee discourse vnder the name of the venerable *Pasquill* of Rome: notwithstanding the things themselues are serious and true. Among others, there is a booke made by the Iesuit *Montaignes*, Principall of the Seminarie of Reims vppon the same subiect, *Arnauld* hauing in his pleading obiected it vnto him, *Montaignes* made no hast to aunswere it, although in things more friuolous, his pen hath euer been too busie. For conclusion, all their actions, all theyr plots, are barbarous and bloodie. Which occasioned a pleasant Gentleman of Fraunce, hauing in a little Poem briefly discouered their deuilish practises, in his conclusion to say thus of them.

Gefum is a warre-like weapon, vfed by the French, as Liuie, Feftus, Nonius, and Sofipater teftifie.

A Gefis funt indita nomina vobis,
Quæ quia facrilegi, Reges torquetis in omnes,
Inde facrum nomen, facrum fumpfiftis
*   & omen.*

Of *Gefum*, not *Iefus*, are Iefuits hight,
A fatall toole the French-men vfed in fight;
Which fith by facriledge at Kings you throw,
From hence your holy name and fortunes flow.

Notwithftanding any thing can be fayde to the contrarie, yet this conclufion ftill muft ftande inuiolable. The particuler offender is to be punifhed, the Order not to be touched, as beeing farre from the thought of fuch impietie. Who is fo braine-ficke to belieue it?

I vvill not abufe your patience, by reckoning vp the tumults and feditions they haue caufed in our ftate. I knovve the great Maifters of our Common-wealth, refpect them as men very zealous ouer the good of their Country, I befeech them to confider, whether that I haue fayd be true or no: Other Rhetoricke I will not vfe to draw them to my opinion. And becaufe I haue begunne this difcourfe vvith the Decree graunted in Rome againft the *Humiliati*, I vvill vrge the fame againe, to make it plaine vnto you with what impudencie the Iefuits ward thys blow.

CHAP.

CHAP. 23.

The impudencie of the Iesuits, to saue themselues from
the processe of the Consistorie of Rome, gran-
ted out against the order of the
Humiliati.

RNauld first of all in the yeere 1594: *Marion* the Kings Attorney since, in 97. declare, that the Order of the *Humiliati,* was in our time suppressed for lesse cause then the Iesuits deserue to be . The one and the other, in few words. This is the position I main-taine . Let vs see how the Iesuits will ward this blow. *Montaignes* writing against *Arnauld* sayth . To strengthen your weake assertion, you bring the exam-ple of the Order of the *Humiliati,* which were suppres-sed in Italy : You are farre wide , the cases are nothing alike. The causes of their suppression are mentioned in the Bull, namely, that they were irregular, imperious, and incorrigible. They conspired against their Prelat, their Protector and reformer : and the executor of the con-spiracie being taken, discouered the rest, who likewise confessed the fact. You cannot affirme the same of the Iesuits, could you, it is like you would not spare them. I am of the Iesuits mind, they are nothing like indeed. For the question was there but of a Prelat, wherof there is plentie ; here of a King, of which sort we had no more, who is Gods true annoynted. The conspirator of the *Humiliati* was punished as soone as he was taken : the Iesuit was not, for after they had brought him backe from Paris (as to them nothing is impossible) they found meanes for his escape. In truth this defence of *Montaignes* is full of preuarication, and therefore *La Fon* denieth it. Concerning the *Humiliati,* (saith hee) it hath beene answered heretofore by *Francis Montaignes,*

Montaig.
ca. 59.

Lii 3.   that

that they were senfual & licentious, vnlearned, irregular, without difcipline, fcandalous, whofe houfes were Princes Pallaces, their chambers garnifhed like Kings Cabinites. Their Cloifters & Galleries, full of lafciuious pictures. Their Prouoft keeping a publique Curtifan, & all the reft, of the Prouofts diet. In the end, they were conuict of treafonable practife againft the perfon of their Prelate, the Cardinall. *Borrhomeo*, a man of verie holy life, labouring by all meanes to reclayme them. Their caufe was exactly heard, the crimes examined, debated, and iudged by our holy Father the Pope, to whom the cognifance of fuch caufes properly belongeth; who condemned them not to depart out of Italy, but to liue confined vnder other religious, as Penfioners depriued of their poffeffiōs, of whom fome liue at this day in Milan. And hereof all Millan is witneffe, togither with the Bull thereof likewife extant. My purpofe was to haue made a comparifon betwixt the *Humiliati* & the Iefuits, therby to fhow, that there is much more reafon to fuppreffe the Iefuits now, then there was caufe then to diffolue the *Humiliati*. But the impudencie of this laft Iefuit preffeth me to encounter him before I paffe any further, What a ftrange comment is this he maketh vpon his fellow *Montaignes*? Where findeth he either in *Montaignes*, or in the Bull, thofe crimes which he mentioneth? where findeth he this fame confpiracie in perfon againft the Cardinal *Borrhomæo*? where findeth he the Prouofts Curtifan? was there but one Prouoft in this order? Had not euery Priory one? Had this Prouoft no name? It is an vfe the Iefuit hath gotten, when hee begins to tell tales, he leaues not till he haue told twentie. But to bring him to the touch. Let vs fee the Bull of Pope *Pius Quintus*, it wil eafily appeare, whether his allegations be Alchimie, or no.

PIVS.

PIVS EPISCOPVS SERVVS
seruorum Dei, ad perpetuam
rei memoriam.

*QVE MAD MODVM sollicitus pater quem v-
nicé carū educauit filium,via salutis egressum reuocare cupiens,primùm hortatur,indulget, prætermit-
tit,increpat, alia præterea atque alia tentare non de-
sinit, dum quod expetit, modo aliquo consequatur, omnia denique expertus, cum nihil iam proficere intelligit desperata
prorsus salute, omnem de illo parentis animum eijcit, domo expellit, indignum existimans, qui parta hæreditate frua-
tur: sic Romanus Pontifex, quem diuina Maiestas patrem
& pastorem omnium Ecclesiæ suæ ordinum constituit,sicubi
quempiam sacrarū congregationū à regula,& vitæ præscripto
aberrare percipit,modo admonendo, modo corripiendo con-
nititur , eam vel primis institutis restituere, vel certè , quo
pacto emendatam in aliquo statu illis magis cohærenti continere: omnibus tandem ad illius sanitatem conquisitis, vbi sa-
lutaria remedia fastidire , & viam iniquitatis obstinatius
procedere, atq̓, adeo in prauum indurescere animaduertit,
vt potius confringi,quam corrigi possit , omni curatione re-
iecta, de ipsa remouenda decernit, ne inueterati atque indo-
miti mali vis, in alias insurgat, eis q̓, exitio sit futura. Quod
(vt nostrum hac in re studium flagrat)cum in plurimis, tum
maximè in fratrum Humiliatorum familia enixè curā-
uimus, nihil inexpertum relinquentes , quin illa multis
iampridem modis affecta, & si non protinus, certè accom-
modâ rerum moderatione directâ ad pristinum institutum
paulatim regrederetur . Etenim post quam dilectus filius noster Carolus , tituli sanctæ Praxedis , præsbiter Cardinalis
Borrhomæus, huius Ordinis protector, & Apostolicæ Sedis
delegatus, animaduertens dictos Fratres in luxū iampridem
effusos esse, multa de ratione cultus diuini, de obedientia &*
vita,

*vita, vt antea communi, deque modo recipiendorum & edu-
candorum religioforum prouidenter ftatuerat, intelligeremus
eos, illa cæteraq̃ omnia regulæ fuæ inftituta, omnino afperna-
ri, itemque omium voluptatum varietate confertam ducere,
re, ac præpofitos, & qui ex eo ordine rerum adminiftrationem
habebant, bonam magnamque fructuum partem veluti propriam in vanitatibus mundanis turpitudinibusque flagitiosè
profundere, innumeraque fcelera committere. Nos vias
omnes quæ illos in aperta huiufmodi pericula atque incommoda coniecerant, excindere conati, pleraque alia de ipforum vita, moribus & proprietate regulæ inimica, deque
modo & tempore gubernandæ cuiufque præpofituræ, nec non
ratione adminiftrationis bonorum, & difpenfatione prouentuum, aliifque muneribus & officijs, ad prolapfi huius fta-
tus, & difciplinæ regularis reparationem maximè confe-
rentibus, edidimus, fperantes illa profperos tandem fucceſ-
fus dicto Ordini allatura. Sed obfistente bonarum rerum
perturbatore plerique omnes (quoniam otio & defidi nimium
affueuerant) regulæ etfi inftituta & emendationem adhor-
rentes, etfi ftatuta & præcepta noftra communi confenfu palam acceptarunt, clam tamen quibus illa modis fupprimerent comminifcentes, nefarias proteftationes
in occulto fecerunt, neceffarios fuos, & alios potentiores lai-
cos ad inteftinas feditiones concitarunt, fuafores præterea &
impulfores ad intimos fummorum principum miniftros demi-
ferunt, qui magnis præmijs & pollicitationibus eos pellice-
rent, in animos prædictorum principum inducere, vt nos
ad illam refcifcendam inclinarent, multaque alia de ea tol-
lenda prauis artibus fuut conati, vt turpem illam & flagi-
tiofam vitam fuam retinerent, letalefque mundi volupta-
tes fequerentur, inter quos non defuit, qui altius præcipi-
tatus, etiam à Catholica fide ad Hæreticos, & impia il-
lorum dogmata declinarit. Quibus cognitis, omnium gra-
uiffimum impœnitentiæ peccatum in eis animaduertimus,
qui toties fruftra correpti, in eadem obftinatione perdura-
re contendunt, non fatis habentes talia attentare, nifi & ijs*

qui

qui inter ipsos qui posse putant, illis imprimis qui saluti e-
orum sedulò inuigilant, exitium machinentur, illius stimu-
lis concitati, qui scelestum Iudam in funestum auaritiæ
morbum iniecisse non contentus, etiam ad prodendum Dominum suum pecunia impulit. Huius nimirum Spiritus ne-
quissimi ductu, quòdam Hieronimus Lignana præpositus præposituræ sancti Christophori Vercellen: & plures alij consce-
lerati huius ordinis, in necem dicti Caroli Cardinalis propi-
tiatoris sui conspirantes, vt pecuniam ad tantum nefas expe-
ditam conficerent, de trucidando in primis dilecto filio Fabio
Simoneta fratre dicti ordinis, prouentuum præposituræ Bre-
dæ Mediolanensis depositario, apud quem nummos inue-
nire credebant, secretò conuenerunt, inde ad ecclesiam
dictæ præpositæ, in qua ipsum orantem, laqueo suffocare
decreuerant, profecti, sed inter se de modo aggrediendi, misericordia Saluatoris nostri, discordes, hoc conatu destite-
runt, mutatoque consilio, sacra aurea & argentea furati
sunt. Quibus clam venditis, seu pignori datis, prædictus
Hieronimus quendam Donatum Faziam comprofessorem
suum, Apostatam, pacta pecunia induxit vt ipsum Caro-
lum Cardinalem occideret, qui nacta loci & temporis op-
portunitate, in eum vesperi de more in sacello cum familia
precantem, vt transuerberaret, sclopum glandibus confer-
tum igne admoto exonerauit, sed telorum parte ad vestes
orantis exinanita, alijs vtrinque in proximo violentia ictus
defixit, innocentem Diuina pietas saluum & incolumem
conseruauit. Quare ambo, & quidam alij huius nefandi
criminis participes postea capitis pœnas debitas persoluerunt.
Quando igitur familiam prædictam, nulli studio ad Ecclesiæ
Dei vtilitatem proficienti incumbentem, nulli disciplinæ Ec-
clesiasticæ deditam, nullum omninò futuræ virtutis speci-
men ostendentem, tam detestandis facinoribus infectam, tam
atroci sacrilegio contaminatam, & præterea inpœnitentem
atque iccorrigibilem agnoscimus, omni de illa spe prorsus
exclusa, ipsam tandem tollere constituimus, tanquam ma-
lam arborem fructus pessimos proferentem. Habita itaque

K k k.   cum

cum fratribus nostris deliberatione matura , de illorum consilio , & nobis attributæ potestatis plenitudine , extinguimus & abolemus ordinem prædictorum fratrum Humiliatorum , officium præpositi generalis ac prouincialium , & quæcunque alia ministeria ordinis sic suppressi , nec non omnia,& quæcumque statuta, consuetudines & decreta eiusdem , etiam iuramento , confirmatione apostolica , vel alia quacumque firmitate munita , & pariter priuilegia , & indulta generalia , & specialia , quorum omnium tenores ac si ad verbum insererentur , præsentibus habemus pro expressis , quibuscumque illa concepta sint formulis , nec non irritantibus alijs decretis , & vinculis roborata : Priuamusque Generalem , ac cæteros omnes præpositos , & fratres omnes, præposituris, dignitatibus , administrationibus , officijs & beneficijs Ecclesiasticis cum cura & sine cura, nec non domibus, conuentibus & bonis immobilibus, mobilibus & se mouentibus in Italia & vbicumque gentium constitutis , sacra quacunque , & communi supellectile ,| ac ipsorum omnium vsu, vsufructa administratione ac possessione spirituali, & temporali, ac etiam iure& actione , siue per statuta nostra , alias quomodolibet pertinente . Ac tollimus eis omnimodam facultatem, vsum & auctoritatem, generalia & prouincialia , & alia capitula de cætero celebrandi . Volumus tamen vt omnes fratres qui nunc sunt, qui professionem regularem emiserunt, deinceps in domibus & locis , quos eis cum victu , & alijs necessarijs proximè assignandos curabimus, omnino redigantur , vt ibi vitam ducant regularem suæ professioni conformem sub cura & visitatione ordinariorum locorum aut alterius , vel aliorum quos eis duxerimus delegandos , vel iuxta iuris communis dispositionem transeant ad pares vel strictiores ordinis approbatos . Nouitij verò & alij quicunque non professi , detracto Religionis habitu ex professorum consortio , & domibus expellantur. Quibus professoribus nominatim præcipimus atque interdicimus ne post hæc quemquam expulsorum, & omnino

alium

alium etiam vouentem , ad professionem , vel habitum ad-
mittant, nec nouas domos, vel loca recipiant, vel acquirant,
quod si secus fiat , professio sit inanis , neminemque obliget,
neque in genere sic professum . Nouarum domorum seu lo-
corū receptiones vel acquisitiones viribus & effectu careant,
& contra facientes, excommunicationis sint sententia eo ipso
innodati, à qua nullus nisi in mortis articulo constitutus absolui
possit , absque Romani Pontificis licentia speciali . Cæte-
rum intendentes & cultui diuino , & Ecclesiæ ministris
quamprimum prospicere , omnes præposituras , dignitates,
personatus, administrationes, officia, cæteraque beneficia Ec-
clesiastica, cum cura & sine cura, quæ deinceps secularia sint,
per priuationem prædictam, apud sedem Apostolicam va-
cantia, nec non domos, conuentus , loca, supellectilem , bona,
fructus, res, actiones & iura supradicta , eorumque propri-
etatem & dominium nostræ & dictæ sedis liberæ dispositioni
specialiter & expresse reseruamus. Decernentes irritum &
inane quicquid secus per prædictos, aut quoscunq, alios sciēter
vel ignoranter contigerit attentari. Voluimus autē vt præsen-
tium exempla notarij publici manu , & personæ in dignitate
Ecclesiastica constitutæ, sigillo obsignata, eandem illam pror-
sus fidem in iudicio & extra illud , vbique locorum faciant,
quam ipsæmet præsentes facerent , si essent exhibita , vel
ostensæ. Nulli ergo. &c. Siquis autem. &c. Datum Romæ
apud sanctum Petrum *, Anno Incarnationis Dominicæ,*
1577. Idibus Februarij , Pontificatus nostri anno sexto.

Kkk 2.   POPE

POPE *PIVS*, SERVANT
of the Seruants of GOD, in
perpetuall memorie of this
matter.

AS a carefull Father ouer that fonne whom he hath brought vp verie tenderly , defirous to reclayme him, when he is ftept out of the way of his faluati-on, firft exhorts him, fauours him , pardons him, rebukes him, moreouer, ceafeth not to trie one thing af-ter another, vntil he attayne vnto that which he defired, & hauing at laft made proofe of all, whē he fees nothing will do him good, vtterly defpayring of his recouerie, caftes off the affection of a Father , and thruftes him out of doores, iudging him vnwoorthie to bee his heire : So the Bifhoppe of Rome, whom the Diuine Maieftie hath appoynted to bee a Father and Paftor of all the Religious orders in his Church, if he per-ceiue any of thefe holy Companies fwarue from the rule and prefcription of life they haue vndertaken, endeauours fometime by admonition, fometime by correction, to reftore their ouncient inftitution, or at leaft, by fome kinde of amendment, bring them in bet-ter order : After he hath fought euerie thing that may make for their good, when hee feeth them loath all wholefome remedies, and ftubbornely goe on ftill in the way of wickedneffe, and perceiueth them to grow worfe and worfe, fo that they may fooner bee broken then bended , careleffe of all cure, hee determineth to remooue them , leaft the power of an inueterate and vntamed euill, ouer-runne iothers, and deftroy them. VVhich thing (becaufe wee are earneft in this poynt)

poynt) both in many others, and especially in the companie of the *Humiliati*, wee haue beene very carefull of, leauing nothing vnattempted, but finding many flawes in them, if not altogether, yet in some conuenient measure and moderation, they might by little and little, be fashioned to their first institution. For, after that our beloued Sonne *(Charles*, of the title *sancta Praxedis*, Priest, Cardinall *Borrhomæus*, Protector of this Order, and Delegat of the Apostolique Sea, of late perceiuing the sayde Friers to breake out into Riot, had prouidently set downe many things, concerning the manner of Gods worship, obedience, & common life, and of the manner of receiuing and education of Religious persons. We vnderstood, that they vtterly despised both those, and all other rules of their owne Order, and liued very voluptuously, & that theyr Gouernours, together with such as had any offices in the administration of their affaires, wickedly wasted a great part of the reuenewes (as if they had beene their owne) in worldlie vanities and filrhines, and committed an innumerable sort of sinnes.

VVee endeuouring to cut off all those meanes that did cast them into so apparant dangers and inconueniences, tooke order for many things hurtfull to their life and manners, and proprietie of theyr rule and Order, and for the manner and time of gouernment in euerie ones commaundement, and also for the menaging their goods, & disposing of their reuenewes: and other places and offices, very profitable to repaire the ruines of this decayed state and regular discipline, hoping that these things would in time to come, bring good successe to the sayd Order. But the enemie of all good things resisting, almost all of them (because they had beene too much inured to ease & idlenes) detesting to liue in order and to be amended, howsoeuer by common consent they outwardly accepted our lawes and precepts,

yet vnderhand they deuised all the wayes they could to
suppresse them. They held wicked conspiracies secret-
lie, they stird vp theyr kindred and others of the Laitie
that were mightie, to sedition; they sent theyr Brokers
and Agents, to the most intrinsecall seruaunts of mightie Princes, to draw them by great rewards and promises, to worke vs by the foresayd Princes meanes, to vn-
doe that wee had done, and many others did they by e-
uill practises attempt to this purpose, that they might
continue theyr filthie and wicked course of life, & follow the deadly pleasures of this world, among whom
was one that fell more high & headlong from the Catholique Fayth to Hereticks, and declined to theyr impious opinions.

Vnderstanding of these things, we found them guiltie of Impenitencie, the greatest sinne of all, who beeing
so often reproued, straue to continue in the same obsti-
nacie, not thinking it enough to haue attempted these
things, vnlesse they contriued the destruction of such
as were of authoritie among them, and chiefely did
watch diligently ouer theyr owne soules, prouoked
heereunto by him, who not contenting himselfe vvith
plunging of *Iudas* into the grieuous sinne of couetousnes, procured him also by mony to betray his Maister.
For by the inticement of of this wicked spirit, *Hierom
Lignana*, once President of the house of Saint *Christopher* at Verselles, and many other confederats of thys
order, cospiring the death of *Charles* the Cardinal theyr
Protector, that they might haue mony, to compasse this
hainous act, they held a conuenticle, to murder first our
beloued sonne *Fabius Simoneta*, a brother of the sayd
Order, Treasurer of the reuenewes of *Breda* at Millan,
thinking to furnish themselues, with such coyne as was
in his keeping: thence determined they to goe to the
Church of the sayd house, to strangle him there, as hee
was at his prayers, but (by Gods mercie) disagreeing a-
mong

mong themselues, about the manner of the assault, they
desisted from that, and changing their minds, they stole
away the sacred gylt vessels of the Church. Which beeing secretly sold, or pawnd, the said *Hierom* hyred one
Donatus Fazia, one of his brotherhoode, an Apostata,
to murder *Charles* the Cardinall, and hee hauing spyed
his time & place, finding him at his prayers (as his manner was) with his familie in a Chappell in the euening,
shot of a pistoll at him to strike him through, but disap-
pointed of his purpose, some of the bullets were defea-
ted by his garments while he prayed, others, by the violence of the blow, stucke in the next on eyther side of
him: the innocent by Gods grace was preserued : wherfore both of them, with others that were pertakers of
this fact, were afterward beheaded.

Thus when we saw this company growne vnprofitable in the Church of God, liue in no order, shewe no
signe of amendement, infected with so grieuous crimes,
defiled with so cruell sacriledge, and furthermore im-
penitent and incorrigible, beeing out of all hope of their
recouerie, we haue at last determined to roote them out,
like an euill tree that carries very badde fruit. Hauing
therefore thoroughly deliberated with our Brethren, by
theyr aduise, and by the absolute authoritie committed
to vs, we vtterly extinguish and abolish the whole Order of the said Friers *Humiliats*, the place of theyr Generall, and Prouincials, and all other offices of theyr Order thus suppressed, and also all, and all manner of Statuts, customs, and decrees of the same; howsoeuer they
haue beene established by any oath, or confirmation A-
postolicall, or any other warrant, and also all priuiledges and graunts, both generall & speciall; the tenors of
all which, as if they were word for word heere inserted,
in these presents we hold them for expressed, whatsoeuer stile or forme they beare, confirmd with other decrees and clauses that may moue vs : And wee depriue

the

the Generall, and all other their Gouernours, and brethren, of commaundements, dignities, administrations,
offices, and ecclesiasticall benefices, with cure, & without cure, and also of their houses, Couents, & goods im-
moouable, mouable, and selfe-moouing, being in Italy
or any other Nation, of all holy things, and common
houshold stuffe, of the vse of all and vsufructuall administration & possession spirituall and temporall, of right
and action also, whether by our statuts, or any other
way they appertaine vnto them. And we take frō them
all power and authoritie, to hold from hence-foorth,
any Generall, Prouinciall, or other Chapters. Yet wee
ordaine, that all the Bretheren now remaining, which
haue made their regular profession, be from henceforth
seated in such houses and places, as wee shall appoynt,
with things necessary for their maintenaunce: that there
they may liue according to theyr rule & profession, vnder the Cure and visitation of the Ordinaries of those
places, or of some others, whō we shall appoynt for that
purpose; or else, that according to the direction of cōmon law, they may goe to theyr equalls, or to some of
straighter order alreadie allowed.

As for the Nouices & others whatsoeuer not yet professed, their habit puld ouer theyr eares, let them be expelled the house and company of the professed. Which
professed, we precisely commaund, & forbid, that from
hence-forth they neuer admit vnto theyr profession or
habite, any of them that are expelled, or any other that
would be deuoted to it : Neither shall they receiue or
purchase anie newe houses or places, if they doe, the
profession shall be voyd, and shall binde no man, not so
much as in generall so professed. All erections of such
like new houses, shall be of no force, and they that shall
doe contrarie, shall thereby incurre the sentence of excommunication : from which none, vnlesse it be vpon
the poynt of death, shall be absolued, without the speciall

ciall licence of the Bishop of Rome.

Furthermore, purposing to prouide with all speede for the seruice of God, and the Ministers of his church, we reserue by the foresaid depriuation, all commaundements, dignities, administrations, offices, and other Ecclesiasticall benefices, with cure & without cure, which be hereafter secular, to the holy Sea, in their vacancie. And also the houses, Couents, places, houshold stuffe, goods, fruits, substances, actions, and foresaid rights, & their proprietie and dominion, specially and expresly to the free dispositon of our said Sea. Decreeing that to be voyd and of none effest, whatsoeuer shall happen to be wittingly or vnwittingly attempted to the contrarie, by the foresaid Friers or any other.

And we will, that the transcript of these presents, taken vnder the hand of a publique Notarie, and sealed by the seale of an Ecclesiasticall person of dignitie, shall be as autenticall, in, or out of iudgment, wheresoeuer they be drawne, as if these presents were exhibited and shewen. Therefore to none. &c. But if any &c. Giuen at Rome in Saint *Peters* Pallace, in the yeere of the incarnation of our Lord, 1 5 7 7, in the Ides of Februarie, the sixt yeere of our Pontificalitie.

This is the Bull at large, the which I tooke out of *Matthæus Toscanus*, in his booke intituled, *Summa constitutionum, & rerum in Ecclesia Romana gestarum à Gregorio nono vsque ad Sixtum quintum*. This fellow besides is a great friend of the Iesuits. But what gather you out of this Bull? that the *Humiliati* were licentious, but no mention of the particulers deuised by *La Fon*. Besides, in expresse termes, that by their plots and practises, they stirred vp troubles and seditions among Princes, *In occulto*. The words are, *necessarios suos & alios potentiores, ad intestinas seditiones concitarunt*. And I pray you, are not our reuerend Iesuits heerein theyr crafts Maisters?

Fur-

Further, you finde not in this Bull, that the Order of the *Humiliati* were at any time assembled to lay violent hands vpon the Cardinall *Borrhomæo*, theyr Reformer, as the Iesuits suggest. If it had beene a rout or an assemblie in person, it could not haue beene auoyded, but their Generall, the Prouincialls of their Order, and the Priors of their Monasteries, must haue beene of the conspiracie, or at the least some part of them. A clause which would not haue beene forgotten in the Decree that Pope *Pius* the fift, & the holy Consistorie of Rome sent out, hauing so great intention finallie to suppresse them.

And this is the reason the Iesuits haue layed this condemnation most falsely vppon all the Order, who had in Chapter (as they say) conspired against *Borrhomeo*. Let vs acknowledge a truth like the children of Christ, and not like the disciples of *Ignacius*. This Order vvas growne very infamous, by reason of their incontinency and licentious life, the which the good Cardinall *Borrhomæo* would haue helpt if it had beene possible. This was (I must confesse) a fault, and that verie foule and scandalous, & yet for this, it is like they should not haue beene suppressed.

It is a vice whereunto naturally wee are prone. Insomuch that hee who would suppresse all houses of Religion where this vice aboundeth, especially those which are seated in places farre from resort, wee may say with *Tacitus, Vt antea vitijs ita tum demũ legibus laboraremus.* And there might be peraduenture more scandale in suppressing, then in winking at theyr vices.

How then? What caused the suppression? It vvas G O D S will, that vnexpectedly, *Lignana*, Pryor of Versellis, and some others, angry with this new reformation, conspired against *Borrhomæo*, as it is expressed in the Bull. And this ryot was the cause of the suppression: and this is the cause the Bull dooth recount theyr disorders

diforders in generall, but fpecially theyr attempt again{t *Borrhomæo*. The which is fet downe verie particularlie, and not the incontinencies which *La Fon* reciteth.

VVhat is there in this ftorie, but will fit the Iefuits as well as if it were made for them? They are notorious throughout the world, for the troubles raifed by them in Fraunce. And as manifeft it is, that they practifed and bargained with a ftranger, to bring in a newe King into this kingdome. The deteftable fact of *Barriere*. The howlings of *Commolet* to the people, to kill the King euen in the time of the truce. The people vvith one mouth, from the youngeft to the moft aged, cried vengeance on them, fo foone as the King reentred Paris. The caufe was pleaded in the name of the Vniuerfitie, and as it falleth out oftentimes, that in matter of iudgement, where the caufe is of confequence, while we feare to be negligent, wee growe ouer-curious: fo heere the caufe was referred to counfaill. GOD would fo haue it, that *Chaftell*, a difciple of the Iefuits, poyfoned vvith theyr damnable pofitions, wounded the King with a knife, and beeing taken, hee maintained in the open face of iuftice, that hee might doe it lawfully.

The haynoufnes of thys fact, aggrauated with other circumftances, gaue occafion of the pronouncing the proceffe againft the whole Order. Nowe I pray you teil mee, if the fame holie Ghoft, which wrought in the fuppreffion of the *Humiliati*, had not a ftroke likewife in driuing the Iefuits out of Paris? They are the fame things, the fame proceedings, vnder feuerall names. Theyr difference is in thefe two poynts: The one, that the *Humiliati*, in being too fubiect to their pleafure, finned, yet committed fuch a finne as our corrupt nature teacheth vs: but the Iefuits, beeing the principall Authours of the troubles wherein two hundred thoufand loft theyr liues, haue finned againft GOD, & againft nature. For nature abhorres nothing more then death,

L ll 2. which

which is so cheape among the Iesuits, to the losse of others. The other difference is, that the attempt of *Ligna-na*, was but against a Cardinall, whō I acknowledge willingly to be one of the holiest men our age yeeldeth: A Cardinall, whom the Colledge would be loth to spare, yet notwithstanding hee liues, and liueth in as great reputation as euer hee did. Whereas the attempt of *Cha-stell*, endangered a King, sole in his kingdome, & such a king, as the world must yeeld to bee as valiant, wise, and curteous, as anie before him; and by whose death, if the treason had sorted to effect, wee were to expect nothing but horrour and confusion, our olde inhabitants. And yet they must be cherrished in some part of the kingdome. But because some not remembring, or not obseruing things past, others not foreseeing, lesse laboring to preuent dangers to come, suffer themselues to be abused by them; accounting them the Champions and protectors of the Catholick faith, I wil make it manifest vnto you, that their sect is as dangerous as *Martin Luthers*, & that there is nothing the Pope hath more to feare, as preiudiciall to his authority and greatnes, then their Generall, what showes and protestations soeuer they make to the contrary notwithstanding.

CHAP. 24.

¶ That the Sect of the Iesuits, is no lesse dangerous to our Church then the Lutherans.

His position may seeme at the first sight Paradoxicall, but it is true. The distribution of the hierarchicall Order of our Church, hath a proportion and correspondēcy with the humane body, wherin the head cōmandeth ouer the other members, amongst the which, there are certaine noble parts, as the hart, the liuer, & the lungs, without which the bodie cannot consist:

fift : So as hee who would take from the head to adde
to the noble parts, or diminifh them to giue vnto the
head, difordering the proportion and correfpondency
which fhould bee betwixt the members, hee fhould
confound & deftroy the bodie: So is it in our hierarchy,
the head of the Church, is our holy father, the Pope, the
noble parts vnder him, are the Archbifhops Bifhoppes,
Cardinals, Priors, & Abbots : I will adde Princes, Lords,
& Vniuerfities; as for the reft of the people, they repre-
fent the other members of the body. *Martin Luther* was
the firft who durft traduce this head, bringing in a form
of *Ariftocratie* into our Church, making all the Bifhops
in their feueral diocefes, equall to the Sea Apoftolique.

There fucceeded him, *Ignactius Loyhola*, fome yeeres
after, who by a contrarie courfe, defended the authoritie of the holy Sea, but after fuch a fafhion, as hee no
leffe endamaged our Church then theirs. For pretending more zeale to the Sea, and our holy Father, then
the reft, and ftill intituling him to more predominant
and new authoritie ouer the Ordinaries, hee and his
fucceffiuely obtaynd from diuers Popes, fo many Priuiledges, Indulgences, and Graunts, in difaduantage of
the Prelats, Monafteries, and Vniuerfities, that fuffering
them to liue in the midft of vs, you disfigure & ftain the
face of the Catholique and Vniuerfall Church. Re-
meber what the Iefuit faid to you this other day, & you
will find my words true. The difference betwixt *Luther*
and *Ignace*, is, that hee troubled our Church, fighting
againft the head : And this, warring againft the noble
parts. All extremitie is a vice, vertue is an vmpiere betwixt both. For mine owne part, I beleeue that the true
Catholique Apoftolick Roman faith, is that, which hath
bin in vfe euer fince the paffion of our Sauiour and Redeemer Iefus Chrift, and that which hath been approoued be all our auncient Doctors of the Church, of
whom the meaneft, had more learning and true Chri-

ſtian feeling in his heart, then *Luther* and all his adherents, then *Ignace* with all his complices. It is the religion
wherein all good and faithfull Chriſtians ought to liue
and die.

I will adde further, that I had rather erre with them,
then runne the Wild-Goofe chafe, endaungering my
foule with thefe night-growne muſhrumps. But wee
will be moderate in a ſubieĉt of ſuch a nature. I will
not ſay then that I had rather, but that I ſhould leſſe
feare to erre. For to ſay that Ieſuits are the onely clubs
to beat downe the blowes of *Caluin* and *Luther*, I am
ſo farre from beleeuing it, as I thinke it is a ſpecial meàne
to confirme them in their erronious opinions. I remember a friend of mine being at a Sermon, rather for
nouelty then deuotion, a Miniſter cryed out to his
diſciples; My brethren, ſaith hee, God hath beheld vs
with a mercifull eye: Although *Martin Luther* had
beene ſufficient to giue the Pope battell: yet ſo it is, that
Ignacius Loyhola is come beſides to ayde vs. For hee
cunningly, vnder colour of ſupport, ſupplanteth him.
What readier meane to ouerthrow a State, then faĉtion
and inteſtine quarrels. And I pray you what other milke
giue theſe Ieſuits in the Church of Rome? Then ſith
this Sect is his laſt refuge, & his principal ſupport, be of
good cheere the day is ours. For without queſtion the
head muſt be verie daungerouſly ſick, if for cure therof,
fauouring this new Sect, they vtterly ouerthrow the noble parts. But what ſhould be the cauſe of this diſorder?
An imaginarie vow of Miſſion, in fauoure whereof
the Pope protecteth their quarrell. For this therefore
let vs prayſe God and ſay as *Demea* ſaid to his brother
Mitio in the Poet, *Conſumat, perdat, pereat, nihil ad me
attinet*.

Theſe ſixe or ſeuen Latine wordes vttered a-
gainſt the holy Sea are blaſphemous. But this is the
vnbridled licence of theſe new Preachers, who when
they

they are tranſported with their prepoſterous zeale, may
ſay any thing. This diſſenſion concerned not the Miniſter : it had beene his part to touch the conſcience of
euerie good Catholique, who deſireth to liue and die
in the boſome of the Catholique Apoſtolique and Romane Church : yet it ſhould be our care, that theſe my
Maiſters the Miniſters inſult not ouer vs, & that their tri-
umphs be not grounded on the Ieſuits. Conſider whether they haue cauſe to ſay thus or no, for among
other particulars of the cenſure of our Diuines, in the
yeere 1 5 5 4. this was, one, that the Ieſuits would become Seminaries of Schiſme, and diuiſion in our
Chriſtian Church, & that they were rather brought in,
for the ruine and deſolation of it then for the edification
thereof. Wherfore, if I may be thought to erre in ſaying
that the Sect of the Ieſuits is no leſſe preiudiciall to the
Church then that of the Lutherans, I doe it not
without iudgement, hauing for my warrant heerein,
the cenſure of that venerable facultie of Diuines in
Paris.

CHAP. 25.

¶ Of the notorious enterprize or vſurpation, of the Ge-
nerall of the Ieſuits ouer the holy Sea, and that there
is no new Sect which in time may bee more pre-
iudiciall to it then this.

Hen the venerable facultie of the Diuines of Paris, cenſured the Sect of
the Ieſuites, in the yeere 1 5 5 4. they
only conſidered of the inferiour orders
aſwell ſpirituall as temporall. But for
matter which concerned the holy Sea,
they went not ſo farre, neither were they acquainted with their Bulls and conſtitutions. But now that
it hath pleaſed God of his grace to enlighten vs, I will
                                                    nœ

not doubt to say, that the Gouernour of the Iesuits, represents the person of *Lucifer*, who would equall himselfe to his Creator. So this fellow being a creature of
the Popes, doth not onely vsurpe equall authoritie ouer
his subiects, but farre greater then the Pope doth exercise ouer the Vniuersall Church. They giue out in
Rome, that they absolutely obey the Pope, not onely in
the matter of Mission, but in all other his commaundements. And vnder this plausible pretence, they haue obtayned, and daily do obtayne verie many extraordinarie priuiledges, in preiudice, and (if I might presume
to say so much) in disgrace of Archbishops, Bishops,
Orders of Religion, Vniuersities, and the whole
Catholique Church. Notwithstanding, the truth is, that
they hauing two Maisters to serue, doe without comparison, more homage to their Generall, then to the
holy Sea.

Rib.lib.1.
Chap.3.

Ignatius Loyhola, a Spaniard, verie honourably dis-
cended, chaunging his condition, chaunged not his
nature. *Ribadinere* reporteth, that when hee was to
leaue his Fathers house, pretending to goe to visite the
Duke of Naiare, *Martin Garsia*, his eldest brother
iealous of his intention, came to him priuately to his
chamber, and said thus vnto him; Brother, all things are
great in you: Wit, Iudgement, Courage, Nobilitie, Fauour of Princes, the peoples loue, Wwisedome, Experience in warre: besides, youth and an able bodie. All
these promise much of you, & are exceeding full of expectation. How then, wil you now frustrate on a sodaine
all these our fayre hopes? will you defeat our house of
those garlands, whereof we in a sort assured our selues
if you would but maintayne the course you haue begunne? Although in yeeres I am much your auncient, yet am I after you in authoritie. Beware then,
that these high hopes, which sometime we conceiued
of you, prooue not abortiue, ending in dishonour.

Whereunto

Whereunto *Ignace* shortly aunswered, that he was not vnmindfull of himselfe and his auncestors, from whom he would not degenerat in the least degree, nor obscure their memorie. And beleeue mee, he kept his promise. For after this vnexpected chaunge of life, he neuer entertained any pettie ambitions, howsoeuer he altered his habit, or any pilgrimage he made to Ierusalem notwithstanding. Cloath an Ape in Tissue, the beast may happily be more proud, but neuer the lesse deformed.

Naturam expellas furca tamen vsque recurret .
Cœlum, non animum mutant, qui trans mare currunt.

Neyther the meanesse of his habit, nor his pilgrimage, could abate those spirits which were borne with him. Whē he & his six first cōpanions, made their first vow at *Mont Marter*, he made himselfe their head without any election of their part. The which you shal finde in *Maffeus*, who witnesseth, that when by the aduise of the Phisitions, he was to chaunge the ayre for the recouerie of his health after a long sicknes, taking his iourny toward Spayne, he left Vicegerent ouer his companions, *Peter Faure*, in whom he reposed a speciall trust . *Cæterum (saith Maffee) nequid é suo discessu res. parisiensis caperet detrimenti, primùm commilitones ad fidē & perseuerantiam paucis adhortatus, Petrum Fabrum & annis & vocatione antiquissimum, illis præposuit, cui interim obtemperarent.* He had then cast off all authoritie and preheminence ouer them , as it is manifest by that which followeth . For it was hee whom they promised to meete at Venice at a certaine day prefixt : It was hee which afterwards assembled them at Vincintia, to deliberate whether they should returne to Rome, or no , there to erect their new Sect : it was he which vndertooke the charge as principall . This was the cause that hee, assuring himselfe, that when they should proceed to elec-

Maff.lib.2.
cap.1.

M m m.   lection

lection, would make choise of him for Generall of their Order, prouided before hand, that this office should not be annuall, but for life and all : with all, that the Generall should haue absolute authority ouer his subiects. *Ergo sine controuersia deligendum videri, cui omnes in terris, tanquam Christo parerent, cuius in verba iurarent, denique cuius sibi nutum ac voluntatem instar diuini cuiusdam oraculi ducerent. His ita constitutis deinceps quæsitum de huius ipsius potestate, vtrum certo dierum spatio definitam, an vero perpetuam esse oporteret : perpetuam esse placuit omnibus.* After the Order was established in Rome, and *Ignatius* chosen Generall, and that vpon termes of an absolute Gouernour : He who from his youth had beene in armes, not in Arts, began to bring in amongst them a tyrannous gouernement, willing that all his Decrees, and the Decrees of his successors, should bee held iust and inuiolable. For although they made shew to vowe like obedience to the holy Sea, & vnder this protestation they were authorized in Rome, yet is it manifest, that they do yeeld more obedience to their Generall, then to the Pope.

I say not onely to their Generall, but to all their other Superiors, as their Prouincials and Rectors, and especially, in their vow of Mission, their Generall hath more commaund ouer them then the Pope : euen all, as I haue more particularly discoursed, speaking aswell of the vow of Mission, as of the blinded or hoodwinckt obedience. Therfore I conclude, & concluding shal not be withstood by any man, which is not verie passionatly partiall, that the commaund which the Pope and the Generall haue ouer the Iesuits, is in all points soueraigne and absolute ; but without comparison, more precise in the things which concerne the General. Which maketh mee beleeue, that if euer the holy Sea receiued a breach, there is no Sect liker to make it, then this of the Iesuit, their General residing in Rome. We exclaime againsts
the

Maff. lib. 2.
chap. 9.

the Lutherans, and not without cause, inasmuch as they were the first in our age that troubled the peace of the Church. Notwithstanding, I hold not the of more dangerous consequence then the Iesuits. Some childish or young scholler, will not sticke to say perhaps, that in maintayning this position, I am an heretique. All those whom we terme in Fraunce of the pretended Religion, of the Reformed, or of the new, haue no head ouer them: If they should admit any, they should contradict themselues, denying the Popes primacie, and yet receiuing another. They liue in an Oligarchy, or an Aristocracy. Insomuch as he, who for his knowledge or antiquity, hath any preheminence ouer the other Ministers, it is an inherent authoritie for time of life, not transmissible from him to his Successors. Besides, they want outward ceremonies, without the which, Religion worketh not easily in the hearts of simple people. He among them is held a great minister, who neuer read ouer but *Caluins* Institutions, or *Peter Martyrs* Commonplaces, and some other moderne writers. So as I doubt not, but this Sect in time will fall of it selfe, as I thinke it had beene downe ere this time, if the vnhappie ambition of the Iesuits, had not so factiously withstood the wise designes of our deceased King. I know this is not a stile greatly to content the Ministers, neyther doe I affect their fauour: all my ambition is, to see our Catholique Apostolique Roman Church in that dignitie, and discipline, wherein it flourished in the dayes of our fore-fathers. For conclusion, our Kings being Catholiques as they must be, if they will raigne, I feare not the Hugonote in Fraunce, who whether he will or no, shall be brought in vnder obedience well ynough.

But I feare the Iesuit aboue all, not onely in Fraunce, but in Rome, becaufe their pollicy tendeth to the establishment of a tyranny ouer all, which they will recouer by little and little, if they be not preuented. They haue a Generall which is not annuall, or for terme, as those of the Friers : But perpetuall, as the Popes. Some one will say, that the like is in the Chartre house, I agree, but they are recluse & lead a solitary life in their Cloysters, seque-stred from trafficke and entercourse with the world. Some will reply, that there are diuers heads of Orders, as of *Clugni*, *Premonstre*, and *Grammond*, which are for terme of life, I graunt it, but yet they haue Statutes and Decrees inuiolable within which they are limited and confined, so that they can do nothing preiudiciall to the rest of the Religious.

It is not so with the Iesuits, for they haue nothing so certaine as the vncertaintie of their constitutions. The which they can change in their Chapters without crauing ayde of the holy Sea : yea, and the Gene-rall himselfe, in ordinarie affayres of his owne absolute authoritie, may doe his pleasure. Euerie man know-eth, that a perpetuall Magistrate is more absolute then a temporary. In the first general congregation which was held by them, in the yeere 1558. Pope *Paule* the fourth, sent to them purposely the Cardinall *Pacochus*, to ad-uertise them his pleasure was, that their Generall should be chosen for certain yeers, foreseeing the extraordinary greatnes which he might grow vnto by this perpetuall regency : Notwithstanding, ouercome with their im-portunities, he was in a sort content, yet sent he the Car-dinal *Taruense*, to signifie, that he held it more côuenient to be temporarie, then perpetuall.

This Generall, beeing thus perpetuall, yet are all the dignities of his Order temporary. Vnder him are the Prouincialls, according to the deuision of Prouinces: vnder them are the Rectors, who haue particuler au-thoritie ouer theyr houses and Colledges; and conse-quently ouer theyr Fathers, & ouer the Coaiutors, spi-rituall and temporall; & ouer the schollers elected: For the heads of Colledges, they are principally appointed to be Superintendents of the ſtranger ſchollers. Theſe offices hold vſually for three yeeres together, yet may they be cõtinued or abridged at the pleaſure of the Generall: he diſpoſeth of the temporalties abſolutly, without any conſent, and exerciſeth a world of prerogatiues, which are not permitted to our Biſhops. I will deliuer you euery particuler in his place.

The Prouincialls are their Biſhops, the Rectors are their Curats: as we likewiſe call in Languedoc, Rectors, thoſe which in all other parts of Fraunce are called Curats. None of theſe I haue named are perpetuall, but at the will of their Generall. No other dignitie of Chriſtendome, is comparable with that of our holy Father, and yet his compared with the Generalls, is leſſe. For after his holineſſe hath confirmd a Biſhoprick, or any other promotion, his hands are bound, he cannot diſplace them of his owne abſolute authoritie; they are not Tenants at will, as the Prouincials & Rectors Ieſuits. Our holy Father, by the ancient Cannons and conſtitutions, cannot giue power to Biſhops and Abbots, to alienate their temporalties, without ſpeciall cogniſance of the cauſe. There is required an eſpeciall aſſemblie to giue aduiſe, and after conſent obtained, one preſenteth himſelfe to the Superior, who appointeth a Proctor for the Church, to ſee if ſuch alienation be neceſſarie.

Theyr Generall may ſell, morgage, allienate, and diſſipate the goods of the Church, and is not accountable when he hath doone. And that which is a tyrannie, the like whereof was neuer heard, hauing deputed ſuch as ſhall pleaſe him to make his ſales, he may fruſtrate and diſanull any act of theirs, although they haue not exceeded the limits of their commiſſion. Our holy Father aſſumeth no ſuch authoritie, to permit ſuch as haue vowed Chaſtitie, Pouertie, or Obedience, to recouer theyr poſſeſſions, much leſſe to marry, except Kings & ſouerainge Princes, and that in caſes of very vrgent neceſſitie.

ceſſitie. The cleane contrarie is practized by the Ieſuits in their firſt vow, which they call the ſimple vow: is not this, to attribute more to theyr Generall, then our holie Father will aſſume?

I told you yeſterday, that in matter of Miſſions, the Generall may ſend all vnder him, whether hee will, not onely of the laſt vowe, but of the firſt and the ſecond. This you may finde in the ninth part of their Conſtitutions, chap. 3. Artic. 9. Heere I deſire to knowe from whence hee deriueth this power, for from the holy Sea he hath it not: ſearch all the Bulls of their Order. Well I know, that in that of 49, of *Paul* the third, it is lawfull for the Generall to ſend as well as the Pope, into diuers countries for the propagation of our fayth. But this clauſe is to be vnderſtood of Fathers, in the laſt ſolemne vow: for the miſſion of the holy Sea extendeth onely to them. Then this muſt proceede from ſome particular dutie the other Ieſuits owe vnto theyr Generall. But where is that? For neither in their ſimple vow, nor in theyr firſt ſolemne vow, they binde themſelues, eyther to the Pope or their Generall to the vow of Miſſion, but onely to the three ſubſtantiall vowes of other religious Orders. Where then is this bond, where lieth this dutie hid? I belieue, in the tyrannie of their Generall, and in their blinded obedience. And that which is ſtrange, this ſame blinded obedience, is by all them promiſed and ſworne vnto the Pope, yet doth hee not exerciſe it, but vppon the Fathers of the great and the laſt vow onely. Whence ſpringeth this diuerſitie? the reaſon is at hand. In a vvorde, our holy Father hath not ſo much power ouer the Ieſuits, as their Generall, who is theyr ſoueraine Pope, and in their irregular gouernment, they acknowledge ours but for faſhion ſake.

Let vs goe a little further, & looke a little into their other behauiours. They ſay they are ſubiect to the ordinances of the holy Sea, I rather think they impoſe lawes

vpon

vpon it. That so it is, before the Bull of the yeere 1540, first foundation of their Order, they exercised of theyr owne authority their assemblies, in the Charter house of Paris, they opened since theyr shops to all comers. Before the permission they obtained in the yeere 1561, they exercised fortie and foure yeeres their simple vow, which is contrarie to all the constitutions of the church, before *Gregory* the 13. had giuen a safe conduit. And as they wrought our Popes still to second theyr greatnes, so this same remissnes & relenting of the holy Sea, hath giuen meanes to theyr Generall, to equall himselfe vnto him.

Let vs consider our holy Father the Pope ordained of G O D, such as he is when hee is chosen by the Colledge. The Cardinalls bow themselues before him, honour him, and kisse his handes. I thinke this honour is proper to his holines. The Generall of the Iesuits hath the selfe same kneeling, and hand-kissing when hee is chosen. And yet I will not wrong him, for I must confesse, that in some Monasteries, this likewise is obserued, specially in publique ceremonies: but to take this homage of others, it is inexcusable. Part. 8. Constit. cap. 6. art. 6.

I will goe no further for an example then Father *Claudius Aquauiua* their present Generall. After that he was chosen in the yeere 1581, and after all his schollers had done their homage, and he had taken his chamber, *Inde pater* saith the first of their Letters annuall for that yeere, *cubiculum ascendens, eo die salutanti turbæ omnis generis hominum, exosculandas manus præbuit.* Which is to say; After that the Father had taken his Chamber, hee offered his handes to kisse to all manner of persons which came to salute him. What newe idolatrie is this? Is not this to erect a newe Pope in Rome, triumphant ouer the true & auncient?

We haue in our Church but one head, whom we acknowledge to be aboue all other Prelats, the Vicar of God.

God. The Generall of the Iesuits arrogats the same title. In al the vowes which the Iesuits make before him, they terme him Gods Lieuetenant : betwixt Lieuetenant & Vicar, the difference is so nice, that I see none. And in one place of their Constitutions, the glosse made by a Iesuit, termeth him expresly Gods Vicar. Nay they are so shamelesse, that they are not content their Generall should assume this state, but forsooth theyr Superiours may exact likewise of their inferiours. *Omnibus itidem commendatum sit vt multum reuerentiæ, & præcipuè in interiore hominis, suis superioribus exhibeant, & Iesum Christum in eisdem considerent & reuereantur.* That it is likewise to all in generall enioyned, to giue great reuerence inwardly in their harts to their Superiours, and that in them, they reuerence and acknowledge Iesus Christ.

The Iesuit *Montaignes*, speaking of the reuerence they vow vnto theyr Generall, without disguising goeth plainly to the poynt. *If they promise* (saith hee) *to obey their Generall, it is in regard that he is Gods Vicar ouer his company.* If hee had said, Vicar of our holy Father, appoynted by him ouer his companie, he had committed lesse incongruitie. But as the Iesuits neuer want pretences to make their shifts more salable, they force a place or two of Scripture, to make good the vsurpation of their Generall the Popes riuall, they say, *Qui vos audit, me audit, & qui vos spernit, me spernit.* And they allude to the place of *Dauid* speaking of the Iudges, *Vos dij estis, & Deus stetit in synagoga Deorum:* And that S. *Basill* said, that the Prelate representh the person of Iesus Christ. And S. *Gregory* of Nazianzene, addressing his speech to the Emperour, sayth, Thou holdest thy Empire with Iesus Christ, with him thou commaundest on earth, thou art the image of God.

I might more strongly alledge one thing which I haue from themselues, for when the Popes, *Paule* and

Iulius

Part.5. constit.cap.3 & part. 6.cap.1

Gl.part.4 Const cap.3.

Part.6.Constit cap.1.

Montag. cap.27.

In the Plea of the Colledge of Clairmont, the yeere 1594. Fol. 61.& Mont. cap.27.

Iulius the fift, in their Bulls of the yeeres 1 5 4 0. & 5 0. speaking of their Generall, sayd: *In illo Christum velut præsentem agnoscant,* was this with any purpose that they should vsurpe ouer theyrs this great title? No question-lesse, but to vse it as we see in the Coūsel of Trent, where it is said, that our Lord ascending into heauen, *Sacerdotes sui ipsius Vicarios reliquit, tanquam præsides & iudices, ad quos mortalia crimina deferantur, in quæ Christi fideles inciderint,* to giue them absolution.

And in another place, when recōmending the poore to the beneficed men, he addeth, *Memores eos qui hospitalitatem amant, Christum in hospitibus recipere.* That is to say, that they remember to be hospitals to the poore, for entertaining them, they entertained Iesus Christ. Words vttered to excite charitie, not to builde an Anabaptisme, which the Iesuits seeme to ground vpon these wordes, that they should acknowledge Iesus Christ in their Generall, as *Iohn Leiden,* the king of Anabaptists, gaue out of himselfe, and would haue had others to belieue it. But because already I haue heereof discoursed at large, I will nowe content my selfe onely to tell you this, that their Generall, taking vpon him the authority of Gods Vicar, hath brought in a schisme and deuision betwixt our holy Father the Pope and him.

And although to maintaine this authoritie, *Montagnes* & his suffragans, ayde him with all the places aboue alledged, they breede withall their cunning another schisme, of more dangerous effect then that: for that Emperours, Kings, and Iudges, may euery one vsurpe the same state. And so at vnawares, wee shall slippe into the heresie of the Lutherans, who would equall Archbishops and Bishops to our holy Father, whom notwithstanding in their seuerall iurisdictions, we acknowledge the Vicars of God: and yet they take not this title vpon them neither, though wee yeeld it them, it is a title which belongeth onely to the Pope, a title which

Sess. 14. ca. 15. where it speakes of confession.

Sess. 24. ca. 8. where it speakes of reformatiō.

Nnn. no

no honeſt and faithfull Chriſtian can denie him, and whereof he may be iuſtly iealous, if any endeuour to rob him of it.

But whether wander we? There is none but knoweth, that they are in their ſeuerall charges, the true creatures and deputies of God, and that ſuch, ſince the time of the Apoſtles, downe to this day they haue cōtinued. There is none likewiſe but knoweth, that the Ieſuits are the Popes creatures: if any ſhould aſſume this title, the Biſhops haue moſt intereſt to challenge it, yet they take it not vpon them, but modeſtly leaue it to our holy Father, and the Ieſuit, who deriueth his reputation from him, will hee be thus immodeſt? By the Counſell of Trent, ſo much renowned in Rome, there are many articles, whereby the Biſhoppes are reſtrained of many things, the which our French Church thinketh to be groūded on ordinary right; yet is it ſo orderd, that they may be knowne to be Vicars vnder the holy Sea: and yet ſhall vvee permit, that theſe vnderminders of our Church, ſhall vſurpe authoritie as immediate Vicars of God, and not as Vicars of the holie Sea?

I confeſſe that ordinarilie, we giue the terme of moſt Reuerend to our Cardinalls, & to thoſe which are princes moſt illuſtrious. Their generall Cōſiſtorie hath not the title of moſt illuſtrious: as we ſee in the great Canoniſt *Nauarre*, *Aduertendum eſt*, ſayth he, *quod per ſolam geſtionem habitus, per vnum, vel plures annos, in illuſtriſſimo ſocietatis Ieſu ordine, non videtur fieri profeſſio tacita.* You muſt conſider (ſaith he) that by wearing the habit onely for one or more yeeres, in the moſt famous order of the ſocietie of Ieſus, a man is not thought to make ſecret profeſſion.

Naua. com. de reg.num. 76.

Nauarre liued in Rome vnder *Gregory* the 13, & did more honour to his hypocrits, then we doe to the great & venerable Conſiſtorie of Cardinals, which are Counſailers in ordinarie to the holy Sea. Writing to Biſhops,

wee

we entitle them, Reuerend Fathers in God, and thinke herein we honour them sufficiently : there is no Father Iesuit of the great vowe, who hath not this title of a Bishop. The Letter written to the king of Spayne in the troubles, by our Sixteene Tygers of Paris, speaking of Father *Mathew* a Iesuit, termes him in three seuerall places, the Reuerend Father *Mathew*. And in a great part of the Booke, there be added to the mention of his name these two Letters *R. P.*

When we speake vnto our holy Father, we say, Your Holinesse; when you speake to the Generall, or other Superiour of this Order, yea but vnto the meanest Father amongst the Iesuits, he taketh his greatnesse much wronged, if you vse not this terme, Your Reuerence : yet wee must say, they encroche not vpon the authorie of the holie seate. But why should they not impeach the authoritie of his holines, sith they vsurpe and insult vpon Christ himselfe, vnto whom onely, our Christian Church permitteth Apostles? Yet suffers the Generall his, in some places, to be called Apostles. This is not to turne our holie Father out of his seate, but to put Iesus Christ out of his throne. This is not to be Gods Vicar, but to belieue that he is God himselfe.

When *Ismaell*, afterwards called the Sophi, about the yeere 1503, attempted, by putting the Easterne parts in combustion, to ouerthrow the Estate; by that means to equal himselfe with the *Othomans*, Emperors of Constantinople, he began first to alter and trouble the auncient religion of *Mahomet*, pretending that hee would reduce it to a farre better passe; alledging that *Mahomet*, who neuer tooke vppon him higher title then the Prophet of GOD, had a brother called *Hali*, vvho brought in vnder the Banner of his Brother, a Religion more austere, whereof *Ismaell* tooke vppon him to be the Restorer. And vnder thys plausible pretext, hee made himselfe to bee called a Prophet as well as *Ma-*

homet, altered the auncient forme of Turban among his owne people, infomuch as they beganne to adore him as the true Image of God, and refolutly to follow his aduertifements. So that he affembled at the firft a handfull of men, after, added to them multitudes, and fhortly after, like another new *Mahomet*, fo encreafed his Armie, that he was followed with fixe hundred thoufand men, both horfe and foote, making the Eaft to tremble. And in thefe his proceedings, fo mingling religion with ftate, conquered a great part of the Country, which his pofterity enioyeth, vnder the great & redoubted name of Sophi.

The comparifons fute not in euerie particuler, but if it pleafe you to confider what hath paffed, and is now in practife among our Iefuits, you fhall find they follow the fame fteps in Chriftianifme, which *Ifmaell* firft trode in Mahumetifme. Their prophet *Ifmaell* is the great *Ignatius*, who with his fabulous vifions, would beare the world in hand, that fometimes hee fpake with G O D, fometimes with Chrift, fometimes with our Ladie, or Saint *Peter*. And as *Ifmaell* fetched out of *Hali*, the pretended Brother of *Mahomet*, a new branch of Religion, taken from the old ftocke : So *Ignatius*, chriftning him felfe with this new name of a Iefuit, in fted of the name of a Chriftian authorized frõ the Apoftles, buildeth vp a religion neuer auncientlie obferued by our Church.

Ifmaell, vnder this new vowe, changed the auncient Turban : *Ignatius* inducing a new Monachifme amõgft vs, yet retaineth not the auncient habite of Munks. *Ifmaell* firft affembled a handfull of people, after rayfed millions : *Ignatius* doth the like. *Ifmaell*, to make himfelfe great, mingled pollicie and religion together; hath not *Ignatius* followed him ? *Ifmaell* and his fucceffours, were adorned and magnified by their followers : *Ignatius* hath been fo idolatrized, and the reft of his fucceffors in the Generalfhip. But they goe beyond him, for the

Generall

Generall of the Iesuits, will not only be honoured by his
followers, but by those which are not of his sect, though
happily somwhat tainted with his superstitious hipocrisie. *Ismael* made himselfe be called the Prophet of God:
The Generall termeth himselfe Gods Vicar. In all these
proceedings and practises, *Ismael* troubled and tormoy-
led the Mahometicall state : And shall not we mistrust in
Rome this same new Iesuited *Sophi* ? Whosoeuer suspec-
teth them not, is no true and legitimate child of the holy
Sea. I pray you obserue a little their encreasing and their
growth. The Iesuits at the first beginning, were content to be some threescore in number ; some three
yeeres after, they kept open house, come who would
and welcome : which was an anticipation preiudiciall
to Ordinaries and Vniuersities, to Kings and their
kingdomes. In the end they were not content to equall
themselues with Bishops in their Diocesse, vsurping
their iurisdiction, but exacted more obedience ouer
their followers, then the Pope ouer vs. And although
there can be no certaine iudgement giuen of future
things, yet I dare say, & it is true, that in matter of State,
the predictions of good or ill, are no lesse infallible then
iudgements Mathematicall.

Toward the declining of the popular state in
Rome, there grew a ciuill warre in Fraunce, betwixt
two great factions, the Sequanois and the Heduans,
which diuersly aspyred to the chiefe gouernment.
The Heduans, confederate with the Romans, deman-
ded their ayde, *Iulius Cæsar*, who from his cradle neuer brooked small attempts, obtayned the command
of the French, aswell on this side the mountaynes, as
beyond, for fiue yeeres. Besides, there were giuen him
foure legions of souldiers, paied by the State. He, as he
was a man of great leading, and verie valiant, soone
brought his affaires to such a passe, that pretending to
succour the Heduans, he made the Gaules tributary

to the people of Rome. In regard whereof, at the inſtance of his friends, he obtayned great priuiledges. As for one, he obtayned that *Pompey*, or his kinſman, might be vndertaker generall, who beſides the bond of alliance, might doe much in fauouring of *Cæſars* greatnes. Hee was of great place in the Towne, and conſequently verie much followed. Wiſe *Cato* the Vticen, ſeeing how theſe things were carried, often tolde him verie earneſtly, hee would ouerthrow the ſtate ere he were aware, by teaching *Cæſar* to play the Tyrant, which he ſhould finde when it was too late. His prediction came to paſſe : for after much ciuill warre, the Empyre fell to his family. I wiſh to God I might be a falſe Prophet.

But when I conſider ſeriouſly the hiſtory of our Ieſuits, I am full of feare and penſiuenes. *Martin Luther* directly oppoſed himſelfe againſt the holy Sea. The Ieſuits, cunning ſtateſmen, couer no leſſe ambition vnder their long caſſocks, then *Cæſar*, and proffer to ſupport the Popedome, but with a propoſition of new obedience; as if I durſt I would ſay, that they make vp a third religion betwixt the true Catholique and the Lutheran. *Cæſar* vanquiſhed the French : theſe if we wil beleeue it, ſubdued a part of the Indies with their prattle, but yet vnder the fauour of the Kings of Portugall, in places where he had command. For, as for our wandring ſoules I do not ſee they had done any great ſeruice in reducing them to the fold. *Cæſar*, in regard of his victories, obtaind of the State, many extraordinarie priuiledges, not before imparted to any : The Ieſuits in recompenſe of their imaginarie conqueſts, in vnknowne countries, haue obtained many priuiledges of the holy Sea, neuer hertofore graunted to them. *Cato* cried out, that the priuiledges giuen to *Cæſar*, would ouerthrow the common-wealth: The great facultie of Diuines in Paris, declared in the yeere 1554. that this Sect would become the vtter

ter defolation and ruine of our Church. And fome
diuining fpirits,foretold long before, the tragedies they
fhould act in Fraunce. *Cæfar* chaunged the popular
State into a Tyrannie : what the Iefuits will attempt a-
gainft the holy Church, is in the hand of God; yet one
thing comforteth me,that this great Sea,is builded vpon
a furer foundation then the Romane common-wealth.
Only this I wil adde, that euen as our Lord Iefus Chrift
lodged his Diuinitie in a humane body for our redemption, fo long as our Prelates harbour holines and integritie in their hearts, all will goe well with them and vs.
But when they fhall fall once a brewing, mingling cunning and pollicie with Religion , thereby thinking to
maintaine their greatnes,then will they ouerthrow them
felues and our whole Church.

CHAP. 26.

¶ That there is no credit to be giuen to the promifes and
protestations of Iefuits , for that they haue no o-
ther faith , but fuch as maketh for the
effecting of their purpofes.

Ou haue hetherto vnderftood, the herefies,Machiauelifms,& Anabaptifmes
of the Sect of Iefuits, the treafons, the
troubles they haue brought to France,
& wherfoeuer elfe they haue remaind:
it is now time to found retreat . And
yet before I do it,we muft haue a little skirmifh with the
reeftablifhment by them procured, againft the proceffe
of the Parliament at Paris,giuen rather by God his iuft
iudgement then by men. Now in this new purfuit, hee
which fhall obferue the time, wherein they beganne to
remoue, aud the authoritie of him whom they imploy,
fhall find them cunning and worldly wife, rather then
religious. I cannot tell whether in the end they wil preuaile

uaile or no : For to speake truly, importunitie, and per-
seuerance, their two principall vertues haue great aduantage ouer the French, which are naturally without
gaule when they are flattered. I assure you, the annals of
the Iesuit *Magius* their Deligate, giue thē leaue to vse all
the faire promises that may be, till they become owners
of their desire, then they may cassiere their promises,
when they can doe them no further seruice. And that
this is their practise, I can verifie by infinite instan-
ces . They were vowed to G O D as they say, in the
Church of Mont-Marter, in the yeere 1 5 3 4. and promised to goe to Ierusalem, to conuert the Turks to the
Catholique Religion . And to this purpose, they came
to Venice in the yeere 1 5 3 7. resolute to take their
iourney, after they had receiued the blessing of Pope
Paule the third, by whom they were well receiued by
the mediation of some who brought them thether, and
there they receiued money for the voyage.

Nothing hindred their enterprise, saue only the fauour
of some Lords , with whom they grew acquainted in
Rome , by whose meanes they hoped to set vp an easier
Sect, excusing the breach of their vow , vnder pretense
that the passage was stopt, by reason of the wars betwixt
the Turke and the Venetian. Yet certaine it was, that the
verie yeere of their approbation, which was in the yeere
1540. there was not onely truce betwixt the Turke and
the Venetian, but a firme peace. What then altered their
resolution ? Marrie euen their ease, and some other busines they had at home.

In the same Church of Mont-Marter , they swore to
vndertake the cōquest of lost soules after they were proceeded Doctors of Diuinitie. That was a promise made
before the face of God, very wise & reasonable. Whereunto, besides ther synceritie of conscience, there was further required soundnes of iudgement & knowledge , to
conuert the Infidels . When they found a better bar-
gaine

gaine at Rome, they remembred to forget their promise. These two first assayes, made them afterward Maisters in matters of deceit & trechery, vpon all
occasions that were offered them for the aduancement
of their designes. In the assembly of Poitly, the yeere
1 5 6 1. they promised to renounce their vowes, and
to submit themselues to the ordinarie discipline of other
Colledges. A promise which afterward they renewed
in open Parliament. Whereupon they were admitted,
onely vnder the title of the Colledge of Clairmont in
Paris. Notwithstanding, in the same yeere, they obtaynd
Buls of Pope *Pius* the fourth, altogether contrarie and
derogatory to all the ancient priuiledges of our Vniuersities. In 64. when they preferred a petition to the Parliament, to be matriculated or incorporated into the
Vniuersity, forgetting the decree of the French Church
confirmed by processe, they entitled themselues *the Societie of Iesus*, an order forbidden them.

Pasquier, hauing at the first beginning of the cause
obiected, that the title they tooke vpon them, disabled
their petition, they denied themselues by the meanes of
Versoris their owne Aduocate, auouching, that this hapned by the fault of *Pons Congordon*, who was their first
principall soliciter in the cause: insomuch, that *Congordan* was driuen to deny himselfe. In Rome they obey the
holy Sea in all things by a blinde obedience, as I haue
showed you by their constitutions: In Fraunce (if you
beleeue it) by the vow of Mission onely, as you may
find in their defence made in 9 4. for the Colledge of
Clairmont, and by *Montaignes* his booke, and by the
humble petition exhibited to the King by a namelesse
Iesuit. In Rome they acknowledge the Pope to be Lord
spirituall and temporall ouer all Christian Princes: Else
they must directly contradict all the extrauagant decretals which impose the same vpon all Monarchies.
It is a proposition verie familiar in the Courte of
Rome.

Rome. And in the Buls appoynted for the publication of the Iubily, in the yeere 1600. Saint *Peter* and Saint *Paule*, are called Princes of the earth. In Fraunce they are of another opinion, for in their pleading in the yeere 94. and in the booke of *Montaignes*, they giue out, that the Pope, hath no title to temporalties, but such as he hath by long succession of time gotten in Italy. *Ribadinere* in the life of *Ignace*, acknowledgeth, that all their order prayed particularly for the health of the deceased King of Spayne : now read their bookes, they know nothing but this particularity , yet pray they generally for all Princes, vnder whose protection they haue built their nestes. In the verie heat of our troubles, there was no Cardinall so much withstood the Duke of Neuers, and the Marquesse of Pisani, sent by the King to his Holines , as the Cardinall of Toledo, a Iesuit, the troubles drawing to an end, none was so forward as he, to further our affayres.

During our last troubles none did so much michiefe as they, if you credit men of great integrity & reputation, who were beholders of their tragedies. Read their humble request and remonstrance preferred to the King, there is nothing which this poore innocent people hath in greater detestation, then that which they sometimes so much adored. This is called among chiefe Pragmaticall fellowes, a fayre pretence for a foule exploit. They neuer made question to mingle their holy deuotions with affaires of State, as they made vs feele to our payne. Seeing our troubles vpon the poynt of appeasing, and the Kings affayres successefull and prospering, they called in *anno*, 39 . a general assembly in Rome, wherin it was forbidden, that any of them should intermeddle, yet they did it. But wil you haue a better and more euident example then this? If you will beleeue them, there is nothing they abhore more then the Hugonots Religion, inasmuch as they inhibit their bookes,

of

of what argumēt soeuer, forbidding expresly their scho-
lers to read them. Oh holy men! Notwithstanding, whē
they presented their request to the king, to be established, they chose a Hugonot to be their spokseman, that
by this retaining him, they might be assured not to haue
him against them. These are states-men & temporisers,
who hold all things honest and lawfull, which serue
their turne. As in former times, whē they spake of a per-
fidious people, they named the Carthagenians, whereof the common prouerbe grew, *Fides Punica.* The like
we may now say of the Iesuit, *Fides Iesuitica* : and apply
that to them, which *Liuie* speaketh of *Hanniball, Perfi-
dia plusquam Punica, nihil veri, nihil sancti, nullus Deûm
metus, nullum iusiurandum, nulla religio*: They priuately
among their friends, make a iest of perfidiousnes & trecherie; for if you aske them, *What is a Iesuit ?* their answere is, *Euery man.* Implying, that they are Creatures
which varie their colours like the Camelion, according
to the obiect. A verie fit comparison for them, for no
more then the Camelion can they borrow the colour of
white, which in holy scripture figureth vertue & innocencie. A little before the King entred Paris, Father *A-
lexander Hays,* a Scot, seeing the affayres of the League
very much decline, it was his chaunce to disgorge out of
the aboundance of his heart, these words in a great audience, in the Colledge of Clairmont, where hee read the
principall lecture; Hetherto to (saith he) we haue beene
Spaniards, but now we are constrained to be French: it
is all one, we must formalize vntill a fitter season. *Ceden-
dum erit tempori.* These were the words he vsed.

And that you may not thinke that this Maxime proceedeth from the pliantnes of their consciences, which
they restraine or extend, as best fitteth their profit, their
good Father *Ignace,* first taught them this dispensation,
whereof since, they haue made a particular constitution.
The other holy Fathers, founders of diuers orders of

Religion

Religion, established diuers ordinances which they faste-
ned, if I may so speake, with nailes of Diamond in tombs
of brasse, which should perpetually be obserued by
their Munks and other Religious. In the Sect of Iesuits,
there is nothing so certaine as their vncertaintie, as I
said of late. In the Bull of Pope *Paule* the third, it is
written as followeth.

*Et quod possint constitutiones particulares, quas ad
Societatis huiusmodi finem, & Iesu Christi Domini nostri gloriam, ac proximi vtilitate conformes esse iudicauerint,
condere: & tam hactenus factas, quam in posterum facien-
das constitutiones, ipsas iuxta locorum, temporu, & reru qua-
litatem & varietatem mutare, alterare, seu in totum cassare
& alias de nouo condere possint & valeant. Qua postea alte-
rata, mutata, seu de nouo condita fuerint, eo ipso, Apostolica sedis authoritate prafata, confirmata censeantur, eadem
Apostolica authoritate, de speciali gratia indulgemus.* That
they may make (saith Pope *Paule*) particular ordinances, which they shal iudge fit for the Societie, to the glory of our Lord Iesus Christ, and the profit of their
neighbour. And that such as are alreadie made, or shall
be made hereafter, they may chaunge, alter or abolish,
according to the varietie of place, time and occasions,
and in steed of them, make new: the which so chaunged, reuoked, or new made, we will that they be confirmed by the foresaid authoritie of the Apostolique
Sea: and by the same authoritie, of our speciall grace
and fauour we confirme them. I haue translated this
place word for word, and yet when the Bull saith in
Latine, that the constitutions may be chaunged as shall
be fit for the Societie, it must be vnderstood, for the
maintenance and aduancement of the Order. Out of
this generall constitution, they haue drawne one particular which is woorthie to be knowne, in the 16. part
of their constitutions, Chaper, 5. the title beginning
thus.

Quod

Quod Constitutiones, peccati obligationem non inducunt.
Cum exoptet Societas, vniuersas suas Constitutiones, decla-
rationes, ac viuendi ordinem, omnino iuxta nostrum institu-
tum, nihil vltra in re declinando, obseruari: Optet etiam ni-
hilominus suos omnes securos esse, vel certè adiuuari, ne in
laqueum vllius peccati, quod ex vi constitutionum huiusmo-
di, aut ordinationum proueniat, incidant, visum est nobis in
Domino, vt excepto expresso voto, quo Societas summo Pon-
tifici pro tempore existente tenetur, ac tribus alijs essentiali-
bus, Paupertatis, Castitatis, & Obedientiæ, nullas Constitu-
tiones, declarationes, vel ordinem vllum viuendi, posse obli-
gationem ac peccatum mortale, vel veniale inducere. Nisi
Superior ea in nomine Domini Iesu Christi, vel in virtute
obedientiæ, iuberet. And a little after, *Et loco timoris offen-*
sæ, succedat amor & desiderium omnis perfectionis, & vt
maior gloria & laus Christi creatoris ac Domini nostri con-
sequatur.

That the constitutions may not bind any man in conscience, sith the Societie desires, that all their constitutions, declarations, and order of life, should be without
euasion, conformable to our direction: and also, neuerthelesse wisheth to be secured, or at least succourd, that
they be not snared in any sin which may grow by theyr
constitutions or ordinances: We haue thought good in
the Lord, (exception taken to the expresse vow, wherewith the societie is bound to the Pope for the time beeing, and the three other essentiall vowes, of Pouertie,
Chastitie, and Obedience,) that no Constitutions, declarations, or any order of life, shall impose any yoake
of mortall or veniall sinne vpon them; vnlesse their Superiour commaund those thinges, in the name of our
Lord Iesus Christ, or in the vertue of obedience. *And a-*
gaine: In stedde of feare of offending, let loue and desire of all perfection come in place, and let the glory &
praise of Christ our Lord and Maker, be the more exalted.

By the firſt article, it is lawfull for them to change & rechange their conſtitutions at their own pleaſure (forſooth) for their good. By the ſecond, their conſtitutions are held (in regard of the ſoule) indifferent; ſo that the Ieſuit may breake them, without committing mortall or veniall ſinne. A law which their great Law-giuer gaue them, to the end, that to Gods honour and glory, there might be fewer ſinners in theyr ſocietie.

Oh holy ſoules! oh pure conſciences! Who reſtrayning their inferiours from ſinne, take themſelues the reines, committing all manner of ſinne vncontrouled. Let vs examine theſe poynts without paſſion, and let vs conſider the ſcope of theſe two propoſitions. By the firſt, no Prince ſhall be aſſured of his eſtate: and by the ſecond, no Prince ſhal be ſecure of his perſon in his own kingdome. Concerning the firſt poynt, call to minde howe matters haue beene carried for theſe 25. or 30. yeeres. There hath beene no Nation, where they be foſtered, but they would be tempering with their affaires of ſtate. I think they are ſuch honeſt men, as what herein they haue done, they haue vndertaken to doe it, by vertue of their ſilent Conſtitutions, (which the auncient Romans termed, *Senatus-Conſulta tacita,*) or if they did it by their owne priuate authoritie, the Generall vvere vnworthy of his place ſhould he ſuffer it. Further, this was forbidden them in the yeere 1593, when they ſawe all their plots meere fruſtrate.

Admit newe troubles ſhould ariſe, theſe gallants will caſſiere and diſanull this laſt Ordinaunce, ſuffering their companions to intermedle as before. This ſame Pauline, will it not breede in them a trouble-ſtate where euer they become? But what are their rules in ſuch affaires? Marry that it is lawfull to kill a Tyrant. That a King breaking and contemning the common lawes of the Land, may be depriued of his Crowne by the people. That there are other cauſes, for the which Princes and

Emanuel Sa in his Aphoriſmes of confeſſion. Montag. cap. 58.

and great perſonages may be ſlaine. In what a miſerable condition ſhall Princes liue, if the aſſurance of theyr Eſtate ſhall depend vpon theſe fellowes?

Let vs ſee their newe conſtitutions of 93. *I will that they meddle not at all in affaires of ſtate in generall termes. And that particulerly, they practiſe not vpon the perſon of Princes.* Are they bound to obey this? Nothing leſſe. Inaſmuch as their Lawgiuer chargeth not their conſciences, but in expreſſe termes, he would otherwiſe haue charged them, by vertue of their blinded obedience. And this is the cauſe that *Commolet,*preaching ſince this new Statute, that there wanted a newe *Ehud* to kill our King, and *Walpoole* furniſhing Squire with poyſon and inſtructions to kill the Queene of England his Miſtres, thought therein they ſinned not, for that in their conſciences they belieued, that they were to preſent theſe two ſoules to God.

The Anabaptiſt, had but one abſolute obedience which hee ought to his Superiour. The Ieſuite hath two. The one depending of his Superiours; and the other, in his particuler conſcience, perſwading himſelfe, that all hee doth, tendeth to the glorie of God, and the aduauncement of his Church.

CHAP. 27.

The concluſion of the third Booke, containing the reſtoring of the Ieſuits, by them procured.

Ou may iudge by this, ſaid the Aduocate, of what conſequence, the reeſtabliſhment is, where-with they dailie haunt and vrge the King, ſith to them all things are indifferent, ſaue ſuch as tend to the diſabling & impeachment of their Sect. All lyes, trecheries, and fraudes, change theyr propertie, and become holy thinges, when they make

make for the aduauncement of their Sect. GOD hath twice miraculously preserued our King from their violence, it is not due to his wisedome & fore-sight, how so euer verie great: he oweth it to God his diuine prouidence. These preseruations are aduertisments, whereof he and his subiects should make their profit. The greater increase of blessings hee hath receiued, the more ought he to acknowledge it in all humiltie.

My Maisters the Iesuits, matchlesse for importunity, vse the authoritie of some great personages, hoping to recouer interest in the King, notwithstanding the processe of Parliament, graunted out against them in Paris. I beseech you call to minde, that these venerable trechers tooke a time to practise against him, not in the heate of our troubles, but when they were well calmed, when he was reconciled to the holy Church, in time of the truce: it was the cōmon place as well of their Preachers as Regents. I humbly beseech his Maiesty to consider, that vpon his safetie, the peace of his subiects dependeth, and that in vaine he blameth the Sea, who hauing escaped two seuerall shipwracks, will try his fortune yet the third time. Further, I beseech him to obserue, what befell in Portugall, and lately likewise hapned within our memory in Fraunce. He who in Portugall most idolatrized this Sect, was the King *Sebastian*, whom the Iesuits, his principall fauourits, counsailed to vndertake the conquest of another kingdome, where the oppinion is he was slaine in the battaile, yet he could not be found amongst the dead. Great pittie, if he there miscarried, the body of a King should want his buriall, but more lamentable, if he liue, as the brute is, that he is not acknowledged.

It fell out much otherwise to our great King *Henrie*, for so soone as he had driuen the Iesuits out of his good towne and Parliament of Paris, God sent him a generall peace aswell within his kingdome as without, and as

prosperous

prosperous successe in all his affaires as he could desire.
These are no faigned, or imaginarie examples which I
place before your eyes, they are generally knowen, and
there is none but may easily iudge, why this mis-for-
tune befell the one, and this blessing fell to the other. In
this most humble request, not fained, as the Petion of
the namclesse Iesuit, consisteth the summe of my desire,
and GOD graunt my discourse may haue accesse vnto
him.

I desire heerein, hee could be pleased to followe the
counsaile of the great Consistorie of Rome, against the
order of the *Humiliati*, who after they were once suppressed, were neuer after restored, although theyr offence was much lesse against the holy Sea, then this of
the Iesuits against his Maiestie : assuring you my Maisters, that there is nothing doth more solicite me to this
quarrell against them, then the generall peace of our
Fraunce, and heerein I appeale to God, before whom I
doe truly and sincerely speake.

The Aduocate, hauing ended his discourse, as the o-
pinions of men are variable and vncertaine, so were wee
diuersly affected with that which was by him deliuered,
some, grieued with the Anatomie made of their order,
others, much meruailing, neuer imagining there had
beene so much shame and abhomination among them,
others, very angry, that with such vnrestrained libertie,
they haue beene suffered to range in many parts of
Fraunce vncontrouled : beeing absolutely of opinion,
that there was nothing neere so great cause to suppresse
the Templers, as to suppresse these Iesuits.

Whereuppon the Iesuit, for the honour which hee
ought to his Faction, said vnto the Aduocate; I cannot
tell wherein you haue been wronged by our companie,
and know as little what hope of reward hath hired you
to this combat; but well I wot, you haue no small enemies that make head against you, and that you must cut

off an infinite number of heads, (which is almost a matter impossible)before you can well come vnto the head. Consider that our company is a venerable Senate, like vnto that which was in Rome in the time of *Pyrrhus*, to whom his Embassadours reported at theyr returne, that they had seene as many Kings as Senators. They were wont to call those auncient Senators, Fathers, so call we ours: and as they were the sinewes of auncient Rome, so are these of the newe, I meane of the Papacie, which farre passeth the vaine greatnes of the olde Romans. Therefore before they attempt against vs, let them be verie well aduised: remember what hapned to *Minos* King of Creet, for his busines with the Athenians. It was there I looked for you, quoth the Aduocate, for your Companie is not the Senate you speake of, but a Monster, which hath farre more heads then a Hydra, against the which I will be another French *Hercules*, to maule and massacre them. Yet one boone I would entreate of you, that when you returne to Rome, you would report to your Generall, as I know you will, all you haue heard discoursed, and would vouchsafe the rather (at my instance) to present him with these foure verses, the which I send him in the nature of a Cartell of defiance.

> *If I haue vsd thee otherwise then well*
> *Iesuit, tis fit that thy reuenge thou take,*
> *But when you aunswere, see no lyes you tell,*
> *If thou speake truth, it would a wonder make.*

Euerie one then beganne to smile, and especially the Gentleman said vnto him: I will not suffer you to goe any further, it is time to cry hola, I will stoppe your mouth, dinner shall decide your difference. And if you will doe me the honour to belieue mee, all which hath hetherto been said, shall be wrapt vp in the cloth: The
lawes

lawes of my Table are, *Odi memorem compotorem.* That
fpeech had beene well vttered, faid the Aduocate, if we
had not difcourfed fafting. Prefently one couerd the table, and after dinner,our horfes beeing made readie, we
thanked the Gentleman for his entertainement, and he
likewife thanked vs for the honour he faid we did him.

We were fome fixe in companie, whereof hee de-
tained the Aduocate, pretending he was to pay him the
arrerage of his long abfence. The other fiue, after they
had paffed the Mountaines, three of them tooke theyr
way to Venice, intending to trauaile to Ierufalem, to
acquite themfelues of a vovve, which they had made
to vifite the holy Sepulcher. The Iefuit and I went toward Rome, hee to yeeld account of his voiage, and I
to fee the Iubile, but efpecially to vifite two great Prelates,both of them bearing the name and qualitie of Fathers: our holy Father Pope *Clement* the 8, a Father of
concord & vnion, hauing by the trauaile & intercourfe
of the Cardinall of Florence his Legate, mediated a
peace betwixt two great Kings,for the which Chriftendome is greatly indebted to him : the other,father *Claudius Aquauina*, Generall of the Iefuits, a Father, or (to
fpeake more properly) a Fountaine of all diuifions,
factions, and difcords, as he who by his bookes,fet them
firft a-broche in Fraunce, to the great damage and
fpoyle of our ftate. God graunt, that by the example of
Tho. Aquinas, frō whofe houfe they fay he is defcended,
hee and his may heereafter, learne the obedience & loy-
altie, which a fubiect oweth in dutie to his King.

Ppp. 2.　　　　To

The third Booke of

To Captaine *Ignatius*, Father and chiefe
Generall ouer the Company of
the Iesuits.

Father Souldiour, where is thy Flaske?
Take vp thy dagger and thy blade,
This Authour pulleth off thy maske
Of craftie vowes, and cogging trade.

That Iesuits are right Preachers, and therefore to be restored to their former place in Paris, a scoffing
Epigram, written to Father *Iames Com-*
molet the Iesuite.

THE *furious speech of a Tribune of Rome,*
Perswadeth men to murder and commotion,
When roaring Commolet *gaue out his doome*
In pulpet, people mus'd at his deuotion:
Hee bid them kill theyr King, his Realme annoy,
Hee stird vp many troubles euery where,
Rage in his mouth his Country to destroy,
This holie doctrine preacht the Iesuit there.
And sith his tongue doth ciuill tempests brew,
I bid this holy Tribune heere adiew.

To *Henrie* the fourth, the most Christian King of
Fraunce and Nauarre.

Great Henrie *by this Epigram is told,*
What course with Iesuits he ought to hold.

FINIS.

A

A Table or short collection of things contayned in all the Chapters of the *three Bookes of the Iesuits* Catechisme.

¶ The first Booke.

¶ The ſecond Booke.

THE TABLE.

¶ The third Booke.

Of

THE TABLE.

FINIS.